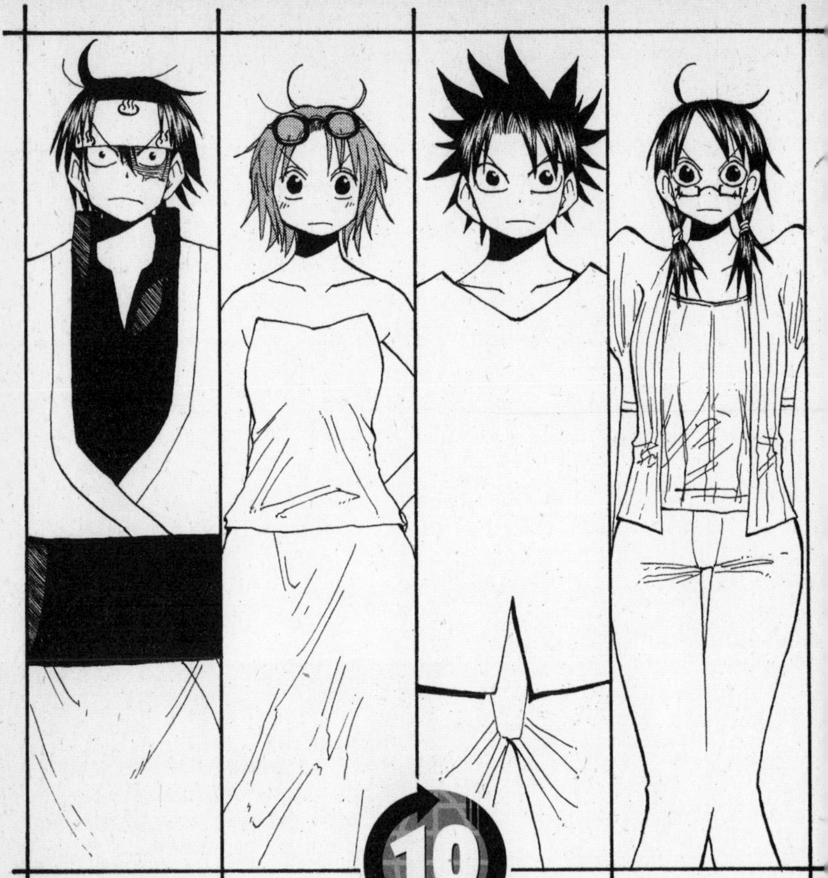

10

The Law of Ueki

うえきの法則

地翼

SA FUKUCHI PRESENTS

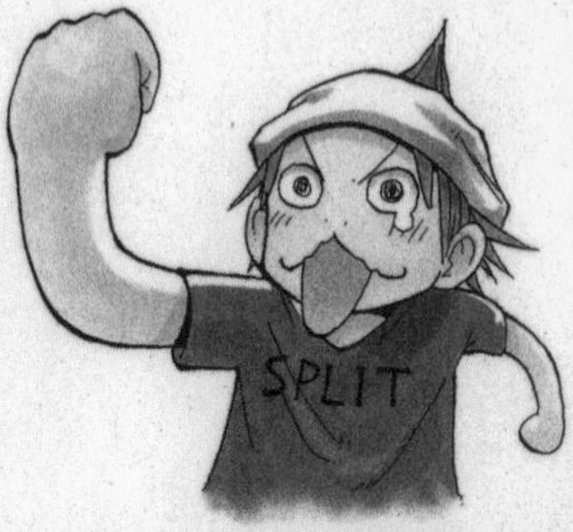
SPLIT

Tsubasa Fukuchi

All right!!! It's cured!!! The ingrown toenail that's been torturing me for three years!!! Goodbye to the old days of excruciating pain as I put on my sock!!! This feeling...is probably not something most people understand.

The Law of Ueki™

うえきの法則

Table of Contents

10

The Characters in The Law of Ueki

Character Profiles — The Law of Ueki

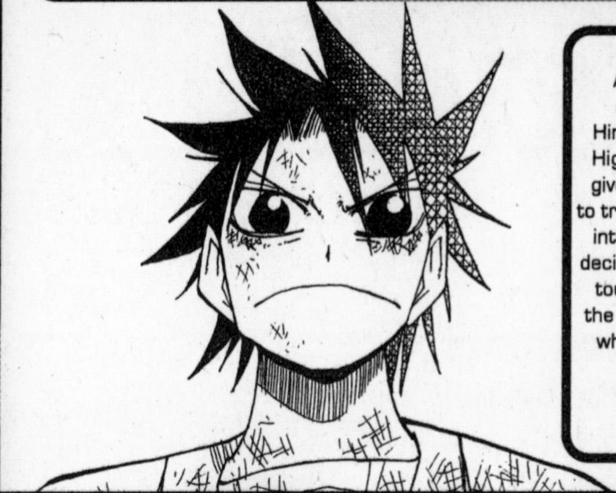

Kosuke Ueki

A first-year student at Hinokuni Junior High. He's been given the power to transform trash into trees. He's decided to win the tournament for the sake of Mr. K, who sacrificed himself to save Ueki.

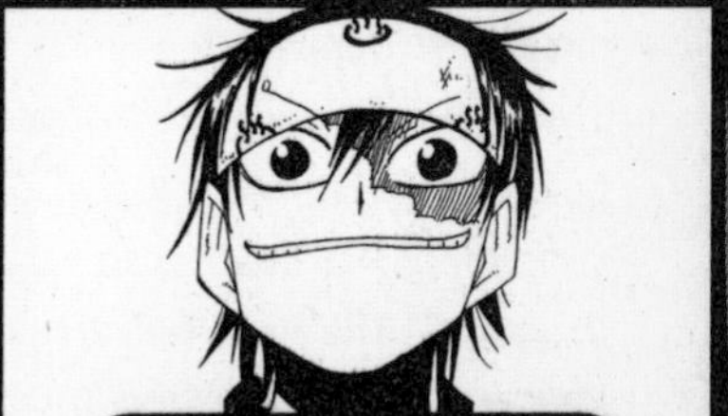

Seiichiro Sano

A former member of Robert's 10. He's a gifted fighter with the power to change towels into iron.

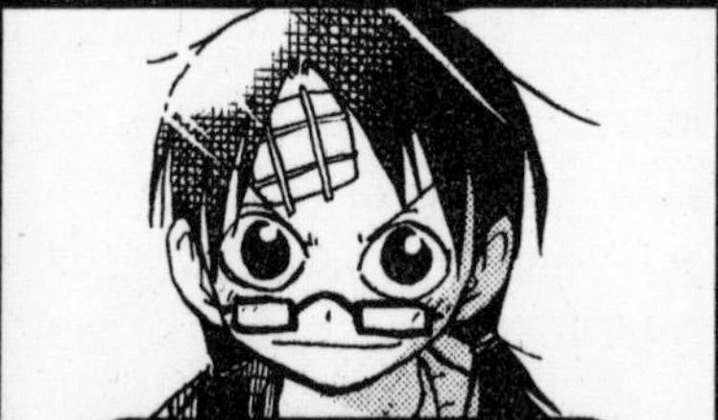

Rinko Jerrard

A former member of Robert's 10. She has the power to change beads into bombs.

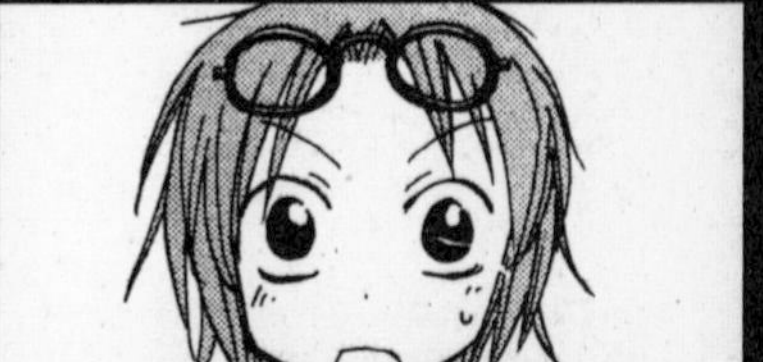

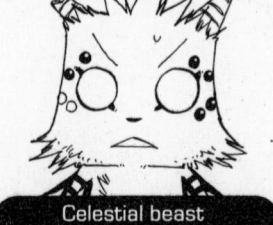

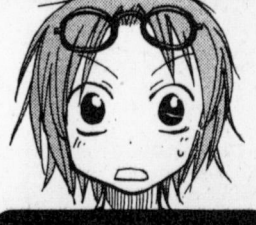

Ai Mori

Ueki's classmate. She learned about the tournament and decided to help Ueki. She's been given a power by Inumaru, but she doesn't know what it is!

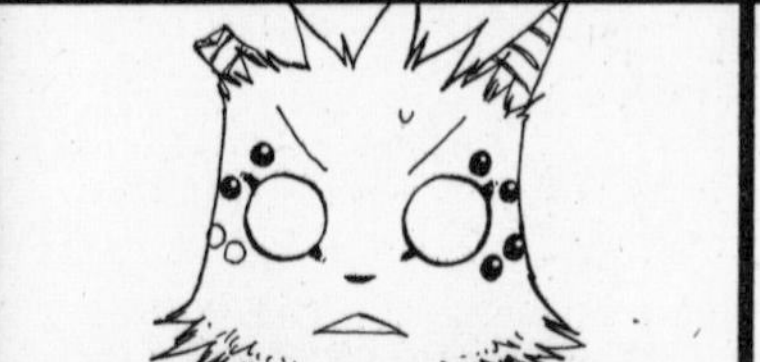

Celestial beast (Tenko)

Celestial beasts act as meters to measure celestial power levels. Tenko was falsely accused and imprisoned in the underworld, but Mr. K helped him escape to the human world.

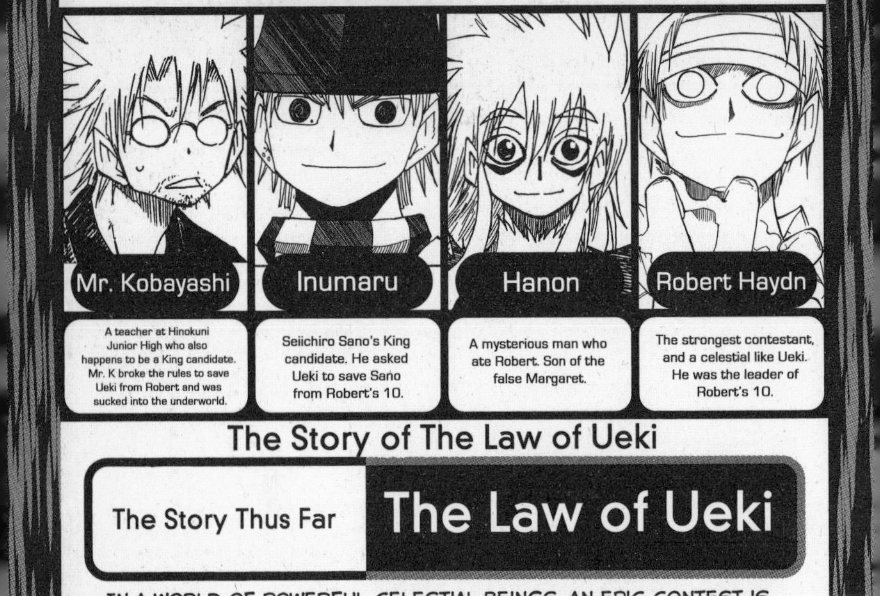
Mr. Kobayashi
Inumaru
Hanon
Robert Haydn

Mr. Kobayashi: A teacher at Hinokuni Junior High who also happens to be a King candidate. Mr. K broke the rules to save Ueki from Robert and was sucked into the underworld.

Inumaru: Seiichiro Sano's King candidate. He asked Ueki to save Sano from Robert's 10.

Hanon: A mysterious man who ate Robert. Son of the false Margaret.

Robert Haydn: The strongest contestant, and a celestial like Ueki. He was the leader of Robert's 10.

The Story of The Law of Ueki

The Story Thus Far — The Law of Ueki

IN A WORLD OF POWERFUL CELESTIAL BEINGS, AN EPIC CONTEST IS BEING HELD TO CHOOSE THE NEXT KING! EACH CELESTIAL SELECTS A KID IN JUNIOR HIGH TO BE HIS CHAMPION AND GRANTS HIM A SPECIAL POWER. THE KIDS BATTLE IT OUT, AND THE LOSERS ARE ELIMINATED. THE GRAND PRIZE FOR THE ULTIMATE WINNER OF THE TOURNAMENT IS THE TALENT OF BLANK, WHERE THE WINNER CAN FILL IN THE BLANK WITH ANY TALENT OF HIS CHOOSING.

KOSUKE UEKI, A FIRST YEAR STUDENT AT HINOKUNI JUNIOR HIGH, ENTERS THE TOURNAMENT AND IS GIVEN A POWER BY HIS KING CANDIDATE, MR. K. BUT MR. K IS SENT TO THE UNDERWORLD FOR SAVING UEKI IN A FIGHT AGAINST ROBERT. UEKI DECIDES TO WIN THE TOURNAMENT AND FULFILL MR. K'S DREAM OF PREVENTING THE TALENT OF BLANK FROM FALLING INTO EVIL HANDS.

SEIICHIRO SANO'S KING CANDIDATE, INUMARU, ASKS UEKI TO SAVE SANO, WHO HAS JOINED ROBERT'S 10. ALONG WITH RINKO, INUMARU AND AI MORI, UEKI MARCHES INTO THE DOGRA MANSION. THERE, THEY ARE FORCED TO BATTLE THE MEMBERS OF ROBERT'S 10, INCLUDING SANO. AFTER LEARNING THAT HE'S A CELESTIAL BEING, UEKI TAKES DOWN ONE FIGHTER AFTER ANOTHER WITH HIS SACRED WEAPONS. HE THEN CHALLENGES ROBERT TO A BATTLE TO STOP HIM FROM ERASING THE WORLD.

ROBERT OVERPOWERS UEKI WITH LEVEL 2 SACRED WEAPONS. WHEN ROBERT MOVES IN TO FINISH HIM, SANO AND RINKO STAND IN THE WAY. DESPITE HIMSELF, ROBERT IS MOVED BY THEIR WILLINGNESS TO SACRIFICE THEMSELVES FOR THEIR FRIENDS.

AFTER THE BATTLE, KOBAYASHI SHOWS UP AS A REPRESENTATIVE OF THE KING, ANNOUNCING THE END OF THE FIRST ROUND. MORI, WHO WAS GIVEN A POWER BY INUMARU, DECIDES TO JOIN THE BATTLE. UEKI AND HIS FRIENDS PLEDGE TO MAKE KOBAYASHI OR INUMARU THE NEXT KING IN ORDER TO SAVE THEM FROM THE UNDERWORLD. A FEW DAYS LATER, A MYSTERIOUS MAN NAMED HANON, WHO HAS TAKEN OVER ROBERT'S BODY AND SOUL, APPEARS BEFORE UEKI!

The Law of Ueki 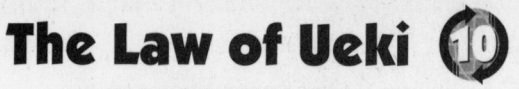 10

STORY AND ART BY TSUBASA FUKUCHI
VIZ Media Edition

Translation & Adaptation/Kenichiro Yagi
Touch-up Art & Lettering/Avril Averill
Cover Design/Amy Martin
Graphic Layout/Nozomi Akashi
Editor/Shaenon K. Garrity

Editor in Chief, Books/Alvin Lu
Editor in Chief, Magazines/Marc Weidenbaum
VP of Publishing Licensing/Rika Inouye
VP of Sales/Gonzalo Ferreyra
Sr. VP of Marketing/Liza Coppola
Publisher/Hyoe Narita

Printed in the U.S.A.

Published by VIZ Media, LLC
P.O. Box 77010
San Francisco, CA 94107

VIZ Media Edition
10 9 8 7 6 5 4 3 2 1
First printing, February 2008

www.viz.com

store.viz.com

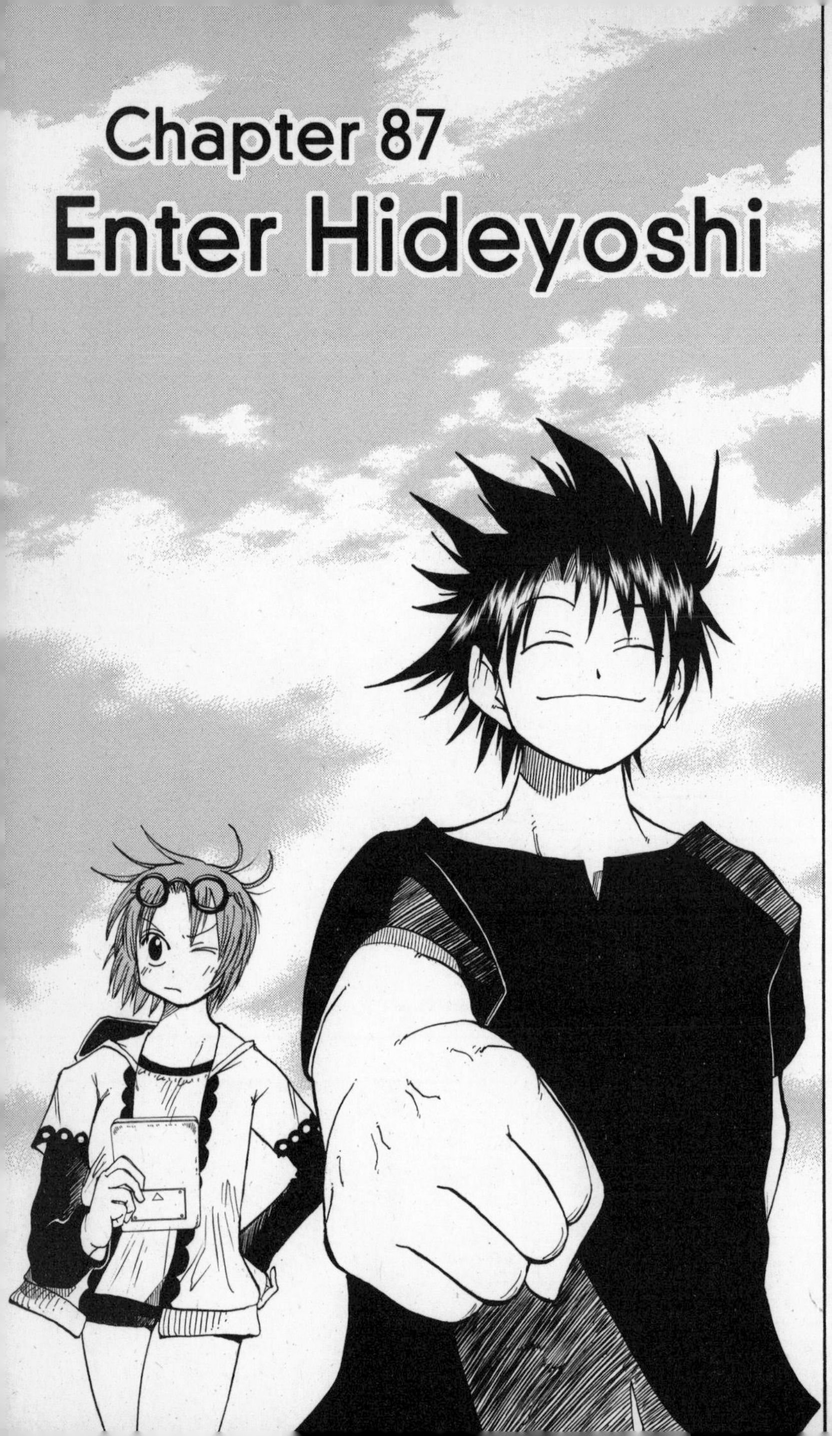
Chapter 87
Enter Hideyoshi

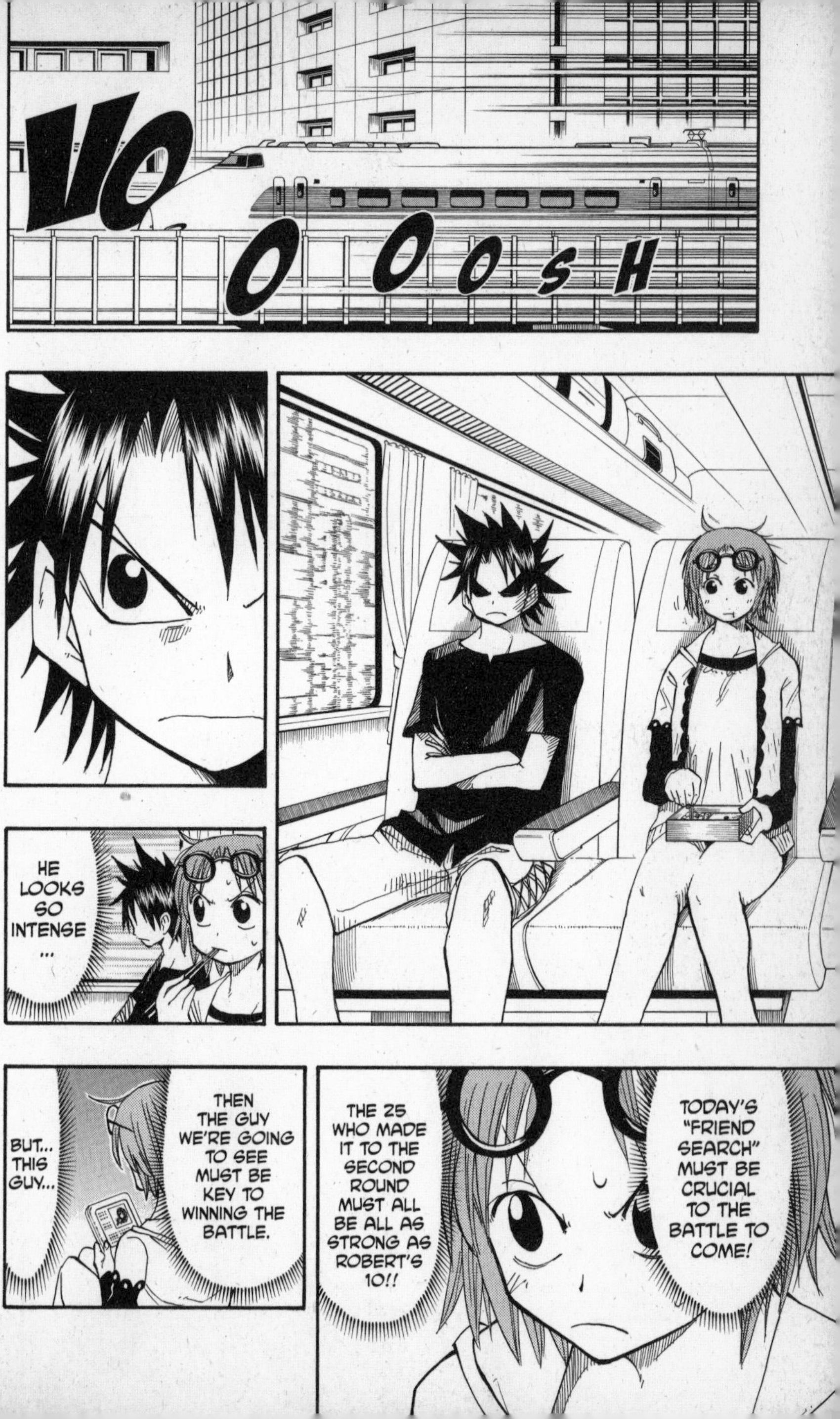
VOOOOSH
HE LOOKS SO INTENSE...
TODAY'S "FRIEND SEARCH" MUST BE CRUCIAL TO THE BATTLE TO COME!
THE 25 WHO MADE IT TO THE SECOND ROUND MUST ALL BE ALL AS STRONG AS ROBERT'S 10!!
THEN THE GUY WE'RE GOING TO SEE MUST BE KEY TO WINNING THE BATTLE.
BUT... THIS GUY...

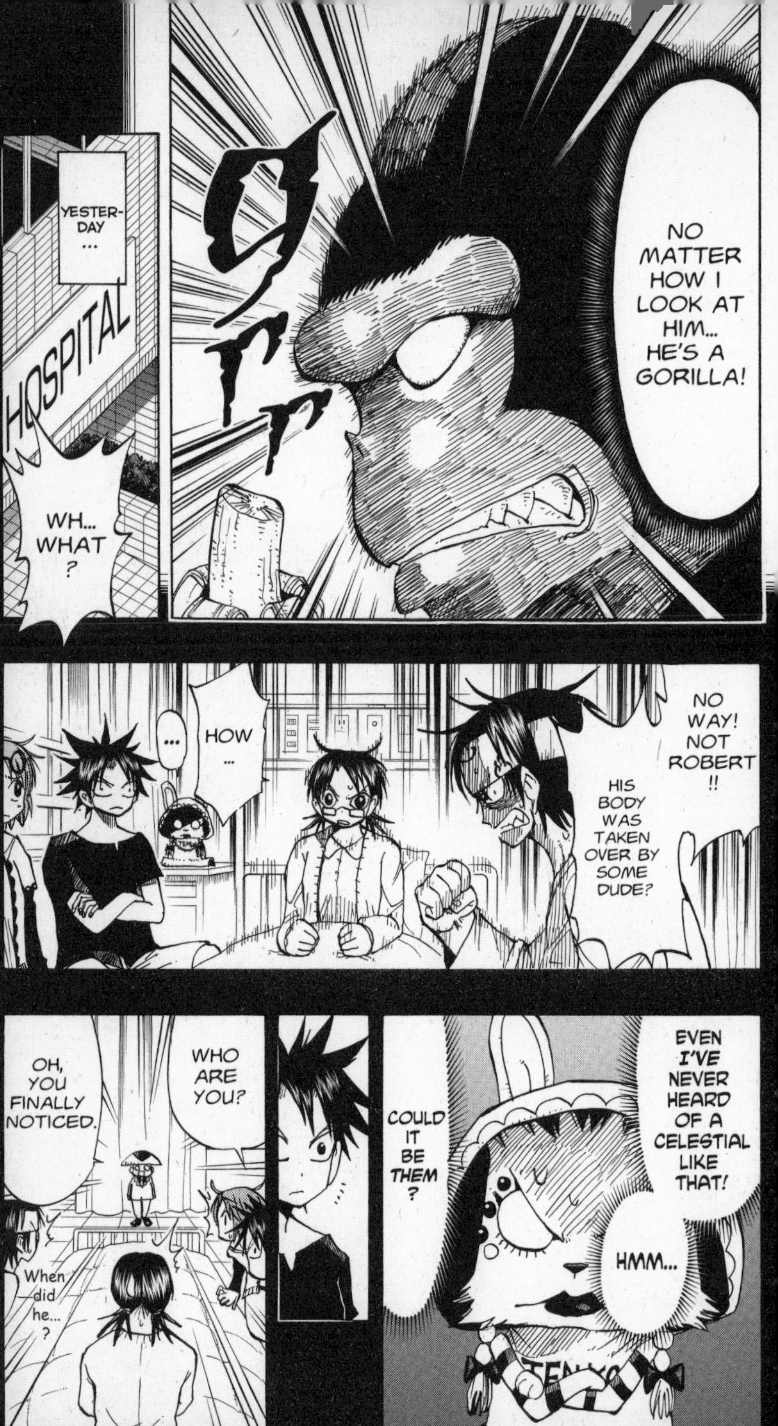
NO MATTER HOW I LOOK AT HIM... HE'S A GORILLA!
YESTER-DAY ...
HOSPITAL
WH... WHAT ?
NO WAY! NOT ROBERT !!
HIS BODY WAS TAKEN OVER BY SOME DUDE?
HOW ...
...
EVEN I'VE NEVER HEARD OF A CELESTIAL LIKE THAT!
HMM...
COULD IT BE THEM ?
WHO ARE YOU?
OH, YOU FINALLY NOTICED.
When did he... ?

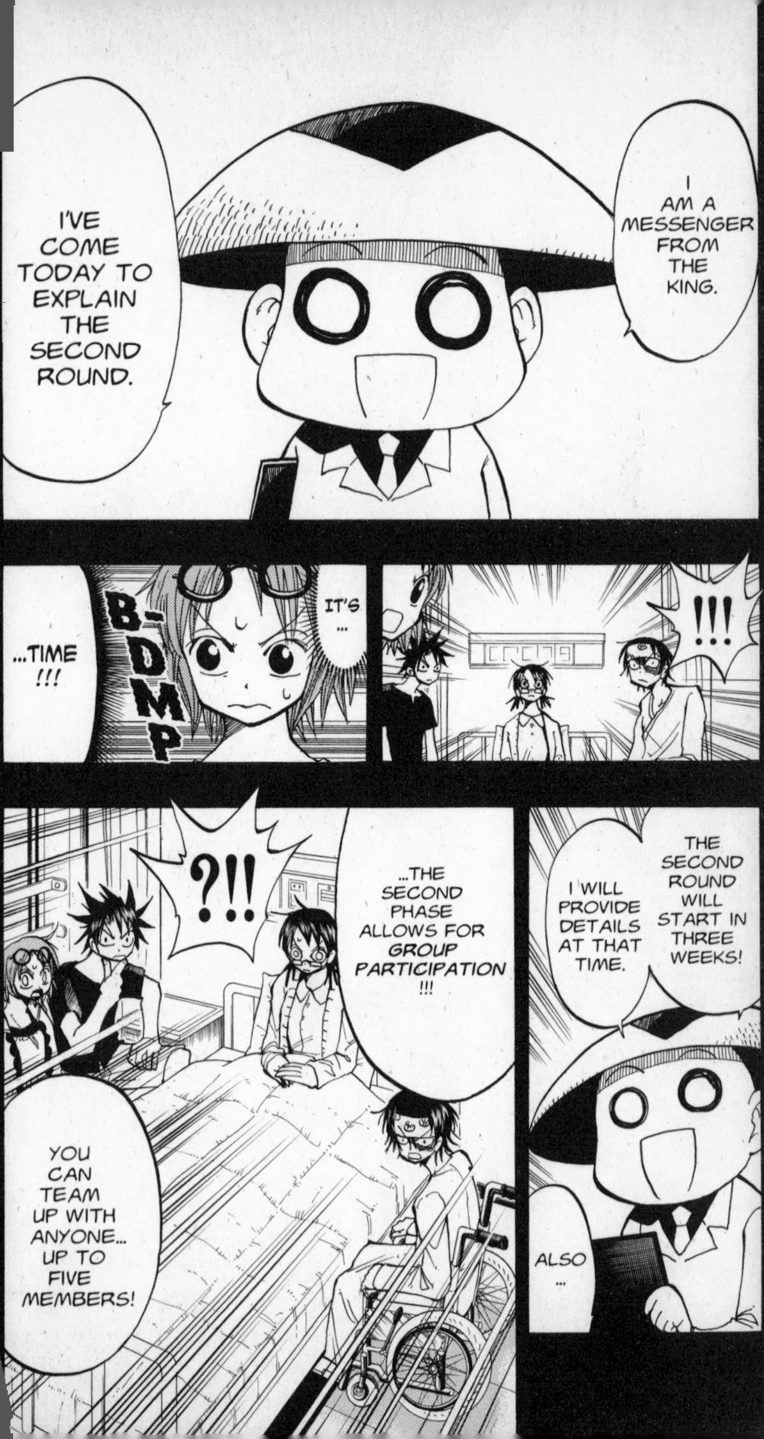
I AM A MESSENGER FROM THE KING.
I'VE COME TODAY TO EXPLAIN THE SECOND ROUND.
!!!
IT'S ...
B-DMP
...TIME !!!
THE SECOND ROUND WILL START IN THREE WEEKS!
I WILL PROVIDE DETAILS AT THAT TIME.
ALSO ...
...THE SECOND PHASE ALLOWS FOR GROUP PARTICIPATION !!!
?!!
YOU CAN TEAM UP WITH ANYONE... UP TO FIVE MEMBERS!

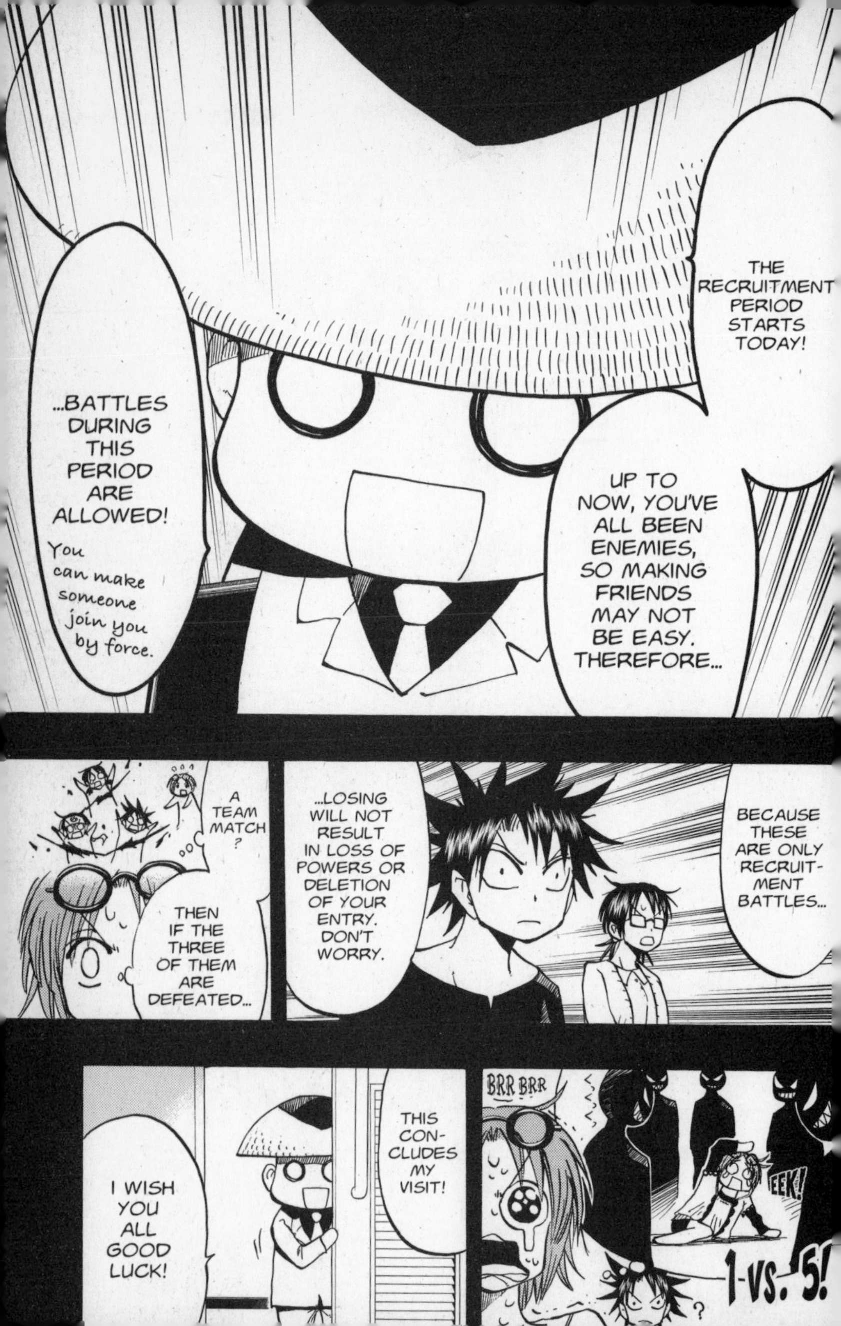
THE RECRUITMENT PERIOD STARTS TODAY!
UP TO NOW, YOU'VE ALL BEEN ENEMIES, SO MAKING FRIENDS MAY NOT BE EASY. THEREFORE...
...BATTLES DURING THIS PERIOD ARE ALLOWED!
You can make someone join you by force.
BECAUSE THESE ARE ONLY RECRUIT-MENT BATTLES...
...LOSING WILL NOT RESULT IN LOSS OF POWERS OR DELETION OF YOUR ENTRY. DON'T WORRY.
A TEAM MATCH?
THEN IF THE THREE OF THEM ARE DEFEATED...
BRR BRR
EEK!
1-VS.-5!
THIS CON-CLUDES MY VISIT!
I WISH YOU ALL GOOD LUCK!

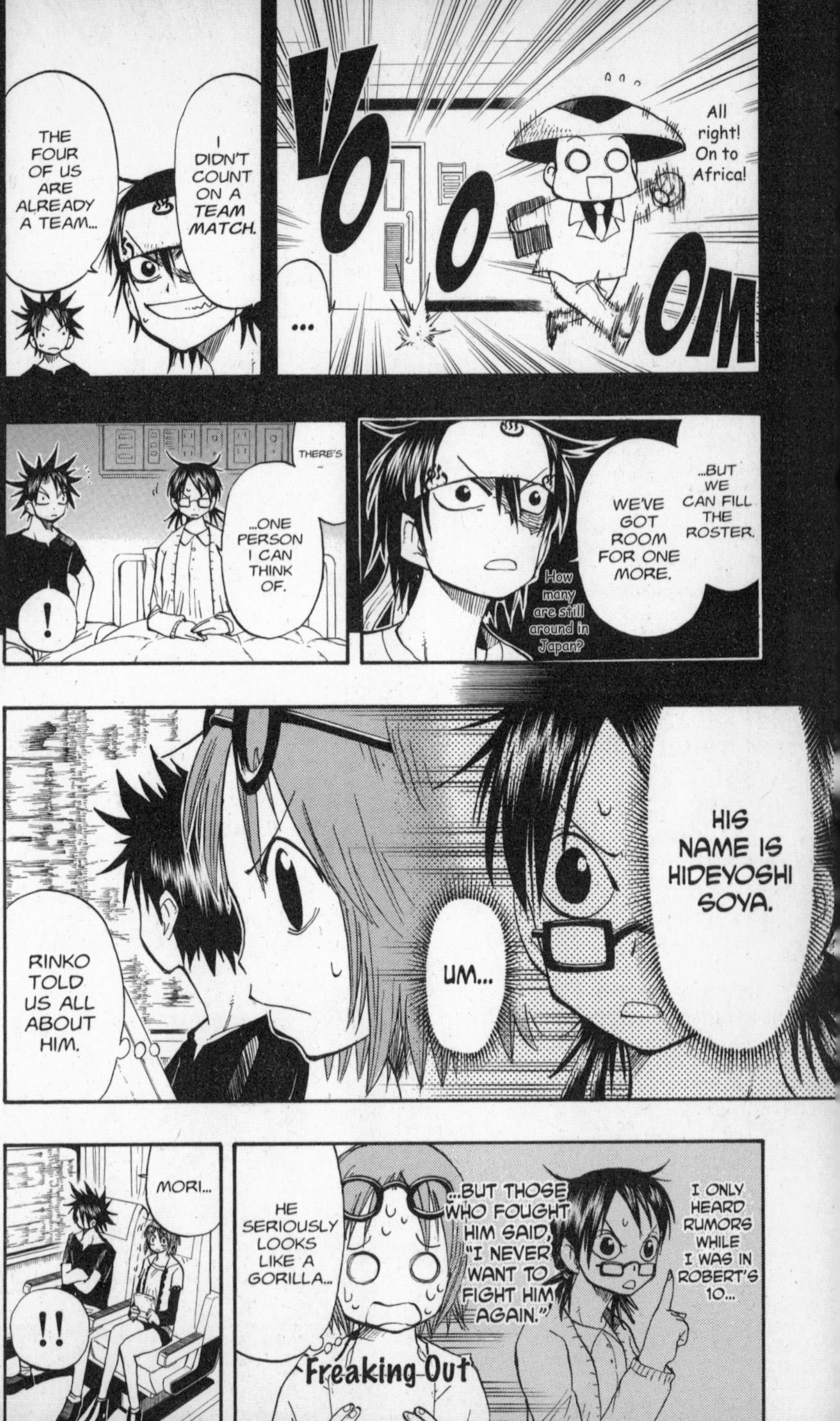
All right! On to Africa!
VOOOOM
...
I DIDN'T COUNT ON A TEAM MATCH.
THE FOUR OF US ARE ALREADY A TEAM...
...BUT WE CAN FILL THE ROSTER.
WE'VE GOT ROOM FOR ONE MORE.
How many are still around in Japan?
THERE'S —
...ONE PERSON I CAN THINK OF.
!
HIS NAME IS HIDEYOSHI SOYA.
UM...
RINKO TOLD US ALL ABOUT HIM.
I ONLY HEARD RUMORS WHILE I WAS IN ROBERT'S 10...
...BUT THOSE WHO FOUGHT HIM SAID, "I NEVER WANT TO FIGHT HIM AGAIN."
HE SERIOUSLY LOOKS LIKE A GORILLA...
Freaking Out
MORI...
!!

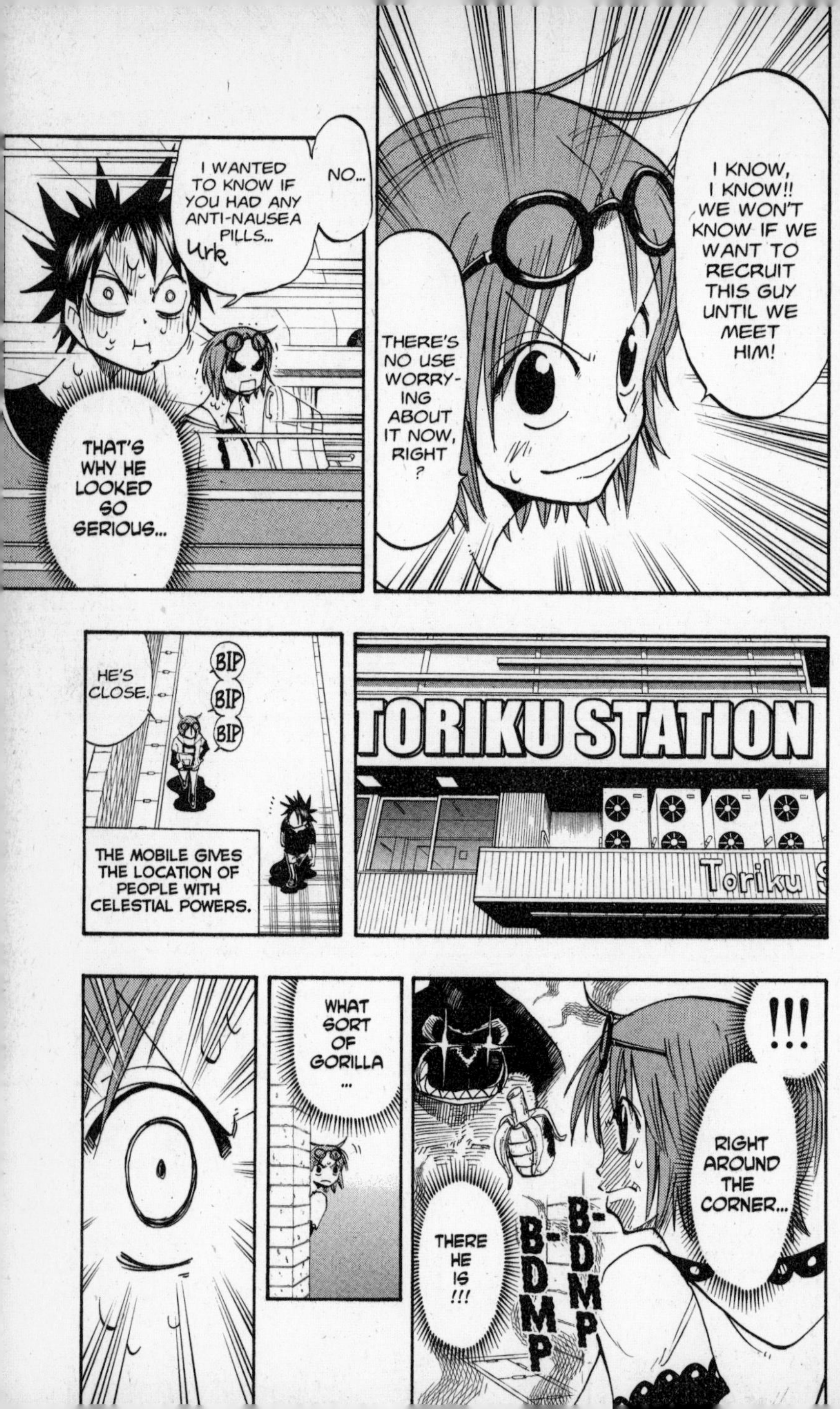
I KNOW, I KNOW!! WE WON'T KNOW IF WE WANT TO RECRUIT THIS GUY UNTIL WE MEET HIM!
THERE'S NO USE WORRY-ING ABOUT IT NOW, RIGHT?
NO...
I WANTED TO KNOW IF YOU HAD ANY ANTI-NAUSEA PILLS...
Urk
THAT'S WHY HE LOOKED SO SERIOUS...
TORIKU STATION
Toriku S
HE'S CLOSE.
BIP
BIP
BIP
THE MOBILE GIVES THE LOCATION OF PEOPLE WITH CELESTIAL POWERS.
!!!
RIGHT AROUND THE CORNER...
B-BDMP
B-BDMP
THERE HE IS!!!
WHAT SORT OF GORILLA...

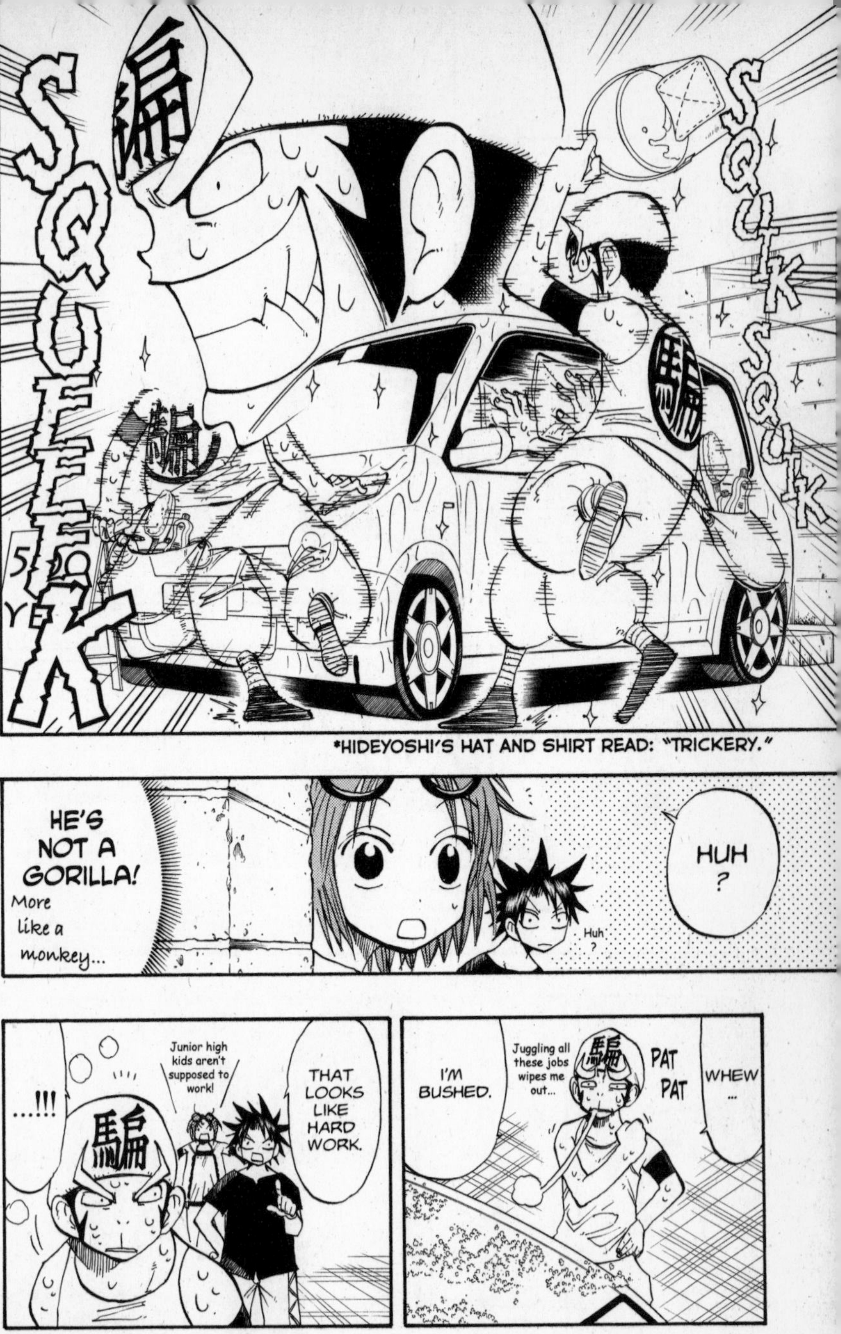
SQUIK SQUIK
SQUEEEK
*HIDEYOSHI'S HAT AND SHIRT READ: "TRICKERY."
HUH ?
Huh ?
HE'S NOT A GORILLA!
More like a monkey...
WHEW ...
PAT PAT
Juggling all these jobs wipes me out...
I'M BUSHED.
THAT LOOKS LIKE HARD WORK.
Junior high kids aren't supposed to work!
...!!!

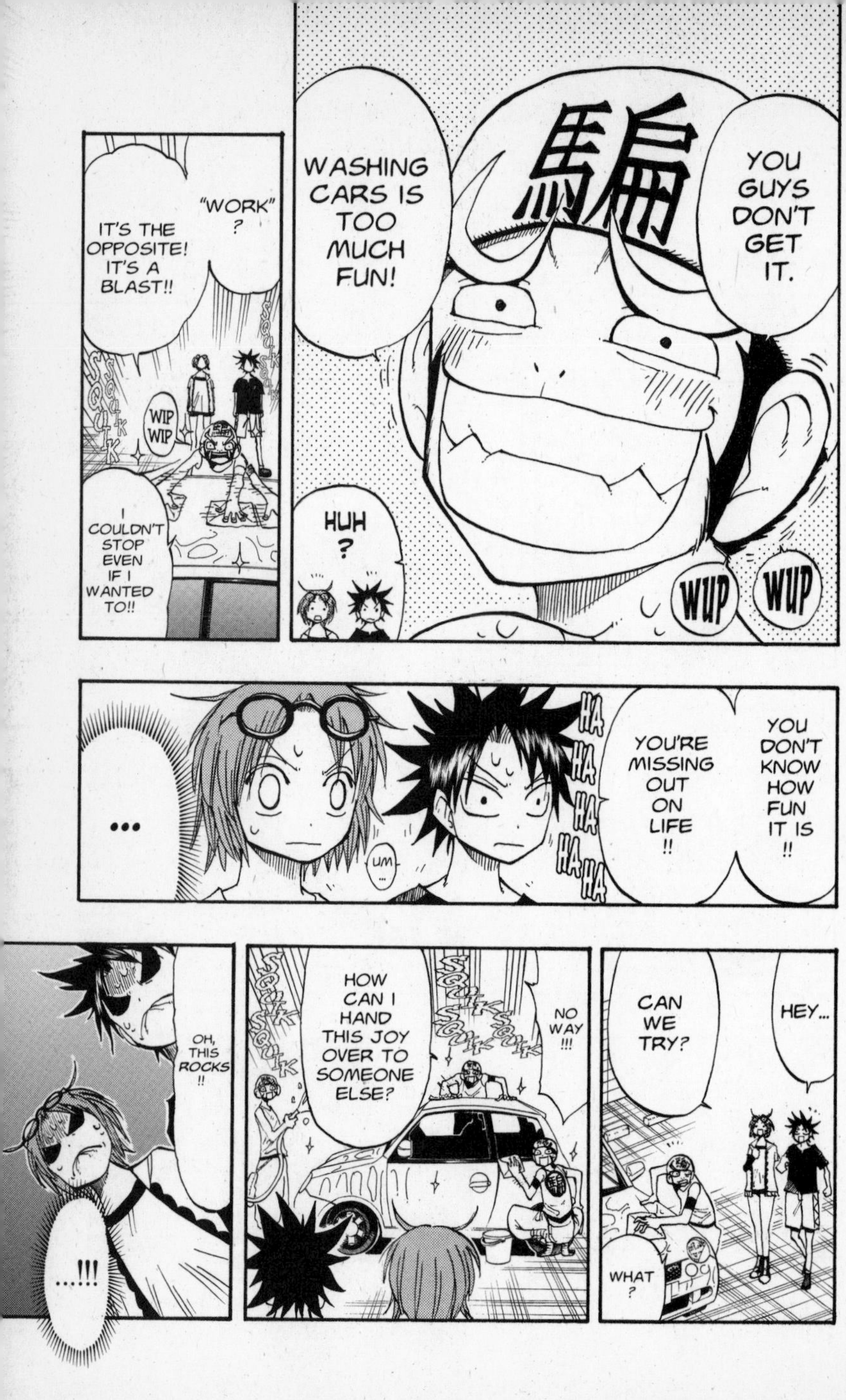
YOU GUYS DON'T GET IT.
馬扁
WASHING CARS IS TOO MUCH FUN!
WUP
WUP
HUH ?
"WORK" ?
IT'S THE OPPOSITE! IT'S A BLAST!!
WIP WIP
I COULDN'T STOP EVEN IF I WANTED TO!!
YOU DON'T KNOW HOW FUN IT IS !!
YOU'RE MISSING OUT ON LIFE !!
HA HA HA HA HA HA
UM ...
...
HEY...
CAN WE TRY?
WHAT ?
NO WAY !!!
HOW CAN I HAND THIS JOY OVER TO SOMEONE ELSE?
OH, THIS ROCKS !!
...!!!

PLEASE!!! JUST A LITTLE BIT !!!
PLEASE? PLEASE?
HMM ...
ALL RIGHT ...
...BUT NOT FOR FREE.
500 YEN PER PERSON.
WE'LL PAY !!
ALL RIGHT !!!
WA HA HA HA HA !!!
FUN! FUN !!
CAN'T STOP US NOW...
AHA HA... HA HA...
...
...?
ER...
IT'S NOT... THAT MUCH FUN...
OH, HEY! IT'S SPARKLING !!
My car!
NO PROBLEM, MISTER !!

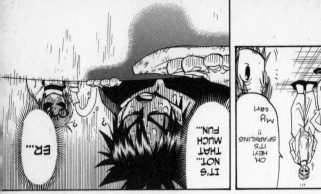

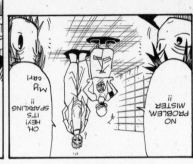

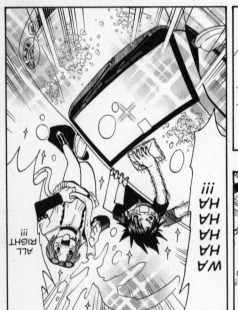

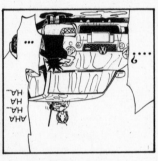

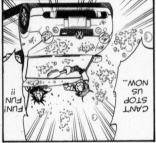

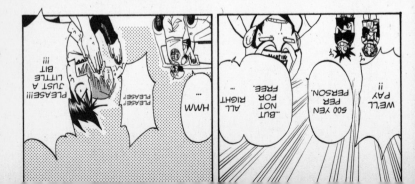

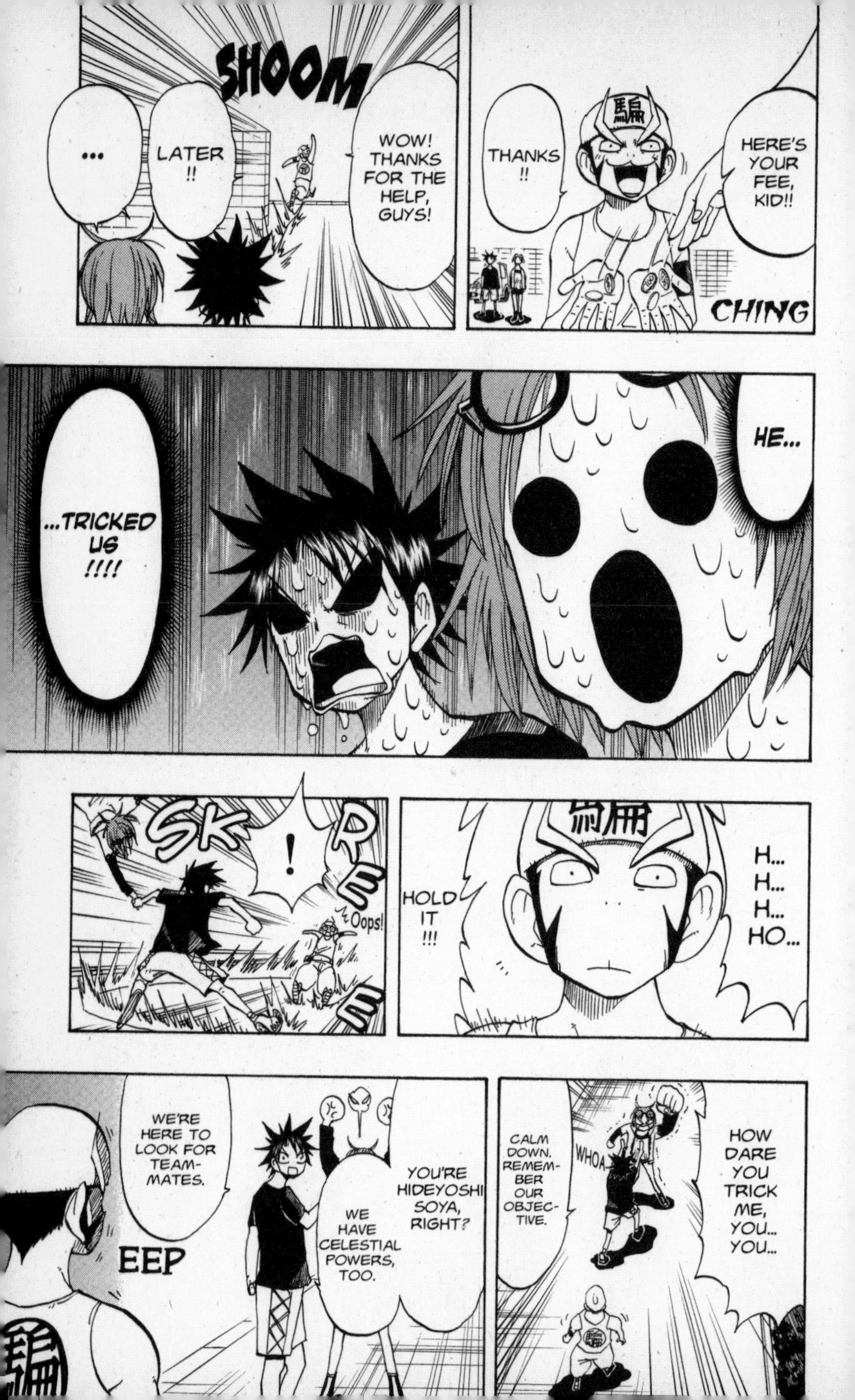
HERE'S YOUR FEE, KID!!
CHING
THANKS !!
WOW! THANKS FOR THE HELP, GUYS!
SHOOM
LATER !!
...
HE...
...TRICKED US !!!!
H... H... H... HO...
HOLD IT !!!
SK
!
RE
Oops!
E
HOW DARE YOU TRICK ME, YOU... YOU...
WHOA
CALM DOWN. REMEMBER OUR OBJECTIVE.
YOU'RE HIDEYOSHI SOYA, RIGHT?
WE HAVE CELESTIAL POWERS, TOO.
WE'RE HERE TO LOOK FOR TEAMMATES.
EEP

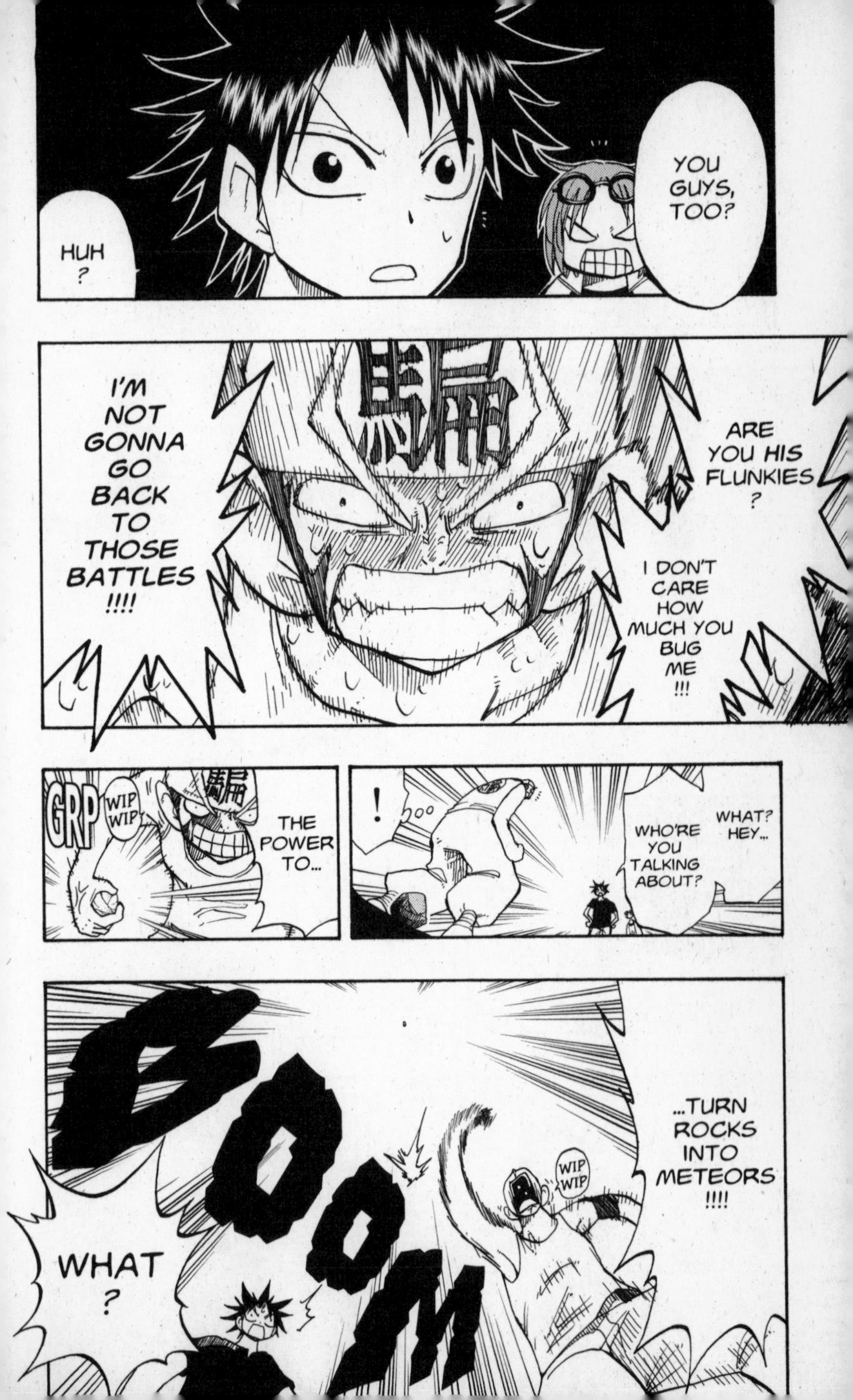
YOU GUYS, TOO?
HUH ?
ARE YOU HIS FLUNKIES ?
I DON'T CARE HOW MUCH YOU BUG ME !!!
I'M NOT GONNA GO BACK TO THOSE BATTLES !!!!
WHAT? HEY...
WHO'RE YOU TALKING ABOUT?
!
THE POWER TO...
WIP WIP
GRP
...TURN ROCKS INTO METEORS !!!!
WIP WIP
BOOM
WHAT ?

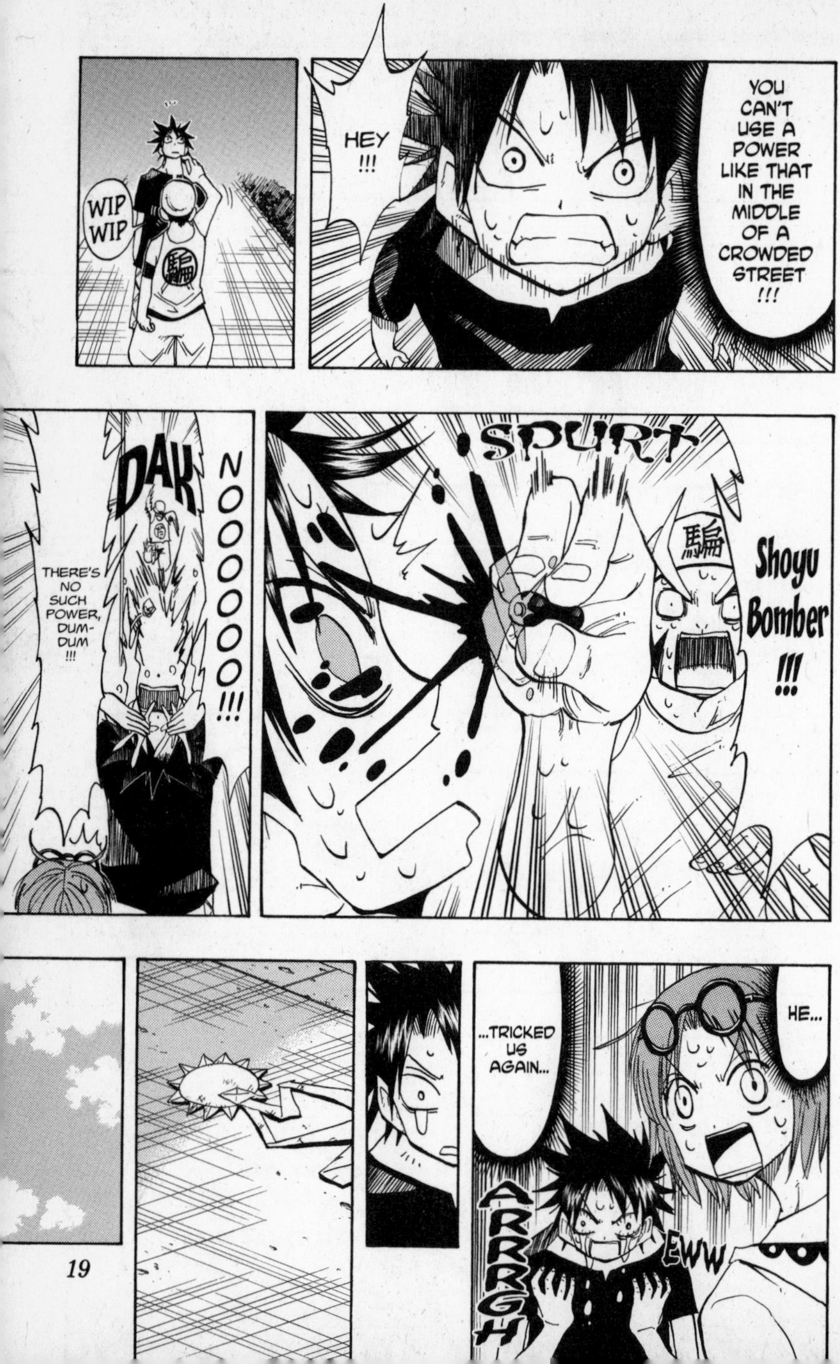
YOU CAN'T USE A POWER LIKE THAT IN THE MIDDLE OF A CROWDED STREET !!!
HEY !!!
WIP WIP
Shoyu Bomber !!!
SPURT
NOOOOOOO!!!
DAK
THERE'S NO SUCH POWER, DUM-DUM !!!
HE...
...TRICKED US AGAIN...
EWW
ARRRGH

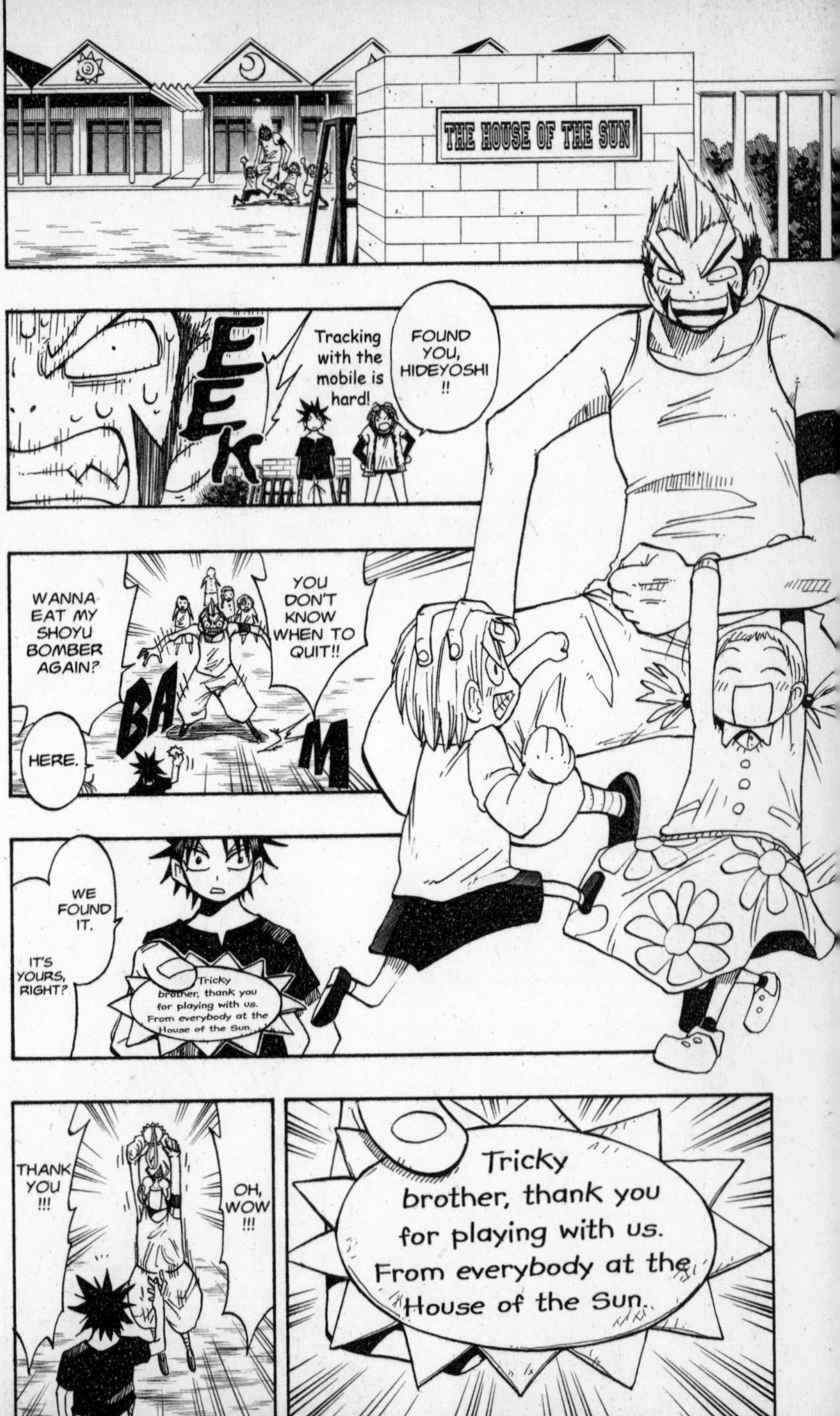
THE HOUSE OF THE SUN
FOUND YOU, HIDEYOSHI !!
Tracking with the mobile is hard!
EEK
YOU DON'T KNOW WHEN TO QUIT!!
WANNA EAT MY SHOYU BOMBER AGAIN?
BAM
HERE.
WE FOUND IT.
IT'S YOURS, RIGHT?
Tricky brother, thank you for playing with us. From everybody at the House of the Sun.
Tricky brother, thank you for playing with us. From everybody at the House of the Sun.
OH, WOW !!!
THANK YOU !!!

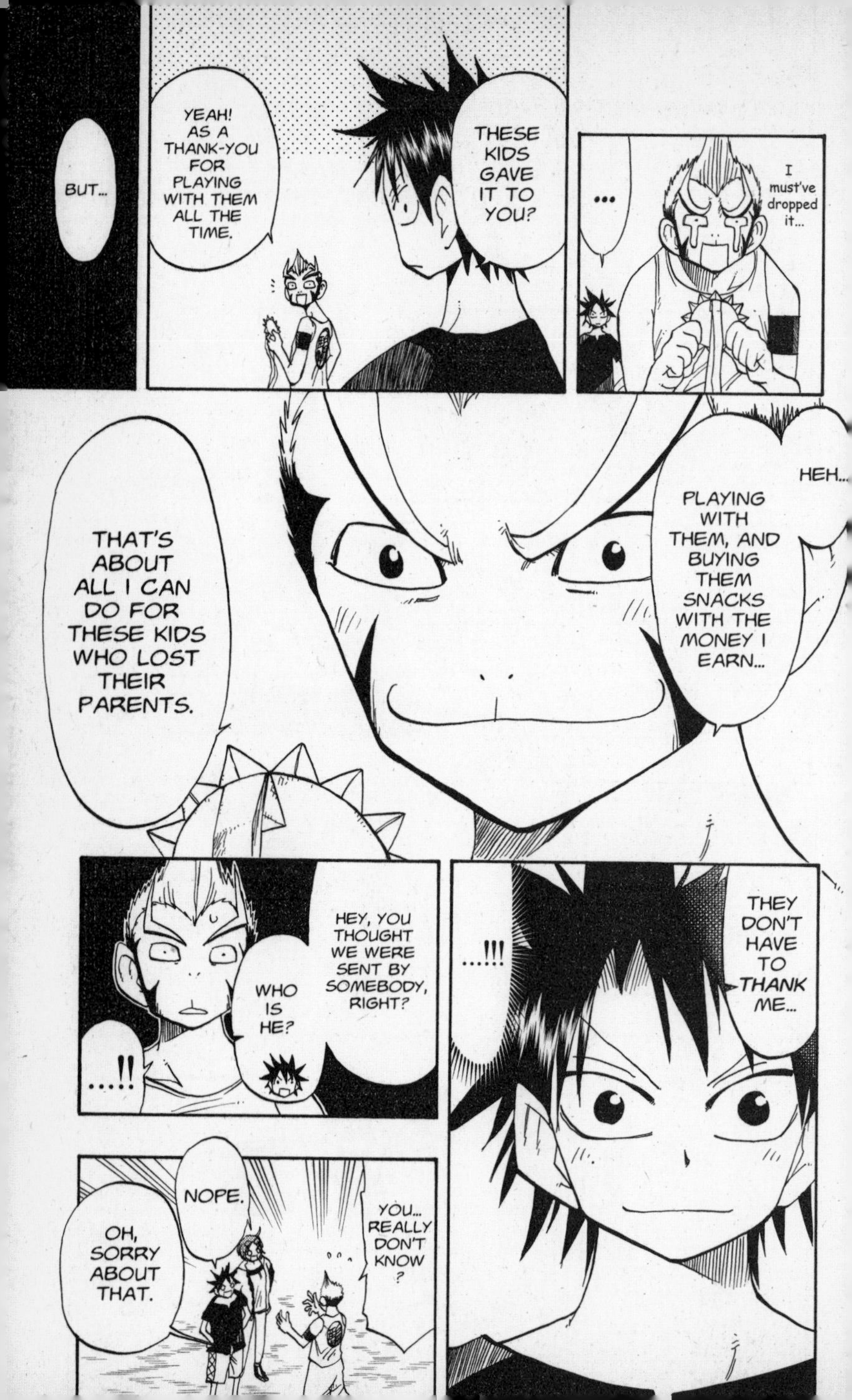

I must've dropped it...
...
THESE KIDS GAVE IT TO YOU?
YEAH! AS A THANK-YOU FOR PLAYING WITH THEM ALL THE TIME.
BUT...
HEH...
PLAYING WITH THEM, AND BUYING THEM SNACKS WITH THE MONEY I EARN...
THAT'S ABOUT ALL I CAN DO FOR THESE KIDS WHO LOST THEIR PARENTS.
THEY DON'T HAVE TO THANK ME...
...!!!
HEY, YOU THOUGHT WE WERE SENT BY SOMEBODY, RIGHT?
WHO IS HE?
....!!
YOU... REALLY DON'T KNOW?
NOPE.
OH, SORRY ABOUT THAT.

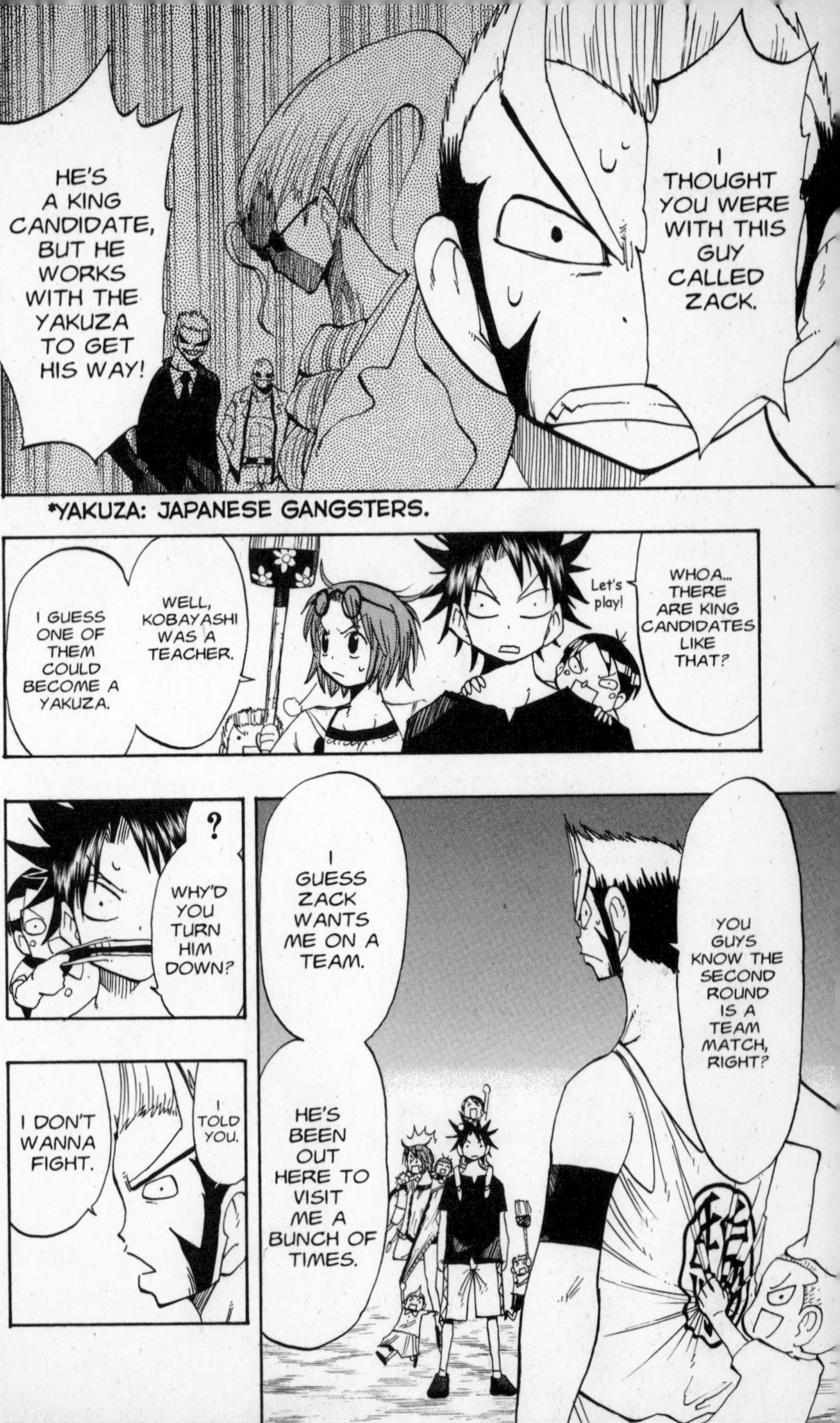
I THOUGHT YOU WERE WITH THIS GUY CALLED ZACK.
HE'S A KING CANDIDATE, BUT HE WORKS WITH THE YAKUZA TO GET HIS WAY!
*YAKUZA: JAPANESE GANGSTERS.
WHOA... THERE ARE KING CANDIDATES LIKE THAT?
Let's play!
WELL, KOBAYASHI WAS A TEACHER.
I GUESS ONE OF THEM COULD BECOME A YAKUZA.
YOU GUYS KNOW THE SECOND ROUND IS A TEAM MATCH, RIGHT?
I GUESS ZACK WANTS ME ON A TEAM.
HE'S BEEN OUT HERE TO VISIT ME A BUNCH OF TIMES.
?
WHY'D YOU TURN HIM DOWN?
I TOLD YOU.
I DON'T WANNA FIGHT.

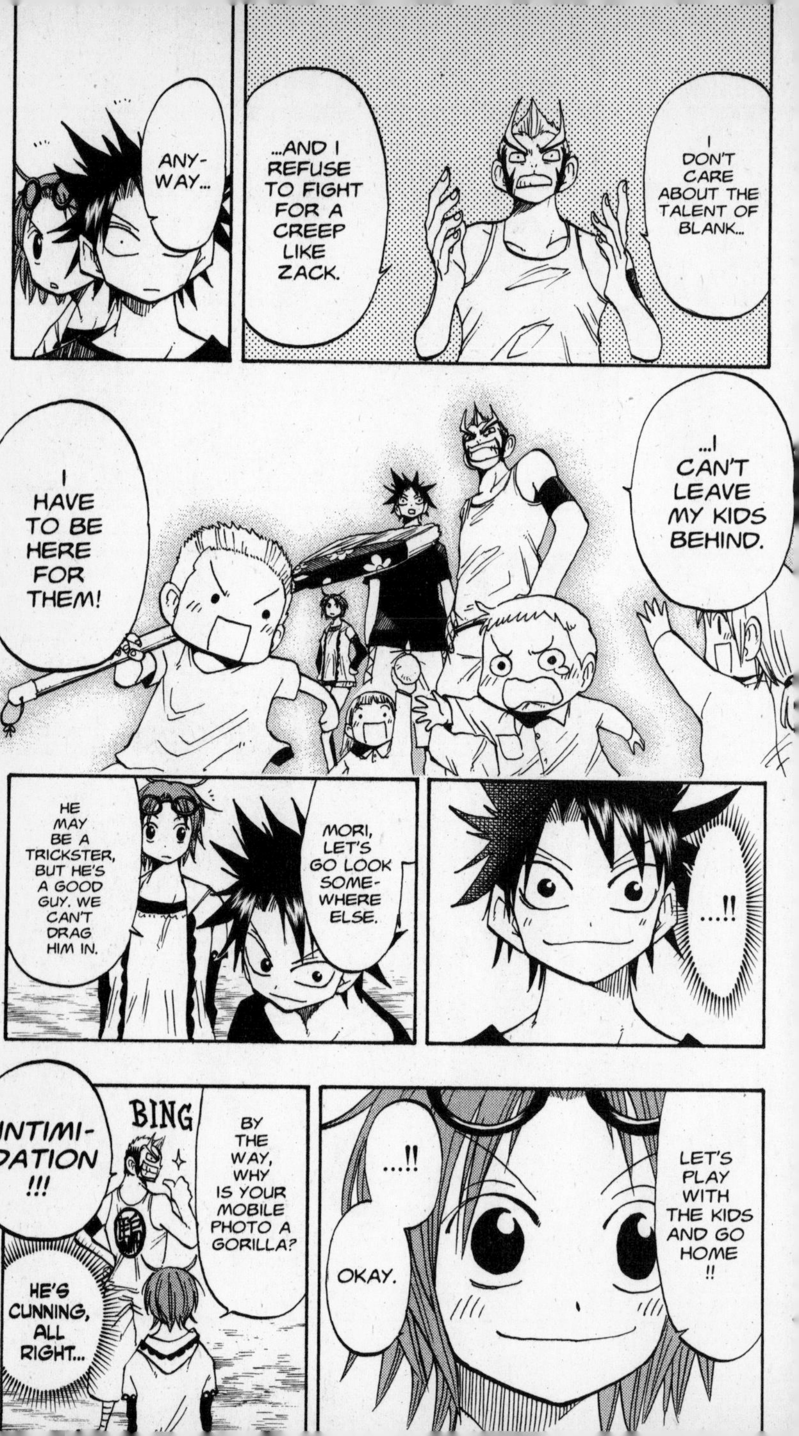
I DON'T CARE ABOUT THE TALENT OF BLANK...
...AND I REFUSE TO FIGHT FOR A CREEP LIKE ZACK.
ANY-WAY...
...I CAN'T LEAVE MY KIDS BEHIND.
I HAVE TO BE HERE FOR THEM!
...!!
MORI, LET'S GO LOOK SOME-WHERE ELSE.
HE MAY BE A TRICKSTER, BUT HE'S A GOOD GUY. WE CAN'T DRAG HIM IN.
LET'S PLAY WITH THE KIDS AND GO HOME !!
...!!
OKAY.
BY THE WAY, WHY IS YOUR MOBILE PHOTO A GORILLA?
BING
INTIMI-DATION !!!
HE'S CUNNING, ALL RIGHT...

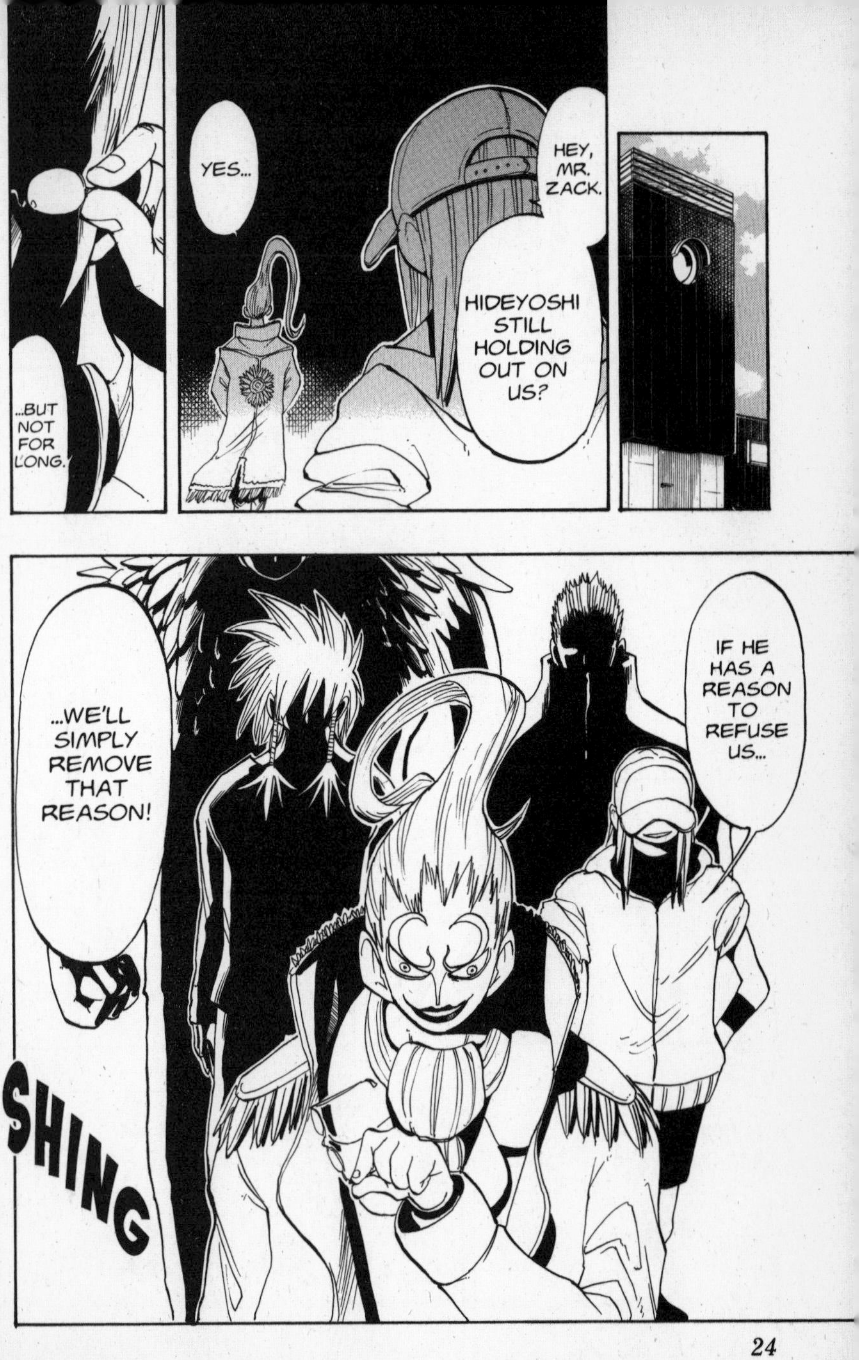
HEY, MR. ZACK.
HIDEYOSHI STILL HOLDING OUT ON US?
YES...
...BUT NOT FOR LONG.
IF HE HAS A REASON TO REFUSE US...
...WE'LL SIMPLY REMOVE THAT REASON!
SHING

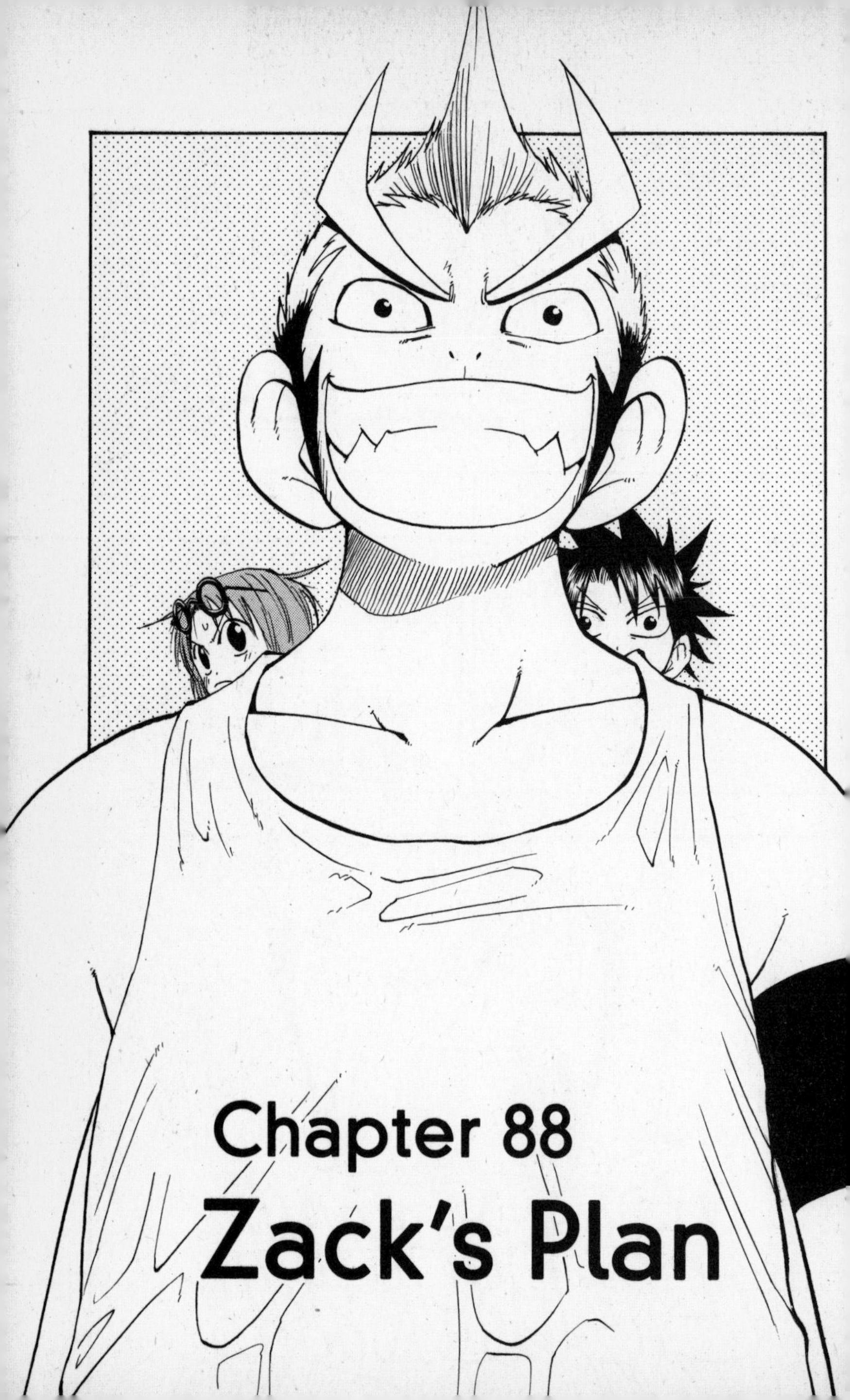
Chapter 88
Zack's Plan

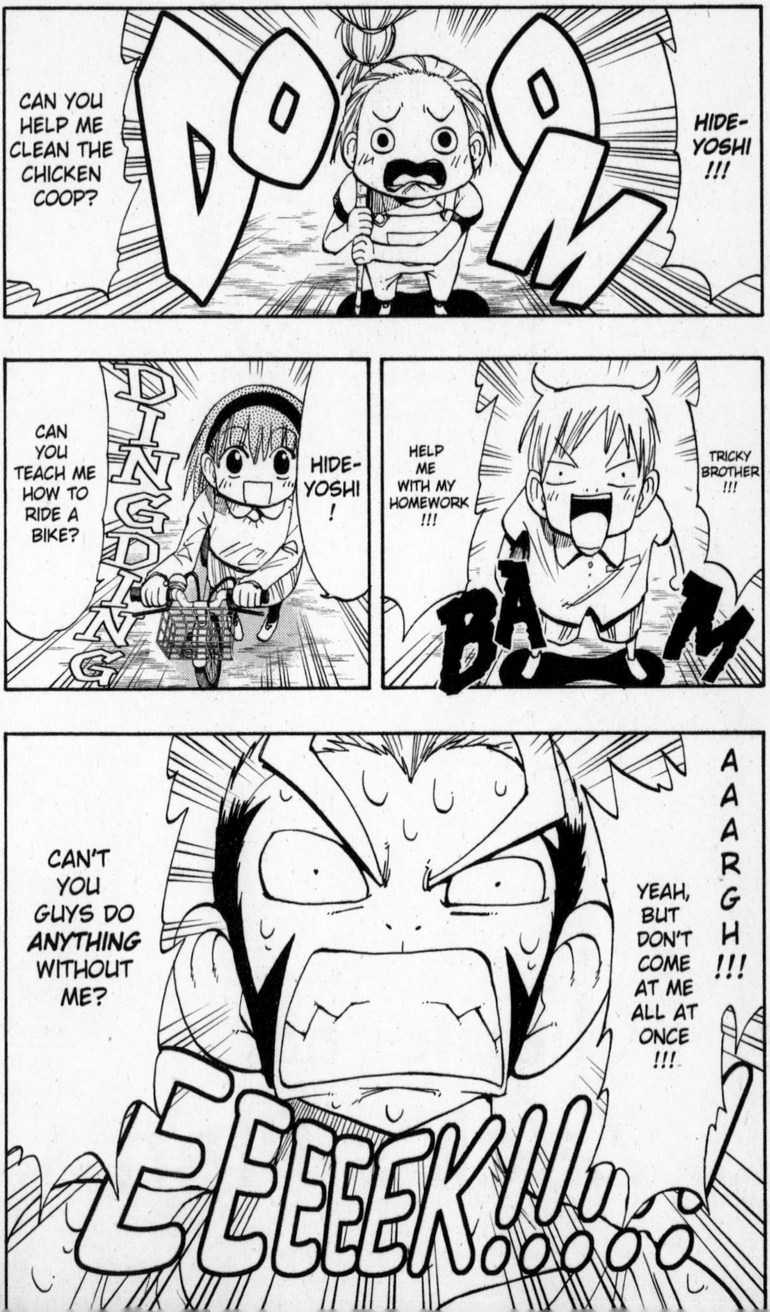
HIDE-YOSHI !!!
DOOM
CAN YOU HELP ME CLEAN THE CHICKEN COOP?
TRICKY BROTHER !!!
HELP ME WITH MY HOMEWORK !!!
BAM
HIDE-YOSHI !
DINGDING
CAN YOU TEACH ME HOW TO RIDE A BIKE?
AAAARGH !!!
YEAH, BUT DON'T COME AT ME ALL AT ONCE !!!
CAN'T YOU GUYS DO ANYTHING WITHOUT ME?
EEEEEK!!!......

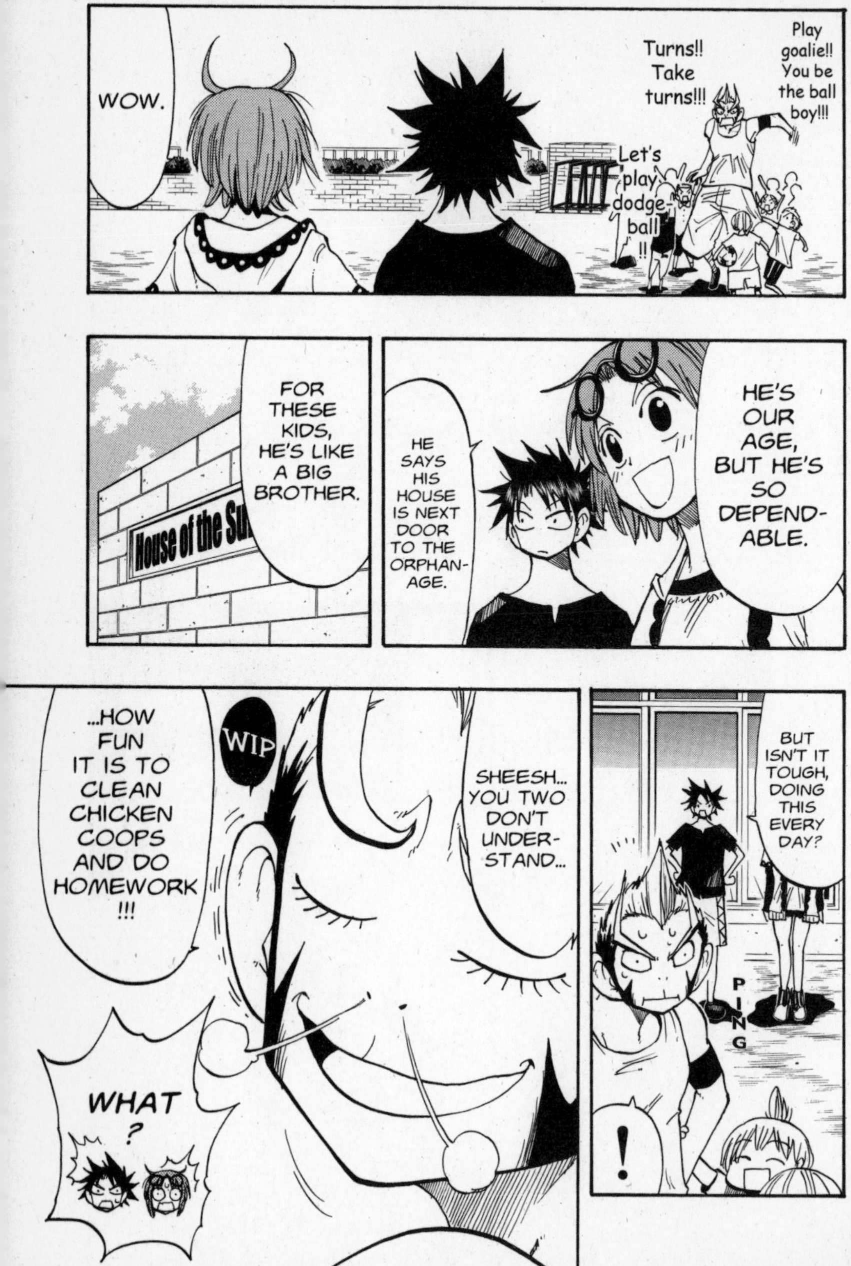
WOW.
Play goalie!! You be the ball boy!!!
Turns!! Take turns!!!
Let's play dodge-ball!!
HE'S OUR AGE, BUT HE'S SO DEPEND-ABLE.
HE SAYS HIS HOUSE IS NEXT DOOR TO THE ORPHAN-AGE.
FOR THESE KIDS, HE'S LIKE A BIG BROTHER.
House of the Su
BUT ISN'T IT TOUGH, DOING THIS EVERY DAY?
PING
!
SHEESH... YOU TWO DON'T UNDER-STAND...
WIP
...HOW FUN IT IS TO CLEAN CHICKEN COOPS AND DO HOMEWORK!!!
WHAT?

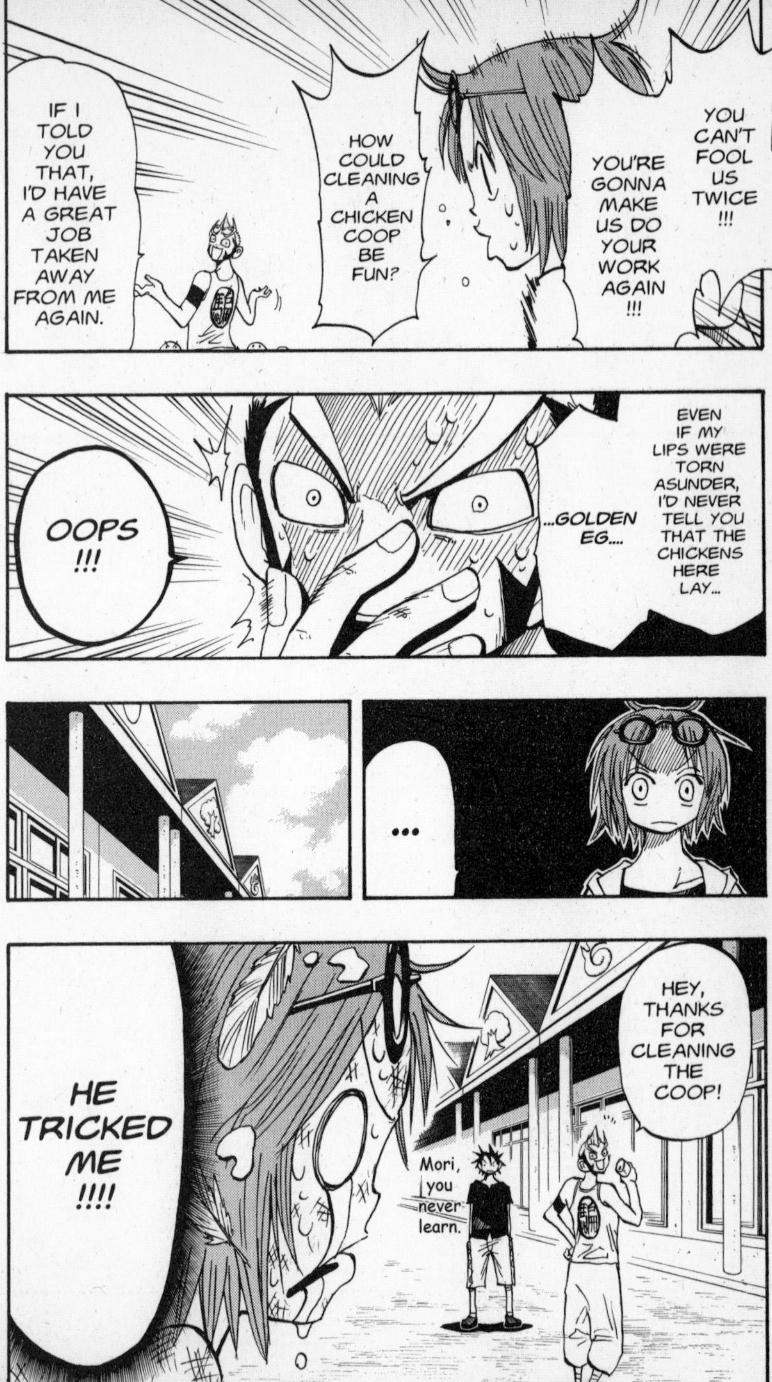
YOU CAN'T FOOL US TWICE !!!
YOU'RE GONNA MAKE US DO YOUR WORK AGAIN !!!
HOW COULD CLEANING A CHICKEN COOP BE FUN?
IF I TOLD YOU THAT, I'D HAVE A GREAT JOB TAKEN AWAY FROM ME AGAIN.
EVEN IF MY LIPS WERE TORN ASUNDER, I'D NEVER TELL YOU THAT THE CHICKENS HERE LAY...
...GOLDEN EG....
OOPS !!!
...
HEY, THANKS FOR CLEANING THE COOP!
Mori, you never learn.
HE TRICKED ME !!!!

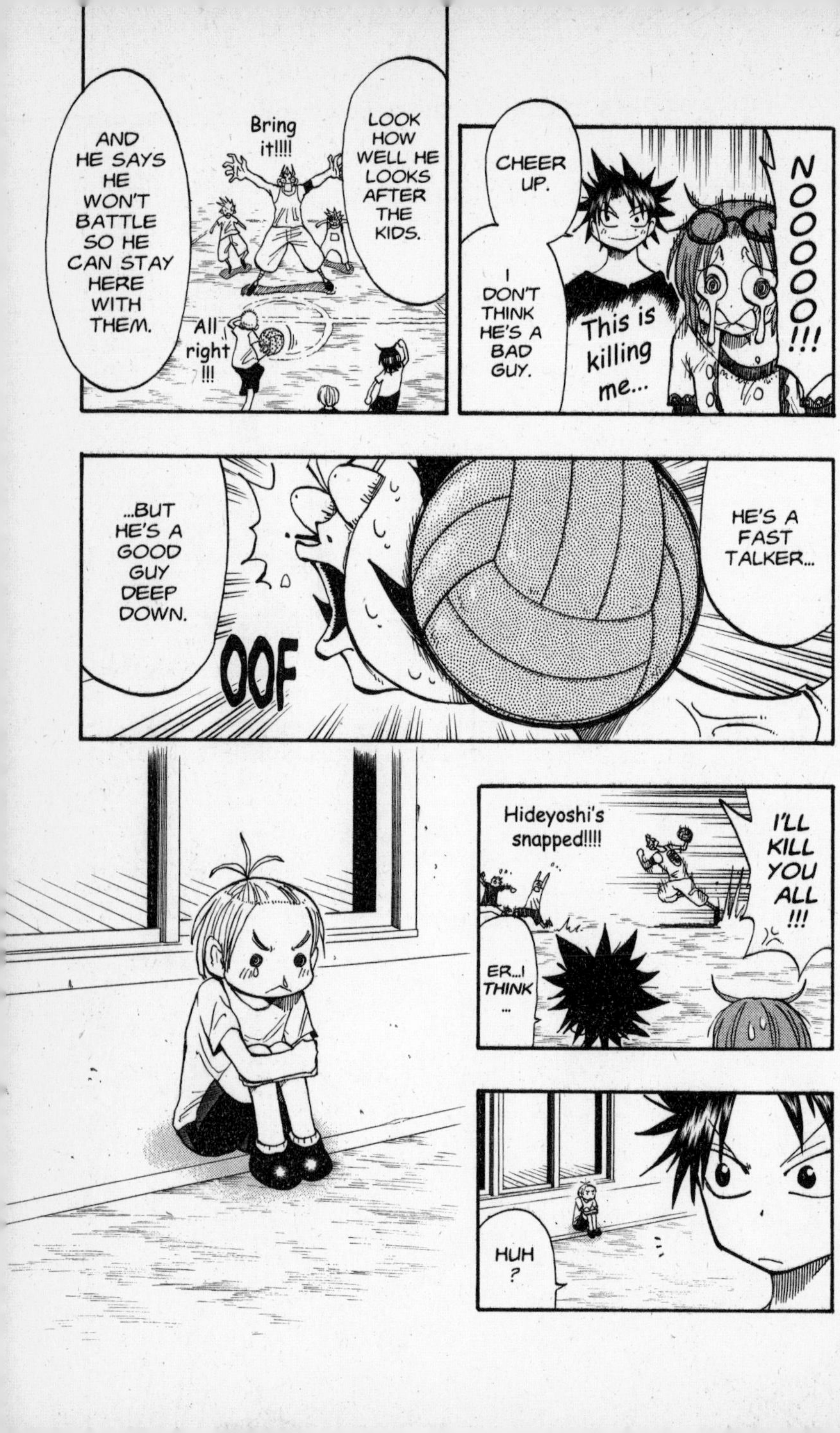
NOOOOOO!!!
CHEER UP.
I DON'T THINK HE'S A BAD GUY.
This is killing me...
LOOK HOW WELL HE LOOKS AFTER THE KIDS.
Bring it!!!!
AND HE SAYS HE WON'T BATTLE SO HE CAN STAY HERE WITH THEM.
All right!!!
HE'S A FAST TALKER...
...BUT HE'S A GOOD GUY DEEP DOWN.
OOF
I'LL KILL YOU ALL!!!
Hideyoshi's snapped!!!!
ER...I THINK...
HUH?

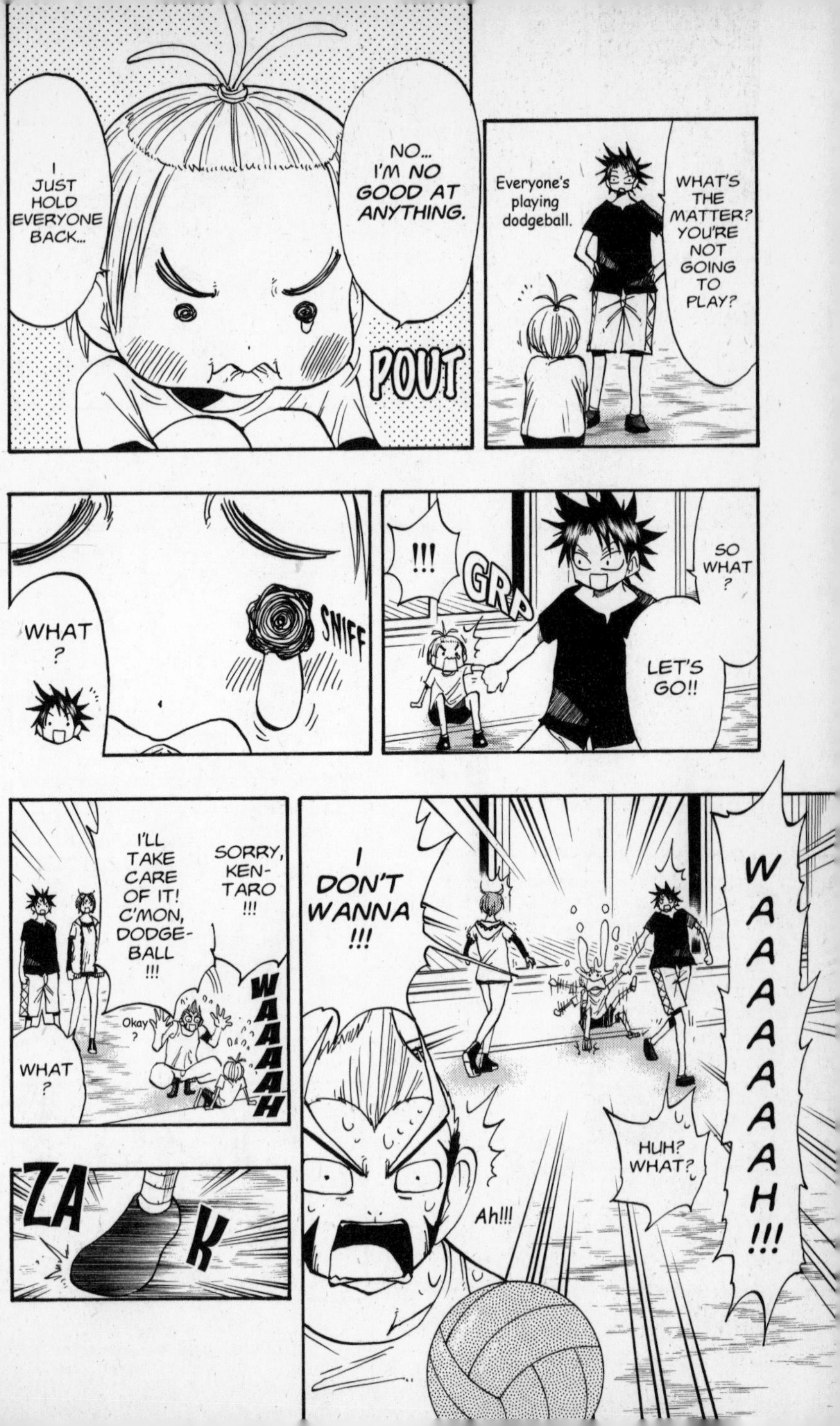
WHAT'S THE MATTER? YOU'RE NOT GOING TO PLAY?
Everyone's playing dodgeball.
NO... I'M NO GOOD AT ANYTHING.
POUT
I JUST HOLD EVERYONE BACK...
SO WHAT?
!!!
GRP
LET'S GO!!
SNIFF
WHAT?
WAAAAAAAAAH!!!
HUH? WHAT?
I DON'T WANNA!!!
Ah!!!
SORRY, KEN-TARO!!!
I'LL TAKE CARE OF IT! C'MON, DODGE-BALL!!!
WAAAAAH
Okay?
WHAT?
ZAK

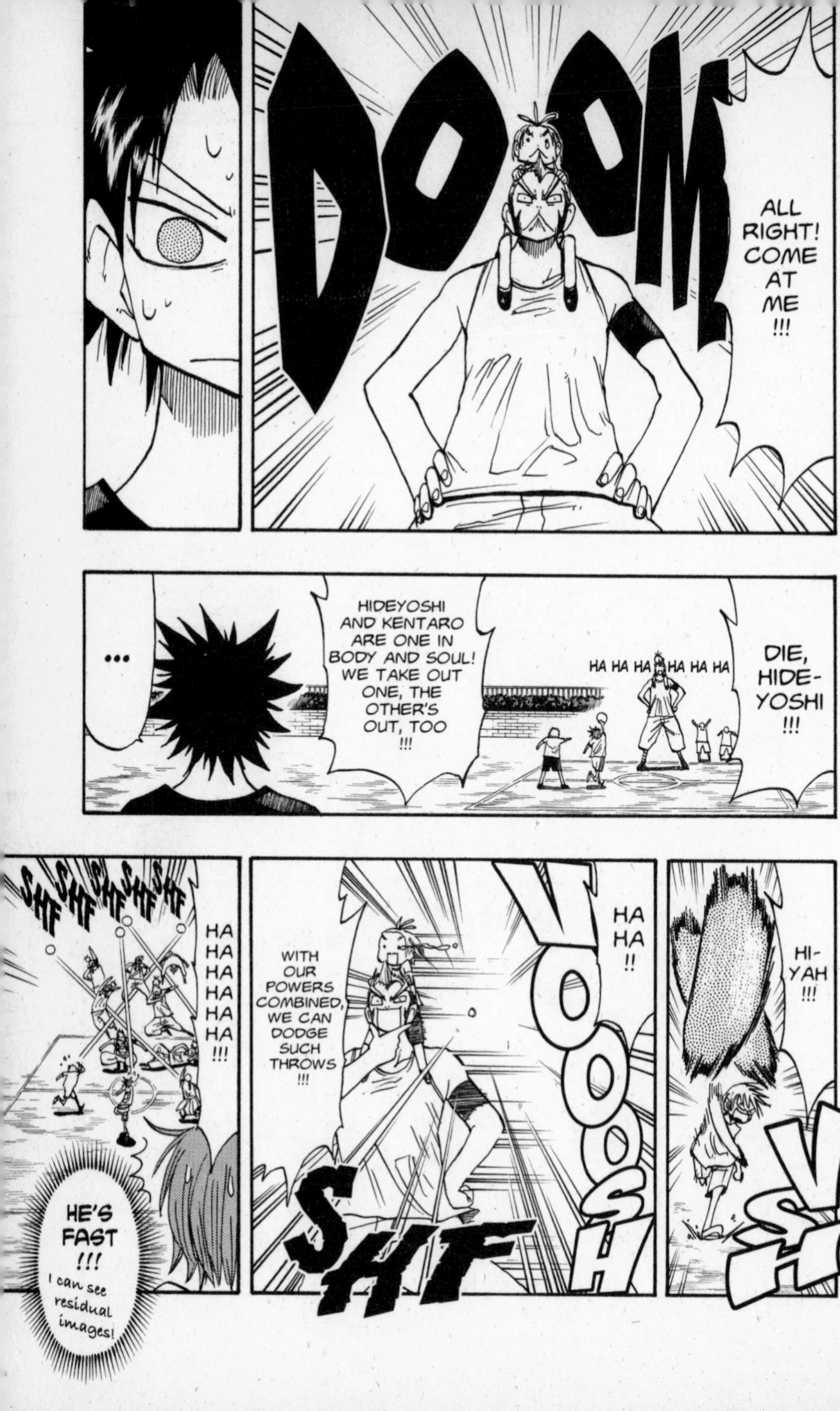
DOOM
ALL RIGHT! COME AT ME !!!
DIE, HIDE-YOSHI !!!
HA HA HA HA HA HA
HIDEYOSHI AND KENTARO ARE ONE IN BODY AND SOUL! WE TAKE OUT ONE, THE OTHER'S OUT, TOO !!!
...
HI-YAH !!!
SV
SH
HA HA !!
VOOOSH
WITH OUR POWERS COMBINED, WE CAN DODGE SUCH THROWS !!!
SHF
HA HA HA HA HA HA !!!
SHF SHF SHF SHF SHF
HE'S FAST !!!
I can see residual images!

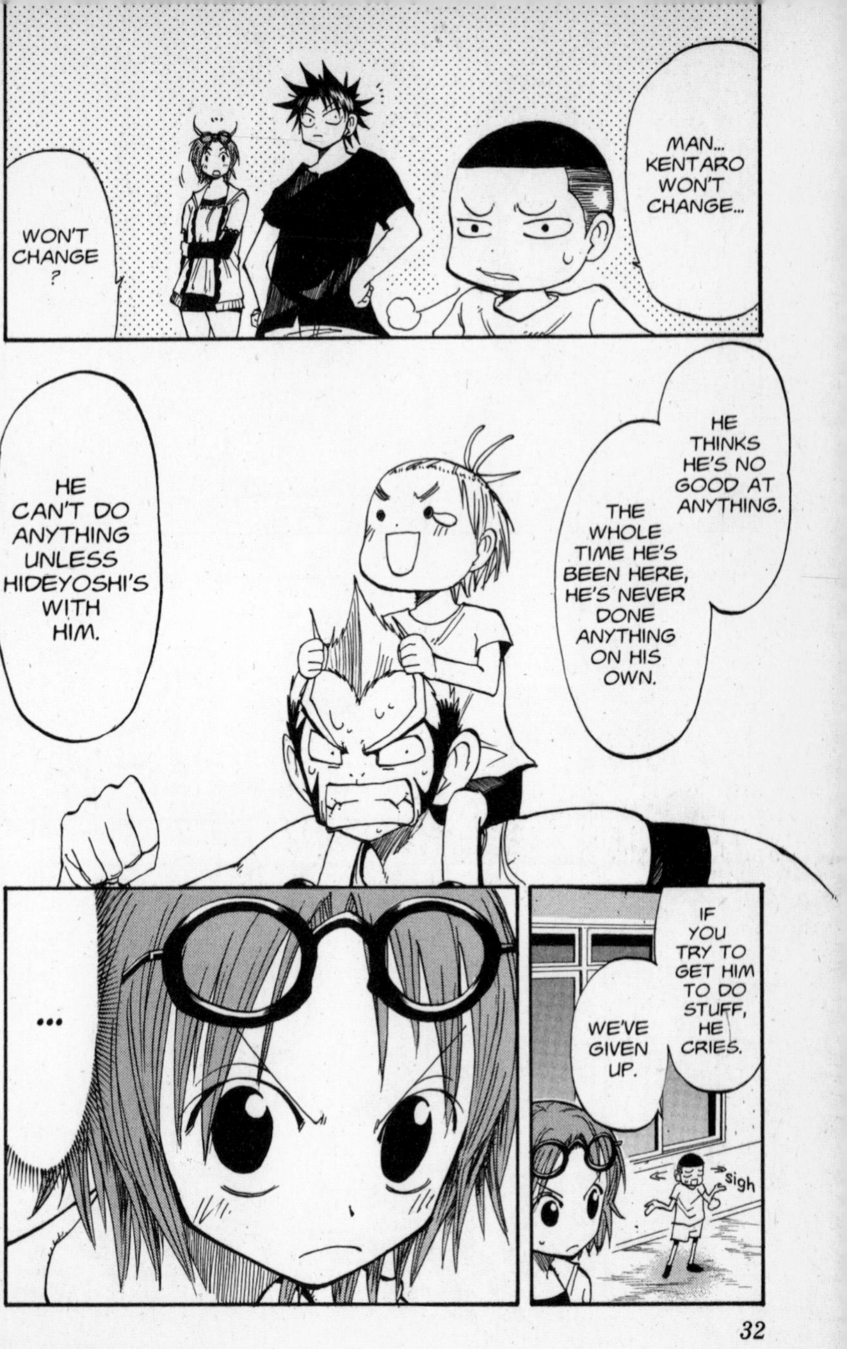
MAN... KENTARO WON'T CHANGE...
WON'T CHANGE ?
HE THINKS HE'S NO GOOD AT ANYTHING.
THE WHOLE TIME HE'S BEEN HERE, HE'S NEVER DONE ANYTHING ON HIS OWN.
HE CAN'T DO ANYTHING UNLESS HIDEYOSHI'S WITH HIM.
IF YOU TRY TO GET HIM TO DO STUFF, HE CRIES.
WE'VE GIVEN UP.
sigh
...

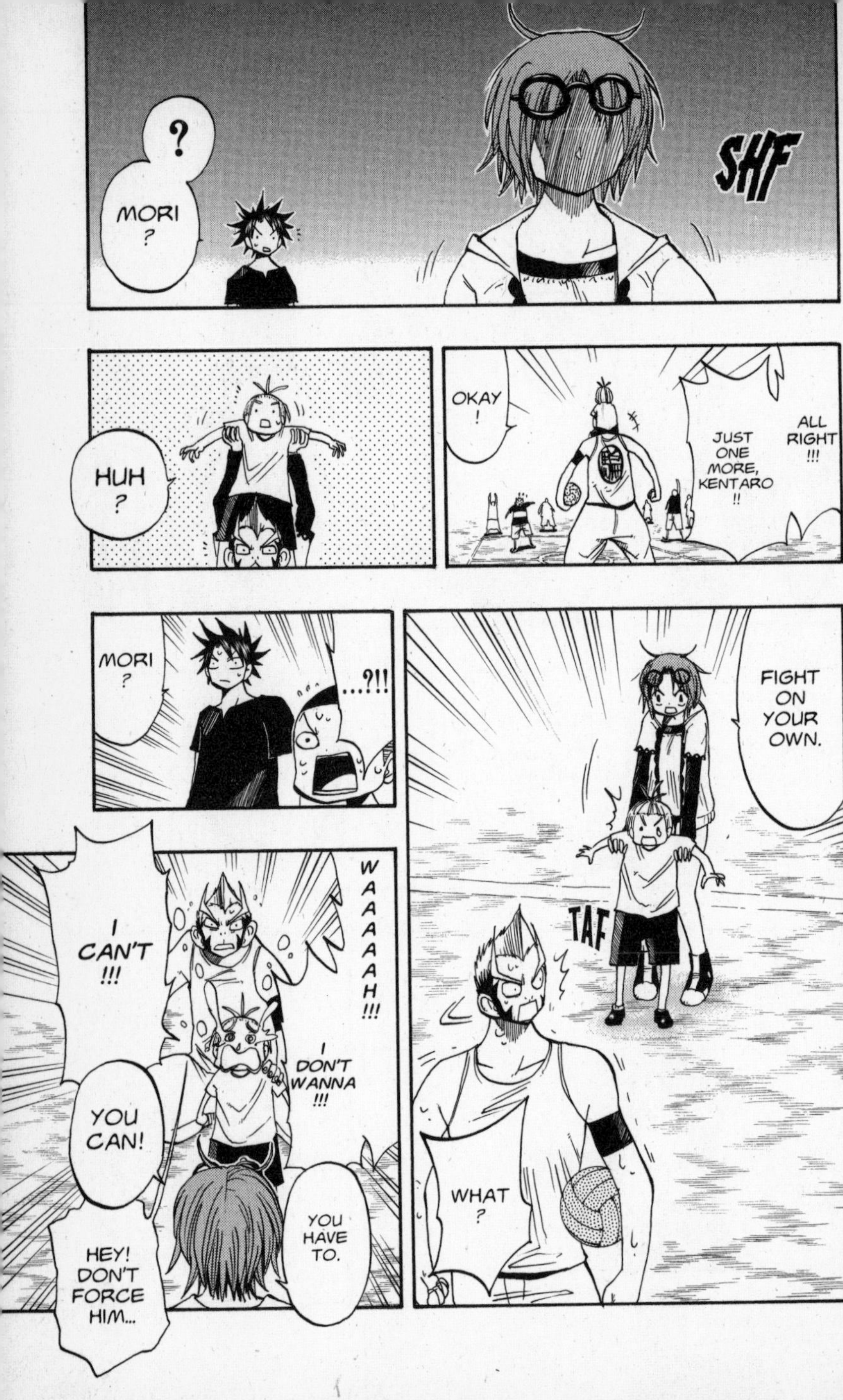
SHF
MORI ?
?
ALL RIGHT !!!
JUST ONE MORE, KENTARO !!
OKAY !
HUH ?
FIGHT ON YOUR OWN.
TAF
WHAT ?
MORI ?
...?!!
I CAN'T !!!
WAAAAAAH !!!
I DON'T WANNA !!!
YOU CAN!
YOU HAVE TO.
HEY! DON'T FORCE HIM...

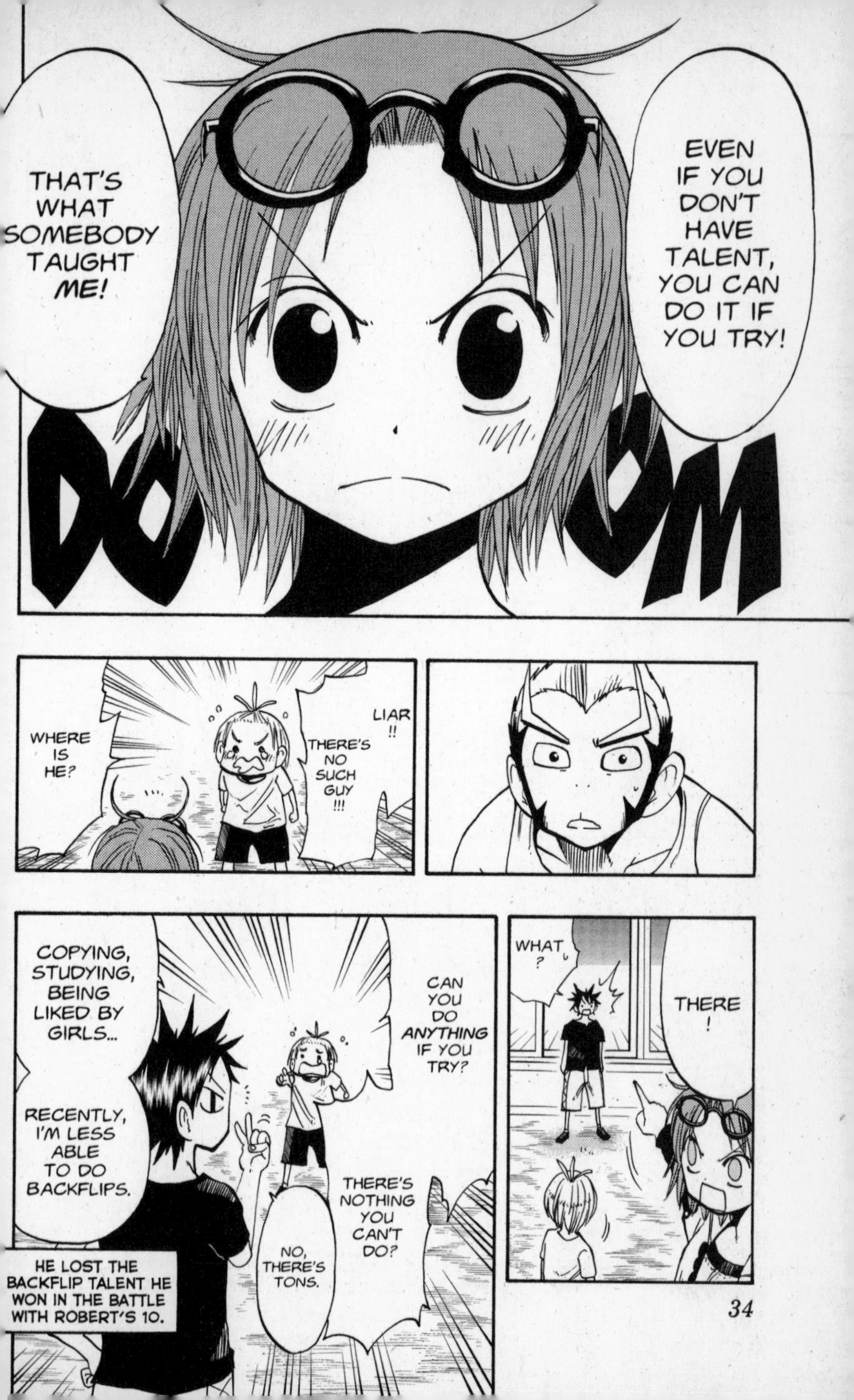
EVEN IF YOU DON'T HAVE TALENT, YOU CAN DO IT IF YOU TRY!
THAT'S WHAT SOMEBODY TAUGHT ME!
DOOOM
LIAR !!
THERE'S NO SUCH GUY !!!
WHERE IS HE?
...
WHAT?
THERE!
CAN YOU DO ANYTHING IF YOU TRY?
THERE'S NOTHING YOU CAN'T DO?
NO, THERE'S TONS.
COPYING, STUDYING, BEING LIKED BY GIRLS...
RECENTLY, I'M LESS ABLE TO DO BACKFLIPS.
HE LOST THE BACKFLIP TALENT HE WON IN THE BATTLE WITH ROBERT'S 10.

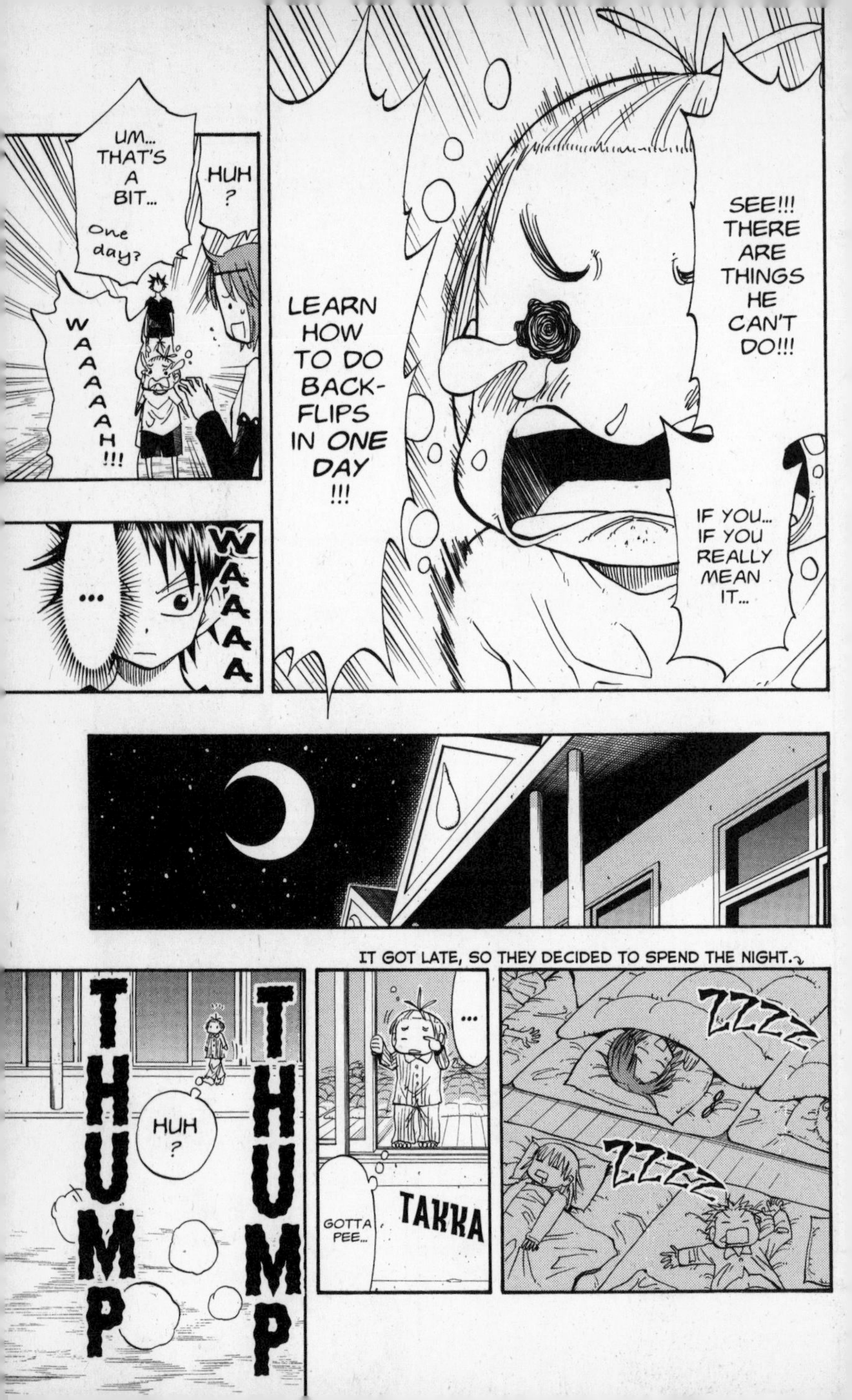
SEE!!! THERE ARE THINGS HE CAN'T DO!!!
IF YOU... IF YOU REALLY MEAN IT...
LEARN HOW TO DO BACK-FLIPS IN ONE DAY!!!
HUH?
UM... THAT'S A BIT...
One day?
WAAAAAAH!!!
WAAAAA
...
IT GOT LATE, SO THEY DECIDED TO SPEND THE NIGHT.
ZZZZ
ZZZZ
...
GOTTA PEE...
TAKKA
THUMP
HUH?
THUMP

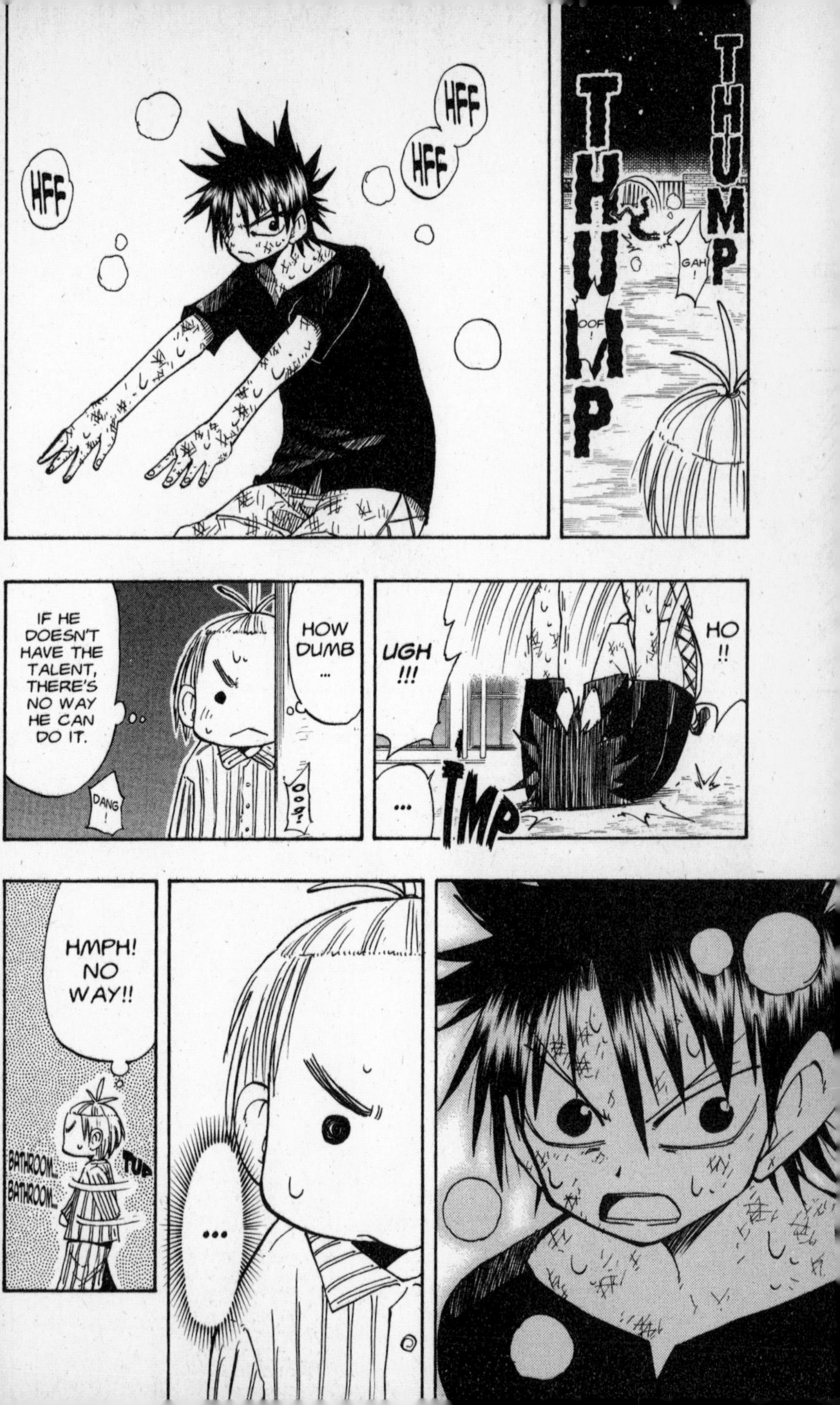
THUMP
THUMP
GAH!
OOF!
HFF
HFF
HFF
HO!!
UGH!!!
TMP
...
HOW DUMB...
OOF!
IF HE DOESN'T HAVE THE TALENT, THERE'S NO WAY HE CAN DO IT.
DANG!
...
HMPH! NO WAY!!
TUP
BATHROOM... BATHROOM...

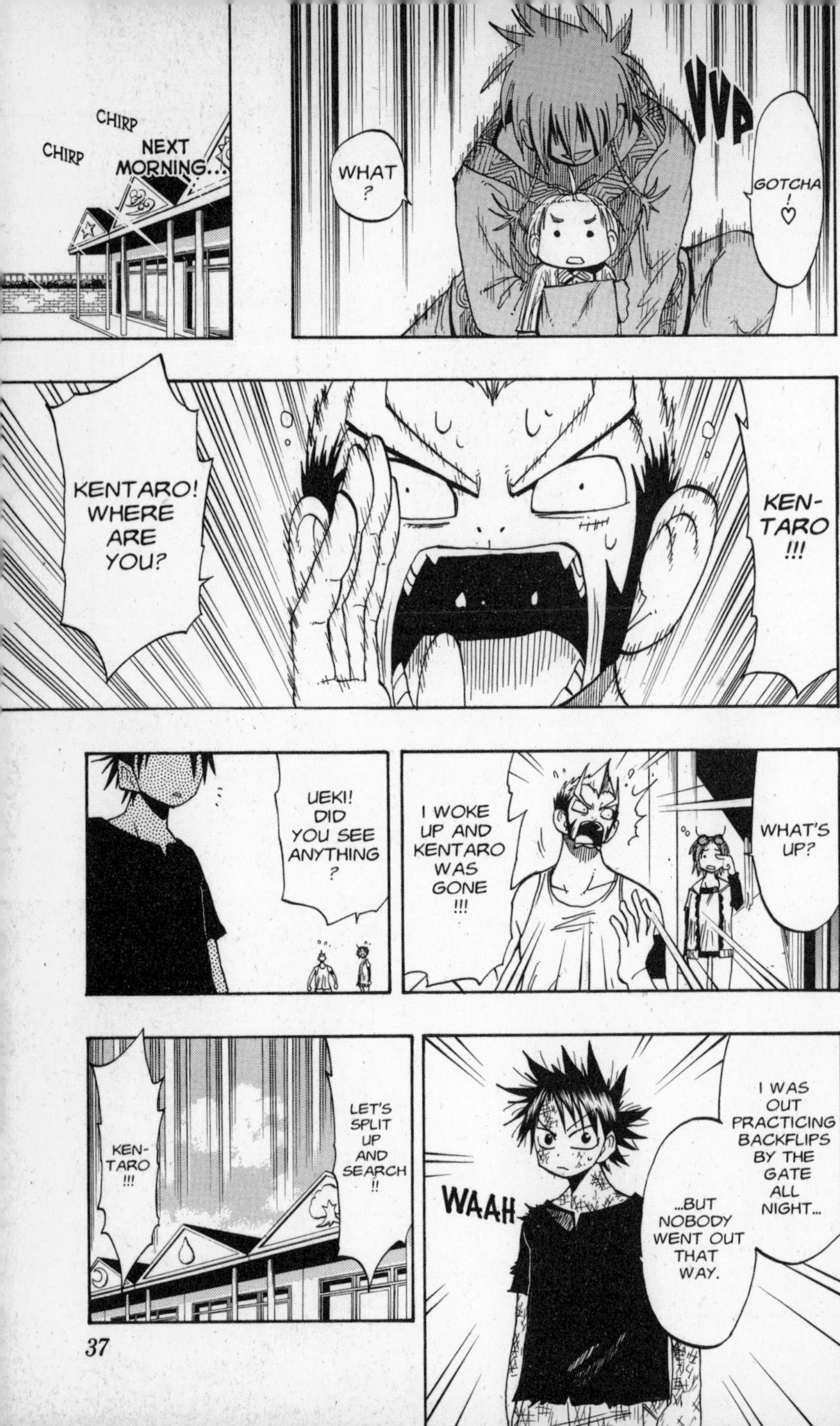
VVP
GOTCHA! ♡
WHAT?
CHIRP
CHIRP
NEXT MORNING...
KEN-TARO!!!
KENTARO! WHERE ARE YOU?
WHAT'S UP?
I WOKE UP AND KENTARO WAS GONE!!!
UEKI! DID YOU SEE ANYTHING?
I WAS OUT PRACTICING BACKFLIPS BY THE GATE ALL NIGHT...
...BUT NOBODY WENT OUT THAT WAY.
WAAH
LET'S SPLIT UP AND SEARCH!!
KEN-TARO!!!

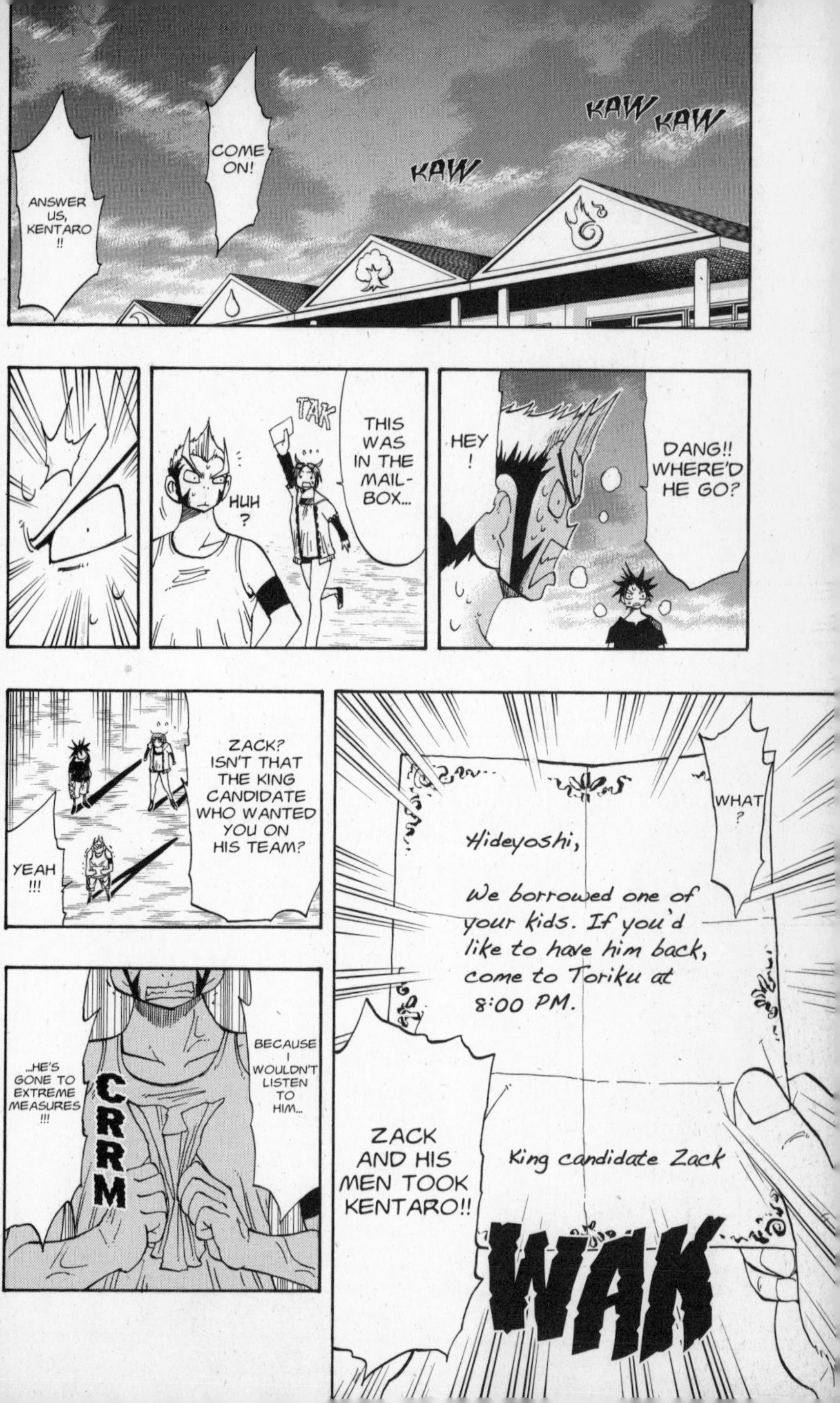
KAW KAW
KAW
COME ON!
ANSWER US, KENTARO !!
DANG!! WHERE'D HE GO?
HEY !
THIS WAS IN THE MAIL-BOX...
TAK
HUH ?
WHAT ?
Hideyoshi,
We borrowed one of your kids. If you'd like to have him back, come to Toriku at 8:00 PM.
King candidate Zack
ZACK AND HIS MEN TOOK KENTARO!!
WAK
ZACK? ISN'T THAT THE KING CANDIDATE WHO WANTED YOU ON HIS TEAM?
YEAH !!!
BECAUSE I WOULDN'T LISTEN TO HIM...
...HE'S GONE TO EXTREME MEASURES !!!
CRRM

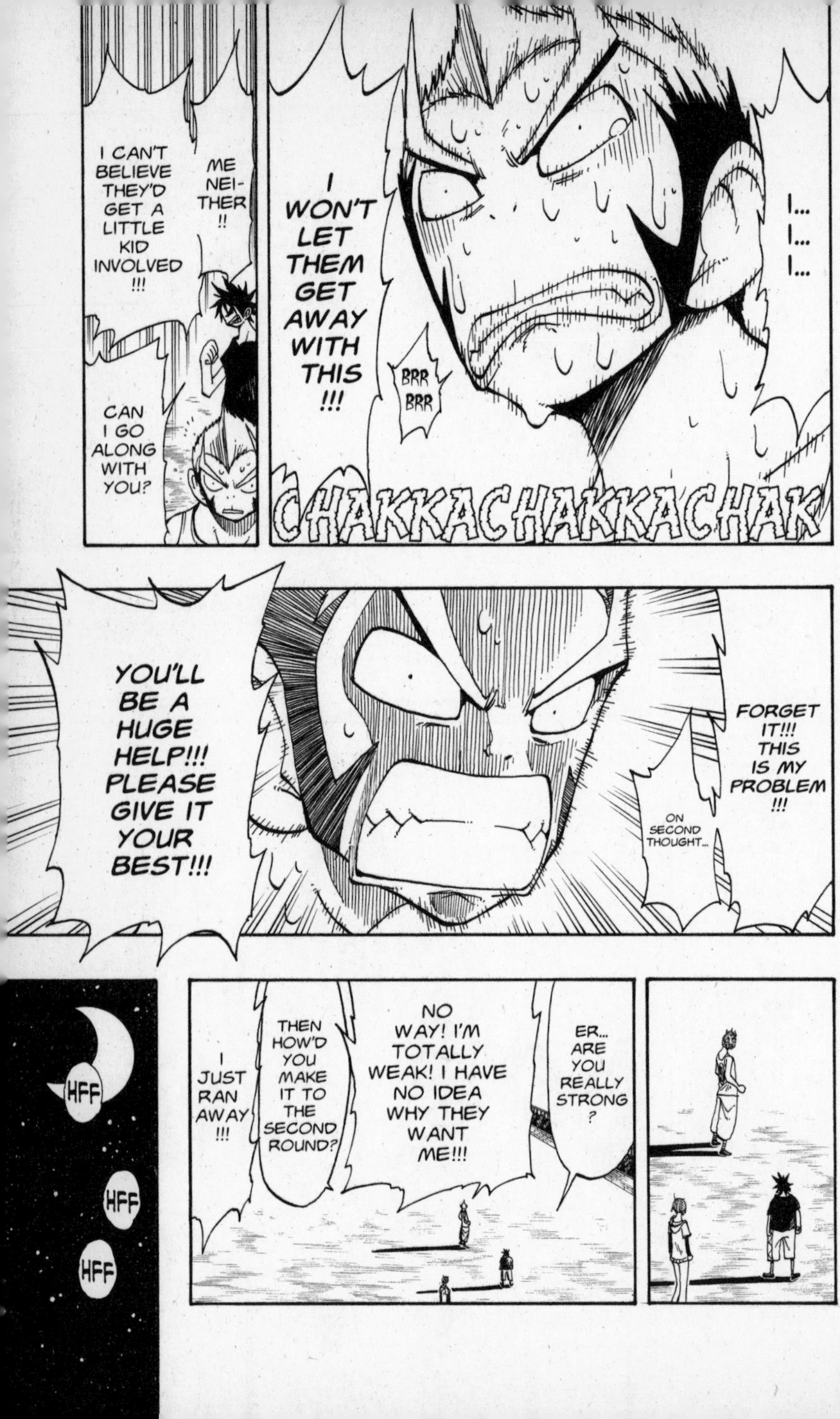
I... I... I...
I WON'T LET THEM GET AWAY WITH THIS !!!
BRR BRR
CHAKKACHAKKACHAK
ME NEI-THER !!
I CAN'T BELIEVE THEY'D GET A LITTLE KID INVOLVED !!!
CAN I GO ALONG WITH YOU?
FORGET IT!!! THIS IS MY PROBLEM !!!
ON SECOND THOUGHT...
YOU'LL BE A HUGE HELP!!! PLEASE GIVE IT YOUR BEST!!!
ER... ARE YOU REALLY STRONG ?
NO WAY! I'M TOTALLY WEAK! I HAVE NO IDEA WHY THEY WANT ME!!!
THEN HOW'D YOU MAKE IT TO THE SECOND ROUND?
I JUST RAN AWAY !!!
HFF
HFF
HFF

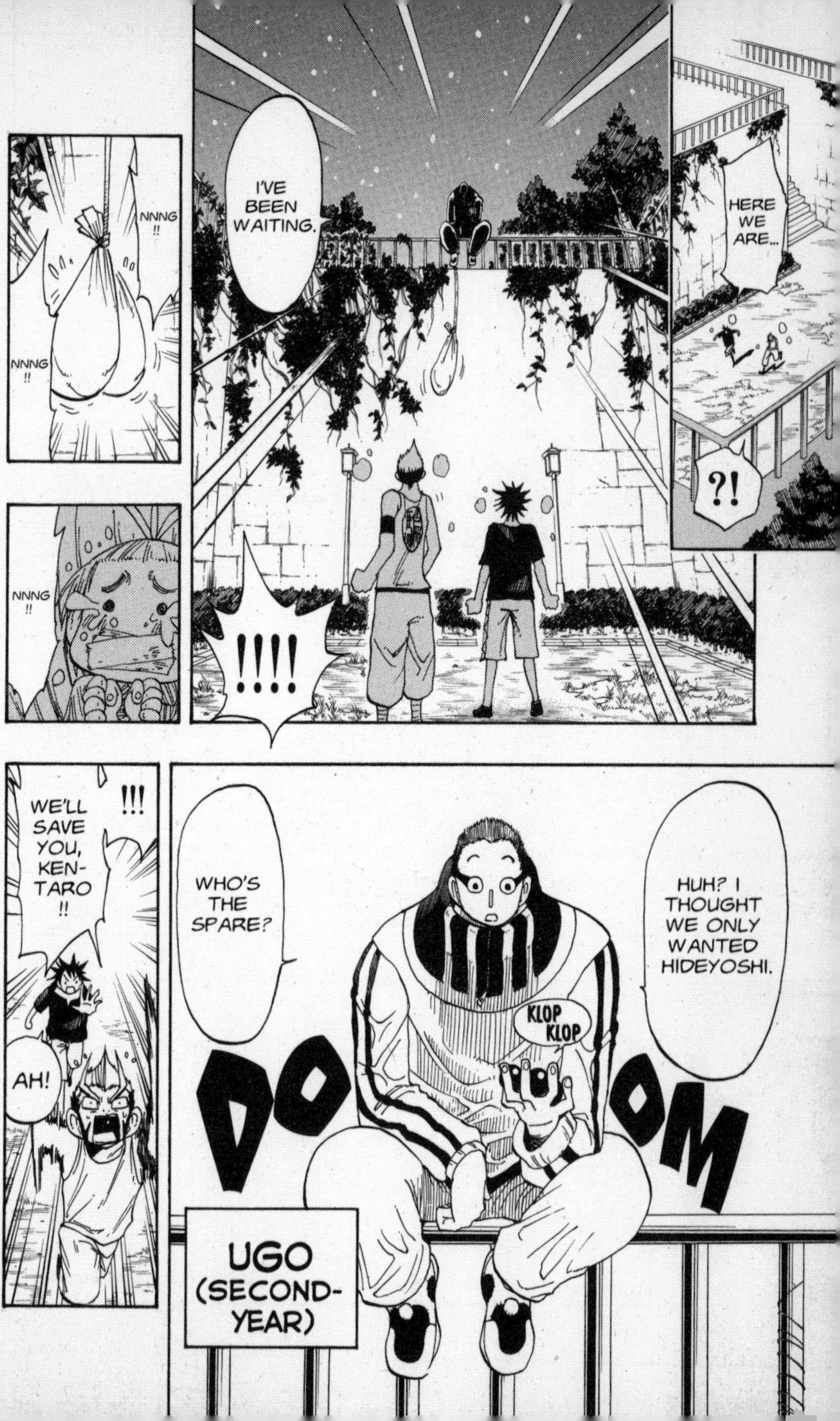
HERE WE ARE...
?!
I'VE BEEN WAITING.
!!!!
NNNG !!
NNNG !!
NNNG !!
HUH? I THOUGHT WE ONLY WANTED HIDEYOSHI.
WHO'S THE SPARE?
KLOP KLOP
DOOM
UGO (SECOND-YEAR)
!!!
WE'LL SAVE YOU, KEN-TARO !!
AH!

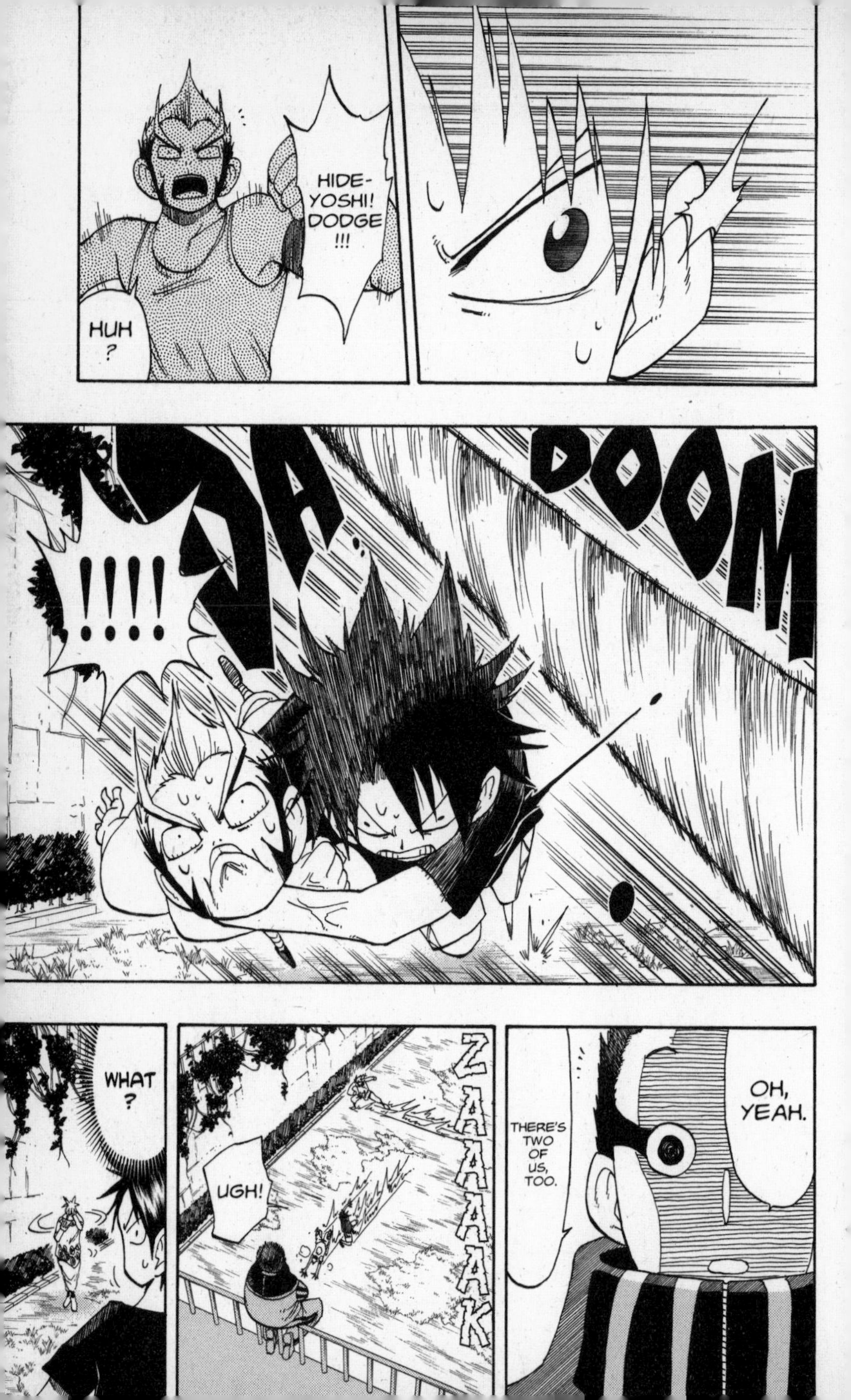
HIDE-YOSHI! DODGE !!!
HUH ?
BOOM
DA
!!!!
OH, YEAH.
THERE'S TWO OF US, TOO.
ZAAAAAK
UGH!
WHAT ?

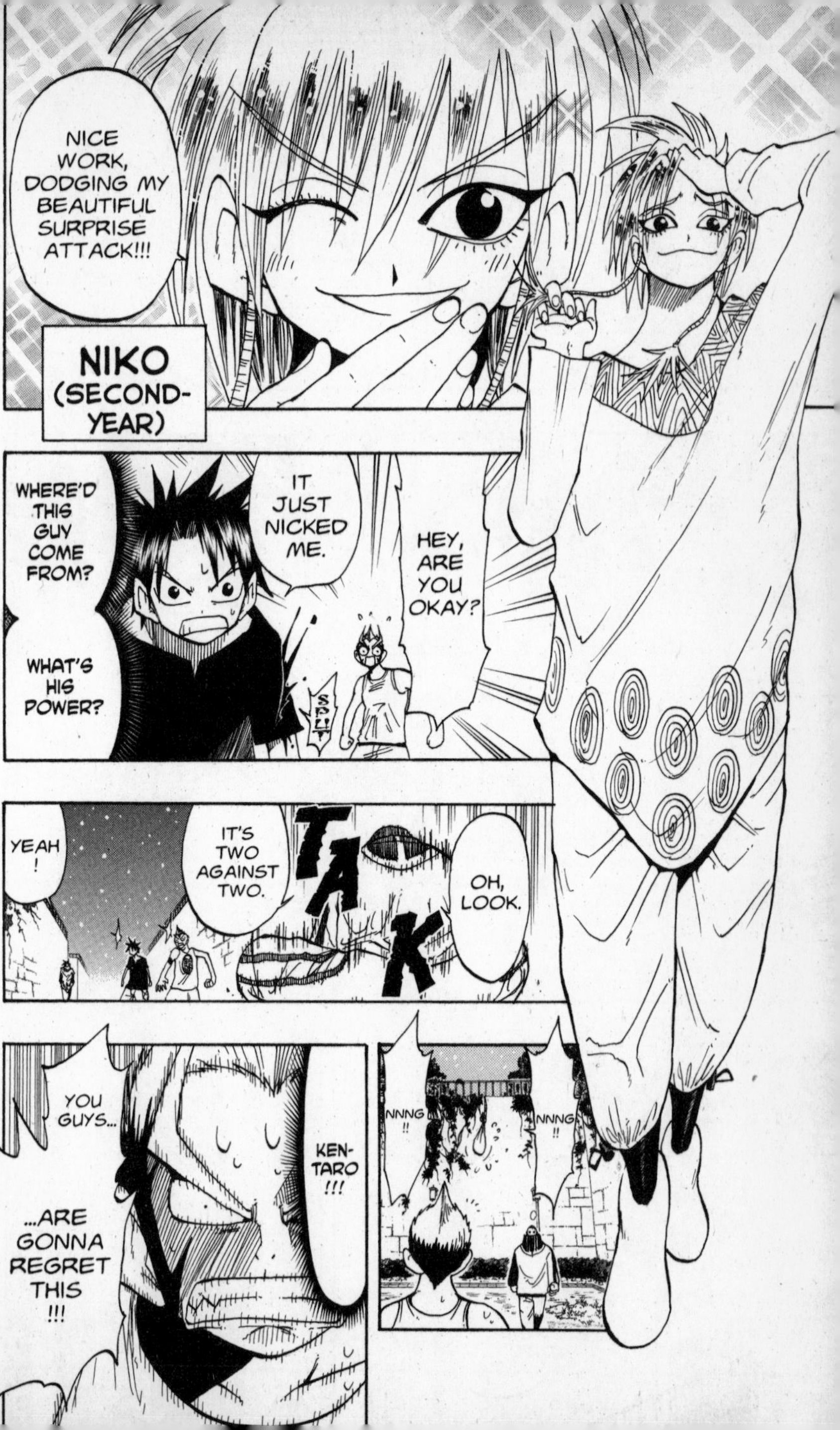
NICE WORK, DODGING MY BEAUTIFUL SURPRISE ATTACK!!!
NIKO (SECOND-YEAR)
HEY, ARE YOU OKAY?
IT JUST NICKED ME.
WHERE'D THIS GUY COME FROM?
WHAT'S HIS POWER?
OH, LOOK.
TAK
IT'S TWO AGAINST TWO.
YEAH!
NNNG!!
NNNG!!
KEN-TARO!!!
YOU GUYS...
...ARE GONNA REGRET THIS!!!

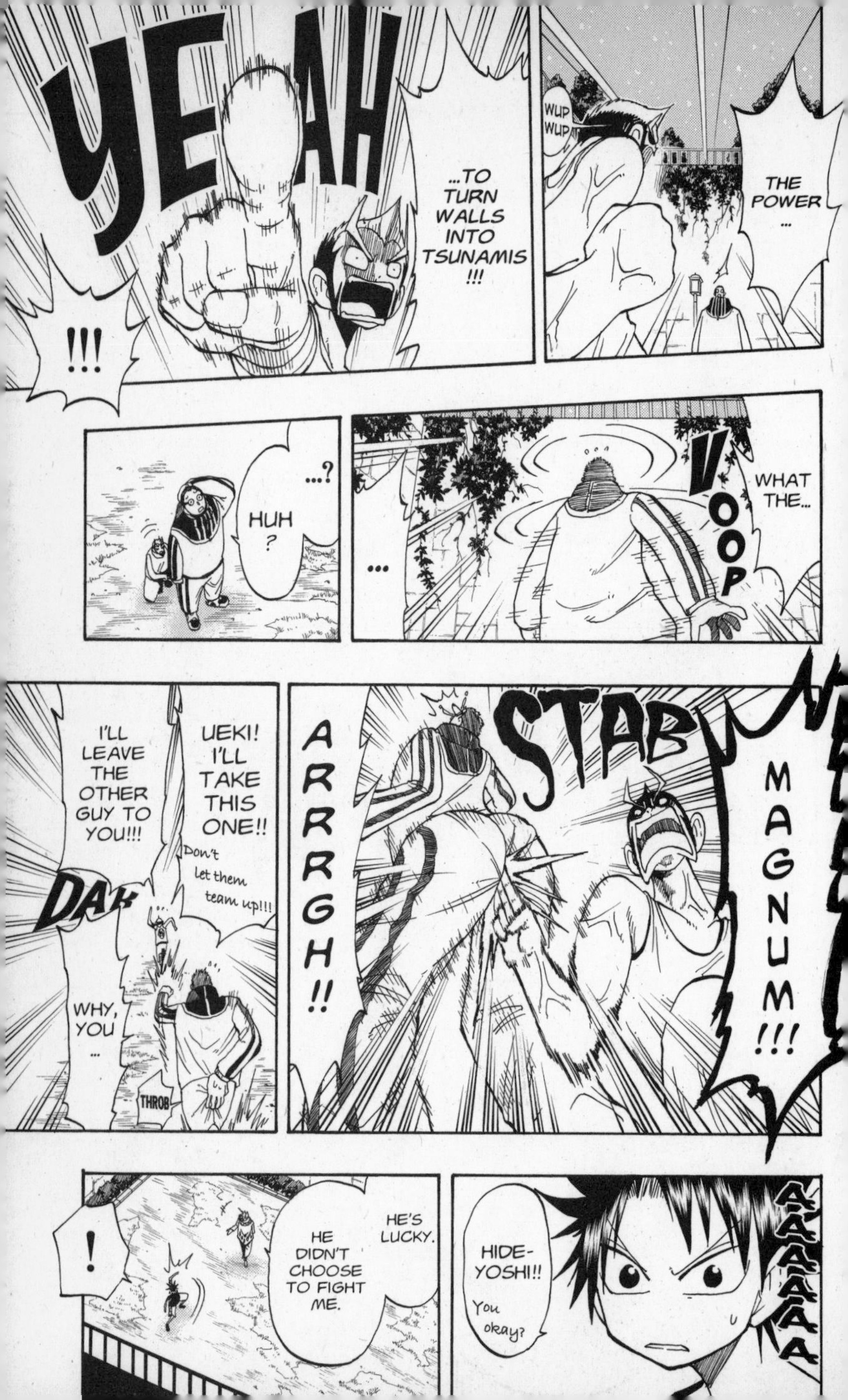
THE POWER...
WUP WUP
...TO TURN WALLS INTO TSUNAMIS!!!
YEAH
!!!
WHAT THE...
VOOP
...
...?
HUH?
MAGNUM!!!
STAB
ARRRGH!!
UEKI! I'LL TAKE THIS ONE!!
I'LL LEAVE THE OTHER GUY TO YOU!!!
Don't let them team up!!!
DAK
WHY, YOU...
THROB
AAAAAAA
HIDE-YOSHI!!
You okay?
HE'S LUCKY.
HE DIDN'T CHOOSE TO FIGHT ME.
!

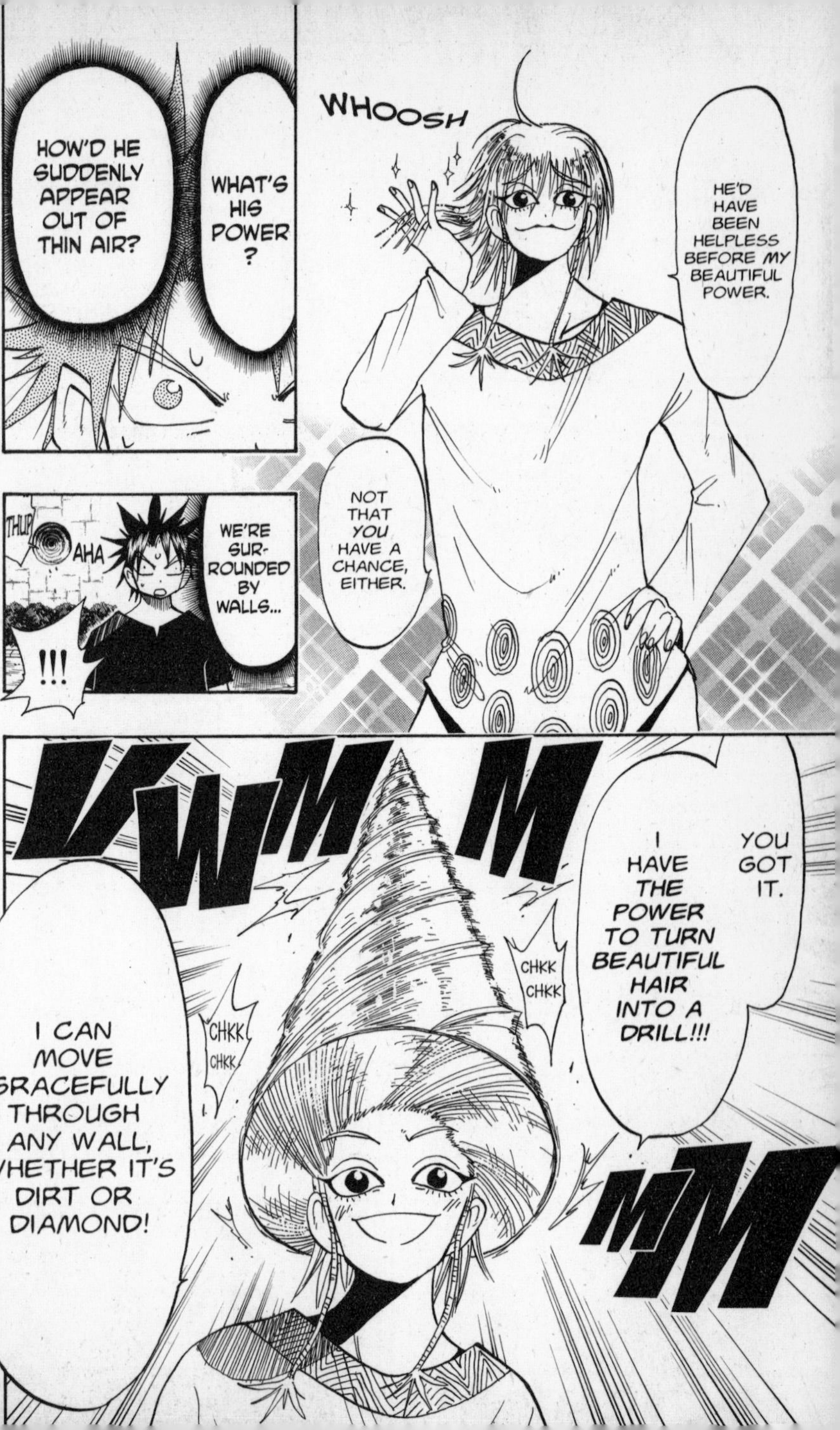
WHOOSH
HE'D HAVE BEEN HELPLESS BEFORE MY BEAUTIFUL POWER.
NOT THAT YOU HAVE A CHANCE, EITHER.
WHAT'S HIS POWER?
HOW'D HE SUDDENLY APPEAR OUT OF THIN AIR?
WE'RE SUR-ROUNDED BY WALLS...
AHA
THUP
!!!
YOU GOT IT.
I HAVE THE POWER TO TURN BEAUTIFUL HAIR INTO A DRILL!!!
VWMM M
CHKK CHKK
CHKK CHKK
MMM
I CAN MOVE GRACEFULLY THROUGH ANY WALL, WHETHER IT'S DIRT OR DIAMOND!

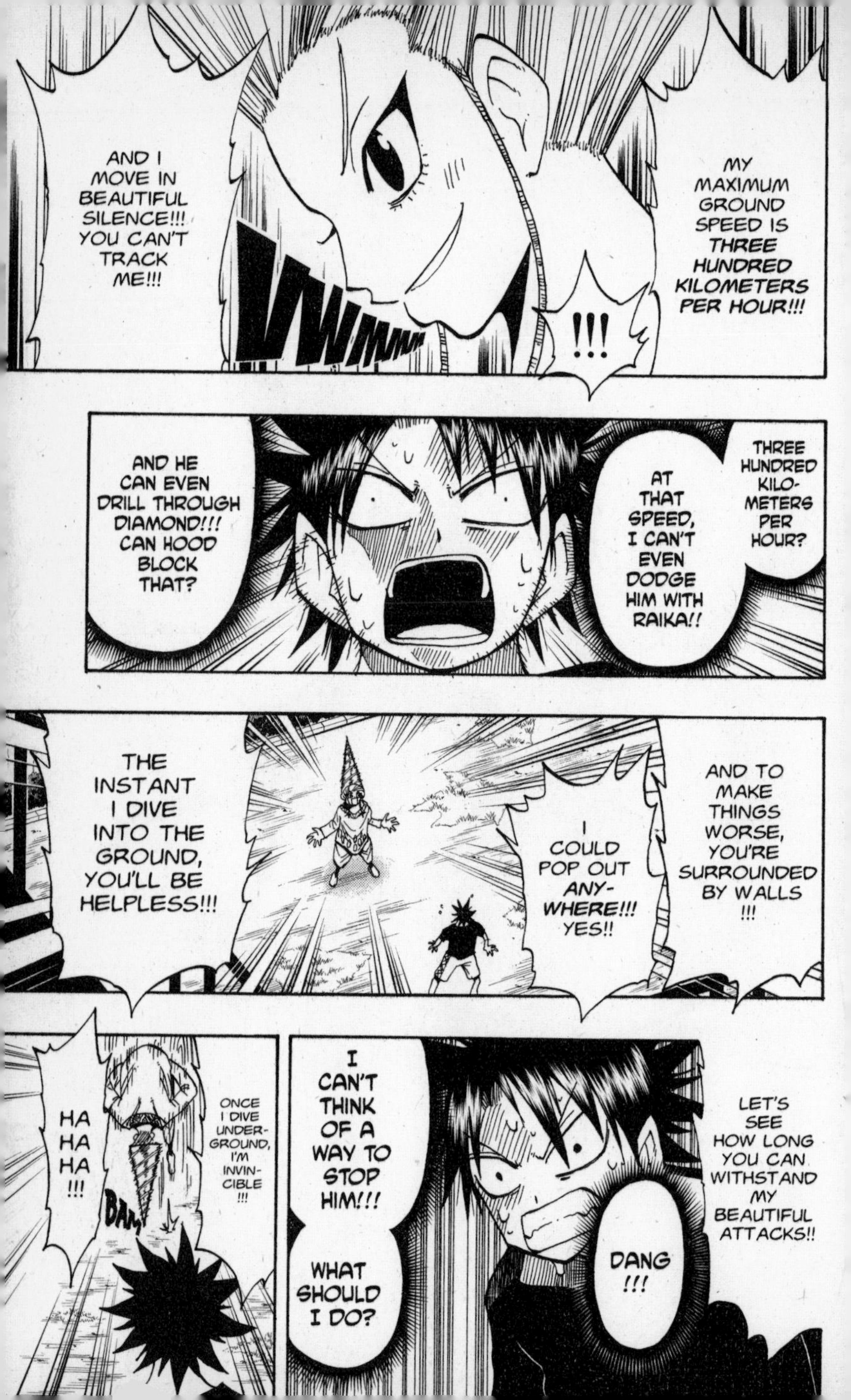
MY MAXIMUM GROUND SPEED IS THREE HUNDRED KILOMETERS PER HOUR!!!
!!!
VWMMM
AND I MOVE IN BEAUTIFUL SILENCE!!! YOU CAN'T TRACK ME!!!
THREE HUNDRED KILO-METERS PER HOUR?
AT THAT SPEED, I CAN'T EVEN DODGE HIM WITH RAIKA!!
AND HE CAN EVEN DRILL THROUGH DIAMOND!!! CAN HOOD BLOCK THAT?
AND TO MAKE THINGS WORSE, YOU'RE SURROUNDED BY WALLS !!!
I COULD POP OUT ANY-WHERE!!! YES!!
THE INSTANT I DIVE INTO THE GROUND, YOU'LL BE HELPLESS!!!
LET'S SEE HOW LONG YOU CAN WITHSTAND MY BEAUTIFUL ATTACKS!!
DANG !!!
I CAN'T THINK OF A WAY TO STOP HIM!!!
WHAT SHOULD I DO?
ONCE I DIVE UNDER-GROUND, I'M INVIN-CIBLE !!!
HA HA HA !!!
BAM

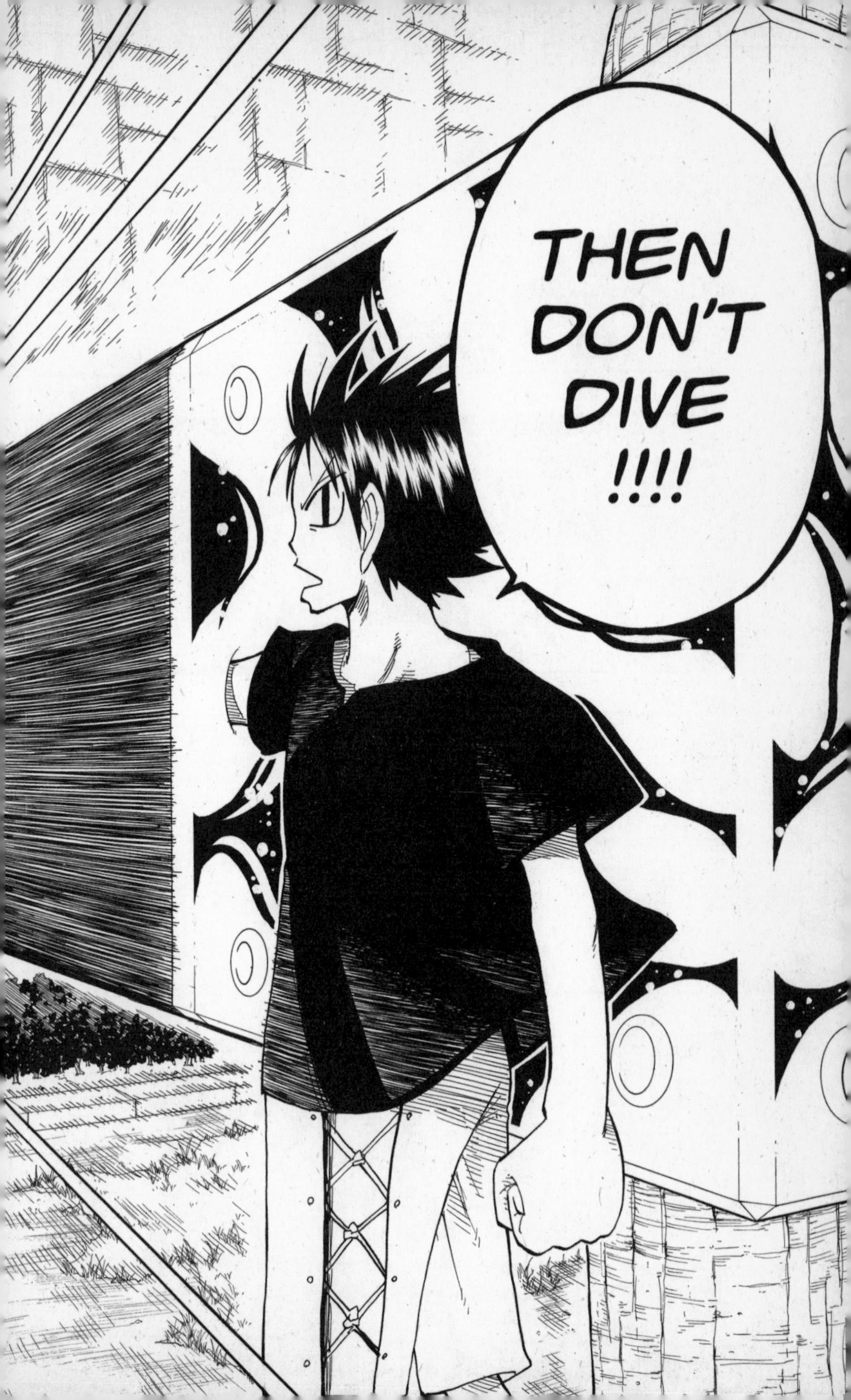
THEN DON'T DIVE !!!!

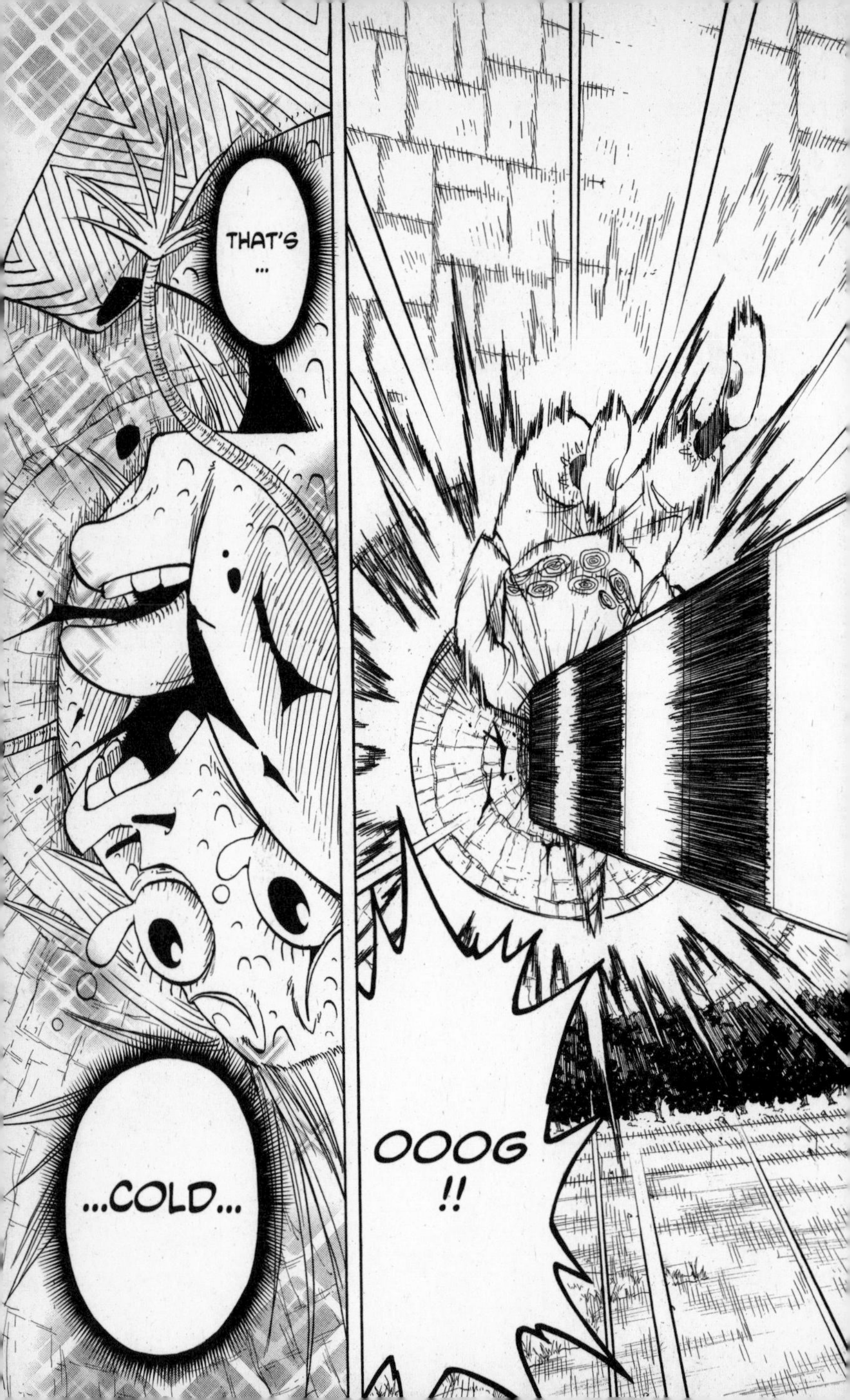
OOOG !!
THAT'S ...
...COLD...

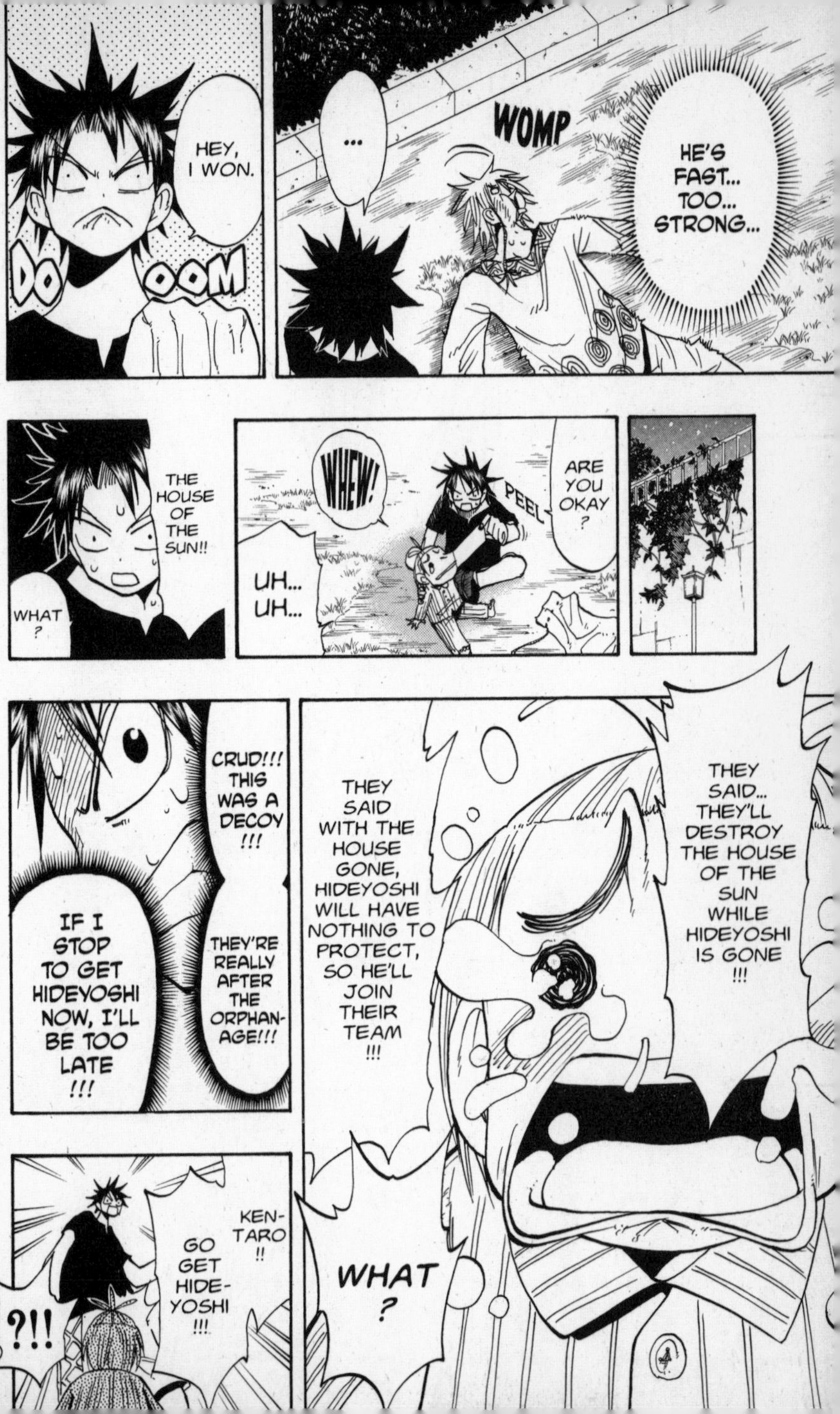
HE'S FAST... TOO... STRONG...
WOMP
...
HEY, I WON.
DOOOM
ARE YOU OKAY?
PEEL
WHEW!
UH... UH...
THE HOUSE OF THE SUN!!
WHAT?
THEY SAID... THEY'LL DESTROY THE HOUSE OF THE SUN WHILE HIDEYOSHI IS GONE!!!
THEY SAID WITH THE HOUSE GONE, HIDEYOSHI WILL HAVE NOTHING TO PROTECT, SO HE'LL JOIN THEIR TEAM!!!
WHAT?
CRUD!!! THIS WAS A DECOY!!!
THEY'RE REALLY AFTER THE ORPHANAGE!!!
IF I STOP TO GET HIDEYOSHI NOW, I'LL BE TOO LATE!!!
KENTARO!!
GO GET HIDEYOSHI!!!
?!!

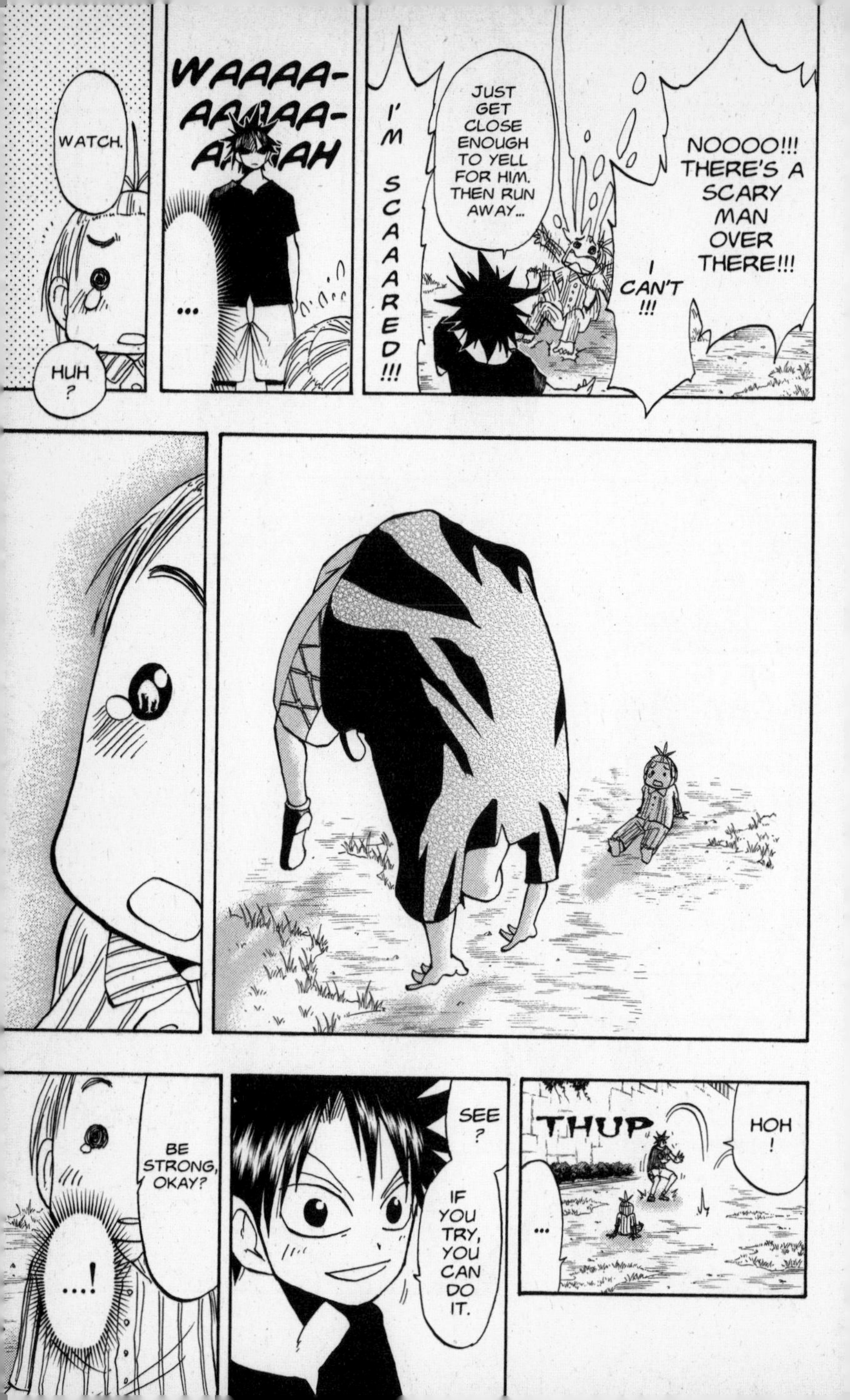
NOOOO!!! THERE'S A SCARY MAN OVER THERE!!!
I CAN'T!!!
JUST GET CLOSE ENOUGH TO YELL FOR HIM. THEN RUN AWAY...
I'M SCAAARED!!!
WAAAA-AAAAA-AAAAH
...
WATCH.
HUH?
HOH!
THUP
...
SEE?
IF YOU TRY, YOU CAN DO IT.
BE STRONG, OKAY?
...!

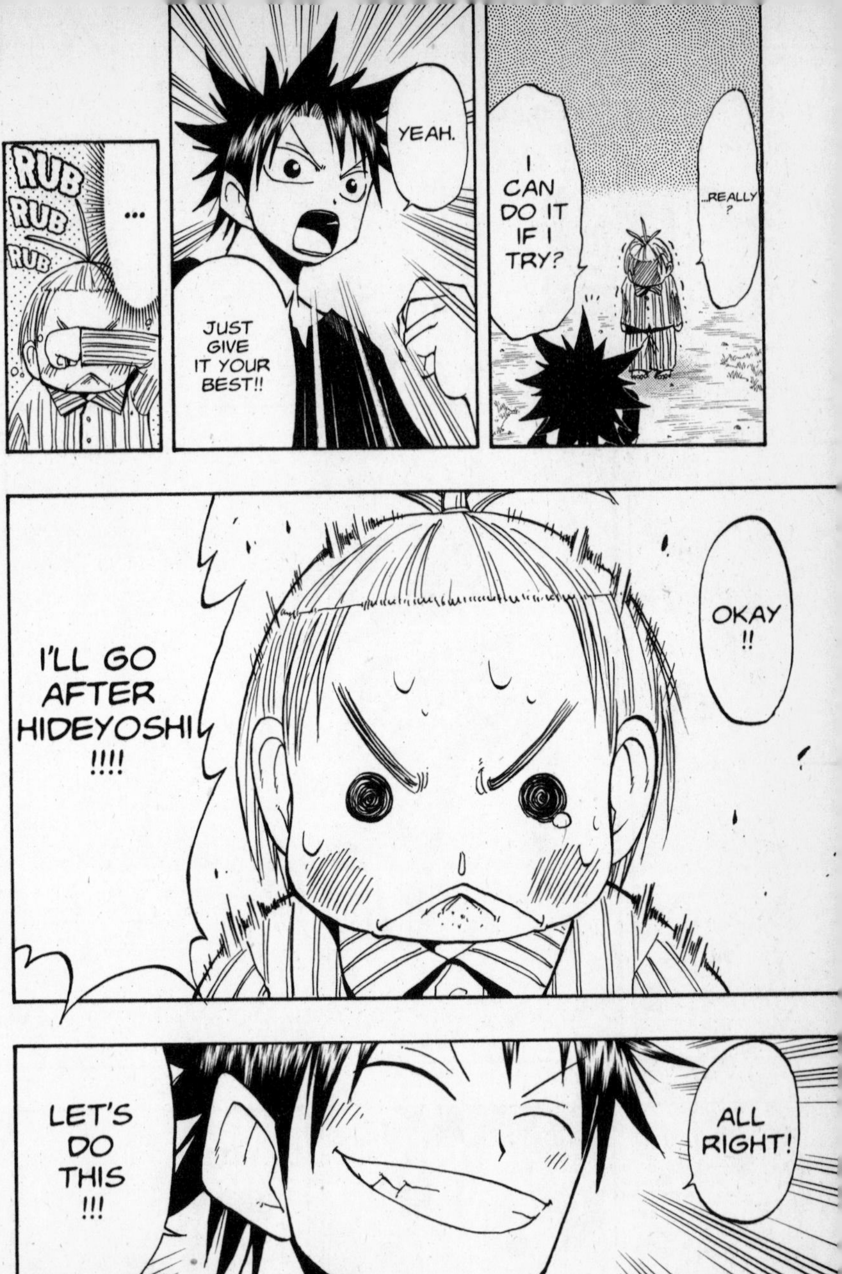
...REALLY?
I CAN DO IT IF I TRY?
YEAH.
JUST GIVE IT YOUR BEST!!
...
RUB RUB RUB
OKAY!!
I'LL GO AFTER HIDEYOSHI!!!!
ALL RIGHT!
LET'S DO THIS!!!

Chapter 89 Hideyoshi Vs. Ugo

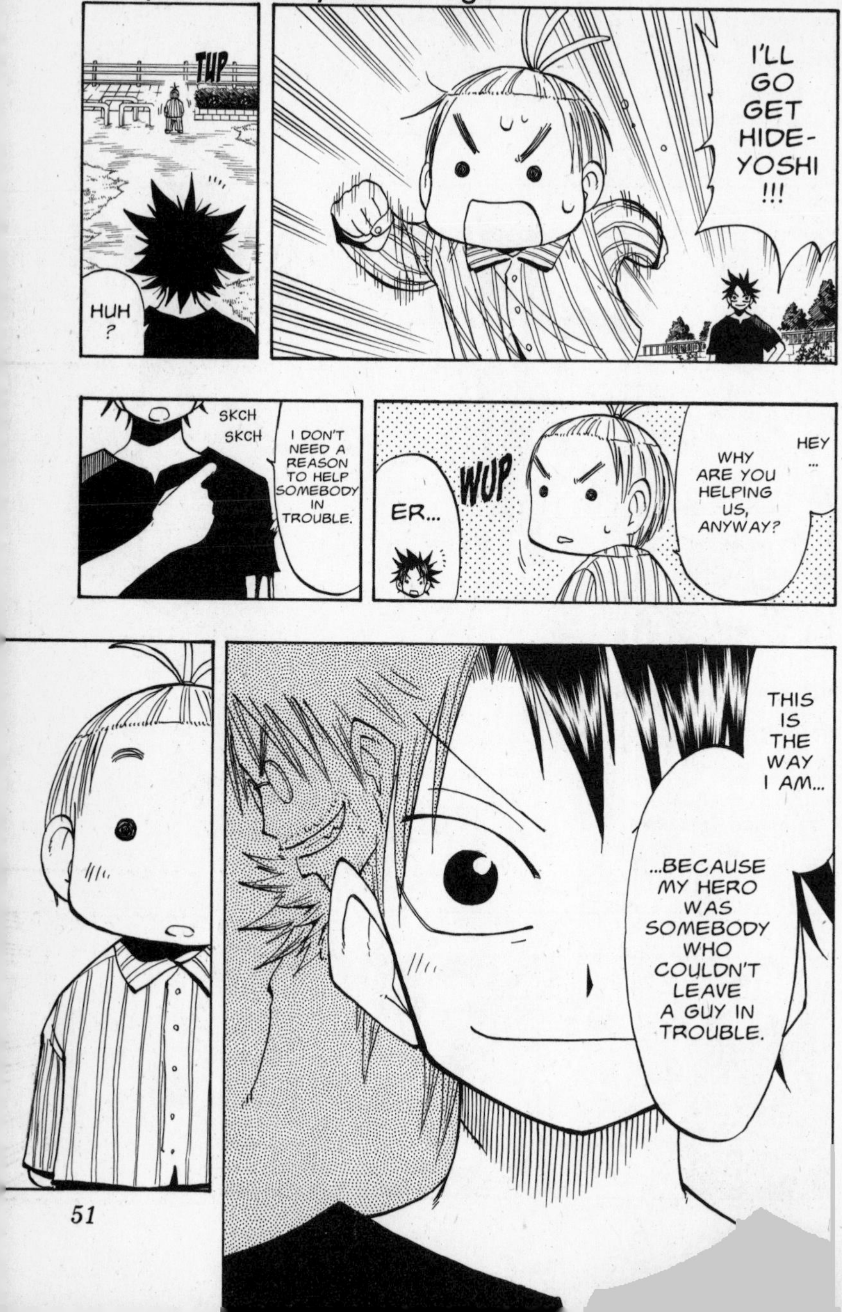
I'LL GO GET HIDE-YOSHI !!!
TUP
HUH ?
HEY ...
WHY ARE YOU HELPING US, ANYWAY?
WUP
ER...
I DON'T NEED A REASON TO HELP SOMEBODY IN TROUBLE.
SKCH SKCH
THIS IS THE WAY I AM...
...BECAUSE MY HERO WAS SOMEBODY WHO COULDN'T LEAVE A GUY IN TROUBLE.

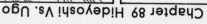

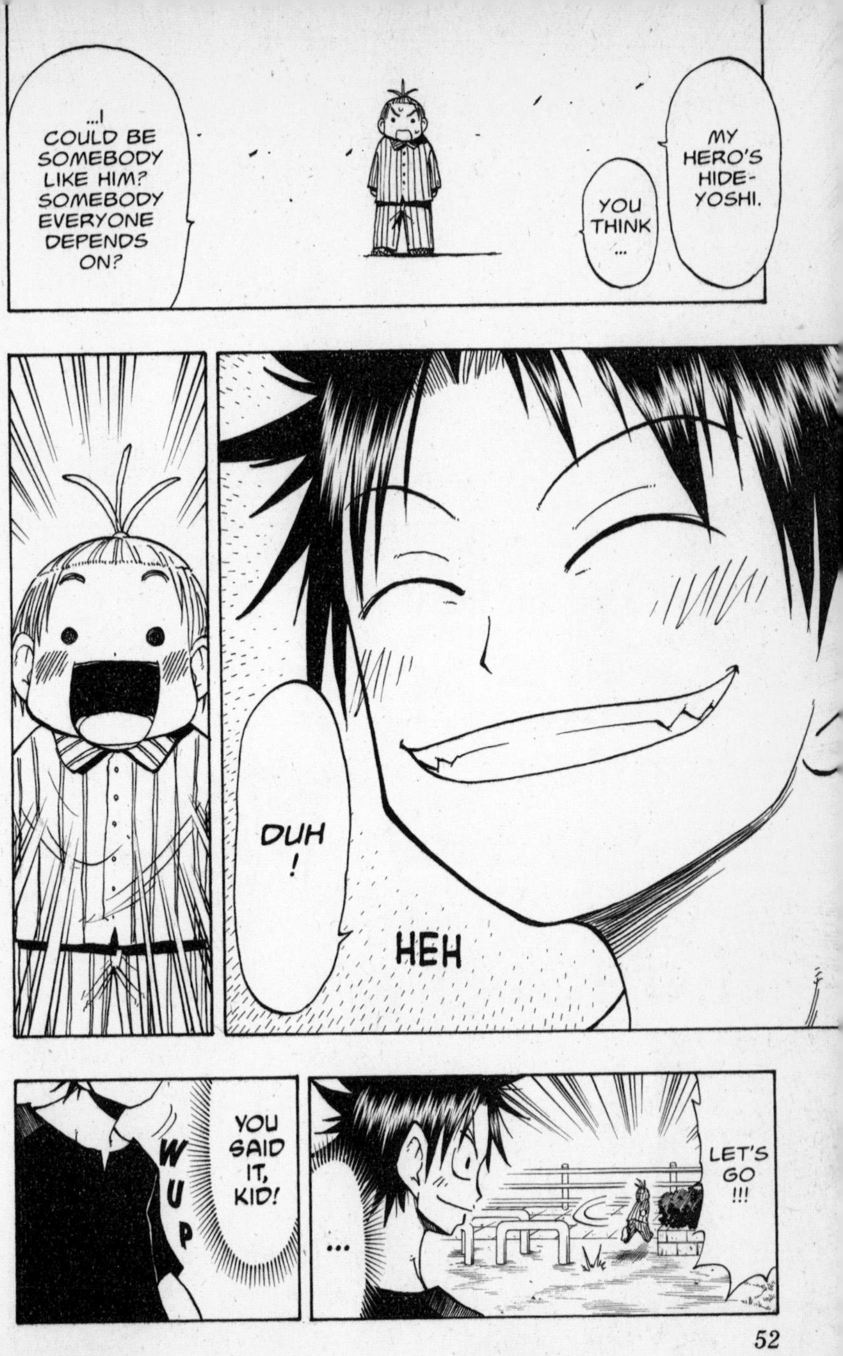
MY HERO'S HIDE-YOSHI.
YOU THINK ...
...I COULD BE SOMEBODY LIKE HIM? SOMEBODY EVERYONE DEPENDS ON?
HEH
DUH !
LET'S GO !!!
...
YOU SAID IT, KID!
WUP

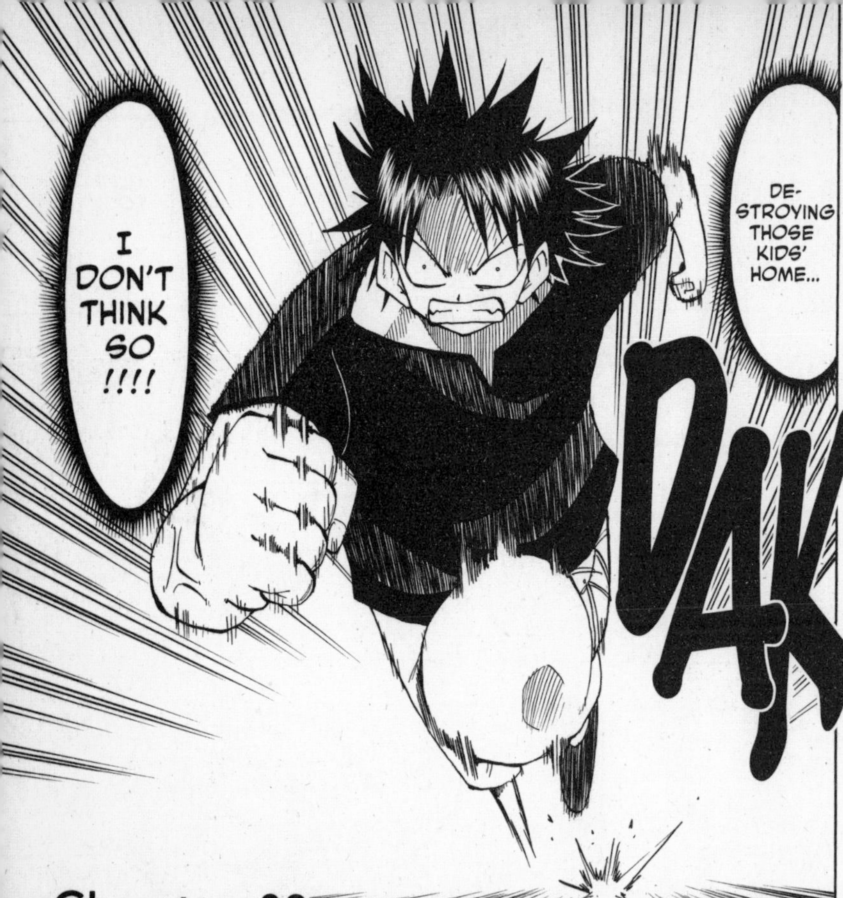
DE-STROYING THOSE KIDS' HOME...
DAK
I DON'T THINK SO!!!!

Chapter 89
Hideyoshi Vs. Ugo

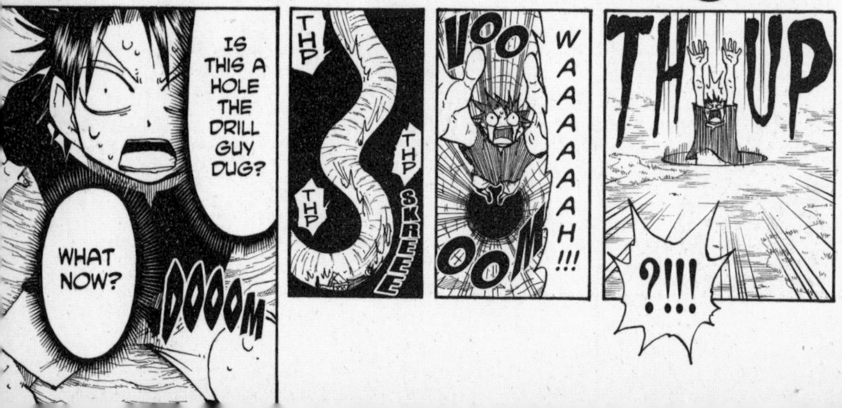
THUP
?!!!
VOOOOM
WAAAAAAAH!!!
THP
THP
THP
SKREEE
IS THIS A HOLE THE DRILL GUY DUG?
DOOOM
WHAT NOW?

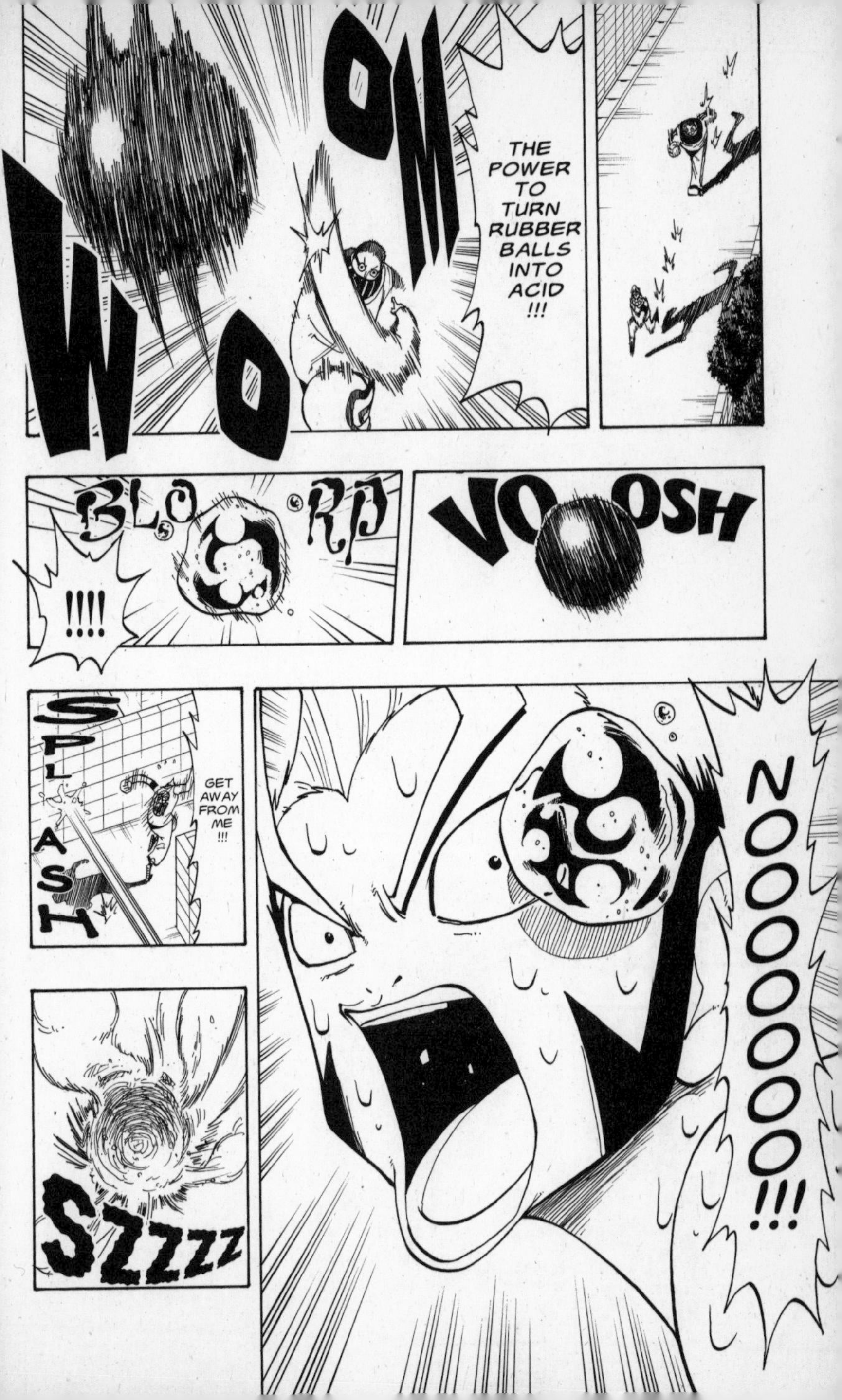
WOOM
THE POWER TO TURN RUBBER BALLS INTO ACID !!!
VO OSH
BLO RP
!!!!
NOOOOOOOOO!!!
SPLASH
GET AWAY FROM ME !!!
SZZZZ

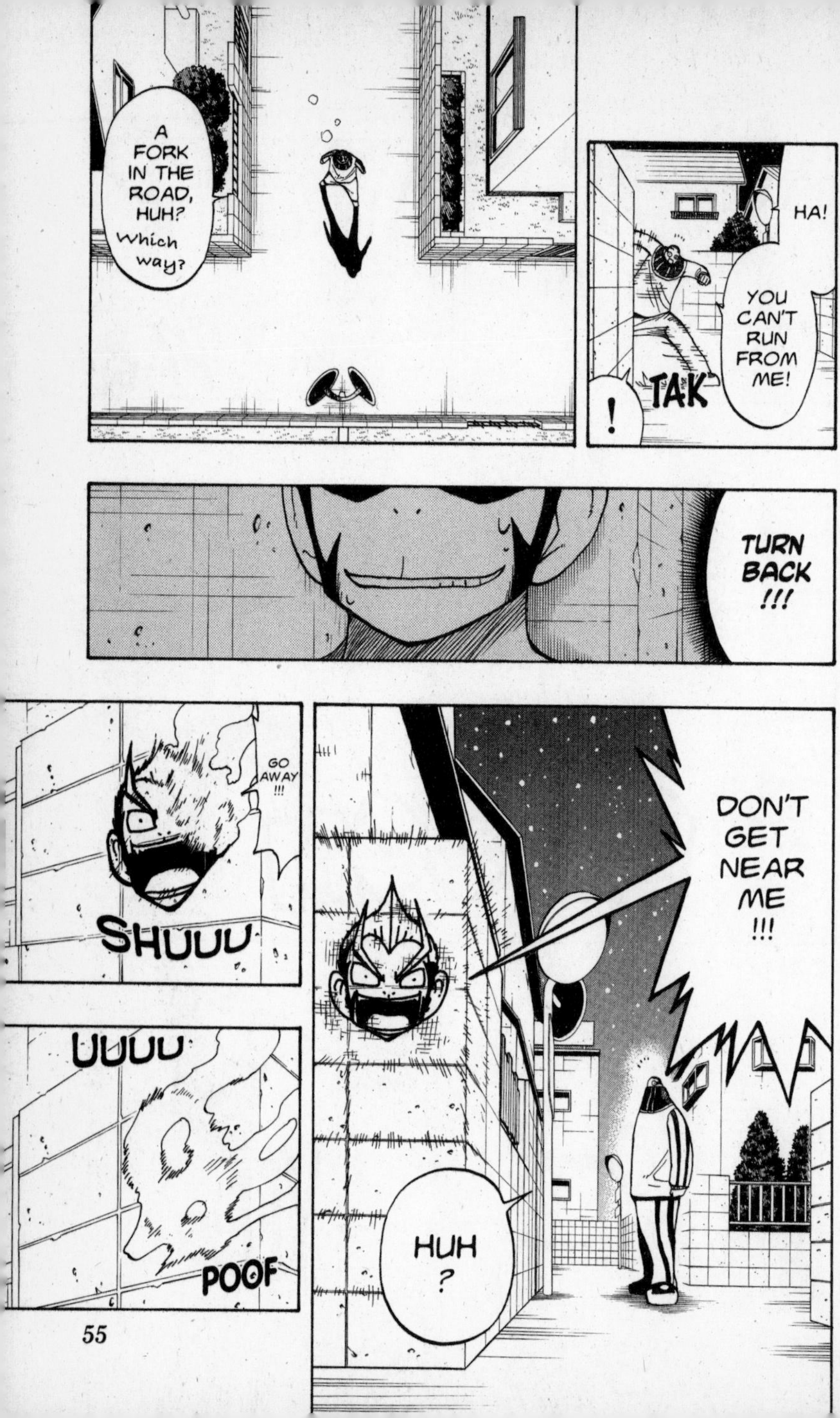
HA!
YOU CAN'T RUN FROM ME!
TAK
!
A FORK IN THE ROAD, HUH? Which way?
TURN BACK !!!
DON'T GET NEAR ME !!!
HUH ?
GO AWAY !!!
SHUUU
UUUU
POOF

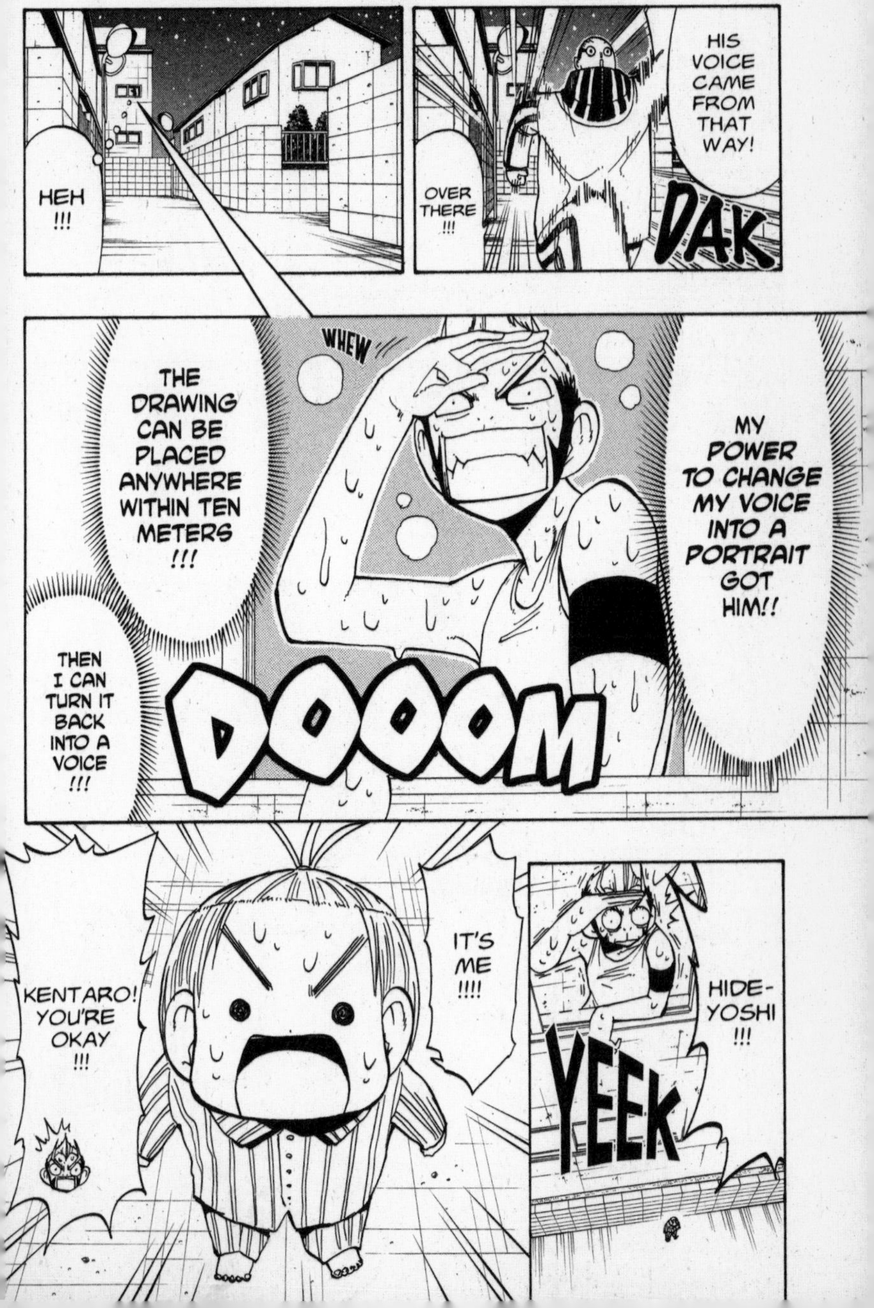
HIS VOICE CAME FROM THAT WAY!
DAK
OVER THERE !!!
HEH !!!
MY POWER TO CHANGE MY VOICE INTO A PORTRAIT GOT HIM!!
WHEW
THE DRAWING CAN BE PLACED ANYWHERE WITHIN TEN METERS !!!
THEN I CAN TURN IT BACK INTO A VOICE !!!
DOOOM
HIDE-YOSHI !!!
YEEK
IT'S ME !!!!
KENTARO! YOU'RE OKAY !!!

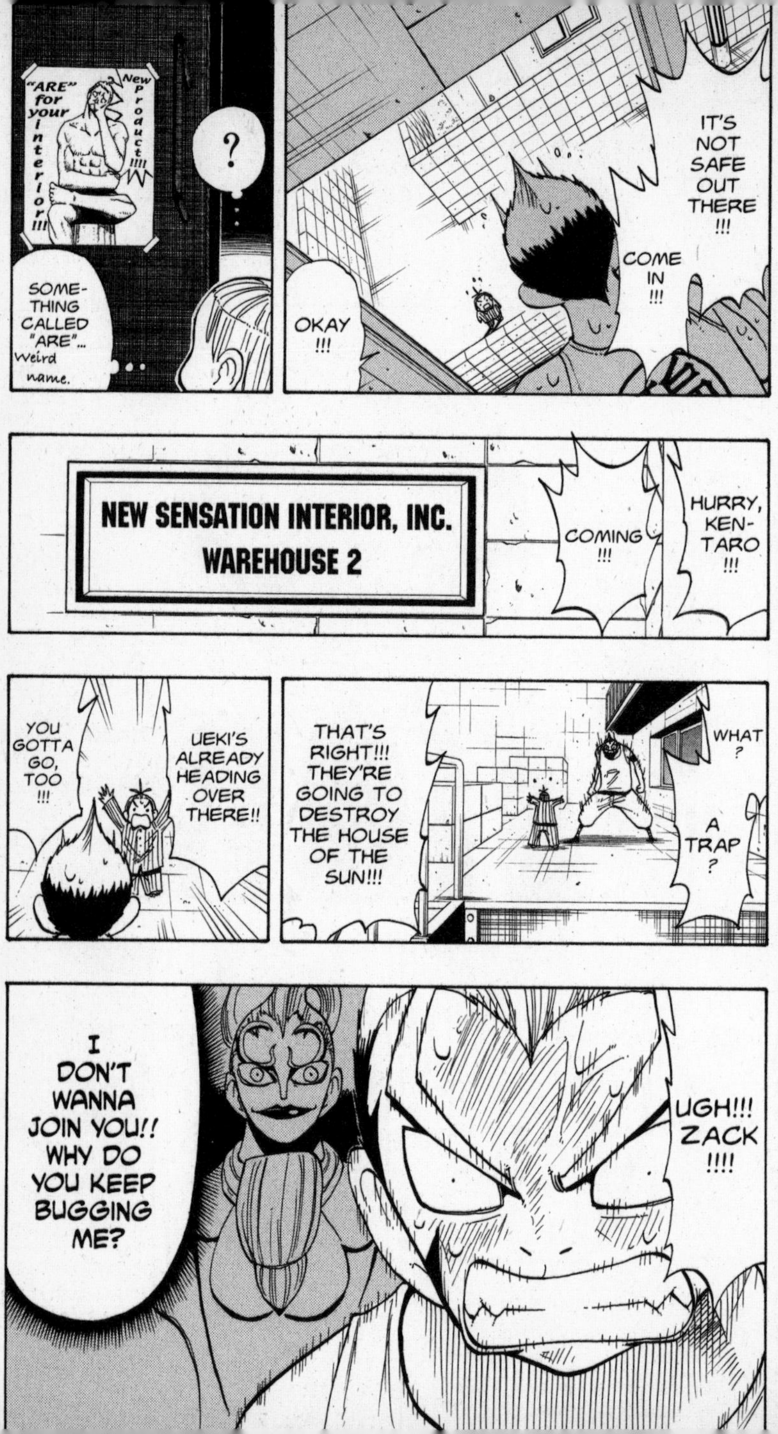
IT'S NOT SAFE OUT THERE!!!
COME IN!!!
OKAY!!!
?
"ARE" for your Interior!!!
New Product!!!!
SOME-THING CALLED "ARE"... Weird name.
HURRY, KEN-TARO!!!
COMING!!!
NEW SENSATION INTERIOR, INC.
WAREHOUSE 2
WHAT?
A TRAP?
THAT'S RIGHT!!! THEY'RE GOING TO DESTROY THE HOUSE OF THE SUN!!!
UEKI'S ALREADY HEADING OVER THERE!!
YOU GOTTA GO, TOO!!!
UGH!!! ZACK!!!!
I DON'T WANNA JOIN YOU!! WHY DO YOU KEEP BUGGING ME?

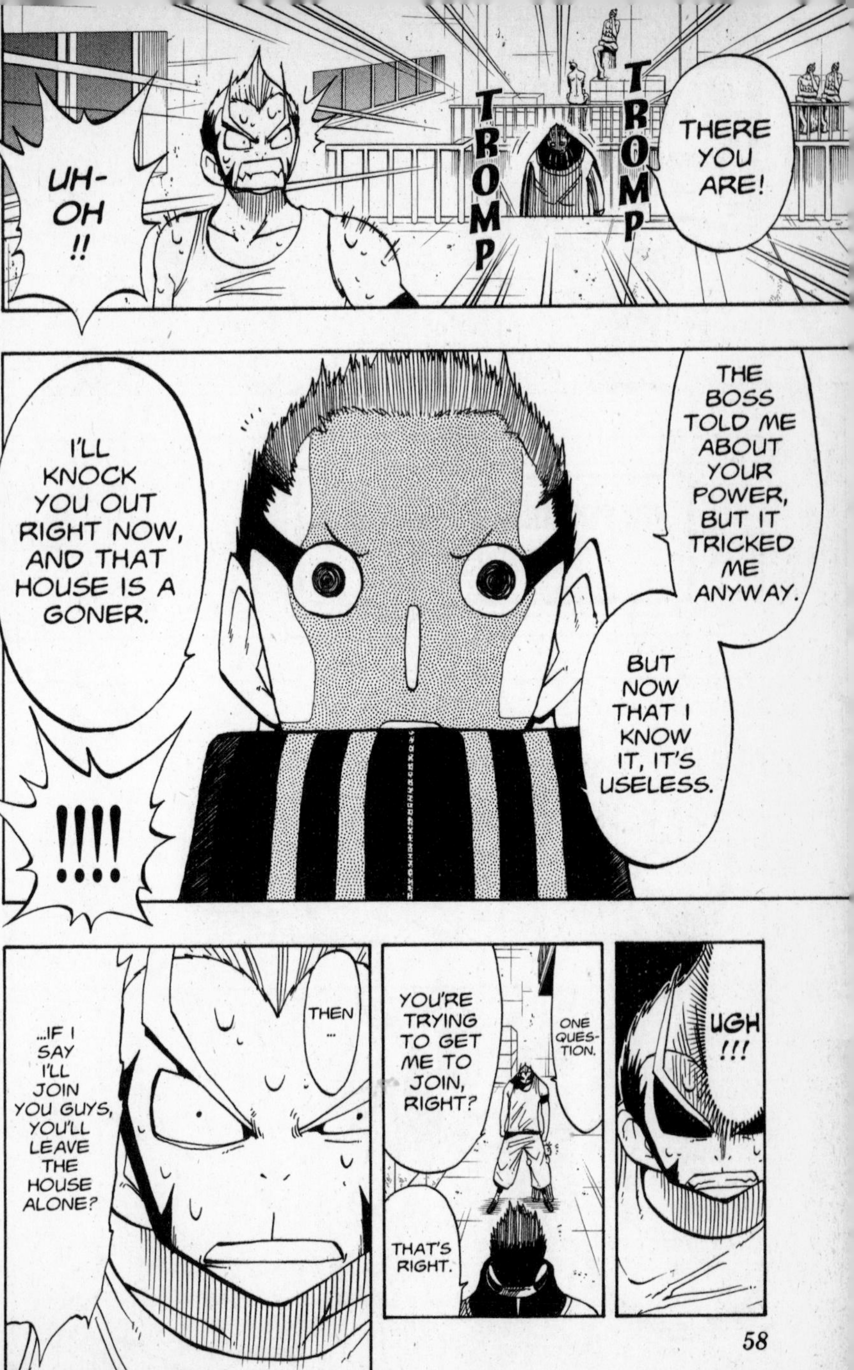
THERE YOU ARE!
TROMP
TROMP
UH-OH !!
THE BOSS TOLD ME ABOUT YOUR POWER, BUT IT TRICKED ME ANYWAY.
BUT NOW THAT I KNOW IT, IT'S USELESS.
I'LL KNOCK YOU OUT RIGHT NOW, AND THAT HOUSE IS A GONER.
!!!!
UGH !!!
ONE QUES-TION.
YOU'RE TRYING TO GET ME TO JOIN, RIGHT?
THAT'S RIGHT.
THEN ...
...IF I SAY I'LL JOIN YOU GUYS, YOU'LL LEAVE THE HOUSE ALONE?

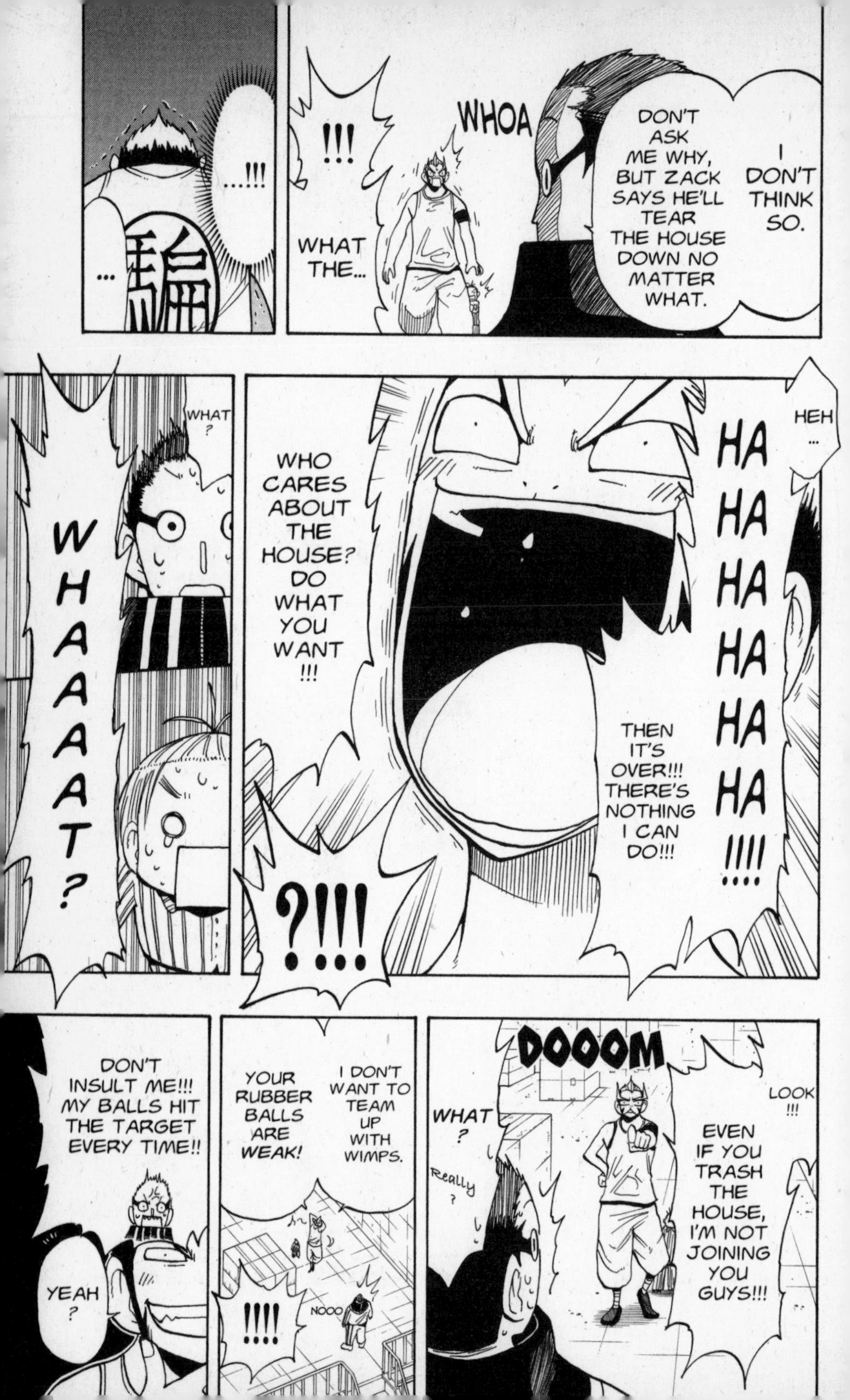
I DON'T THINK SO.
DON'T ASK ME WHY, BUT ZACK SAYS HE'LL TEAR THE HOUSE DOWN NO MATTER WHAT.
WHOA
!!!
WHAT THE...
...!!!
...
HEH ...
HA HA HA HA HA HA !!!!
THEN IT'S OVER!!! THERE'S NOTHING I CAN DO!!!
?!!!
WHO CARES ABOUT THE HOUSE? DO WHAT YOU WANT !!!
WHAT ?
WHAAAAT?
LOOK !!!
EVEN IF YOU TRASH THE HOUSE, I'M NOT JOINING YOU GUYS!!!
DOOOM
WHAT ?
Really ?
I DON'T WANT TO TEAM UP WITH WIMPS.
YOUR RUBBER BALLS ARE WEAK!
!!!!
NOOO
DON'T INSULT ME!!! MY BALLS HIT THE TARGET EVERY TIME!!
YEAH ?

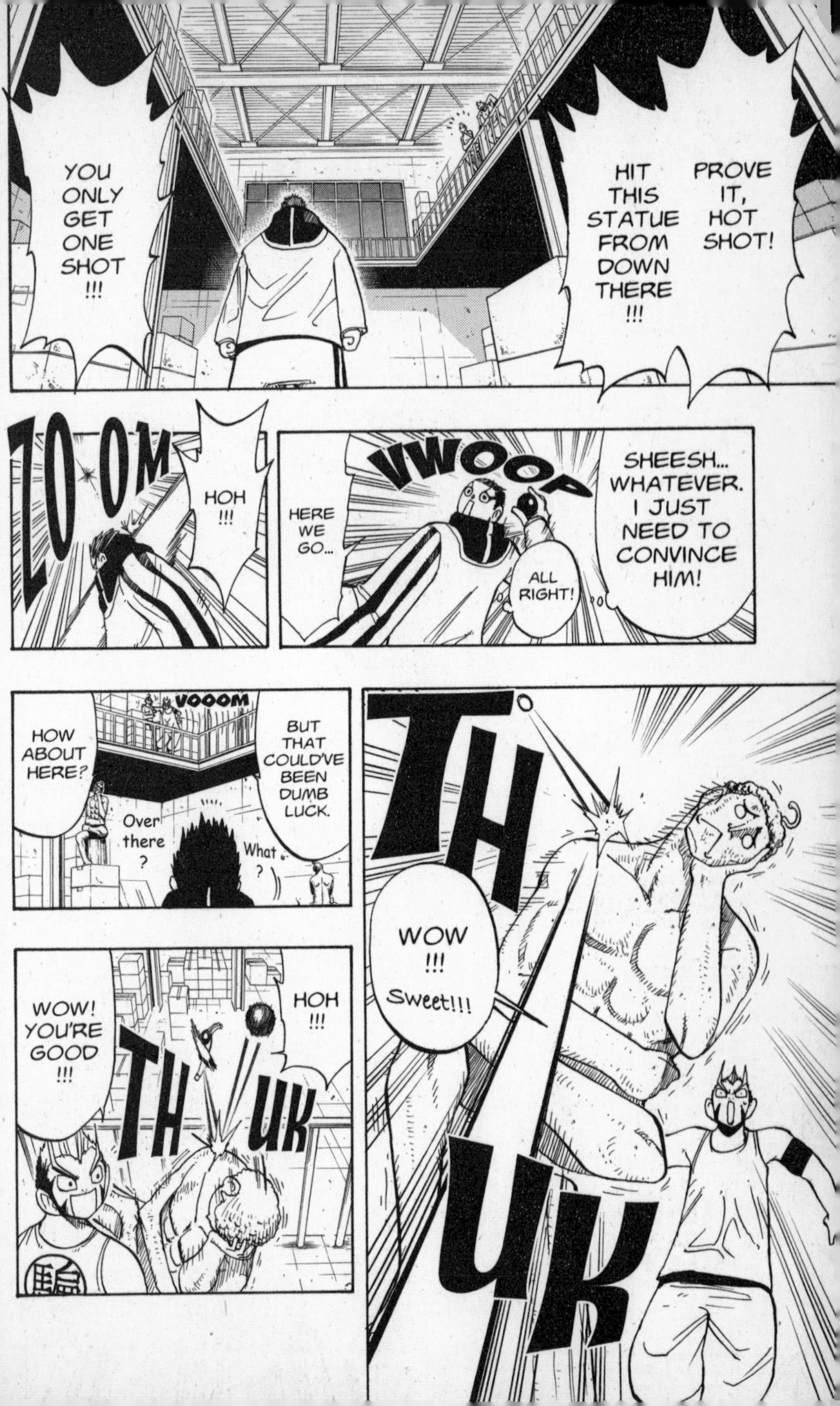
PROVE IT, HOT SHOT!
HIT THIS STATUE FROM DOWN THERE !!!
YOU ONLY GET ONE SHOT !!!
SHEESH... WHATEVER. I JUST NEED TO CONVINCE HIM!
VWOOP
ALL RIGHT!
HERE WE GO...
HOH !!!
ZOOM
THUK
WOW !!! Sweet!!!
BUT THAT COULD'VE BEEN DUMB LUCK.
What ?
Over there ?
VOOOM
HOW ABOUT HERE?
HOH !!!
THUK
WOW! YOU'RE GOOD !!!

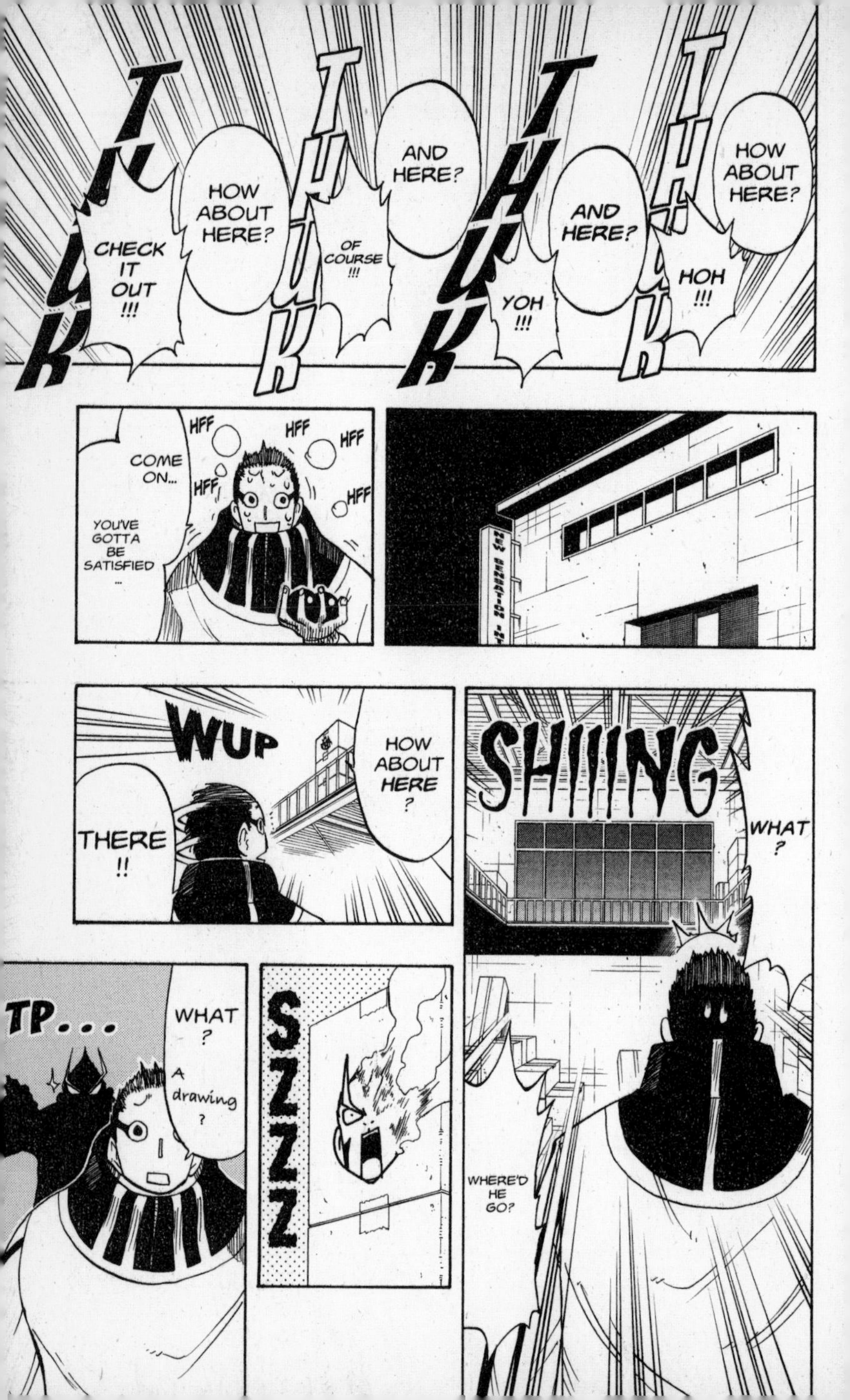
HOW ABOUT HERE?
HOH!!!
AND HERE?
YOH!!!
AND HERE?
OF COURSE!!!
HOW ABOUT HERE?
CHECK IT OUT!!!
NEW SENSATION
HFF HFF HFF HFF HFF
COME ON...
YOU'VE GOTTA BE SATISFIED ...
SHIIING
WHAT?
HOW ABOUT HERE?
WUP
THERE!!
WHERE'D HE GO?
SZZZ
TP...
WHAT?
A drawing?

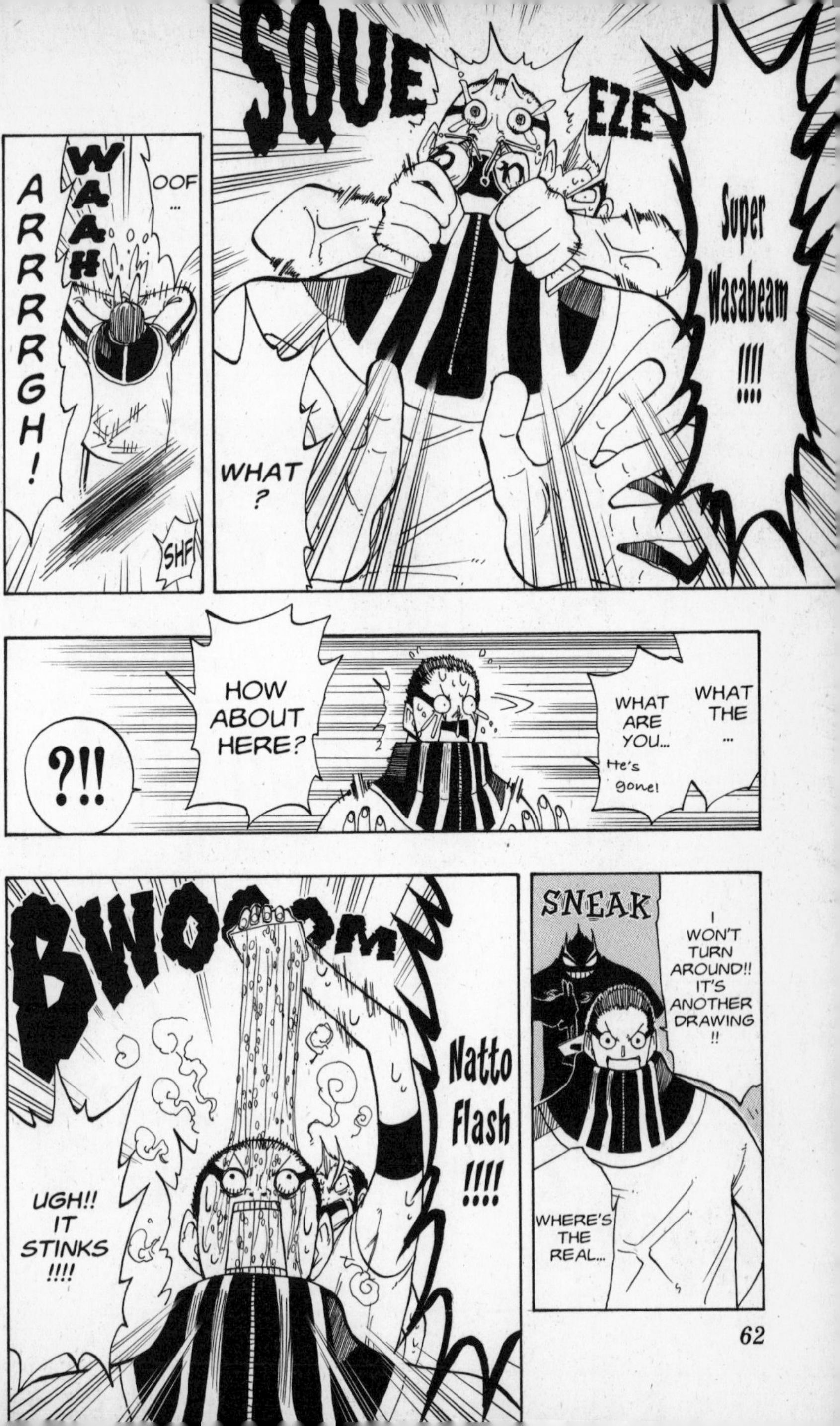
SQUE
EZE
Super Wasabeam !!!!
WHAT ?
WAAH
OOF ...
ARRRRGH!
SHF
WHAT THE ...
WHAT ARE YOU...
He's gone!
HOW ABOUT HERE?
?!!
SNEAK
I WON'T TURN AROUND!! IT'S ANOTHER DRAWING !!
WHERE'S THE REAL...
BWOOOM
Natto Flash !!!!
UGH!! IT STINKS !!!!

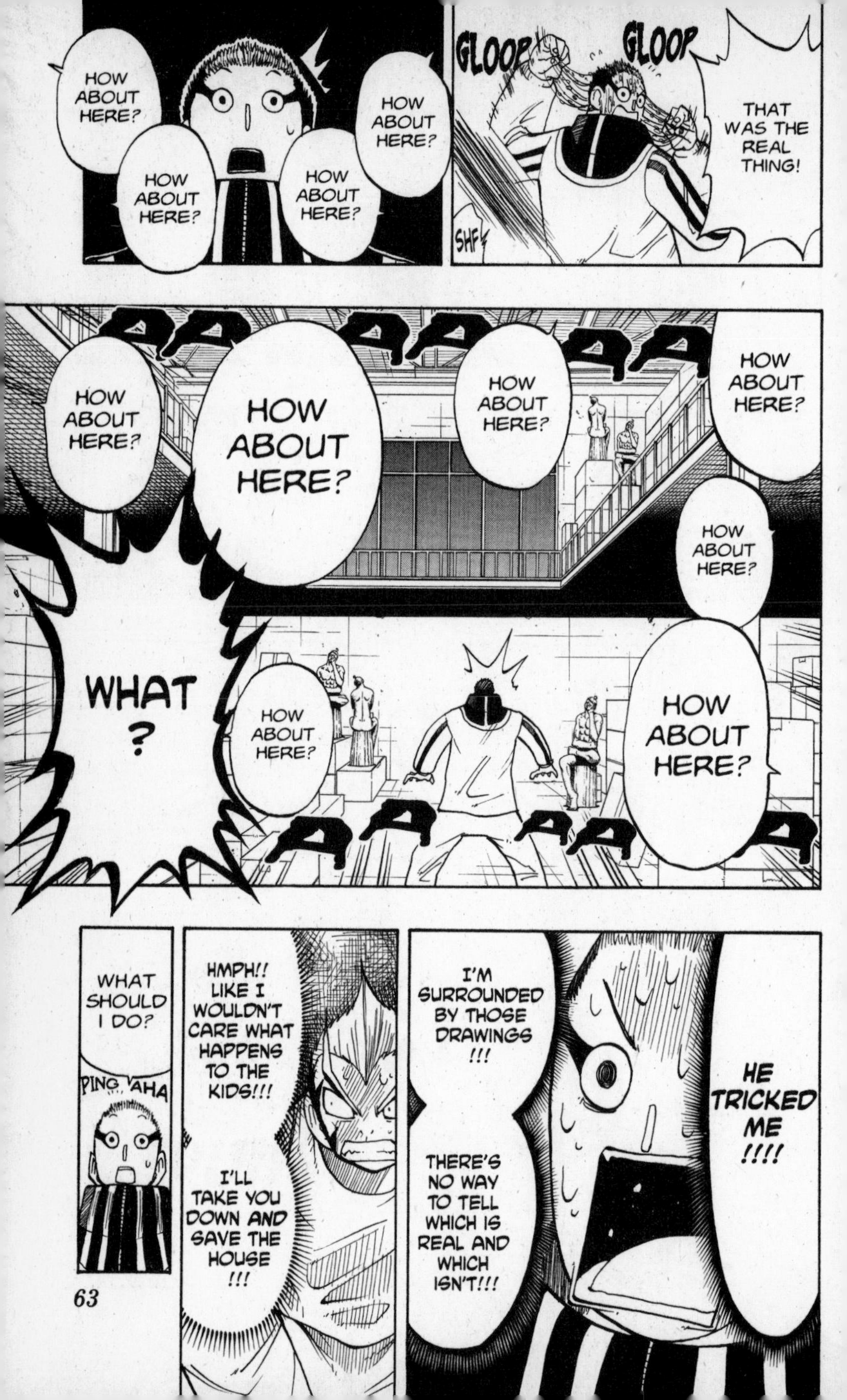
GLOOP GLOOP
THAT WAS THE REAL THING!
SHF
HOW ABOUT HERE?
HOW ABOUT HERE?
HOW ABOUT HERE?
HOW ABOUT HERE?
HOW ABOUT HERE?
HOW ABOUT HERE?
HOW ABOUT HERE?
HOW ABOUT HERE?
HOW ABOUT HERE?
HOW ABOUT HERE?
HOW ABOUT HERE?
WHAT ?
HE TRICKED ME !!!!
I'M SURROUNDED BY THOSE DRAWINGS !!!
THERE'S NO WAY TO TELL WHICH IS REAL AND WHICH ISN'T!!!
HMPH!! LIKE I WOULDN'T CARE WHAT HAPPENS TO THE KIDS!!!
I'LL TAKE YOU DOWN AND SAVE THE HOUSE !!!
WHAT SHOULD I DO?
PING AHA

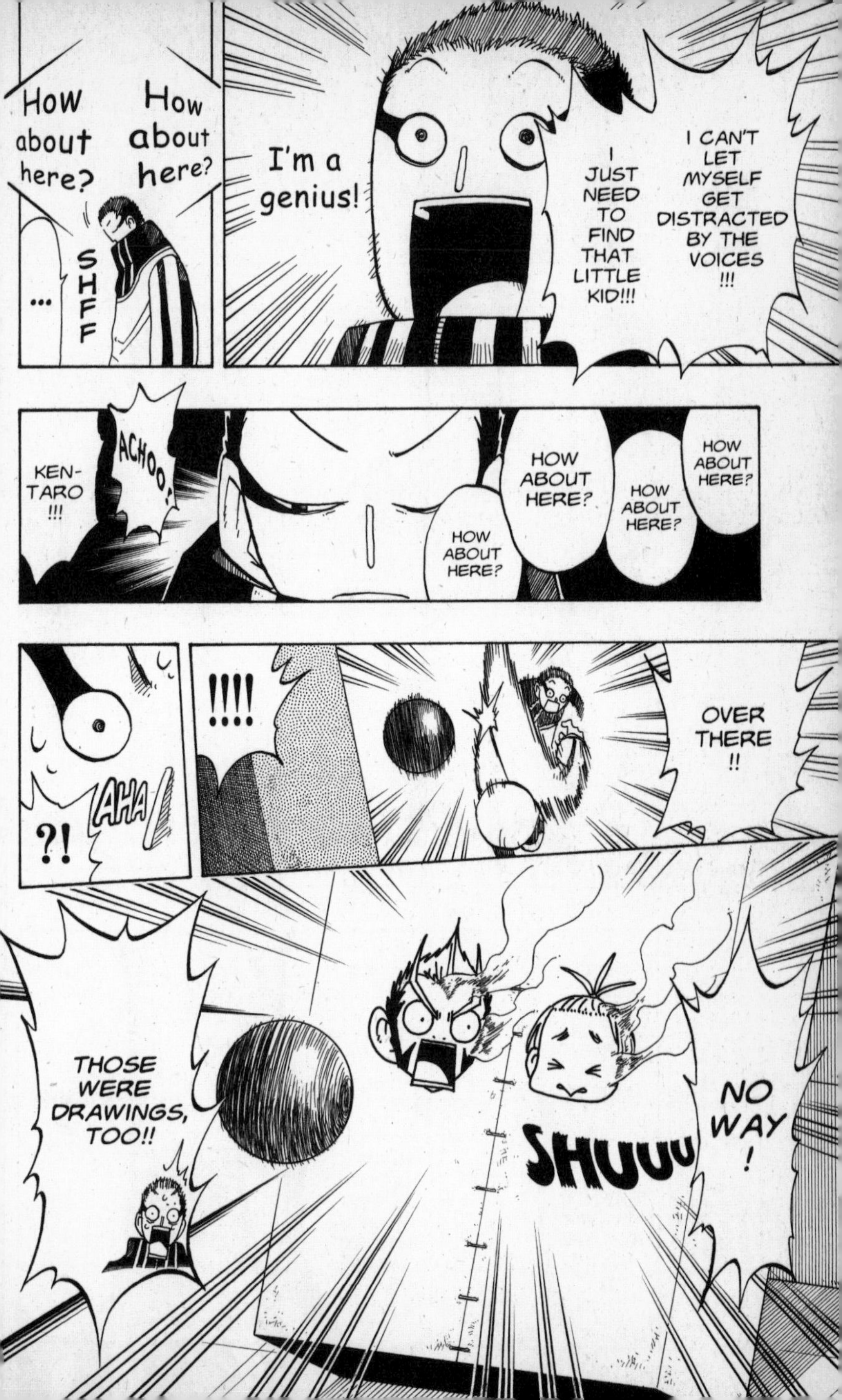
I CAN'T LET MYSELF GET DISTRACTED BY THE VOICES !!!
I JUST NEED TO FIND THAT LITTLE KID!!!
I'm a genius!
How about here?
How about here?
SHFF
...
HOW ABOUT HERE?
HOW ABOUT HERE?
HOW ABOUT HERE?
HOW ABOUT HERE?
ACHOO!
KEN-TARO !!!
OVER THERE !!
!!!!
AHA
?!
NO WAY !
SHUUU
THOSE WERE DRAWINGS, TOO!!

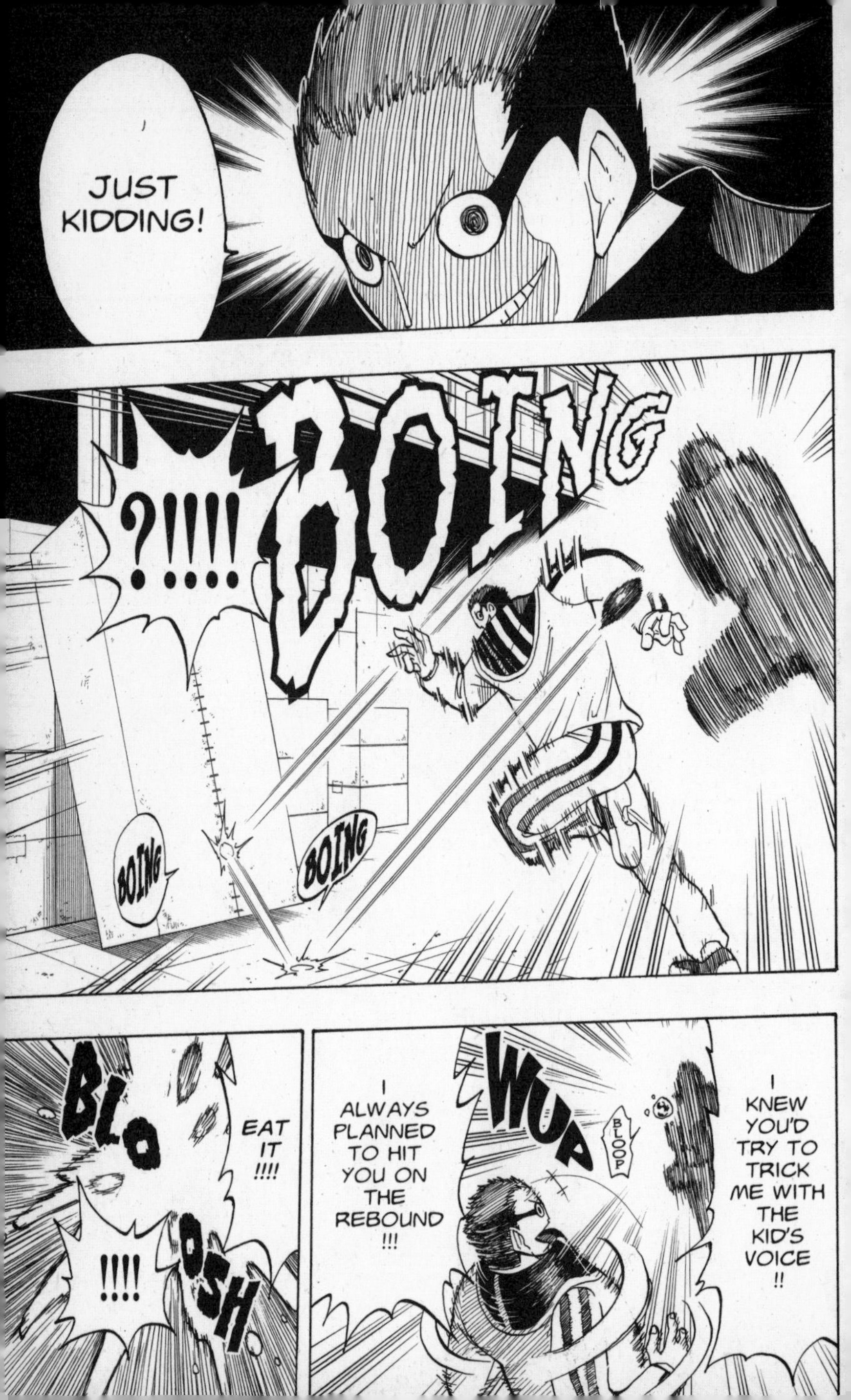
JUST KIDDING!
BOING
?!!!!
BOING
BOING
I KNEW YOU'D TRY TO TRICK ME WITH THE KID'S VOICE !!
BLOOP
WUP
I ALWAYS PLANNED TO HIT YOU ON THE REBOUND !!!
EAT IT !!!!
BLOOSH
!!!!

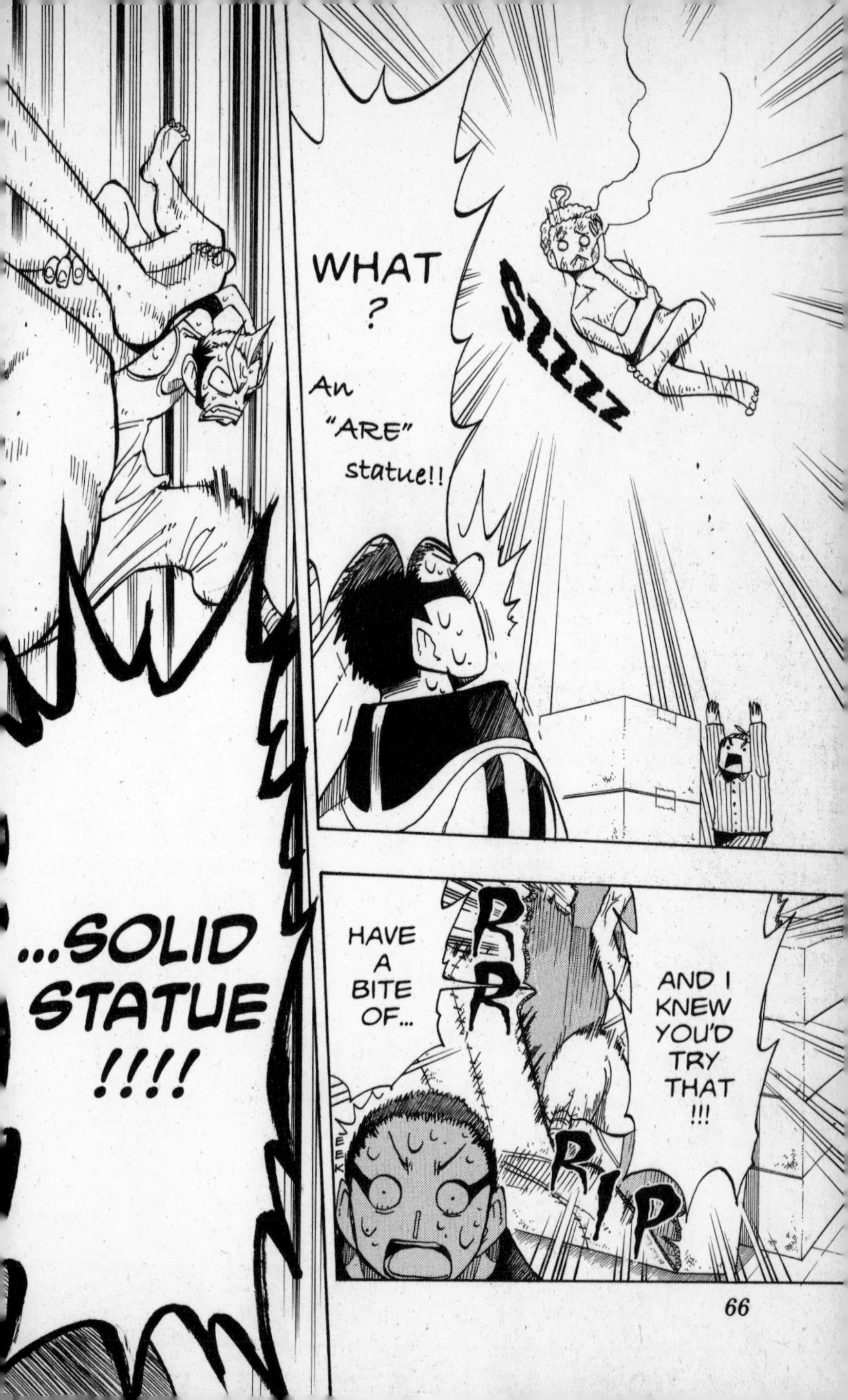
WHAT
?
An "ARE" statue!!
SZZZZ
AND I KNEW YOU'D TRY THAT!!!
HAVE A BITE OF...
RRRIP
EEK
...SOLID STATUE!!!!

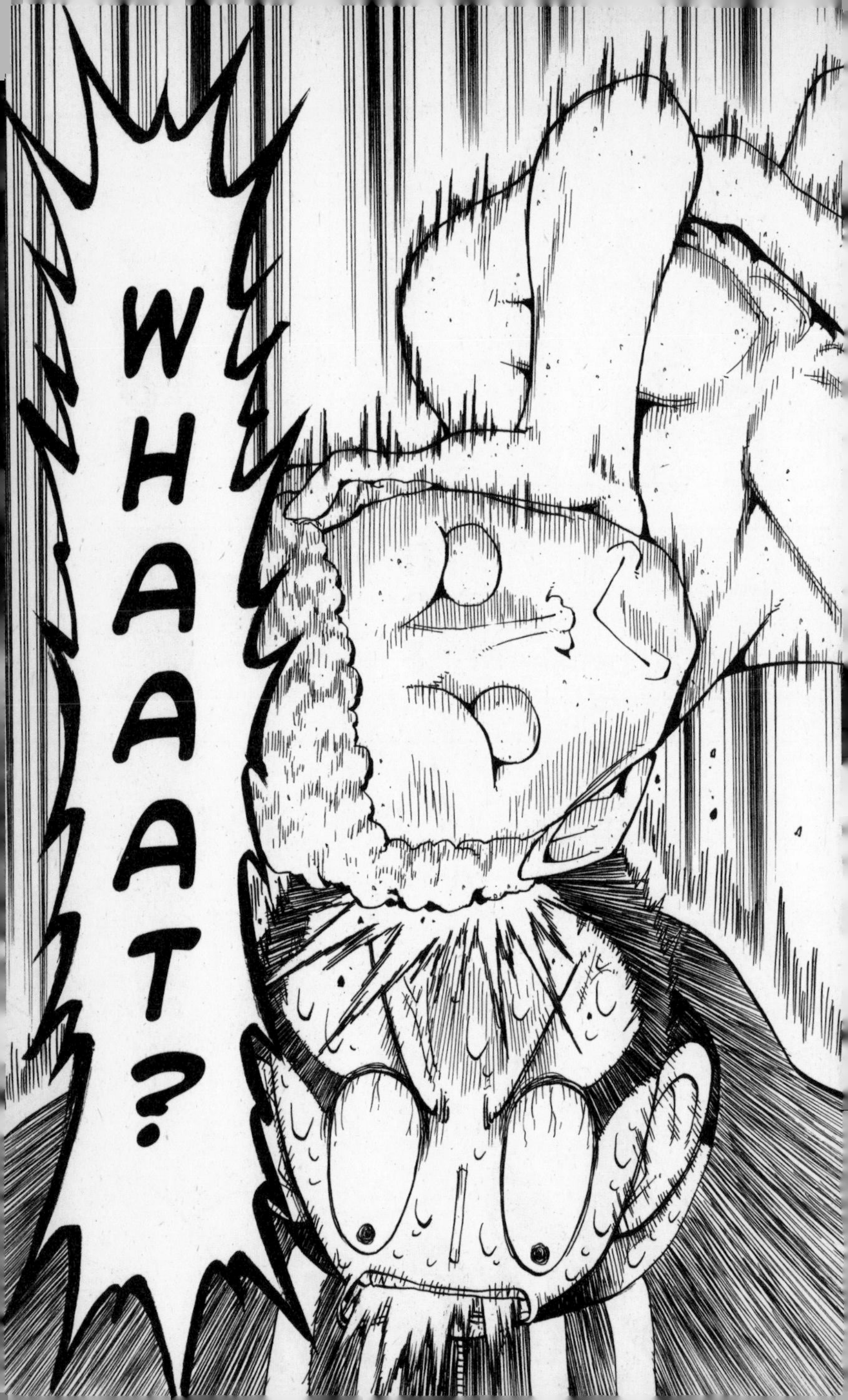
WHAAAT?

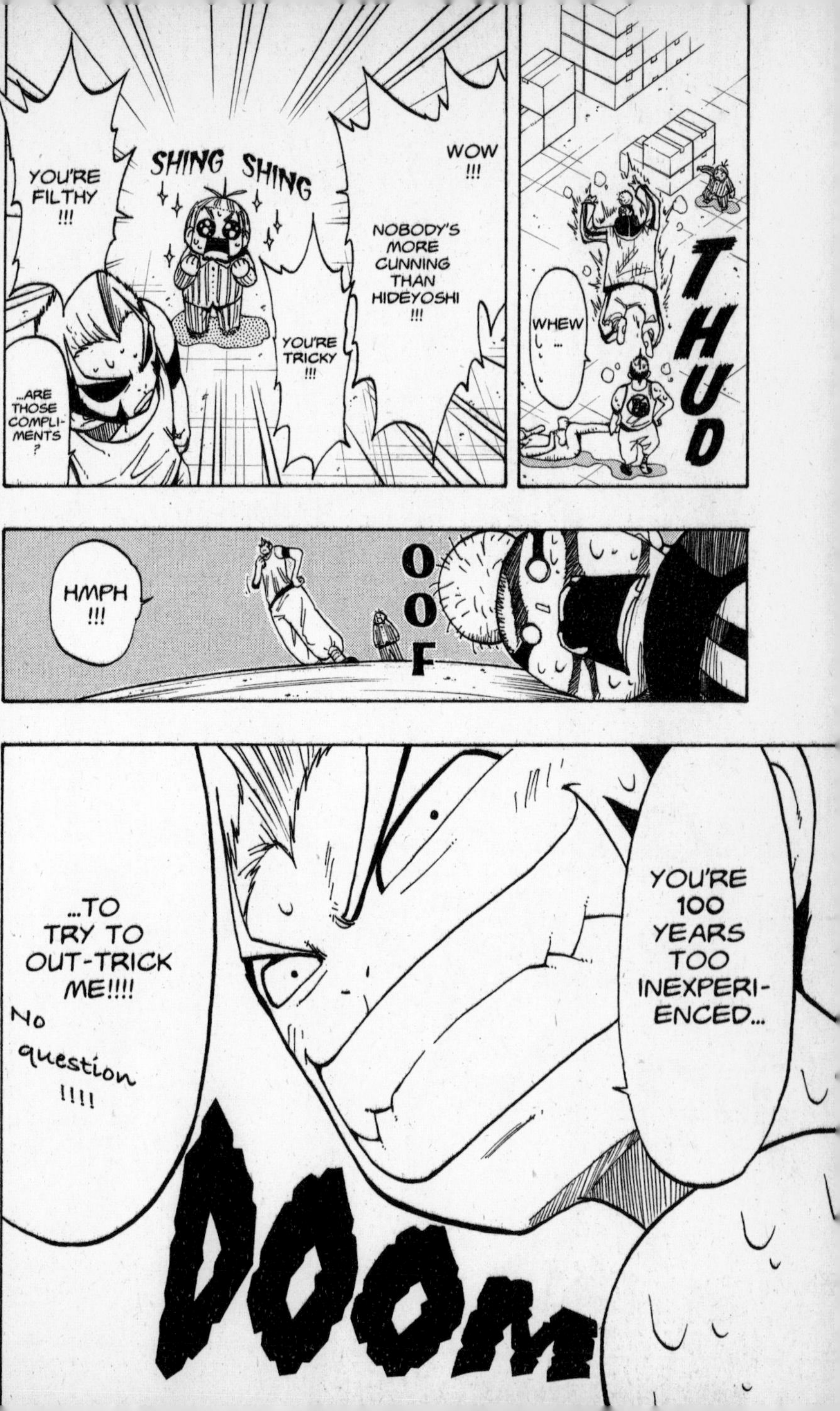
THUD
WHEW ...
WOW !!!
NOBODY'S MORE CUNNING THAN HIDEYOSHI !!!
YOU'RE TRICKY !!!
SHING SHING
YOU'RE FILTHY !!!
...ARE THOSE COMPLI-MENTS ?
OOF
HMPH !!!
YOU'RE 100 YEARS TOO INEXPERI-ENCED...
...TO TRY TO OUT-TRICK ME!!!!
No question !!!!
DOOM

Chapter 90
Defense Line

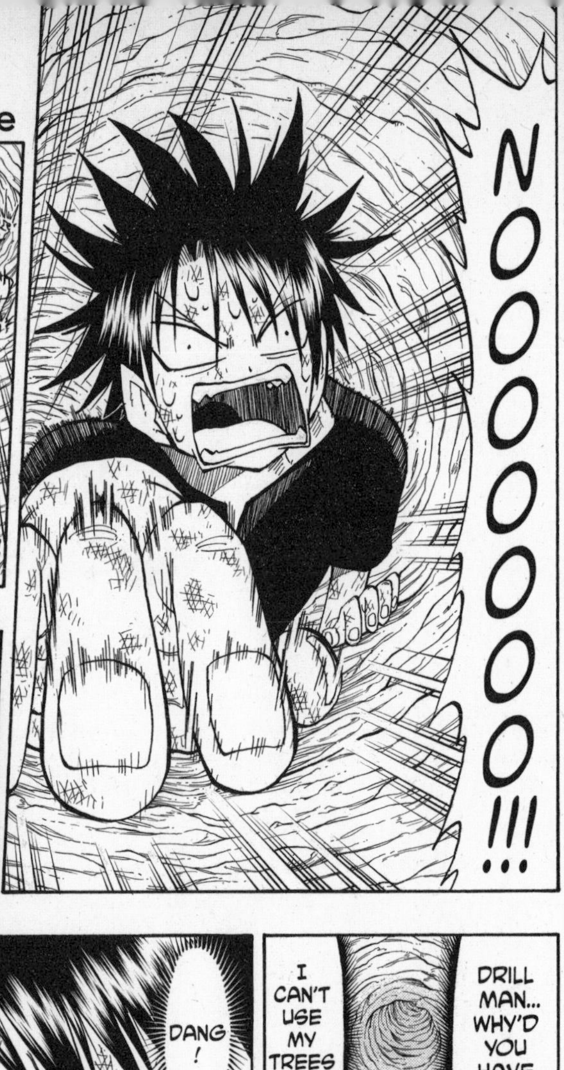
NOOOOOOOOO!!!

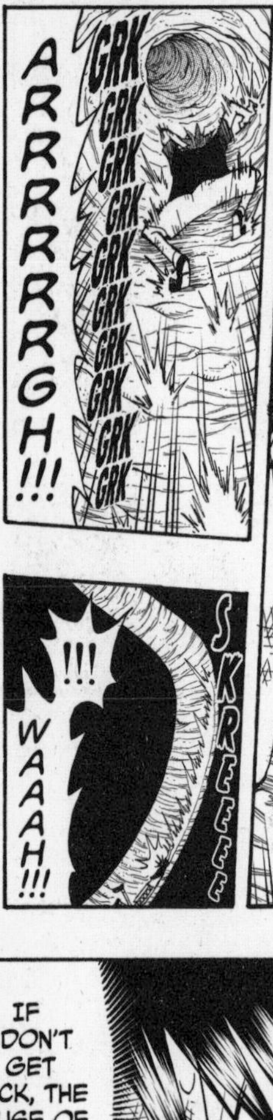
GRK GRK GRK GRK GRK GRK GRK GRK GRK GRK GRK
ARRRRRRRGH!!!
SKREEEE
!!!
WAAAAH!!!

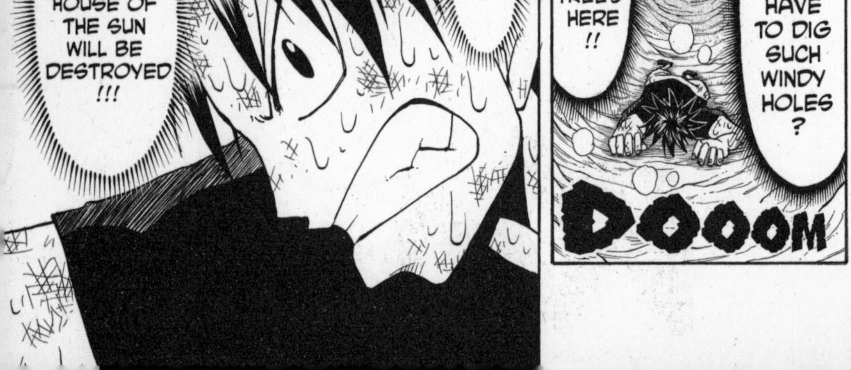
DRILL MAN... WHY'D YOU HAVE TO DIG SUCH WINDY HOLES?
I CAN'T USE MY TREES HERE!!
DOOOM
DANG!
IF I DON'T GET BACK, THE HOUSE OF THE SUN WILL BE DESTROYED!!!

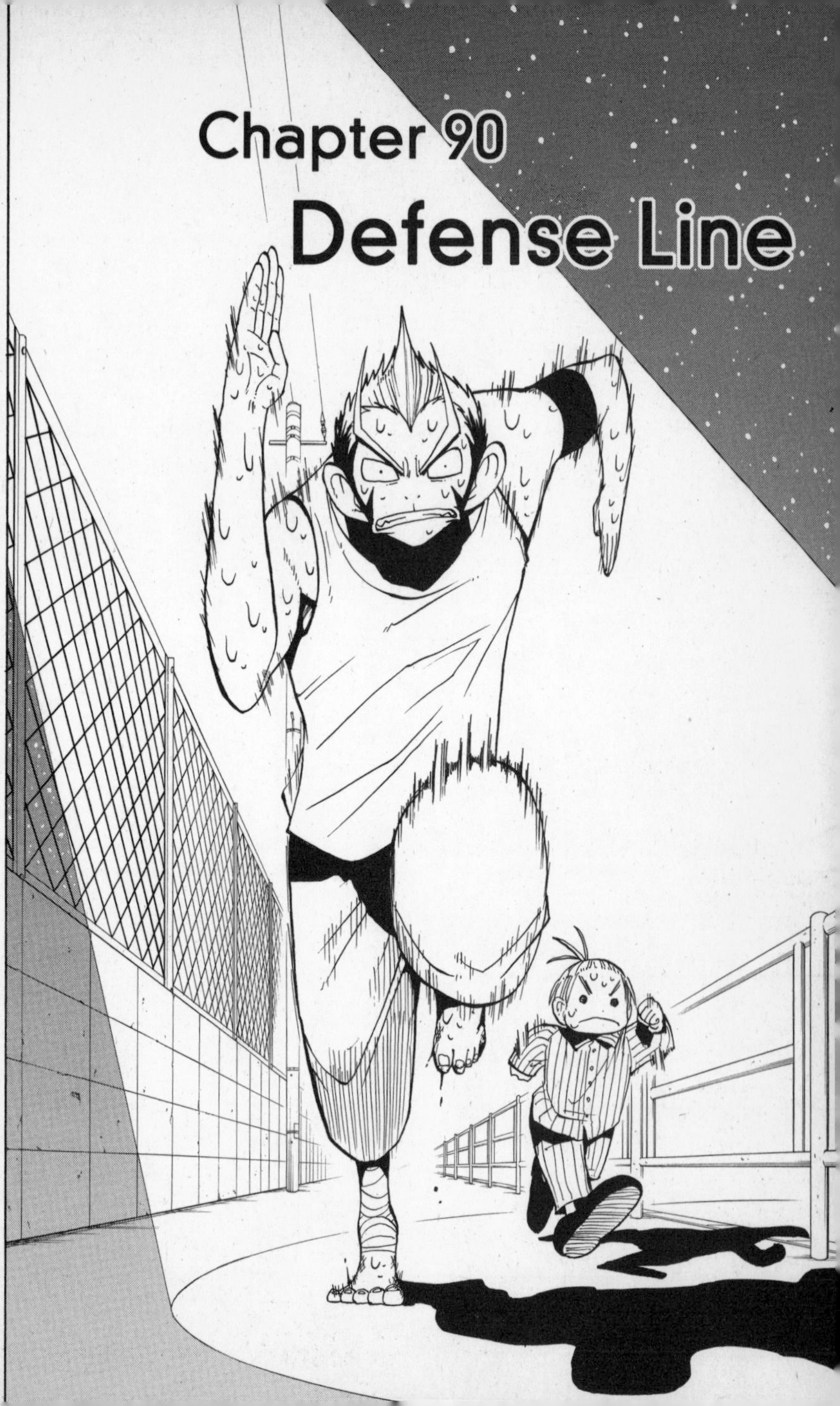
Chapter 90
Defense Line

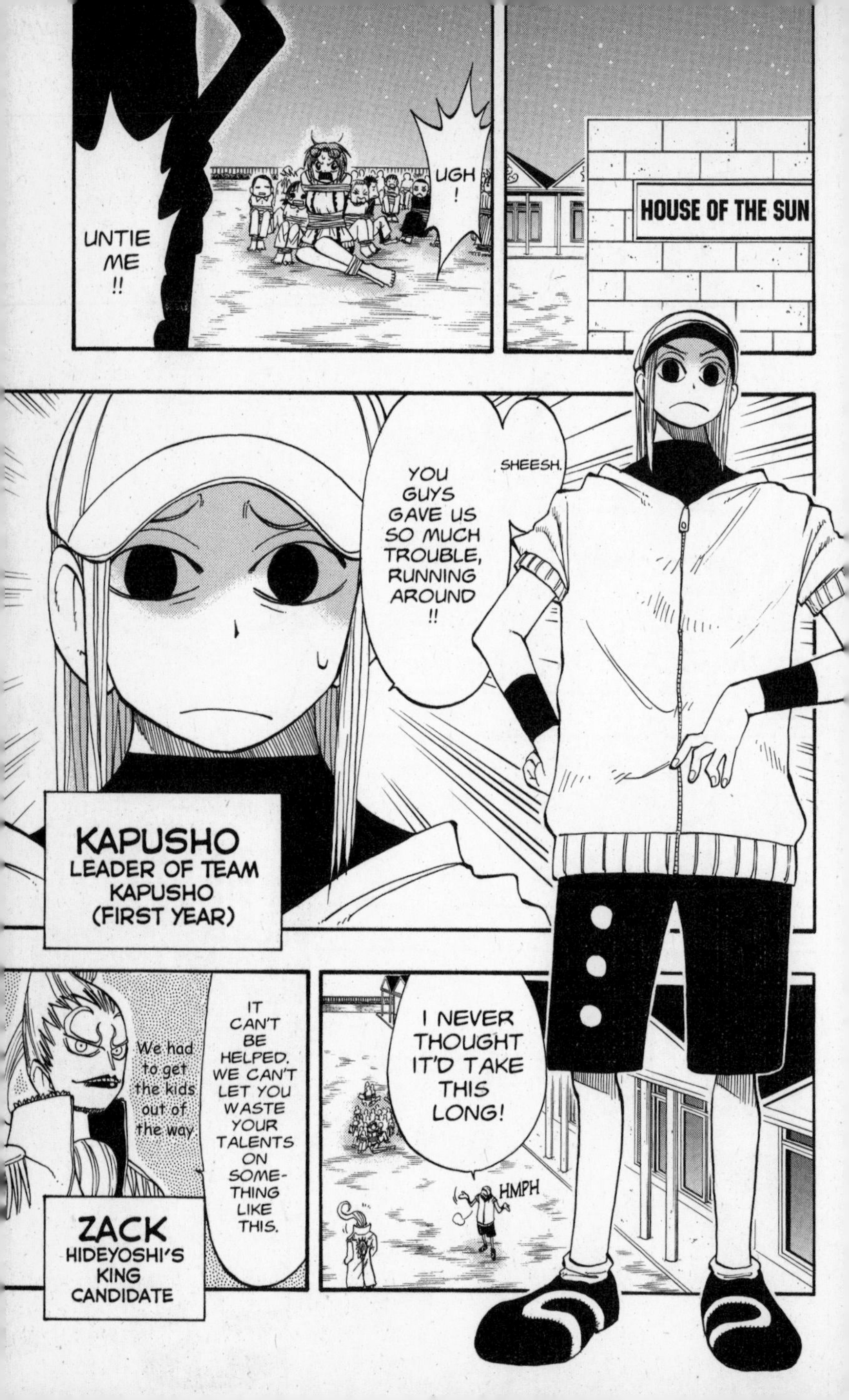
HOUSE OF THE SUN
UGH !
UNTIE ME !!
SHEESH.
YOU GUYS GAVE US SO MUCH TROUBLE, RUNNING AROUND !!
KAPUSHO
LEADER OF TEAM KAPUSHO (FIRST YEAR)
I NEVER THOUGHT IT'D TAKE THIS LONG!
HMPH
IT CAN'T BE HELPED. WE CAN'T LET YOU WASTE YOUR TALENTS ON SOME-THING LIKE THIS.
We had to get the kids out of the way.
ZACK
HIDEYOSHI'S KING CANDIDATE

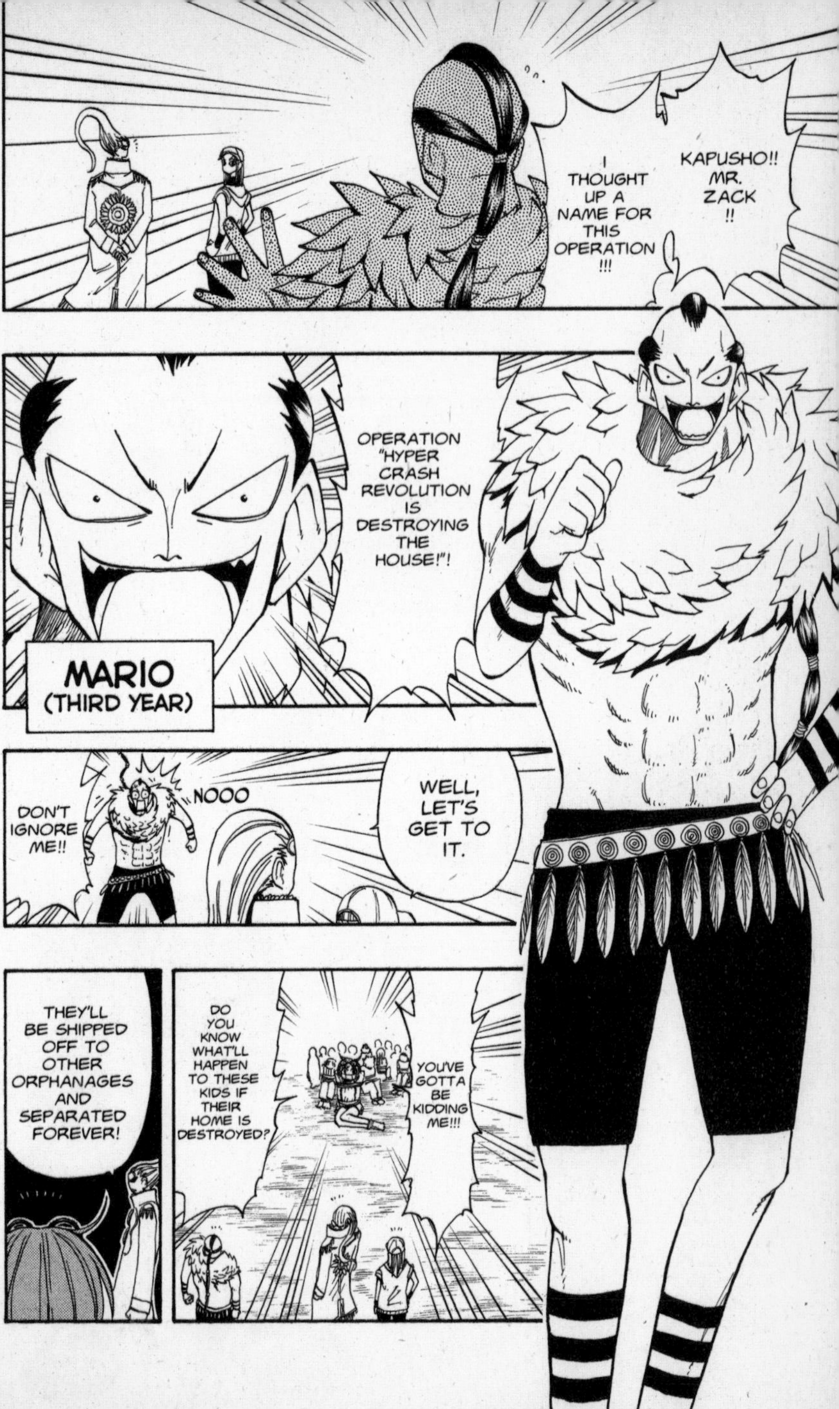
KAPUSHO!! MR. ZACK !!
I THOUGHT UP A NAME FOR THIS OPERATION !!!
OPERATION "HYPER CRASH REVOLUTION IS DESTROYING THE HOUSE!"!
MARIO (THIRD YEAR)
WELL, LET'S GET TO IT.
NOOO
DON'T IGNORE ME!!
YOU'VE GOTTA BE KIDDING ME!!!
DO YOU KNOW WHAT'LL HAPPEN TO THESE KIDS IF THEIR HOME IS DESTROYED?
THEY'LL BE SHIPPED OFF TO OTHER ORPHANAGES AND SEPARATED FOREVER!

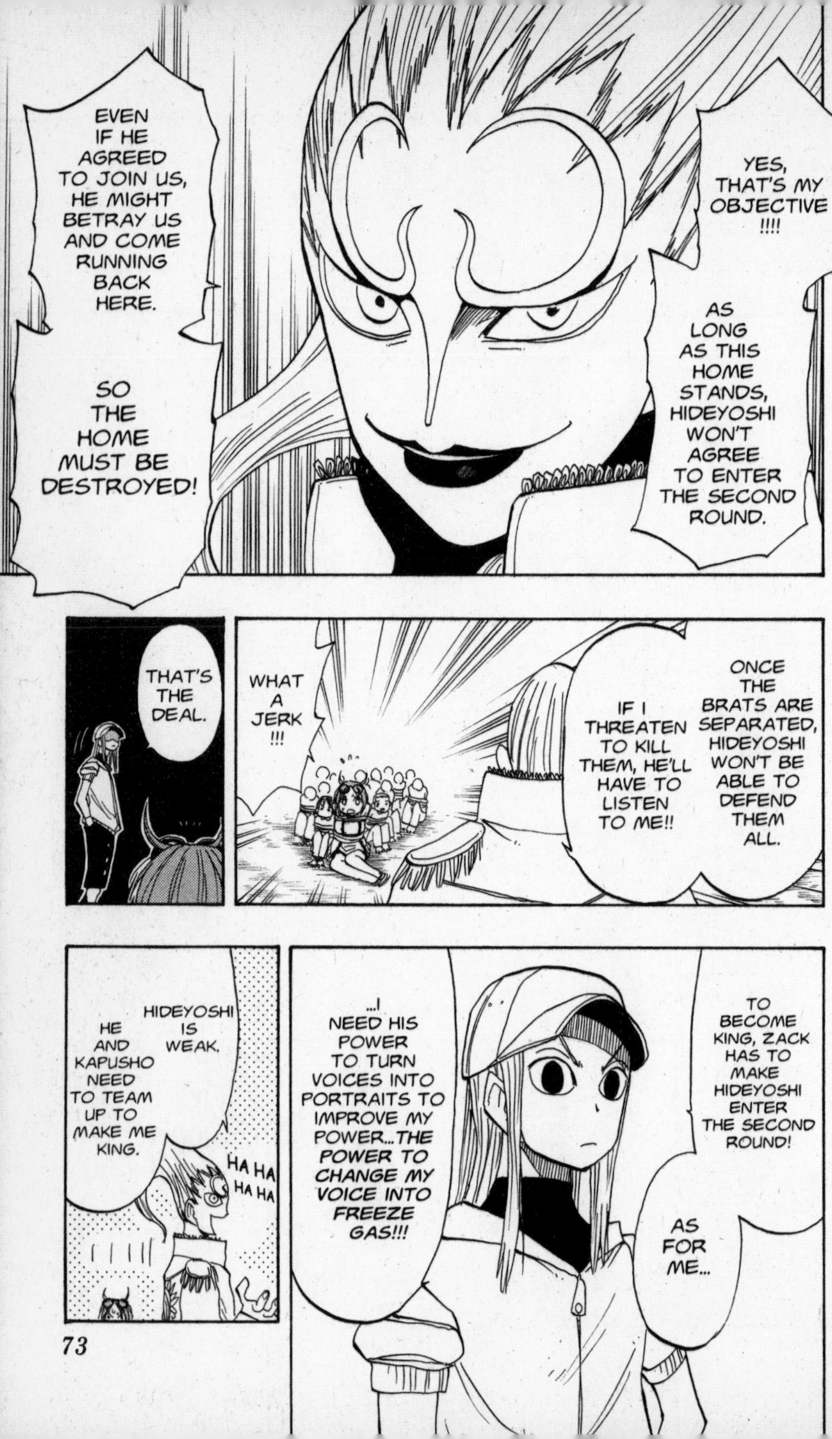
YES, THAT'S MY OBJECTIVE !!!!
AS LONG AS THIS HOME STANDS, HIDEYOSHI WON'T AGREE TO ENTER THE SECOND ROUND.
EVEN IF HE AGREED TO JOIN US, HE MIGHT BETRAY US AND COME RUNNING BACK HERE.
SO THE HOME MUST BE DESTROYED!
ONCE THE BRATS ARE SEPARATED, HIDEYOSHI WON'T BE ABLE TO DEFEND THEM ALL.
IF I THREATEN TO KILL THEM, HE'LL HAVE TO LISTEN TO ME!!
WHAT A JERK !!!
THAT'S THE DEAL.
TO BECOME KING, ZACK HAS TO MAKE HIDEYOSHI ENTER THE SECOND ROUND!
AS FOR ME...
...I NEED HIS POWER TO TURN VOICES INTO PORTRAITS TO IMPROVE MY POWER...THE POWER TO CHANGE MY VOICE INTO FREEZE GAS!!!
HIDEYOSHI IS WEAK.
HE AND KAPUSHO NEED TO TEAM UP TO MAKE ME KING.
HA HA HA HA

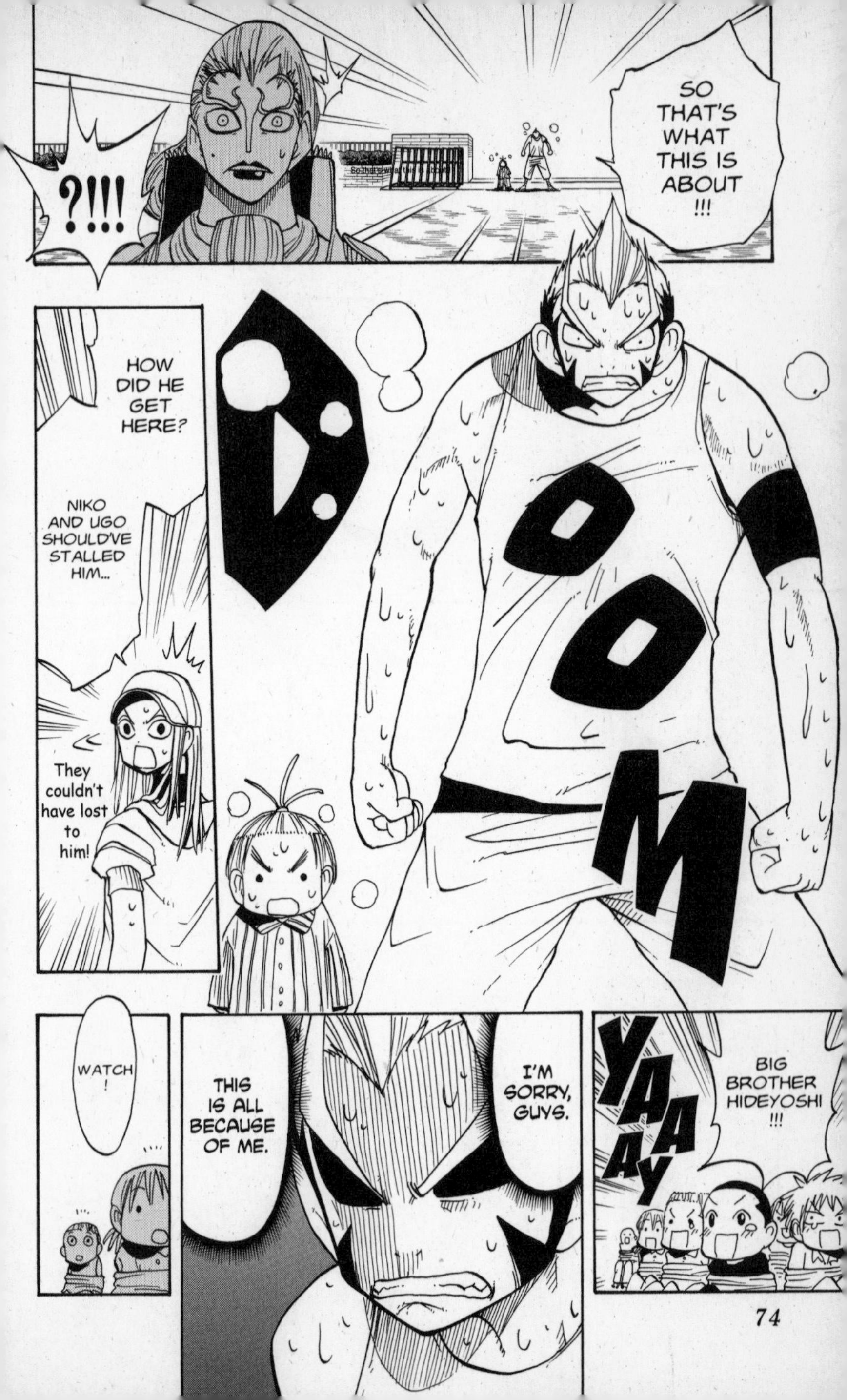
SO THAT'S WHAT THIS IS ABOUT !!!
?!!!
DOOM
HOW DID HE GET HERE?
NIKO AND UGO SHOULD'VE STALLED HIM...
They couldn't have lost to him!
BIG BROTHER HIDEYOSHI !!!
YAAAAY
I'M SORRY, GUYS.
THIS IS ALL BECAUSE OF ME.
WATCH !
...
...

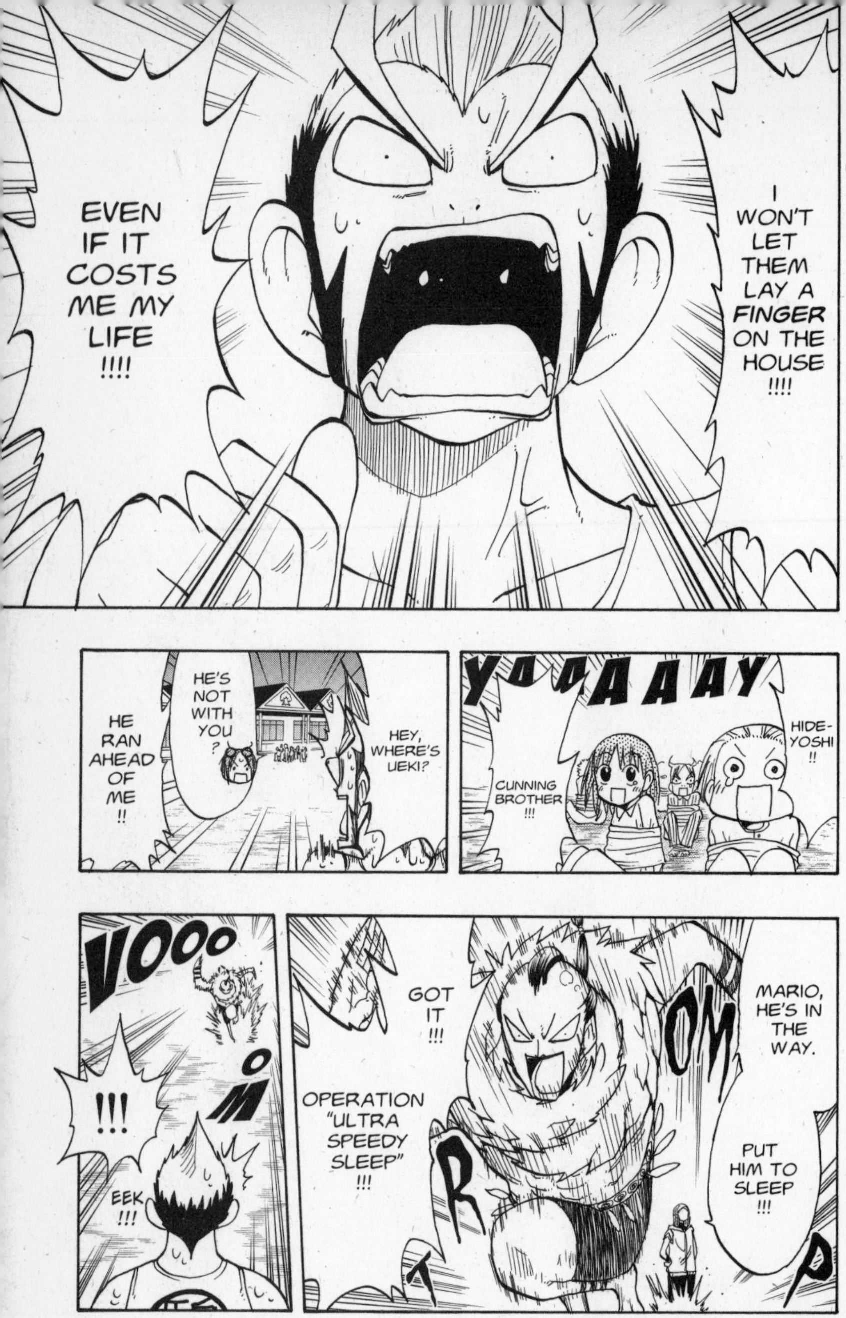
I WON'T LET THEM LAY A FINGER ON THE HOUSE !!!!
EVEN IF IT COSTS ME MY LIFE !!!!
YOOAAAAY
HIDE-YOSHI !!
CUNNING BROTHER !!!
HEY, WHERE'S UEKI?
HE'S NOT WITH YOU ?
HE RAN AHEAD OF ME !!
MARIO, HE'S IN THE WAY.
PUT HIM TO SLEEP !!!
OM
GOT IT !!!
OPERATION "ULTRA SPEEDY SLEEP" !!!
R
T
P
VOOO
M
O
!!!
EEK !!!

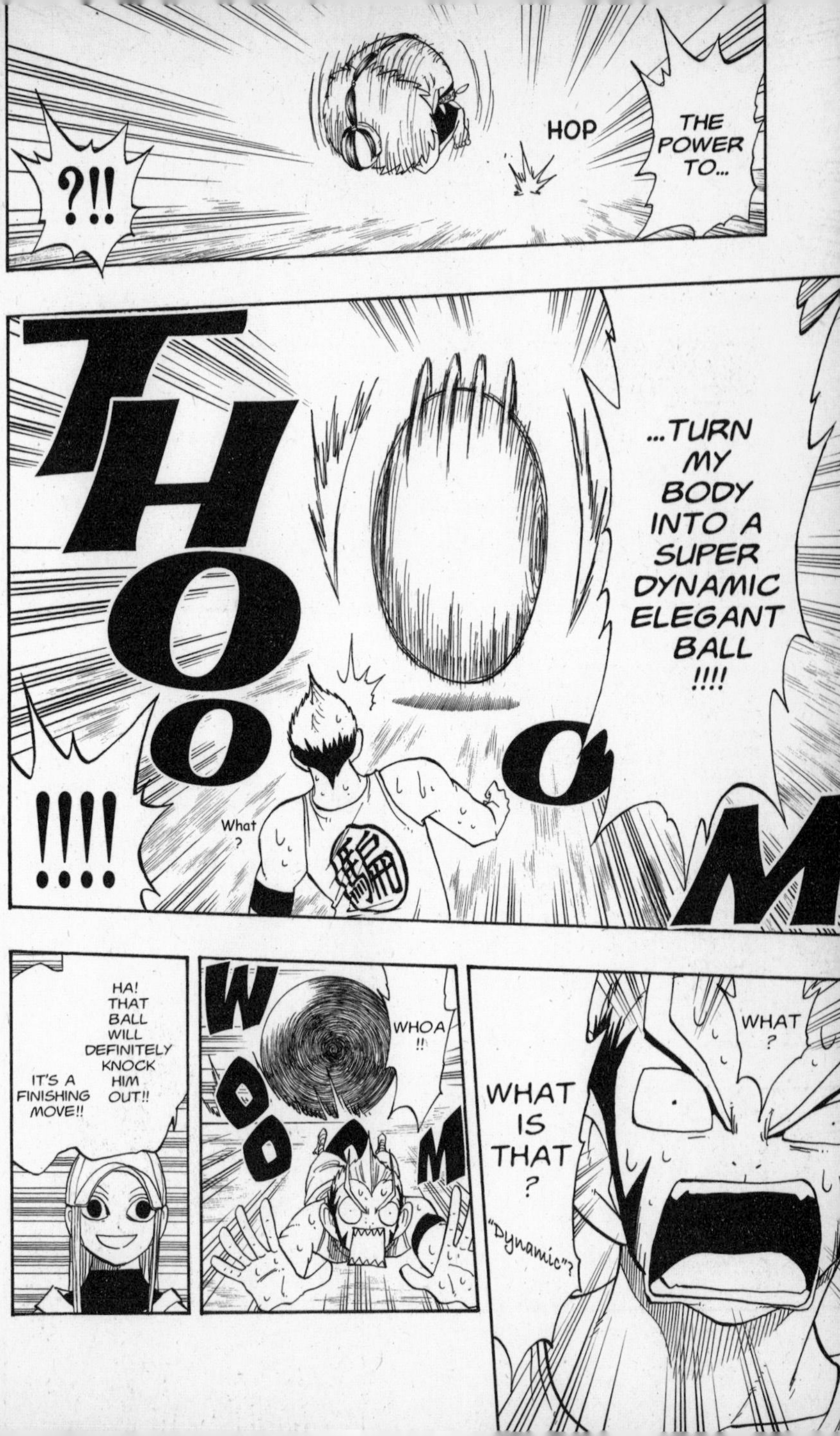
THE POWER TO...
HOP
?!!
...TURN MY BODY INTO A SUPER DYNAMIC ELEGANT BALL !!!!
THOOOOM
What ?
!!!!
WHAT ?
WHAT IS THAT ?
"Dynamic"?
WHOA !!
WOOOM
HA! THAT BALL WILL DEFINITELY KNOCK HIM OUT!!
IT'S A FINISHING MOVE!!

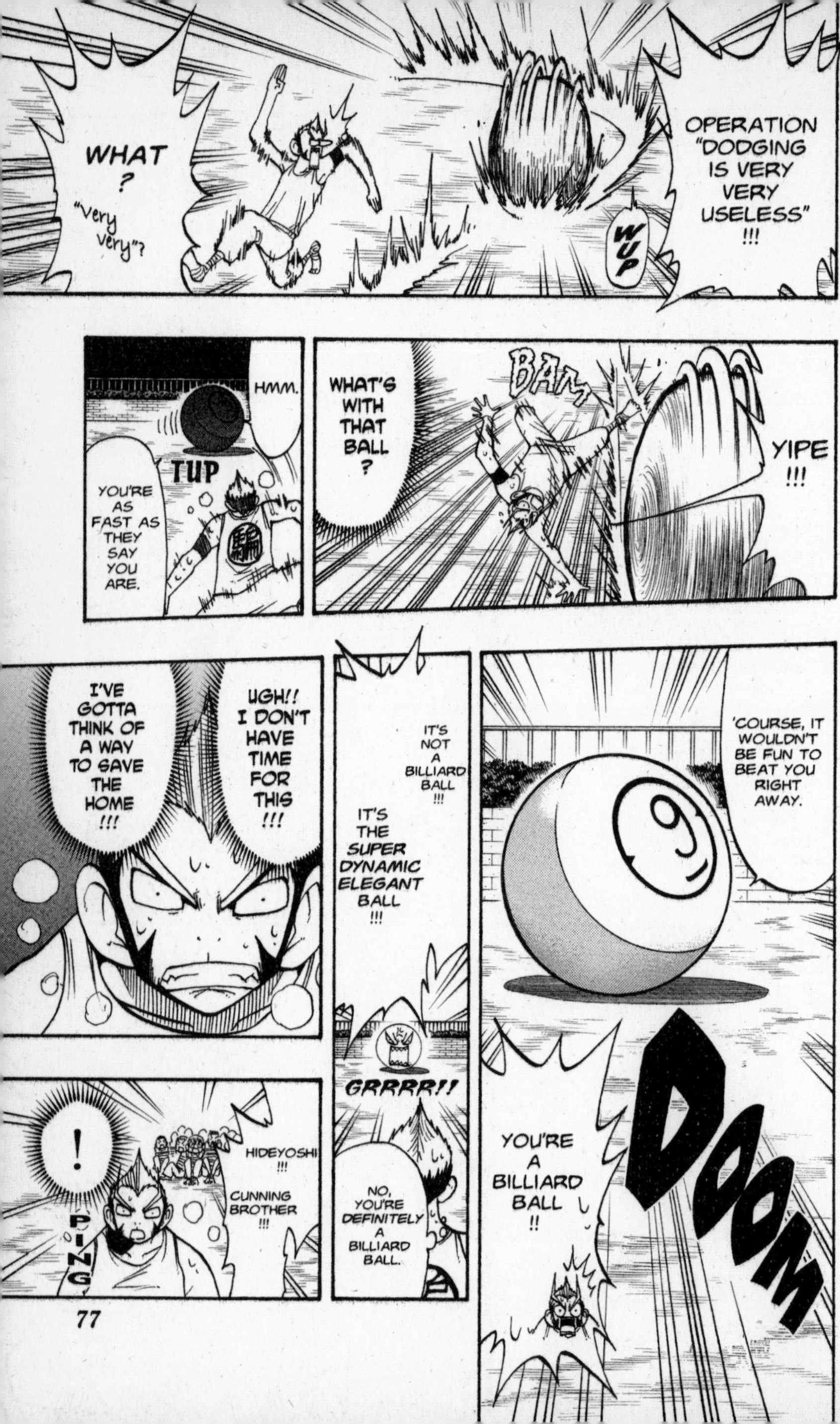
OPERATION "DODGING IS VERY VERY USELESS" !!!
WUP
WHAT ? "very very"?
YIPE !!!
BAM
WHAT'S WITH THAT BALL ?
HMM.
TUP
YOU'RE AS FAST AS THEY SAY YOU ARE.
'COURSE, IT WOULDN'T BE FUN TO BEAT YOU RIGHT AWAY.
DOOM
YOU'RE A BILLIARD BALL !!
IT'S NOT A BILLIARD BALL !!!
IT'S THE SUPER DYNAMIC ELEGANT BALL !!!
GRRRR!!
NO, YOU'RE DEFINITELY A BILLIARD BALL.
UGH!! I DON'T HAVE TIME FOR THIS !!!
I'VE GOTTA THINK OF A WAY TO SAVE THE HOME !!!
!
HIDEYOSHI !!!
CUNNING BROTHER !!!
PING

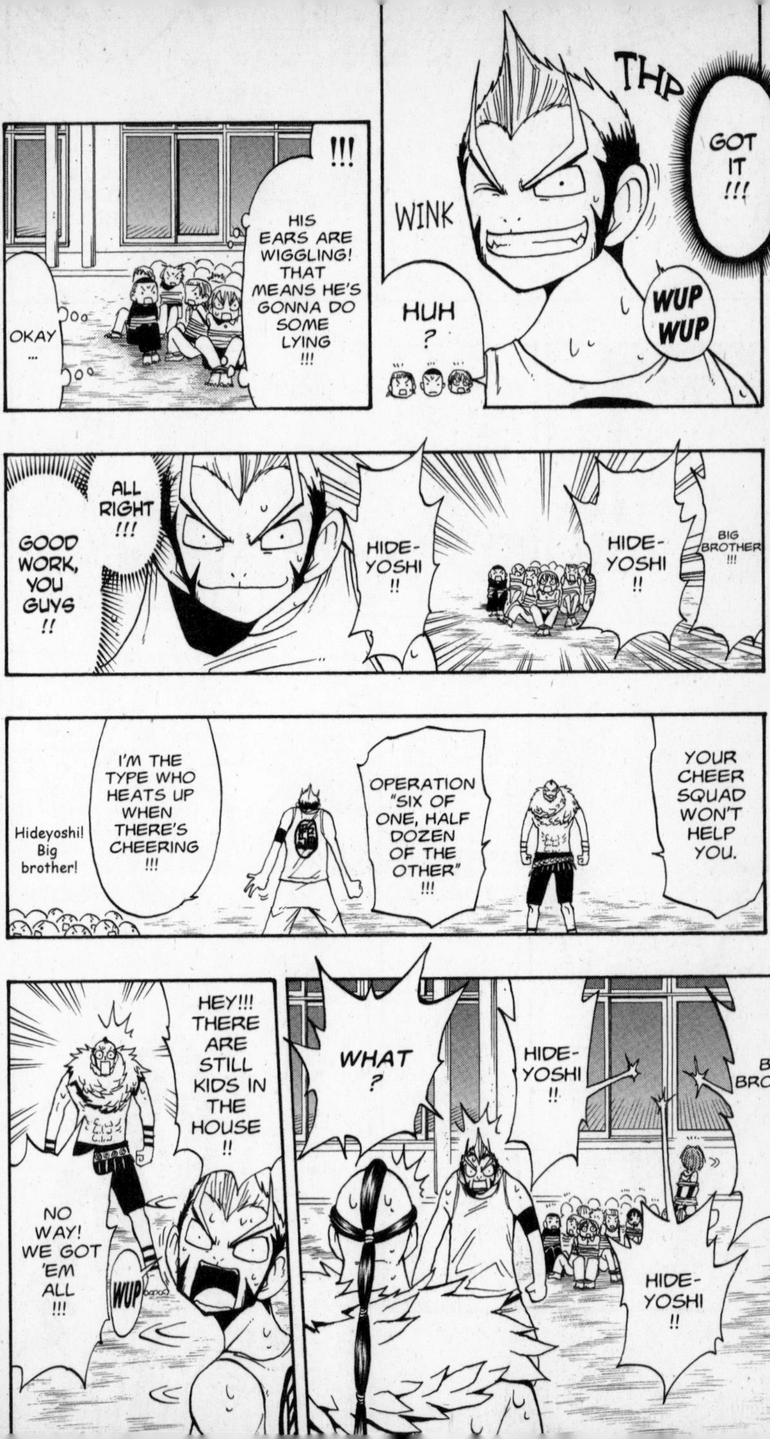
THP
GOT IT !!!
WINK
WUP WUP
HUH ?
!!!
HIS EARS ARE WIGGLING! THAT MEANS HE'S GONNA DO SOME LYING !!!
OKAY ...
BIG BROTHER !!!
HIDE-YOSHI !!
HIDE-YOSHI !!
ALL RIGHT !!!
GOOD WORK, YOU GUYS !!
YOUR CHEER SQUAD WON'T HELP YOU.
OPERATION "SIX OF ONE, HALF DOZEN OF THE OTHER" !!!
I'M THE TYPE WHO HEATS UP WHEN THERE'S CHEERING !!!
Hideyoshi! Big brother!
BIG BROTHER !!!
HIDE-YOSHI !!
HIDE-YOSHI !!
WHAT ?
HEY!!! THERE ARE STILL KIDS IN THE HOUSE !!
NO WAY! WE GOT 'EM ALL !!!
WUP

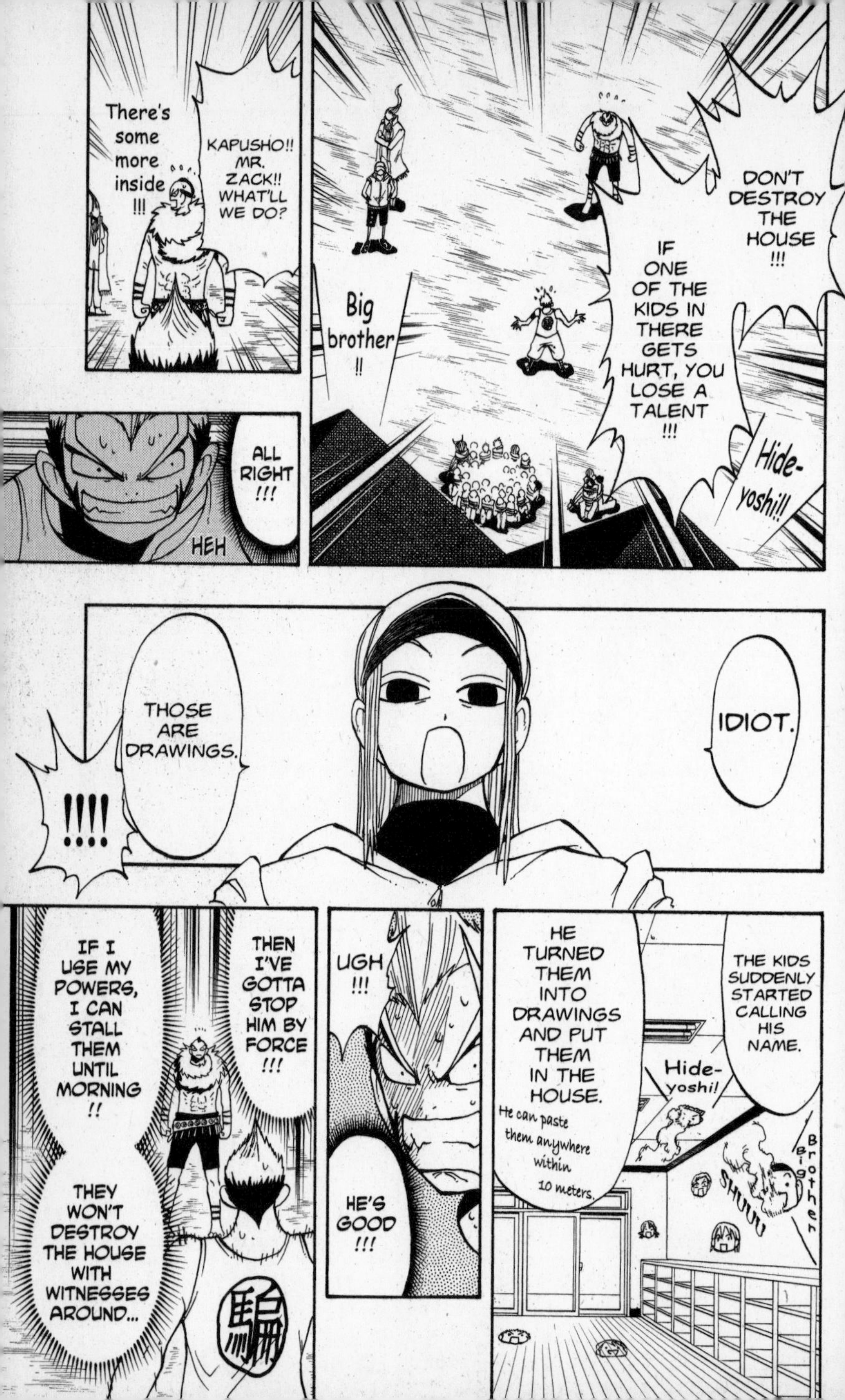
DON'T DESTROY THE HOUSE !!!
IF ONE OF THE KIDS IN THERE GETS HURT, YOU LOSE A TALENT !!!
Big brother !!
Hide-yoshi!!
KAPUSHO!! MR. ZACK!! WHAT'LL WE DO?
There's some more inside !!!
ALL RIGHT !!!
HEH
IDIOT.
THOSE ARE DRAWINGS.
!!!!
THE KIDS SUDDENLY STARTED CALLING HIS NAME.
Hide-yoshi!
Big Brother
SHUUU
HE TURNED THEM INTO DRAWINGS AND PUT THEM IN THE HOUSE.
He can paste them anywhere within 10 meters.
UGH !!!
HE'S GOOD !!!
THEN I'VE GOTTA STOP HIM BY FORCE !!!
IF I USE MY POWERS, I CAN STALL THEM UNTIL MORNING !!
THEY WON'T DESTROY THE HOUSE WITH WITNESSES AROUND...
騙

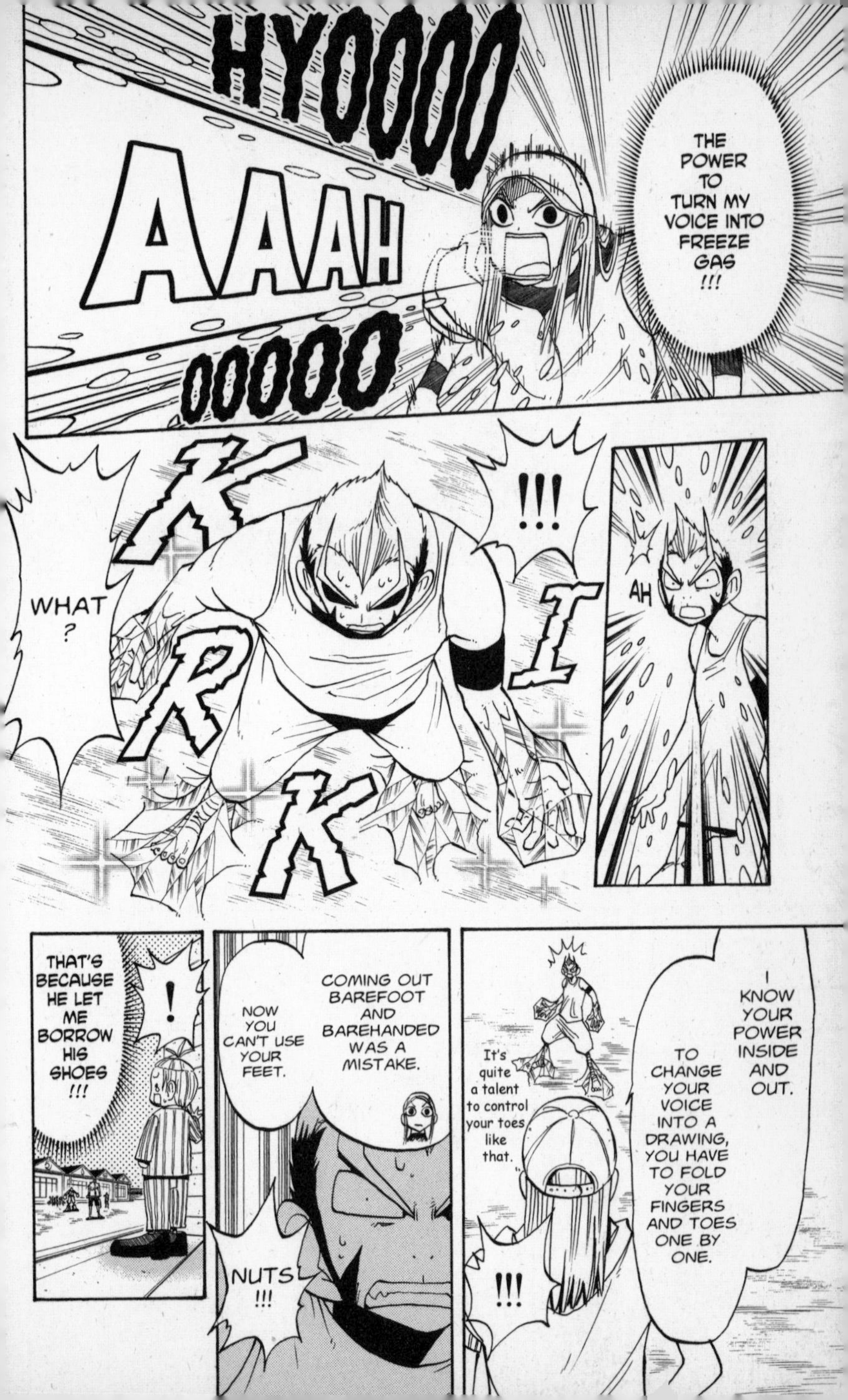
THE POWER TO TURN MY VOICE INTO FREEZE GAS !!!
HYOOOO AAAH OOOOO
AH
!!!
KIRK
WHAT ?
I KNOW YOUR POWER INSIDE AND OUT.
TO CHANGE YOUR VOICE INTO A DRAWING, YOU HAVE TO FOLD YOUR FINGERS AND TOES ONE BY ONE.
It's quite a talent to control your toes like that.
!!!
COMING OUT BAREFOOT AND BAREHANDED WAS A MISTAKE.
NOW YOU CAN'T USE YOUR FEET.
NUTS !!!
!
THAT'S BECAUSE HE LET ME BORROW HIS SHOES !!!

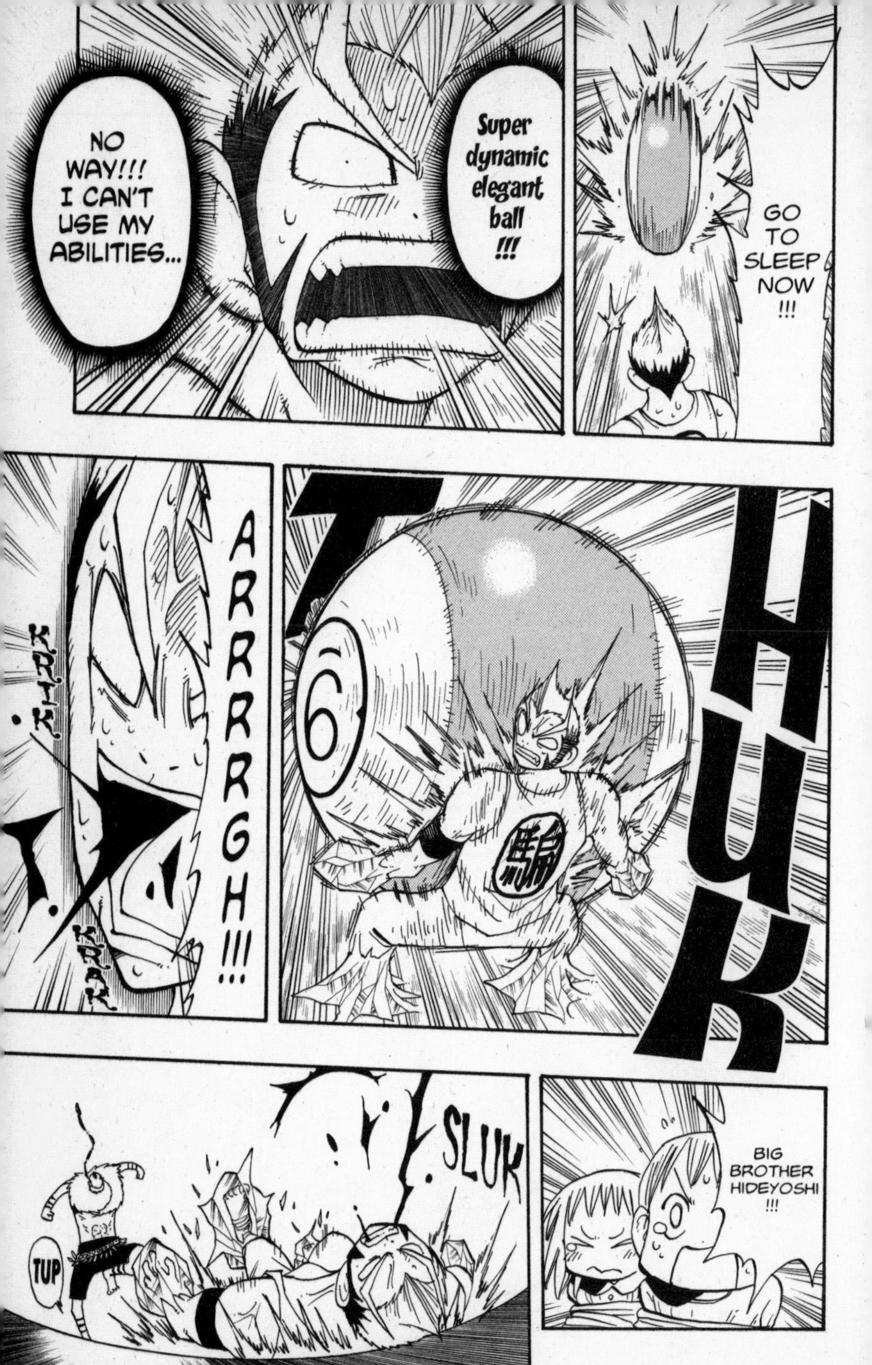
GO TO SLEEP NOW !!!
Super dynamic elegant ball !!!
NO WAY!!! I CAN'T USE MY ABILITIES...
THUK
ARRRRGH!!!
KRIK
KRAK
BIG BROTHER HIDEYOSHI !!!
SLUK
TUP

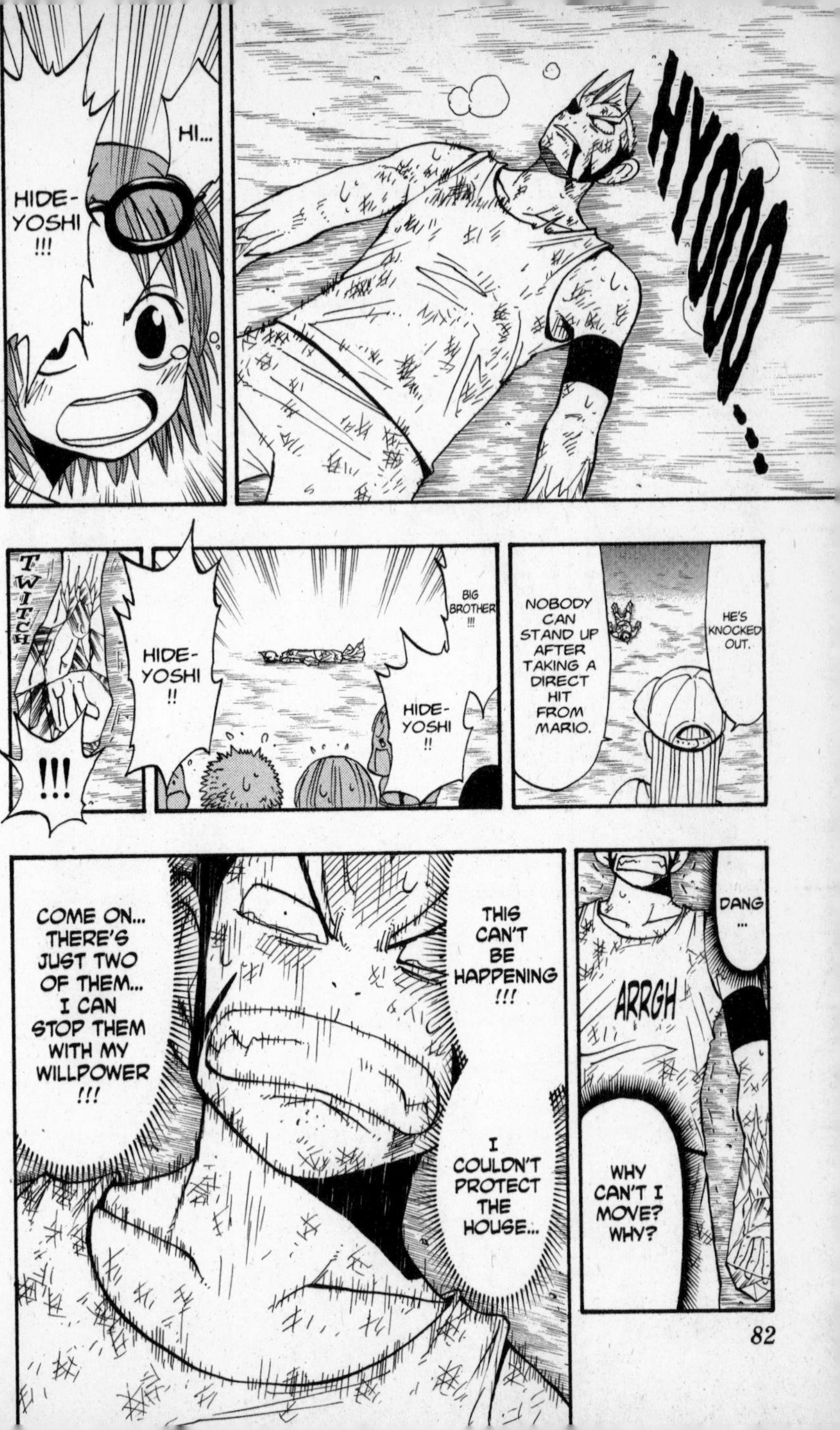
HYOOO...
HI...
HIDE-YOSHI!!!
HE'S KNOCKED OUT.
NOBODY CAN STAND UP AFTER TAKING A DIRECT HIT FROM MARIO.
BIG BROTHER!!!
HIDE-YOSHI!!
HIDE-YOSHI!!
TWITCH
!!!
DANG...
ARRGH
WHY CAN'T I MOVE? WHY?
THIS CAN'T BE HAPPENING!!!
I COULDN'T PROTECT THE HOUSE...
COME ON... THERE'S JUST TWO OF THEM... I CAN STOP THEM WITH MY WILLPOWER!!!

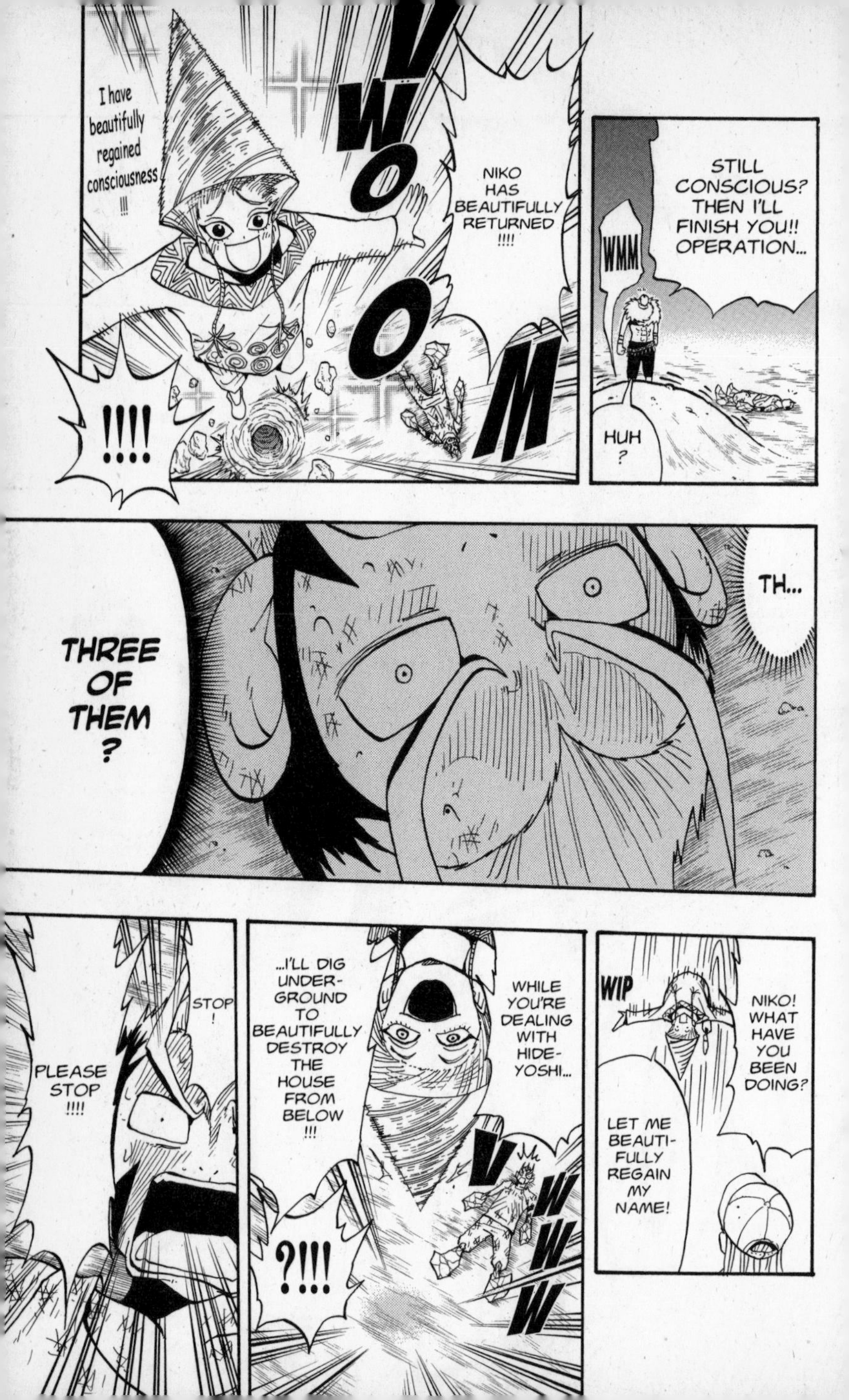
STILL CONSCIOUS? THEN I'LL FINISH YOU!! OPERATION...
WMM
HUH?
NIKO HAS BEAUTIFULLY RETURNED !!!!
VWOOOM
I have beautifully regained consciousness !!!
!!!!
TH...
THREE OF THEM?
NIKO! WHAT HAVE YOU BEEN DOING?
WIP
LET ME BEAUTIFULLY REGAIN MY NAME!
WHILE YOU'RE DEALING WITH HIDEYOSHI...
...I'LL DIG UNDERGROUND TO BEAUTIFULLY DESTROY THE HOUSE FROM BELOW !!!
VWWW
?!!!
STOP!
PLEASE STOP !!!!

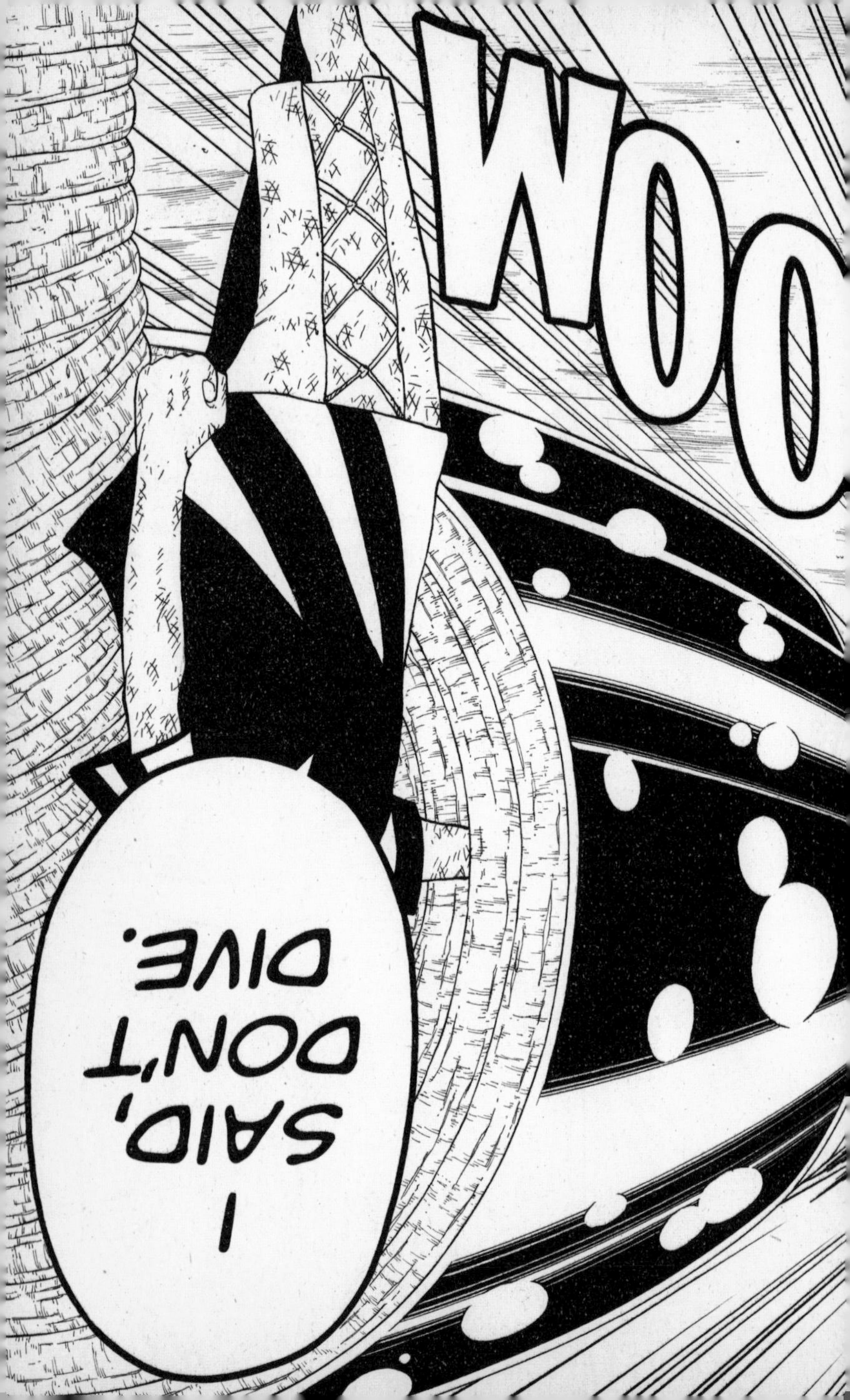
WOO
I SAID, DON'T DIVE.

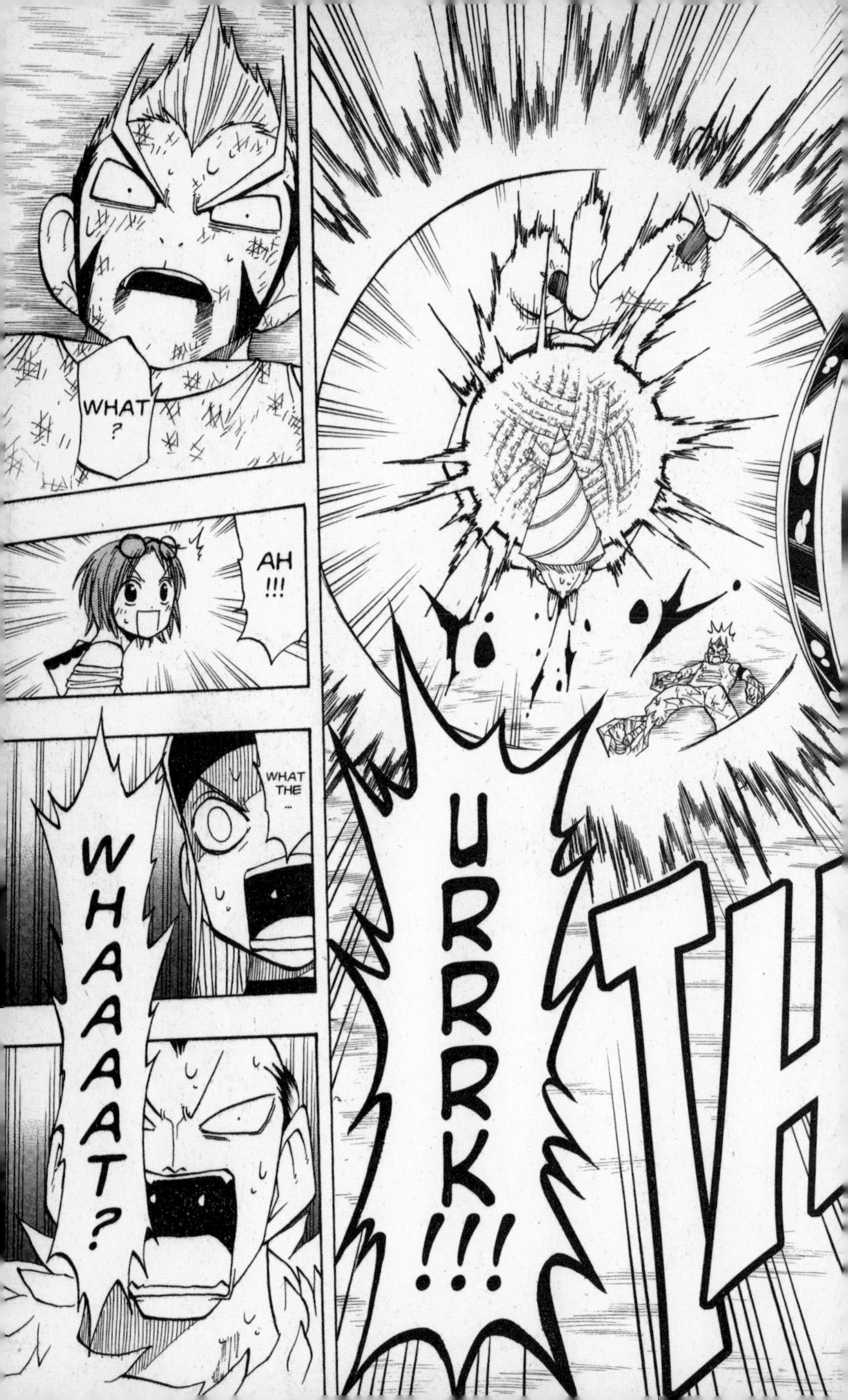
URRRK!!!
TH
WHAT?
AH!!!
WHAT THE...
WHAAAAT?

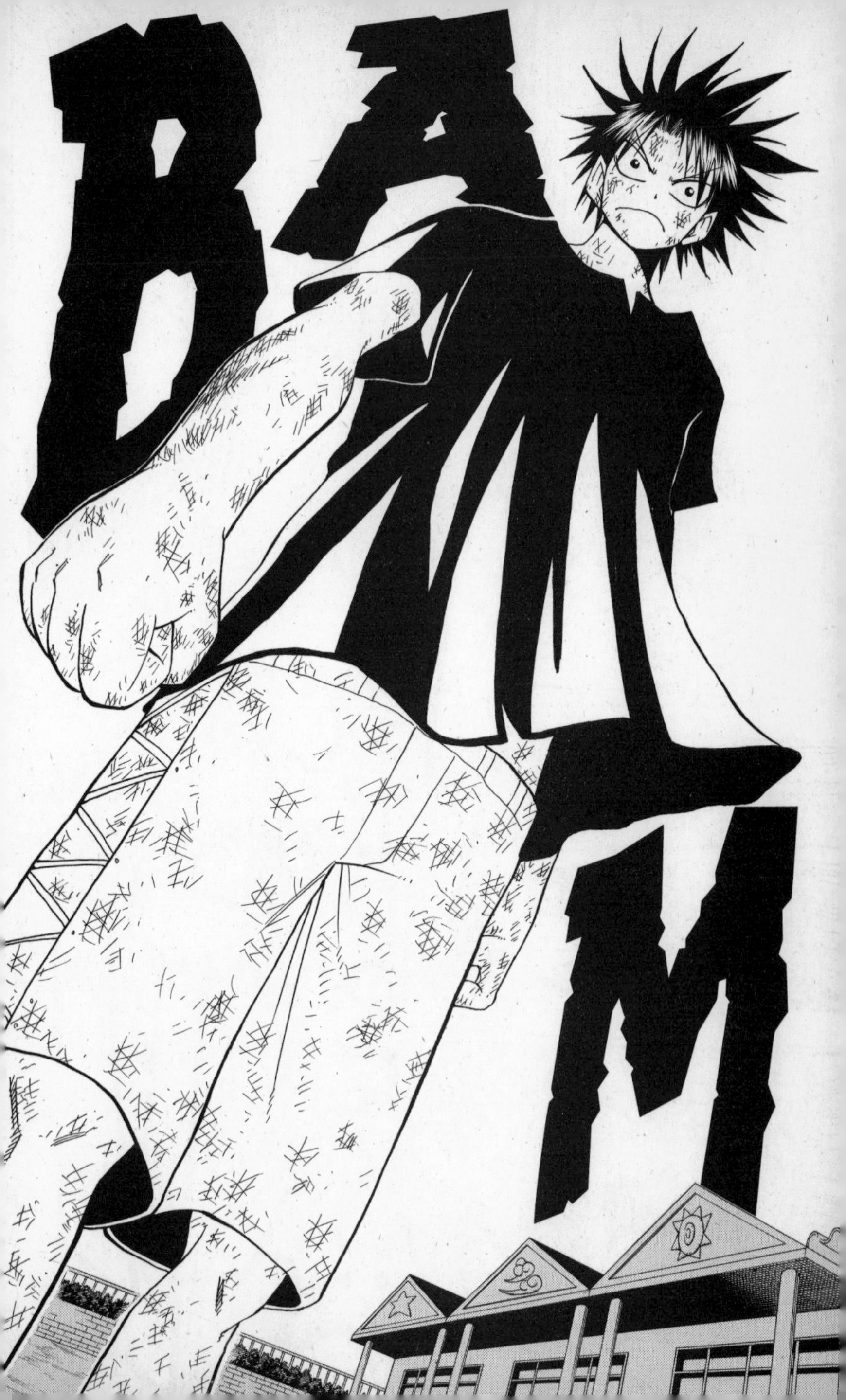
BAM

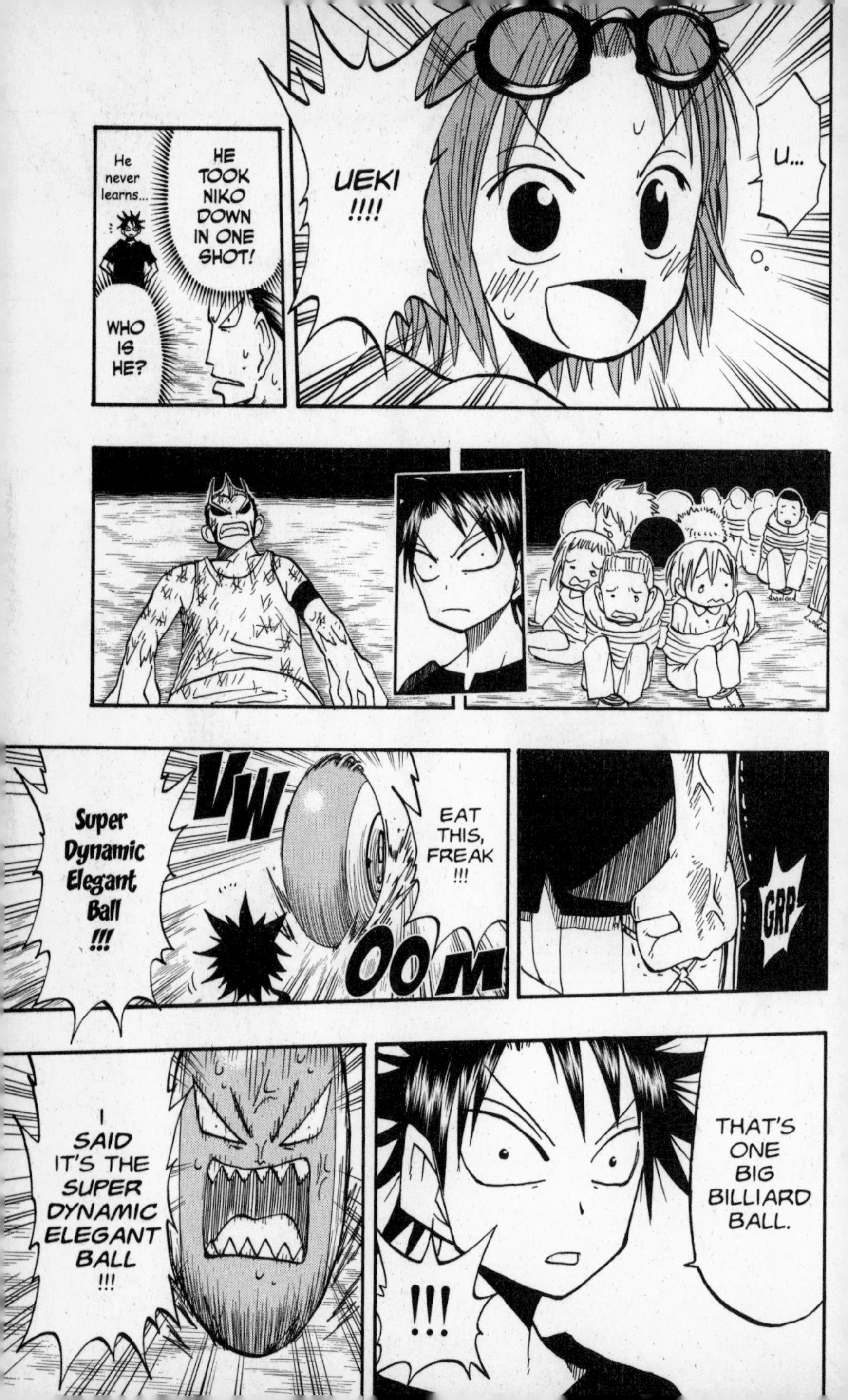
U...
UEKI !!!!
HE TOOK NIKO DOWN IN ONE SHOT!
He never learns...
WHO IS HE?
GRP
EAT THIS, FREAK !!!
VWOOM
Super Dynamic Elegant Ball !!!
THAT'S ONE BIG BILLIARD BALL.
!!!
I SAID IT'S THE SUPER DYNAMIC ELEGANT BALL !!!

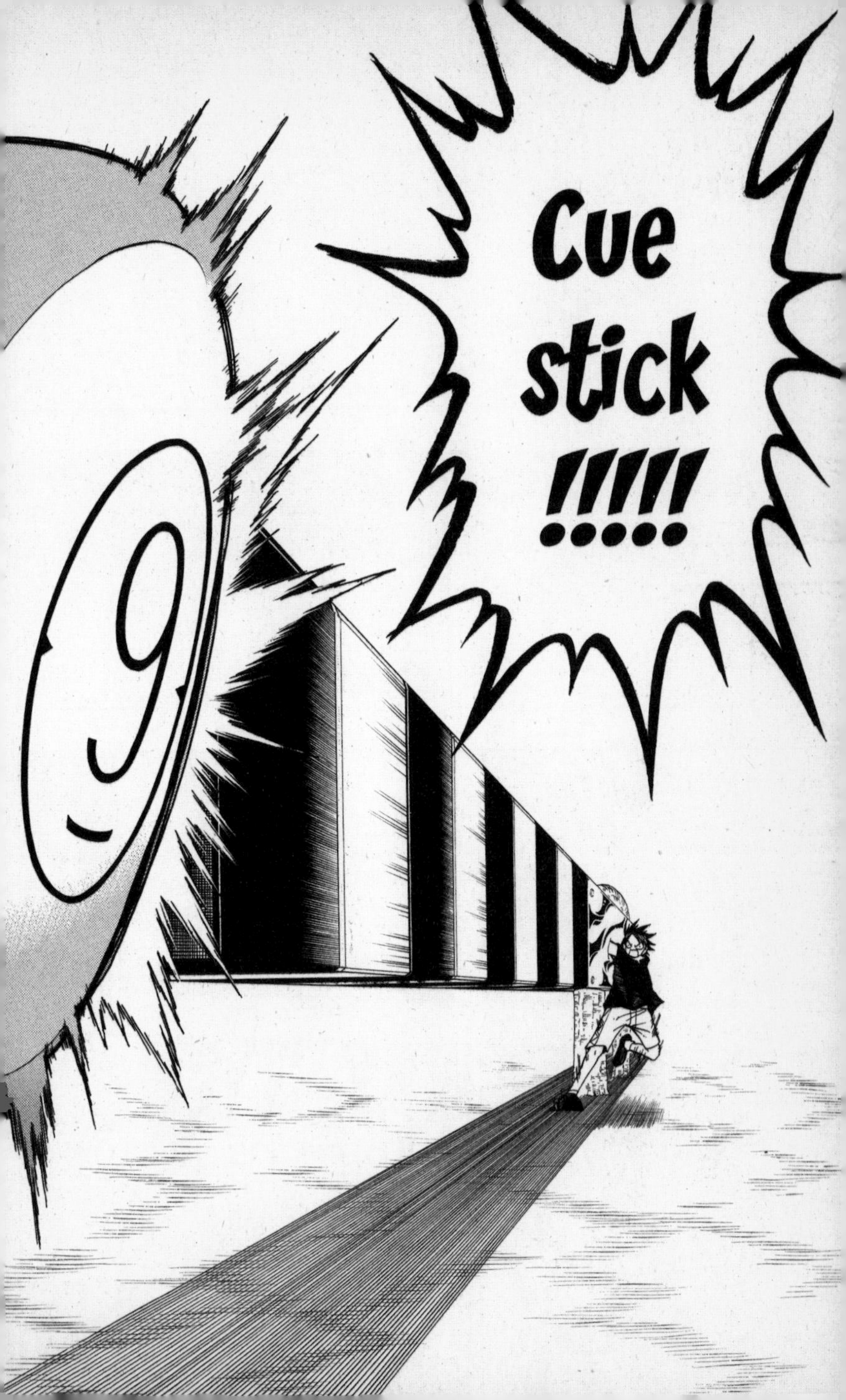
Cue stick!!!!!

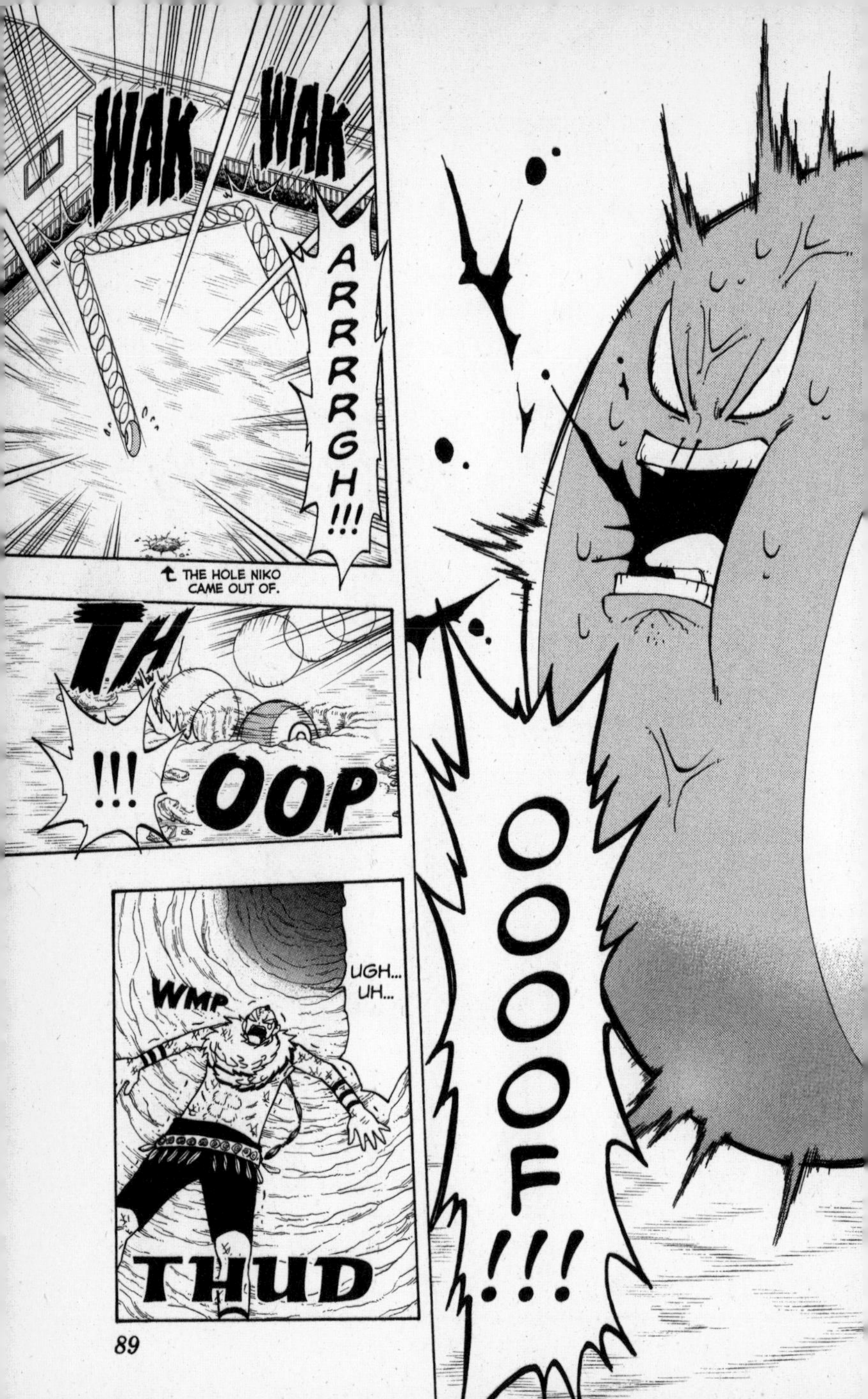
OOOOOF!!!
WAK WAK
ARRRRGH!!!
THE HOLE NIKO CAME OUT OF.
TH
OOP
!!!
UGH... UH...
WMP
THUD

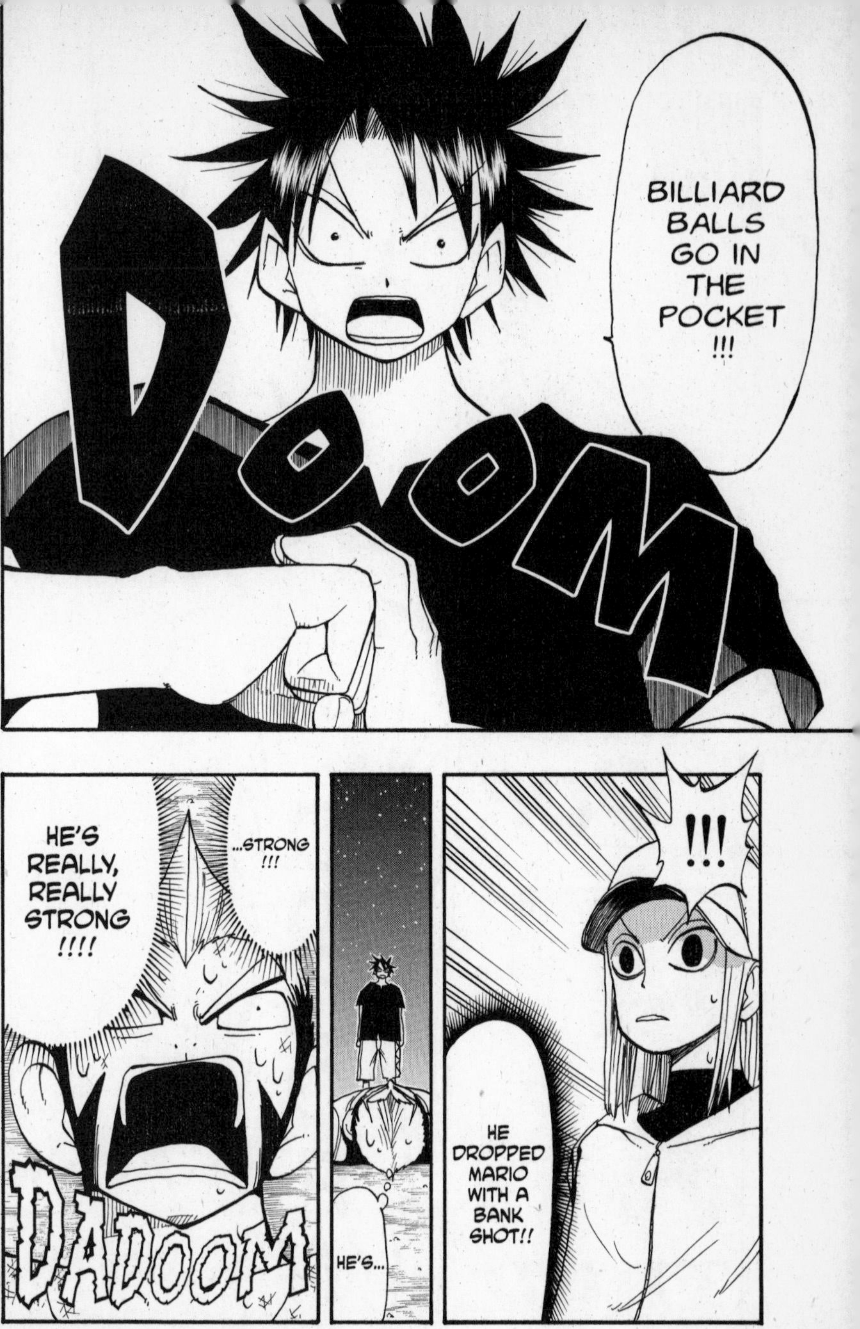
BILLIARD BALLS GO IN THE POCKET !!!
DOOM
!!!
HE DROPPED MARIO WITH A BANK SHOT!!
HE'S...
...STRONG !!!
HE'S REALLY, REALLY STRONG !!!!
DADOOM

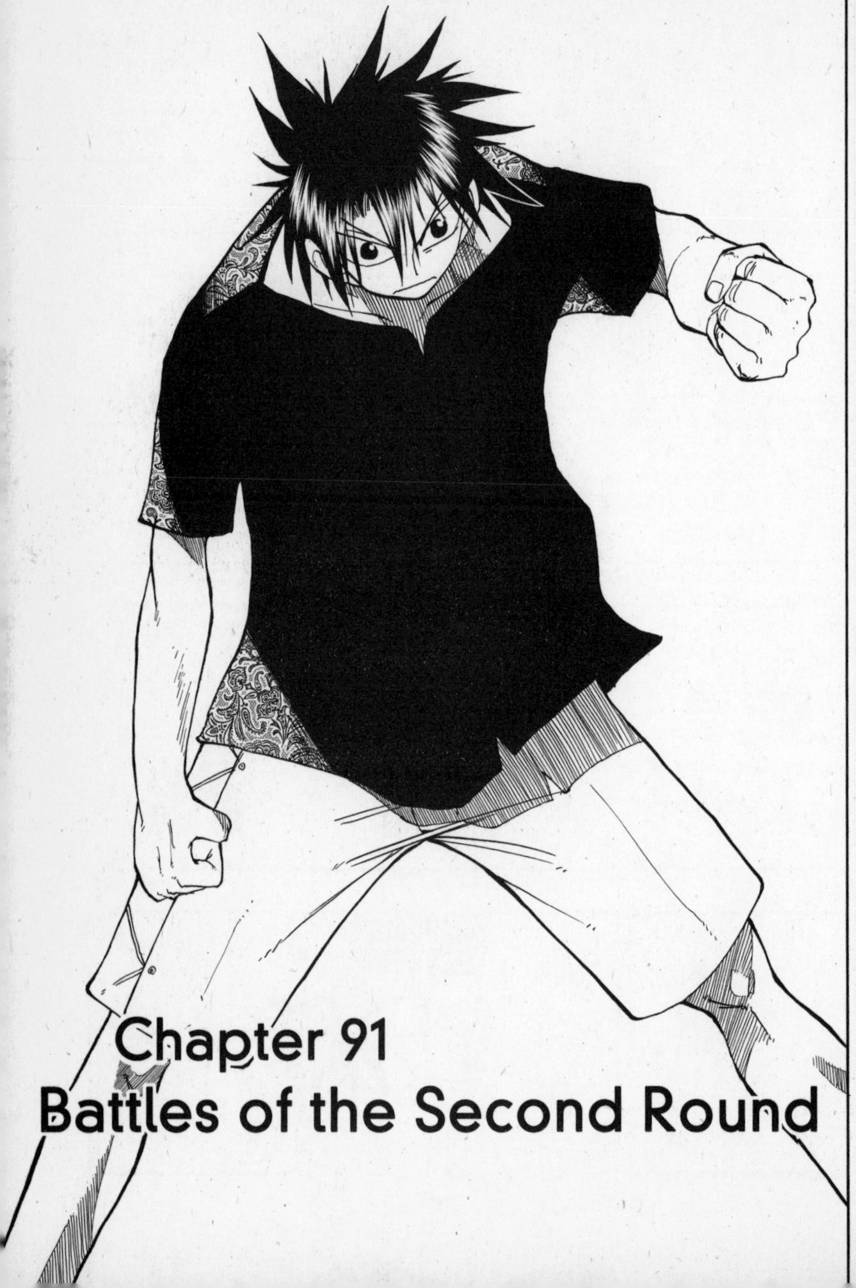

Chapter 91
Battles of the Second Round

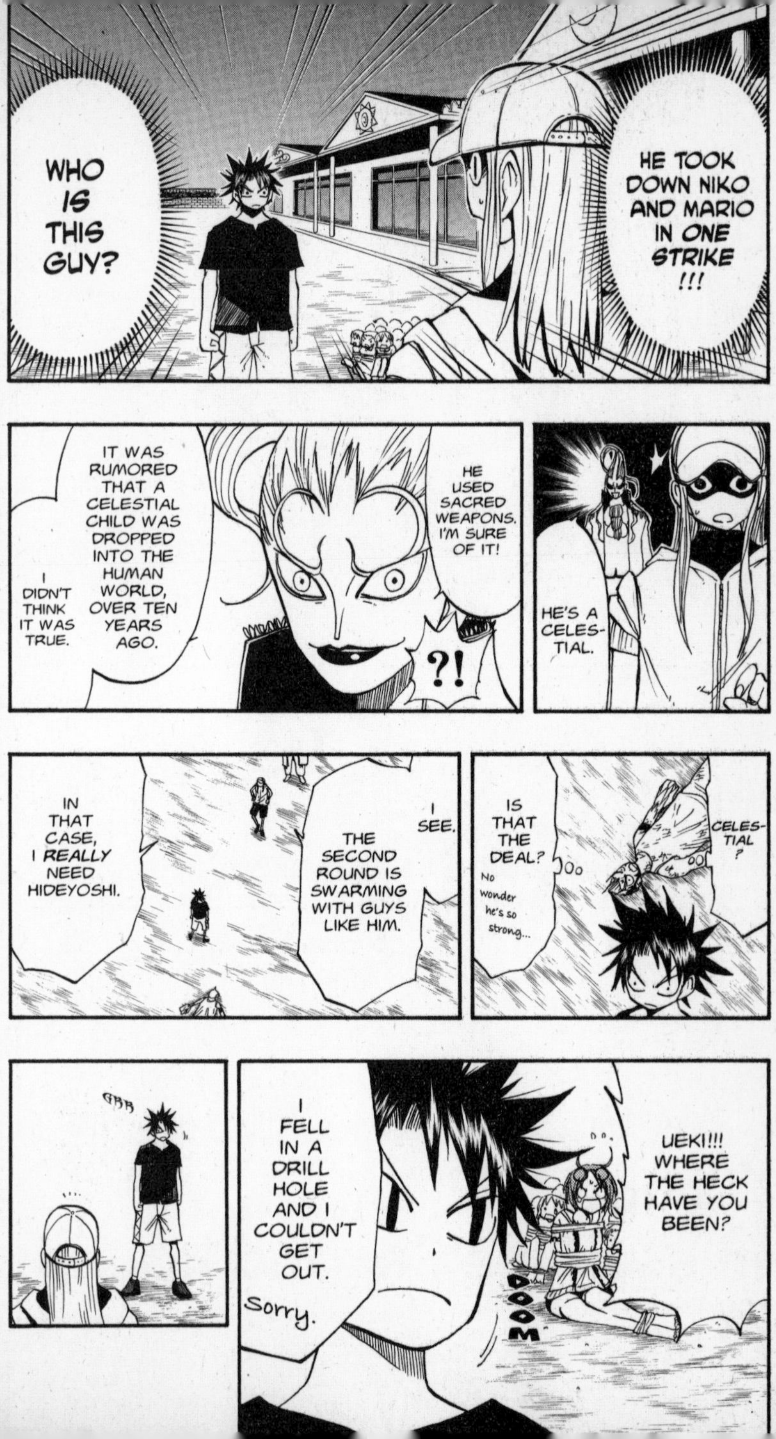
HE TOOK DOWN NIKO AND MARIO IN ONE STRIKE !!!
WHO IS THIS GUY?
HE'S A CELES-TIAL.
HE USED SACRED WEAPONS. I'M SURE OF IT!
?!
IT WAS RUMORED THAT A CELESTIAL CHILD WAS DROPPED INTO THE HUMAN WORLD, OVER TEN YEARS AGO.
I DIDN'T THINK IT WAS TRUE.
CELES-TIAL?
IS THAT THE DEAL?
No wonder he's so strong...
I SEE.
THE SECOND ROUND IS SWARMING WITH GUYS LIKE HIM.
IN THAT CASE, I REALLY NEED HIDEYOSHI.
UEKI!!! WHERE THE HECK HAVE YOU BEEN?
DOOM
I FELL IN A DRILL HOLE AND I COULDN'T GET OUT.
Sorry.
GRR

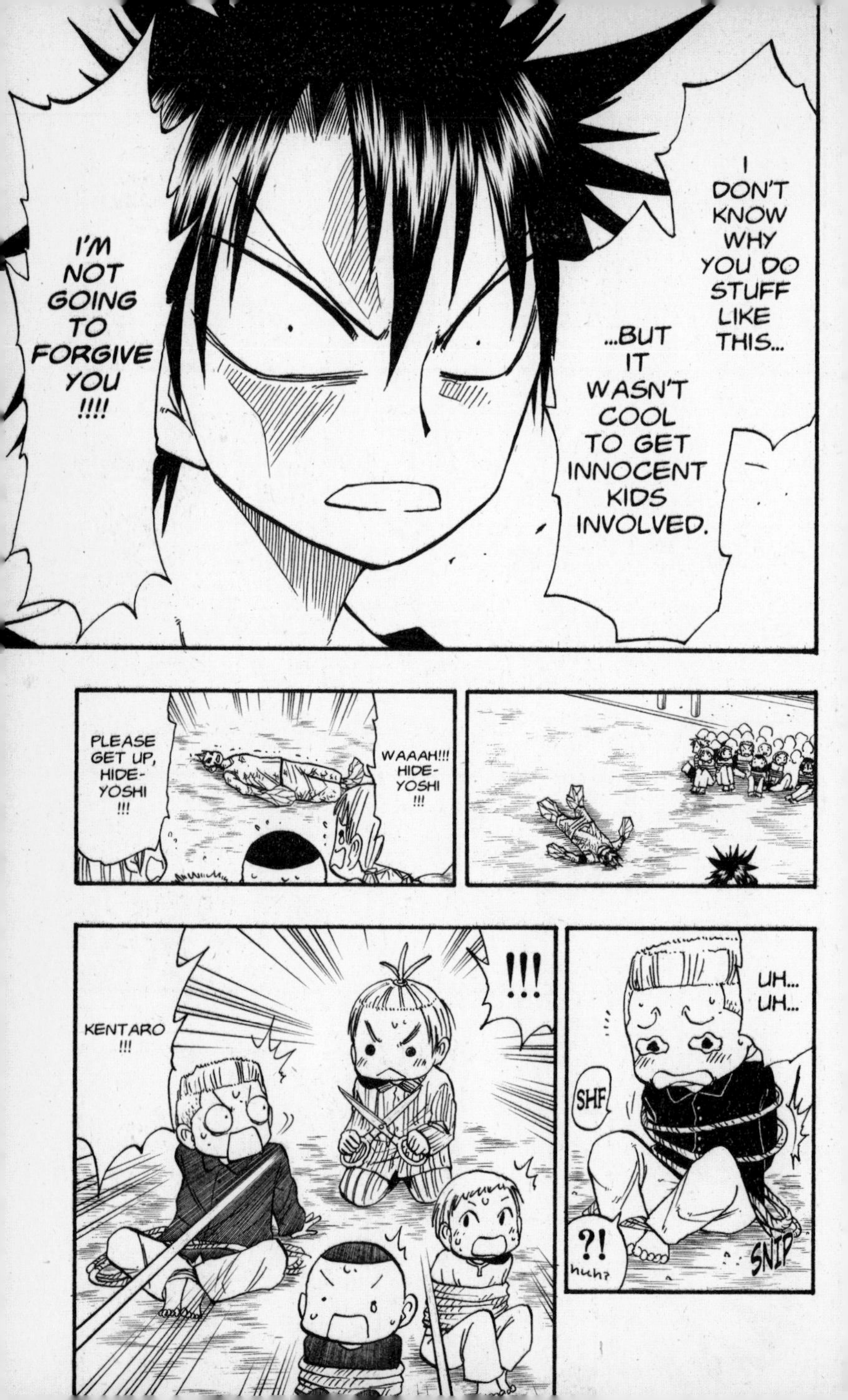
I DON'T KNOW WHY YOU DO STUFF LIKE THIS...
...BUT IT WASN'T COOL TO GET INNOCENT KIDS INVOLVED.
I'M NOT GOING TO FORGIVE YOU !!!!
WAAAH!!! HIDE-YOSHI !!!
PLEASE GET UP, HIDE-YOSHI !!!
UH... UH...
SHF
SNIP
?!
huh?
!!!
KENTARO !!!

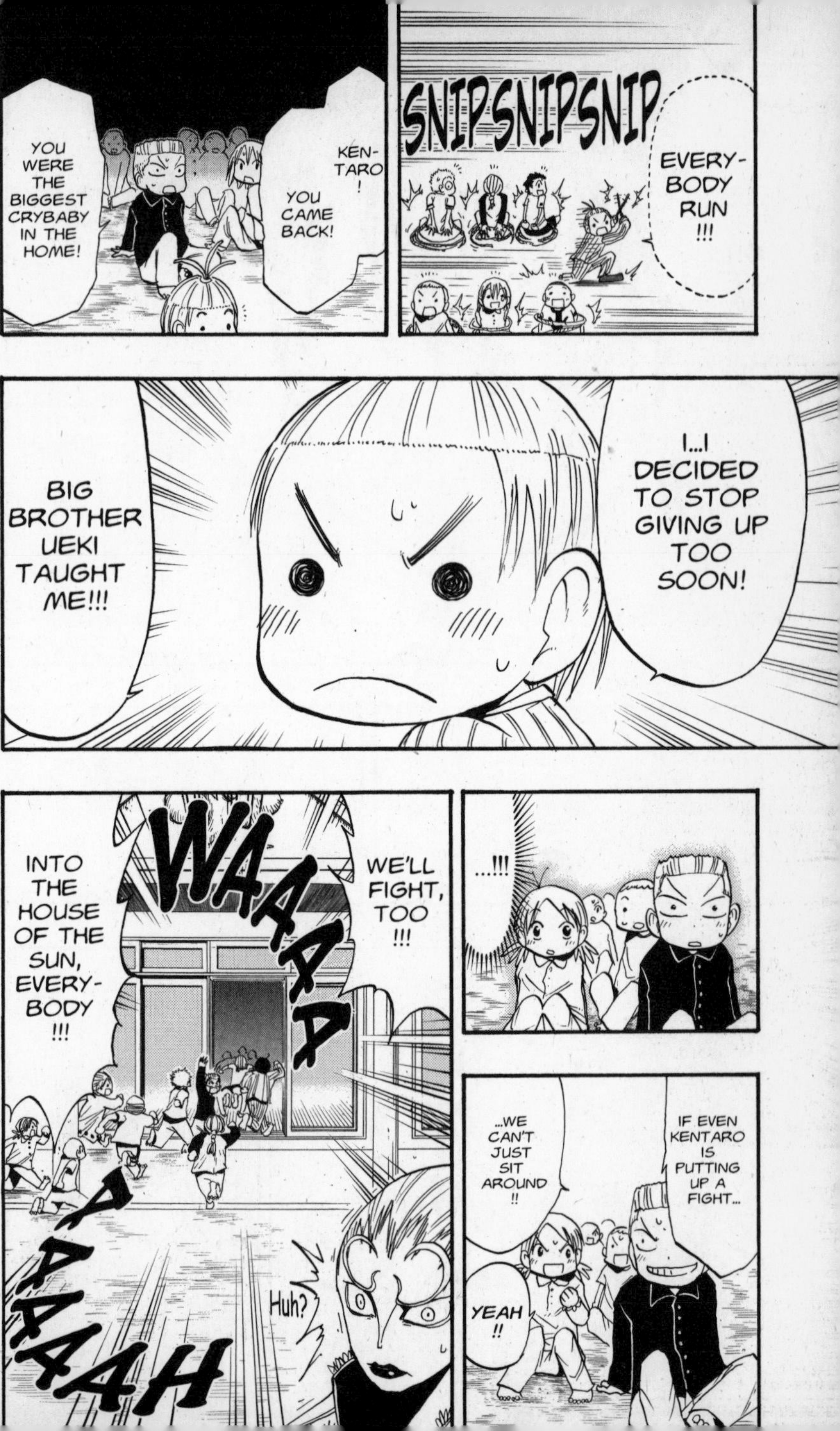
SNIPSNIPSNIP
EVERY-BODY RUN !!!
KEN-TARO !
YOU CAME BACK!
YOU WERE THE BIGGEST CRYBABY IN THE HOME!
I...I DECIDED TO STOP GIVING UP TOO SOON!
BIG BROTHER UEKI TAUGHT ME!!!
...!!!
IF EVEN KENTARO IS PUTTING UP A FIGHT...
...WE CAN'T JUST SIT AROUND !!
YEAH !!
WE'LL FIGHT, TOO !!!
INTO THE HOUSE OF THE SUN, EVERY-BODY !!!
WAAAAA
Huh?
YAAAAH

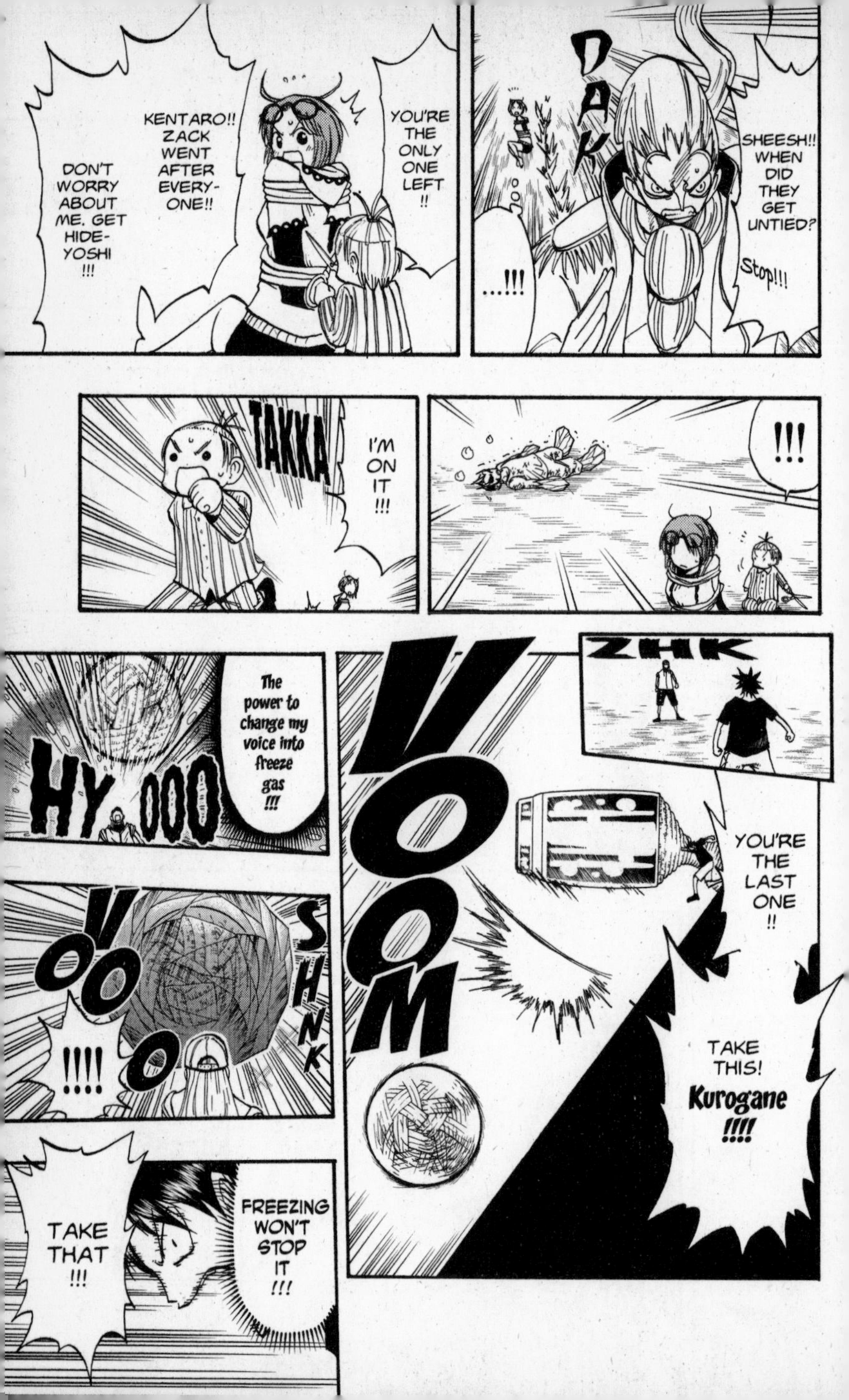
DAK
SHEESH!! WHEN DID THEY GET UNTIED?
Stop!!!
...!!!
YOU'RE THE ONLY ONE LEFT !!
KENTARO!! ZACK WENT AFTER EVERY-ONE!!
DON'T WORRY ABOUT ME. GET HIDE-YOSHI !!!
!!!
I'M ON IT !!!
TAKKA
ZHK
YOU'RE THE LAST ONE !!
VOOM
TAKE THIS!
Kurogane !!!!
The power to change my voice into freeze gas !!!
HY..OOO
SHNK
VOOOO !!!!
FREEZING WON'T STOP IT !!!
TAKE THAT !!!

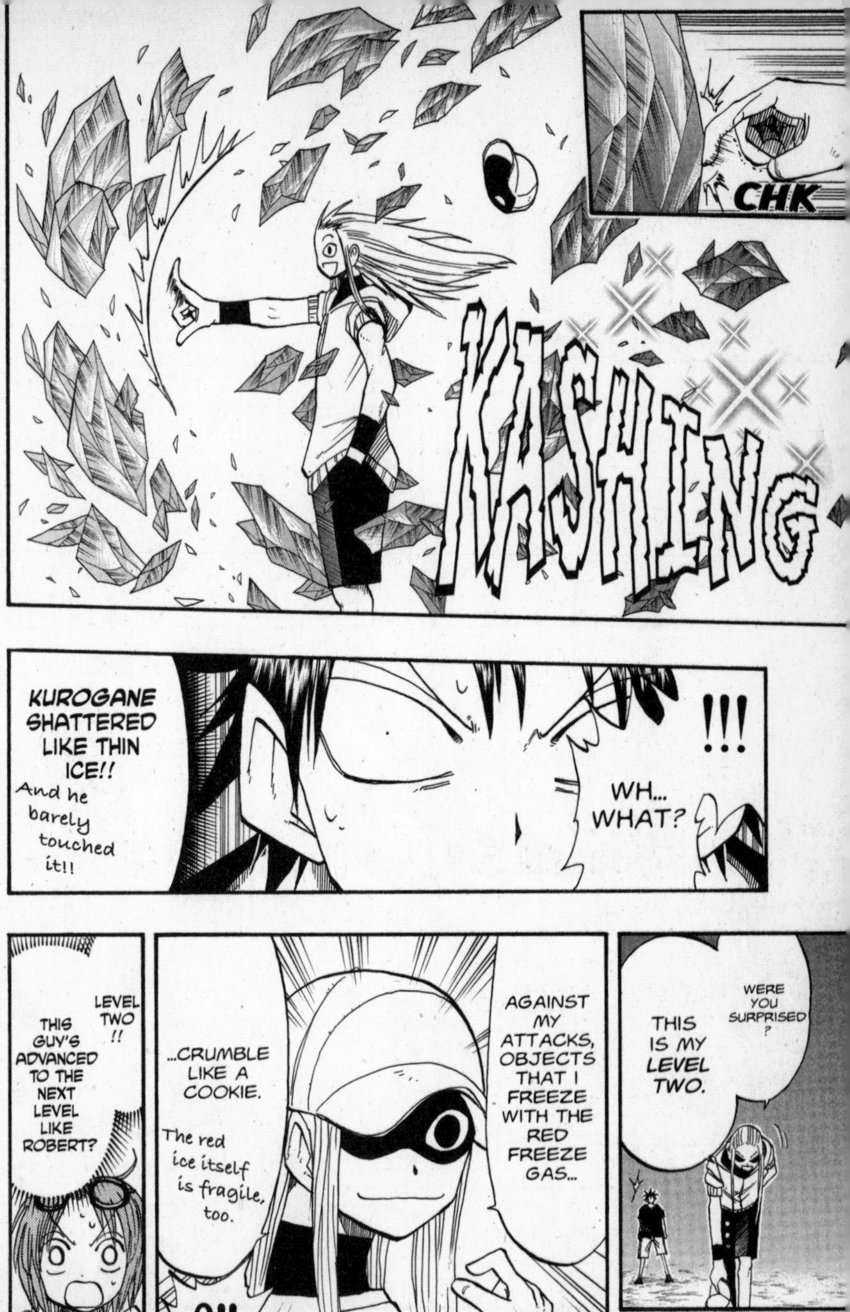

CHK
KASHING
!!!
WH... WHAT?
KUROGANE SHATTERED LIKE THIN ICE!!
And he barely touched it!!
WERE YOU SURPRISED?
THIS IS MY LEVEL TWO.
AGAINST MY ATTACKS, OBJECTS THAT I FREEZE WITH THE RED FREEZE GAS...
...CRUMBLE LIKE A COOKIE.
The red ice itself is fragile, too.
?!!
LEVEL TWO!!
THIS GUY'S ADVANCED TO THE NEXT LEVEL LIKE ROBERT?

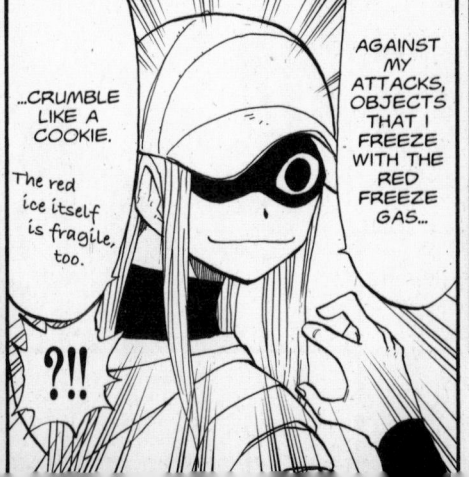

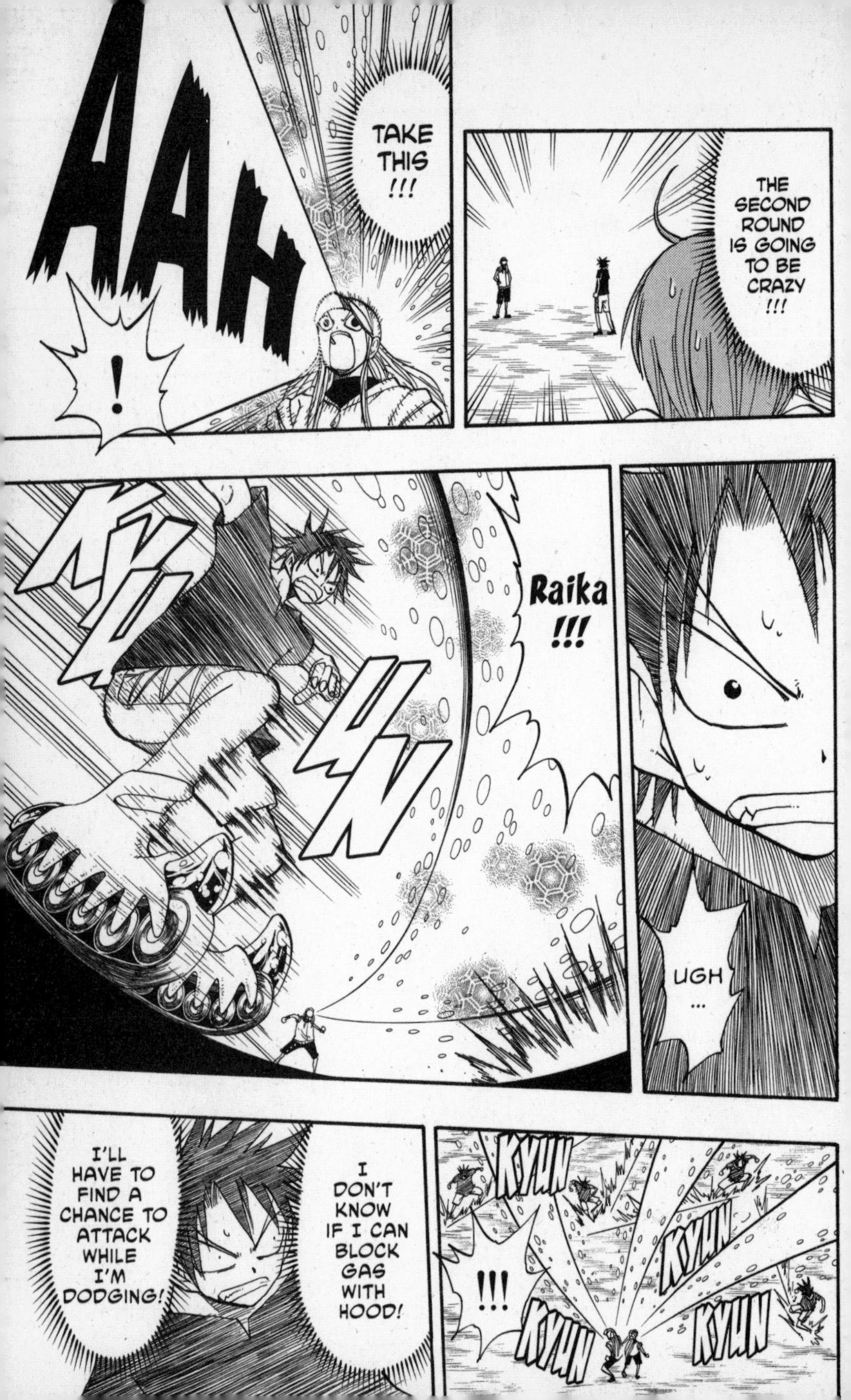
THE SECOND ROUND IS GOING TO BE CRAZY !!!
TAKE THIS !!!
AAH
!
UGH ...
Raika !!!
KYUUN
KYUN
KYUN
!!!
KYUN
KYUN
I DON'T KNOW IF I CAN BLOCK GAS WITH HOOD!
I'LL HAVE TO FIND A CHANCE TO ATTACK WHILE I'M DODGING!

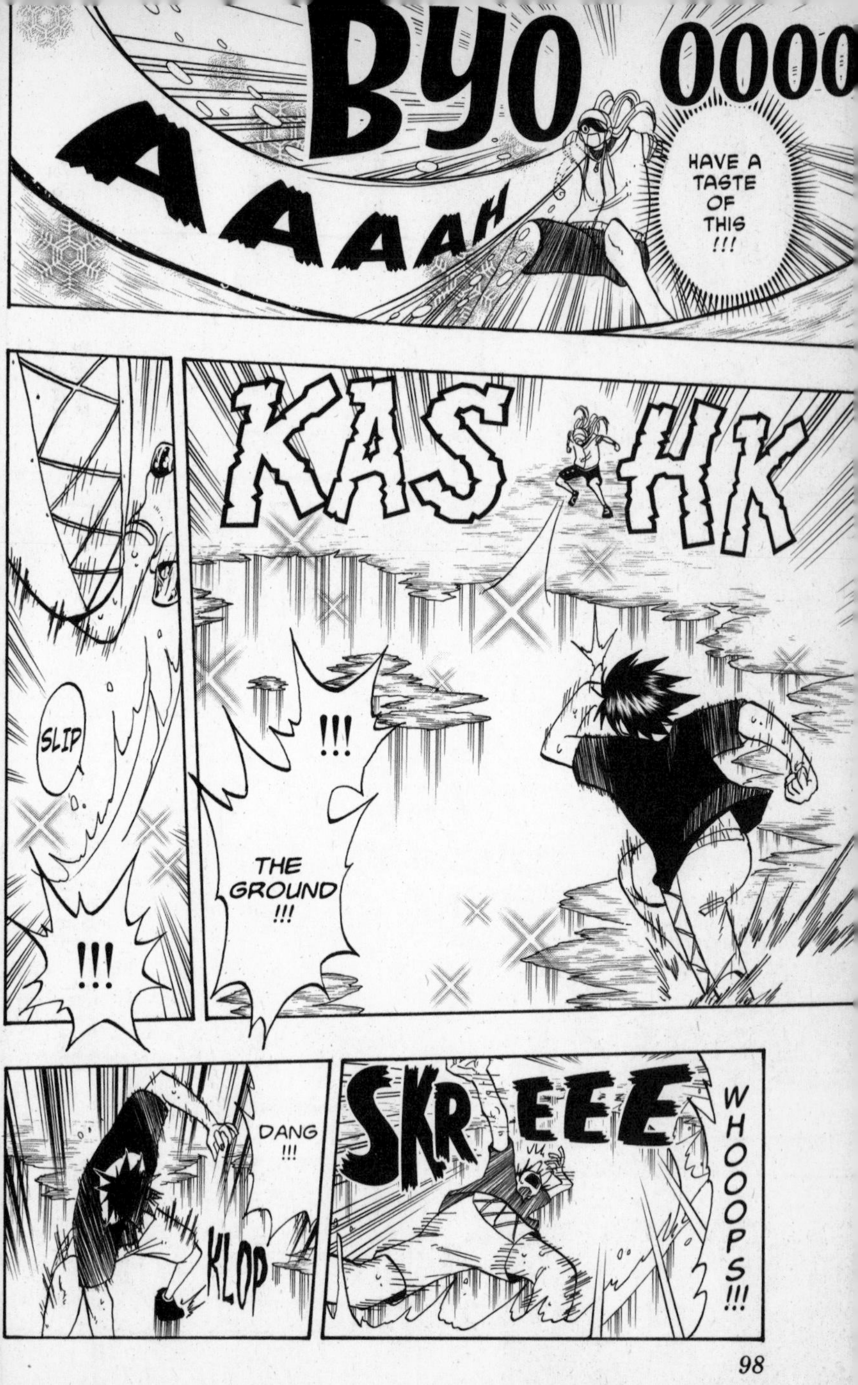
HAVE A TASTE OF THIS!!!
BYOOOOO
AAAAAH
KAS HK
!!!
THE GROUND!!!
SLIP
!!!
SKREEE
WHOOOOPS!!!
DANG!!!
KLOP

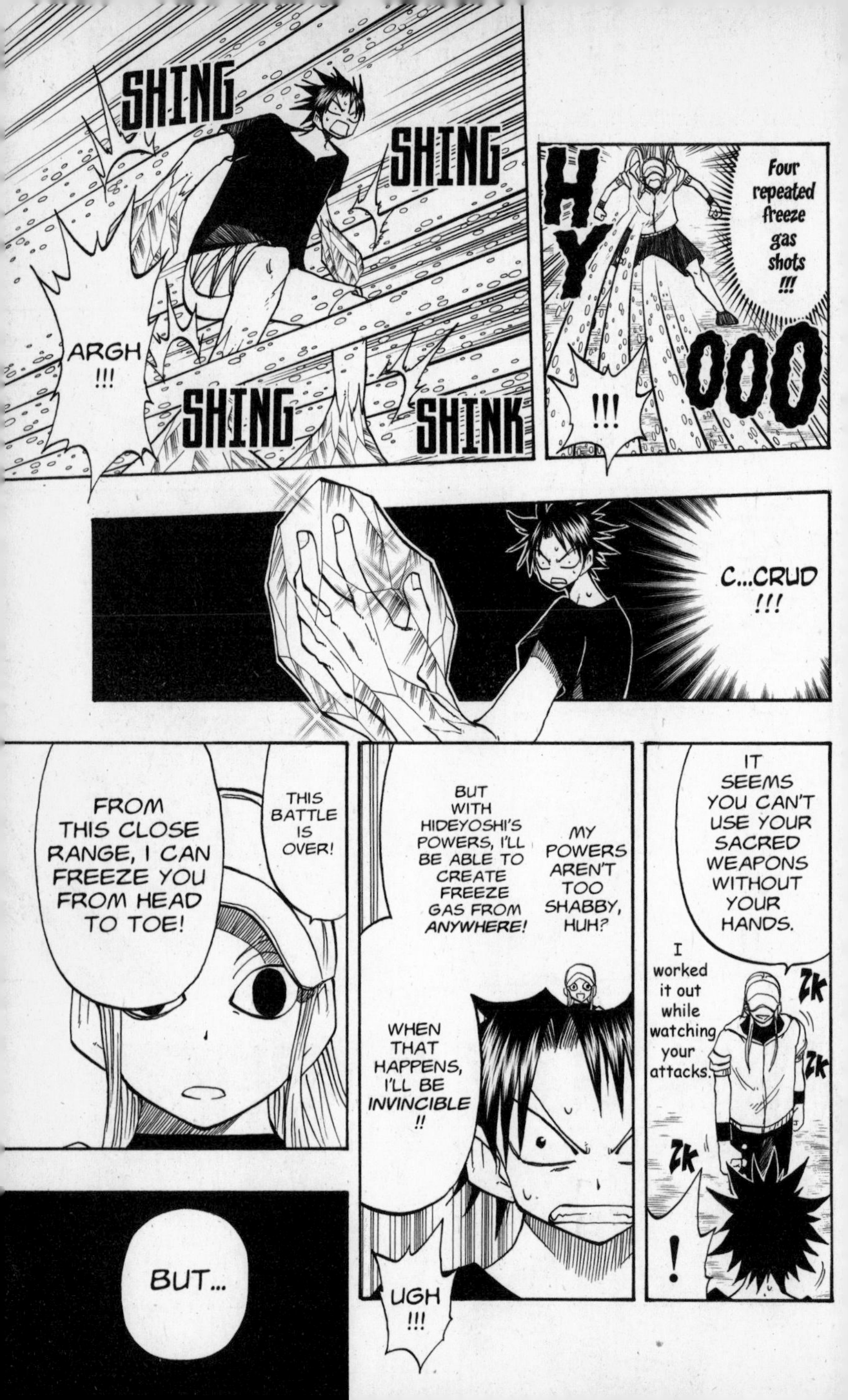
Four repeated freeze gas shots !!!
HYOOO
!!!
SHING
SHING
SHING
SHINK
ARGH !!!
C...CRUD !!!
IT SEEMS YOU CAN'T USE YOUR SACRED WEAPONS WITHOUT YOUR HANDS.
I worked it out while watching your attacks.
ZK
ZK
ZK
!
BUT WITH HIDEYOSHI'S POWERS, I'LL BE ABLE TO CREATE FREEZE GAS FROM ANYWHERE!
MY POWERS AREN'T TOO SHABBY, HUH?
WHEN THAT HAPPENS, I'LL BE INVINCIBLE !!
UGH !!!
THIS BATTLE IS OVER!
FROM THIS CLOSE RANGE, I CAN FREEZE YOU FROM HEAD TO TOE!
BUT...

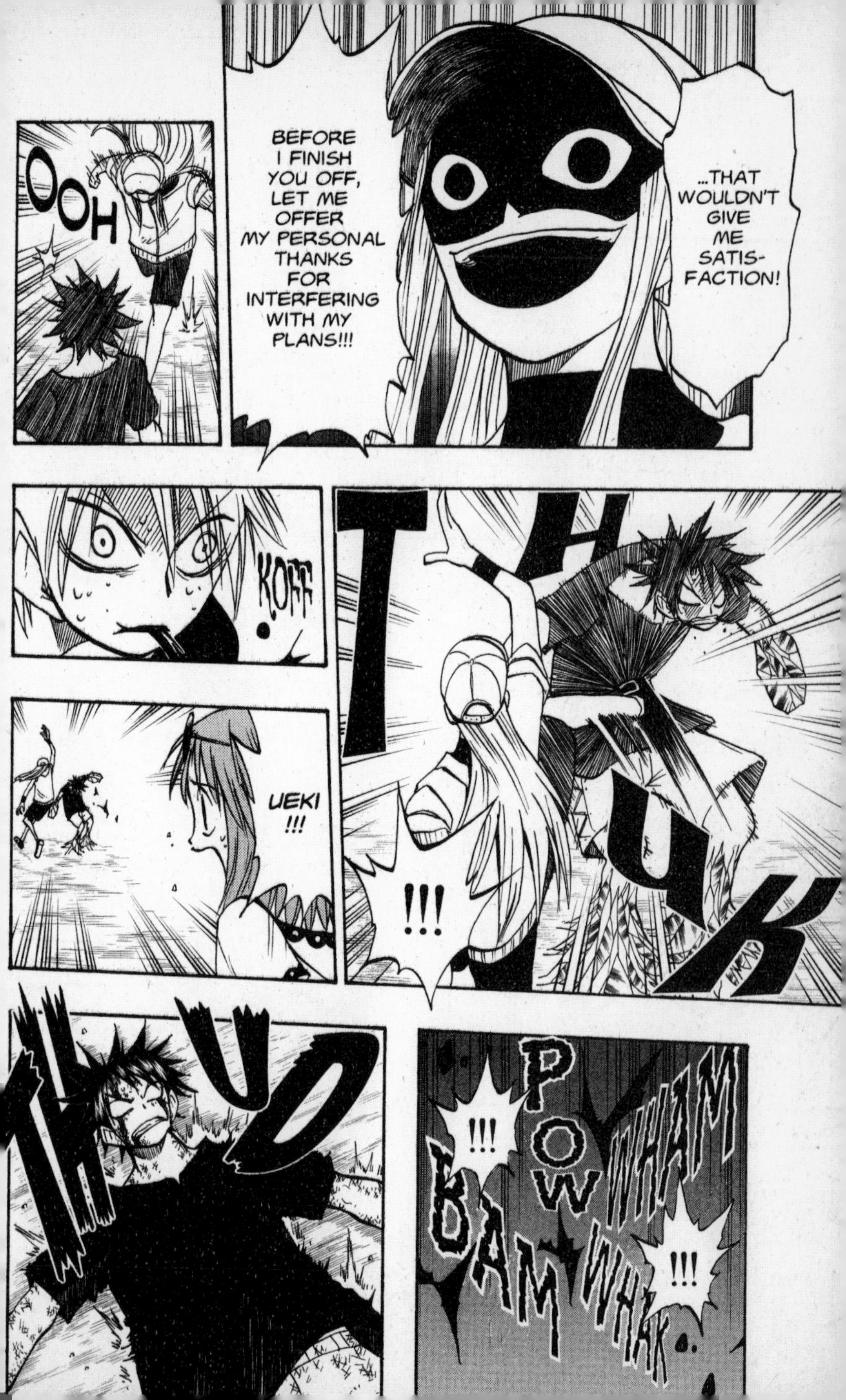
...THAT WOULDN'T GIVE ME SATIS-FACTION!
BEFORE I FINISH YOU OFF, LET ME OFFER MY PERSONAL THANKS FOR INTERFERING WITH MY PLANS!!!
OOH
THUNK
!!!
KOFF
UEKI !!!
POW
WHAM
BAM
WHAK
!!!
!!!
THUD

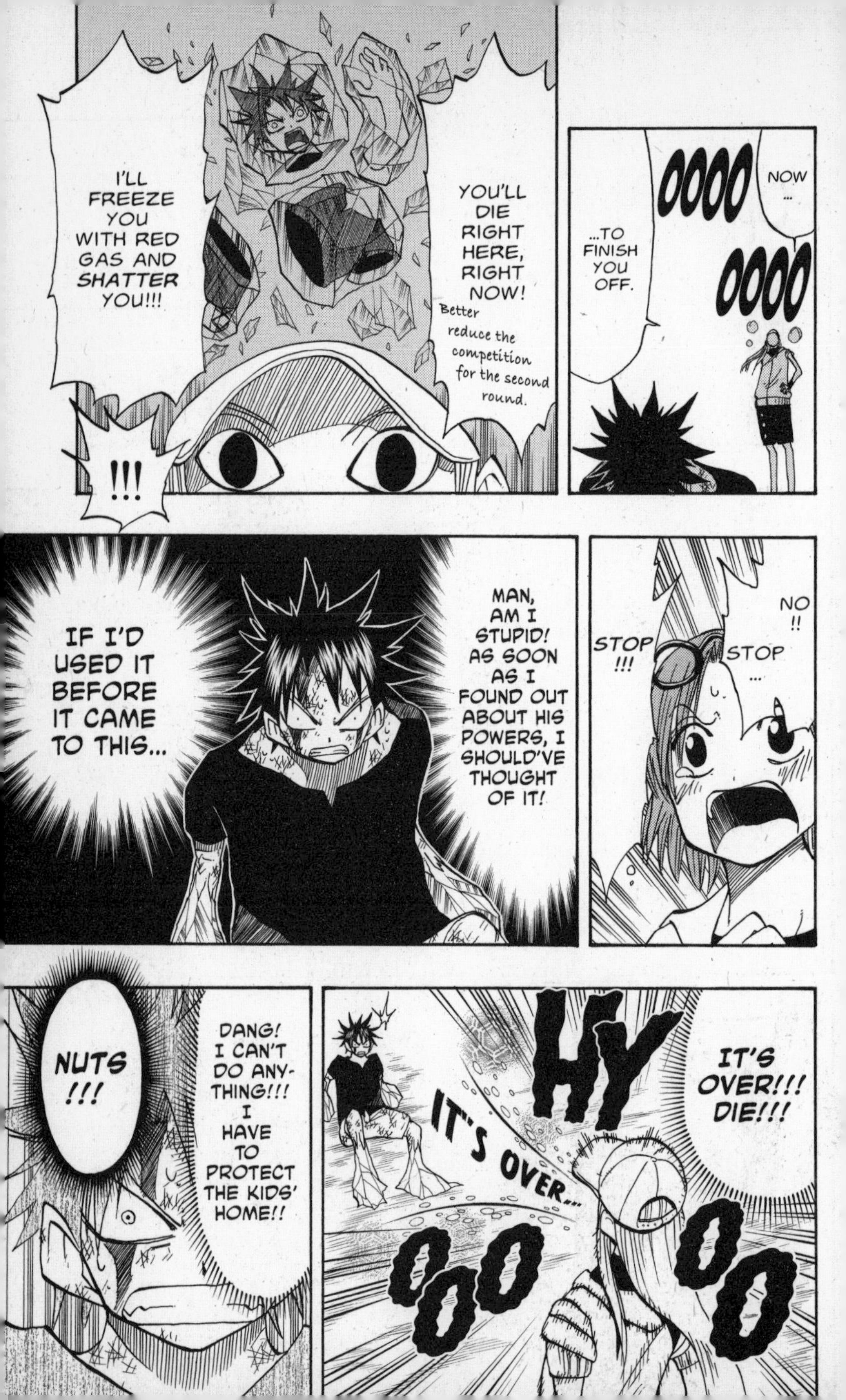
NOW ...
OOOO
OOOO
...TO FINISH YOU OFF.
YOU'LL DIE RIGHT HERE, RIGHT NOW!
Better reduce the competition for the second round.
I'LL FREEZE YOU WITH RED GAS AND SHATTER YOU!!!
!!!
NO !!
STOP ...
STOP !!!
MAN, AM I STUPID! AS SOON AS I FOUND OUT ABOUT HIS POWERS, I SHOULD'VE THOUGHT OF IT!
IF I'D USED IT BEFORE IT CAME TO THIS...
IT'S OVER!!! DIE!!!
HY
IT'S OVER...
OOO
OOO
DANG! I CAN'T DO ANY-THING!!! I HAVE TO PROTECT THE KIDS' HOME!!
NUTS !!!

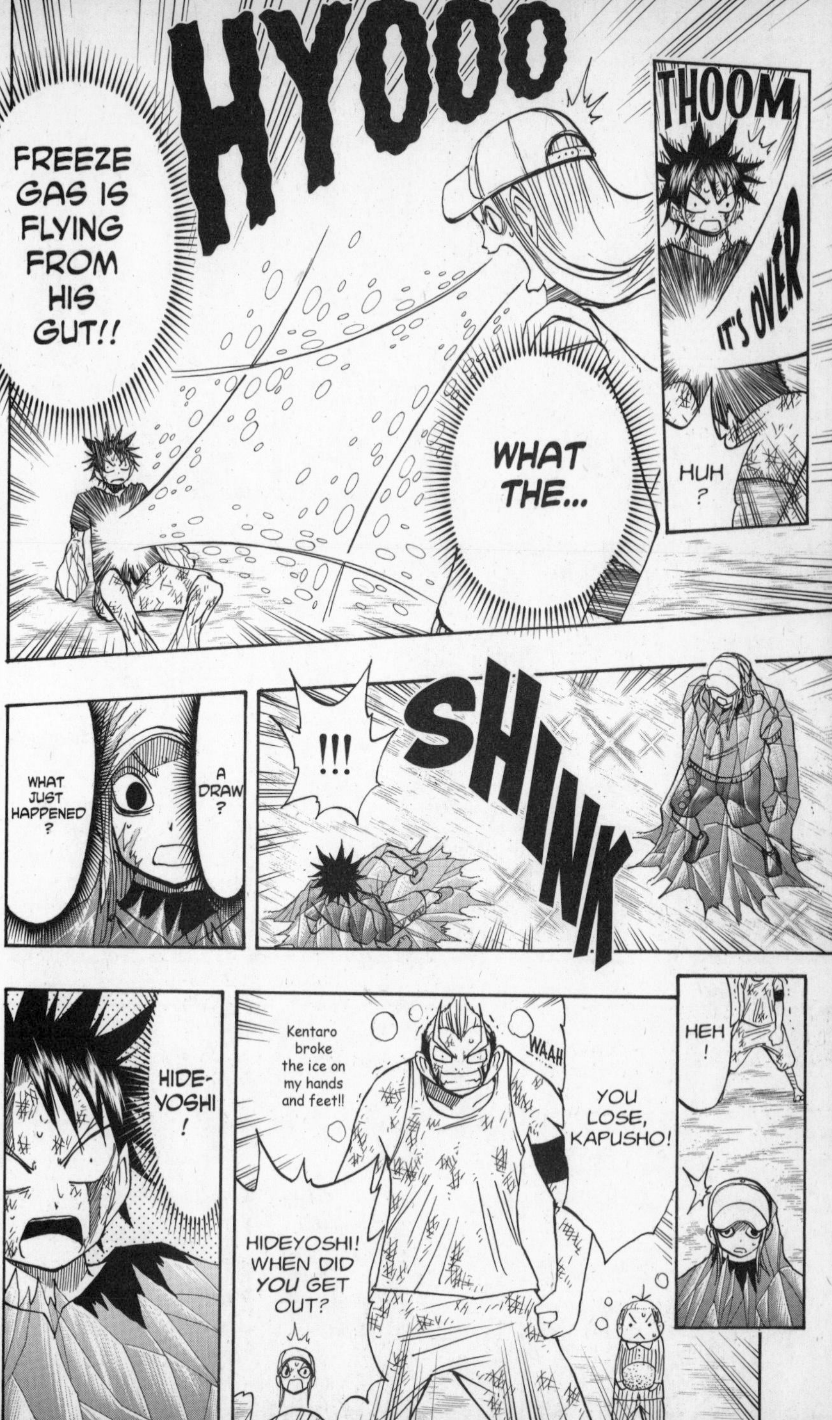
THOOM
IT'S OVER
HUH?
HYOOO
FREEZE GAS IS FLYING FROM HIS GUT!!
WHAT THE...
SHINK
!!!
A DRAW?
WHAT JUST HAPPENED?
HEH!
YOU LOSE, KAPUSHO!
WAAH
Kentaro broke the ice on my hands and feet!!
HIDEYOSHI! WHEN DID YOU GET OUT?
HIDE-YOSHI!

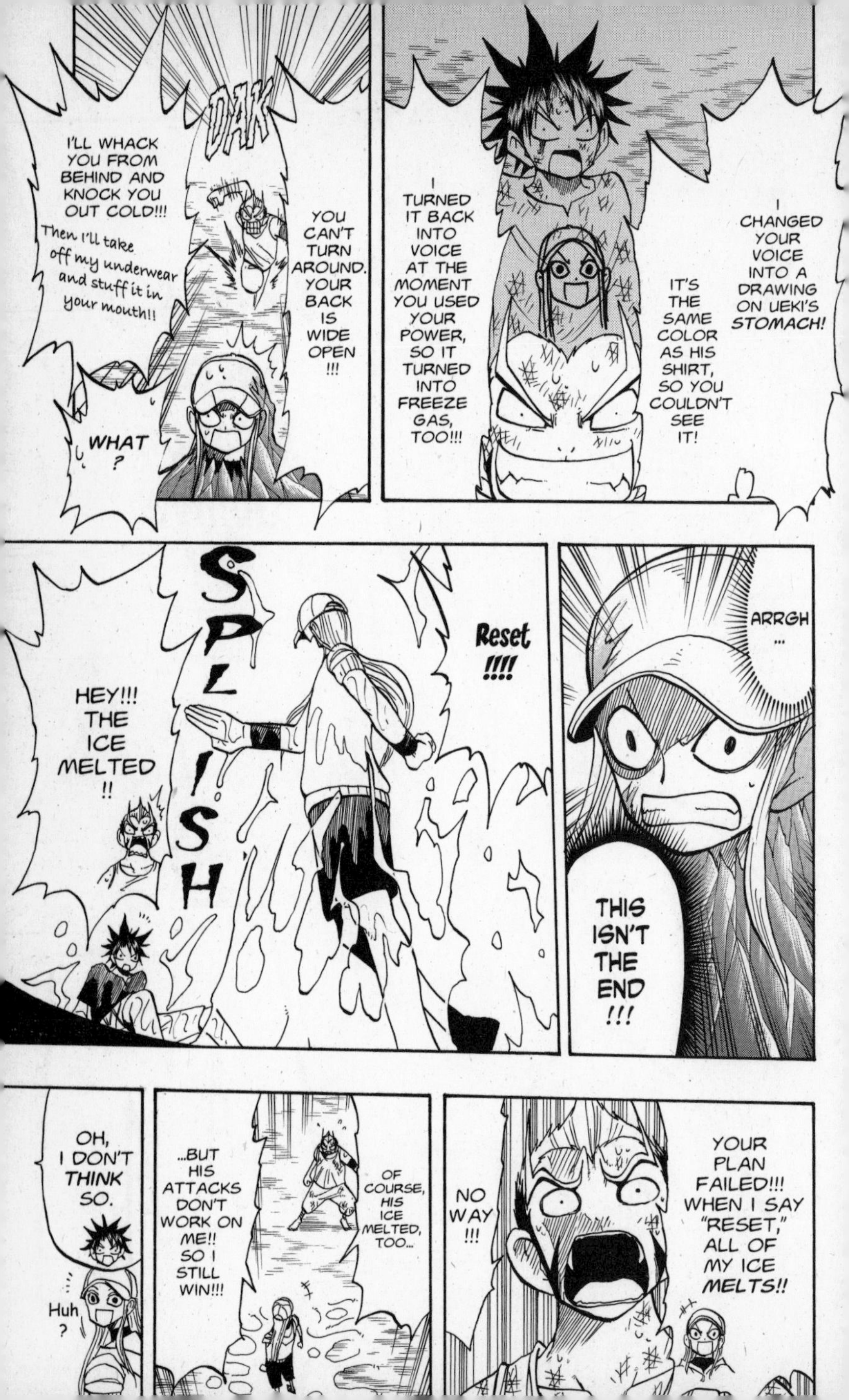
I CHANGED YOUR VOICE INTO A DRAWING ON UEKI'S STOMACH!
IT'S THE SAME COLOR AS HIS SHIRT, SO YOU COULDN'T SEE IT!
I TURNED IT BACK INTO VOICE AT THE MOMENT YOU USED YOUR POWER, SO IT TURNED INTO FREEZE GAS, TOO!!!
YOU CAN'T TURN AROUND. YOUR BACK IS WIDE OPEN!!!
DAK
I'LL WHACK YOU FROM BEHIND AND KNOCK YOU OUT COLD!!!
Then I'll take off my underwear and stuff it in your mouth!!
WHAT?
ARRGH...
THIS ISN'T THE END!!!
Reset!!!!
SPLISH
HEY!!! THE ICE MELTED!!
YOUR PLAN FAILED!!! WHEN I SAY "RESET," ALL OF MY ICE MELTS!!
NO WAY!!!
OF COURSE, HIS ICE MELTED, TOO...
...BUT HIS ATTACKS DON'T WORK ON ME!! SO I STILL WIN!!!
OH, I DON'T THINK SO.
Huh?

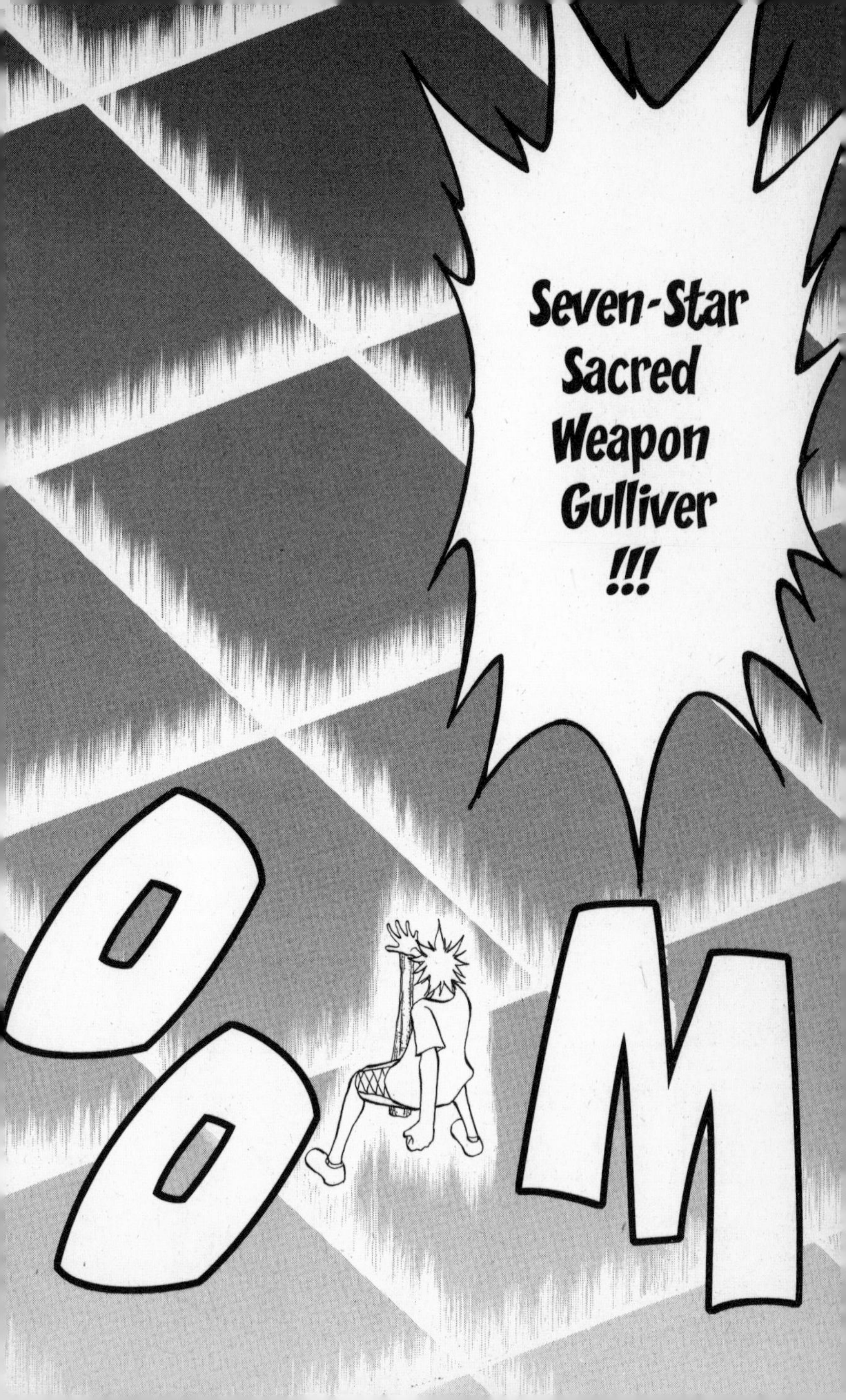

Seven-Star Sacred Weapon Gulliver !!!
OOM

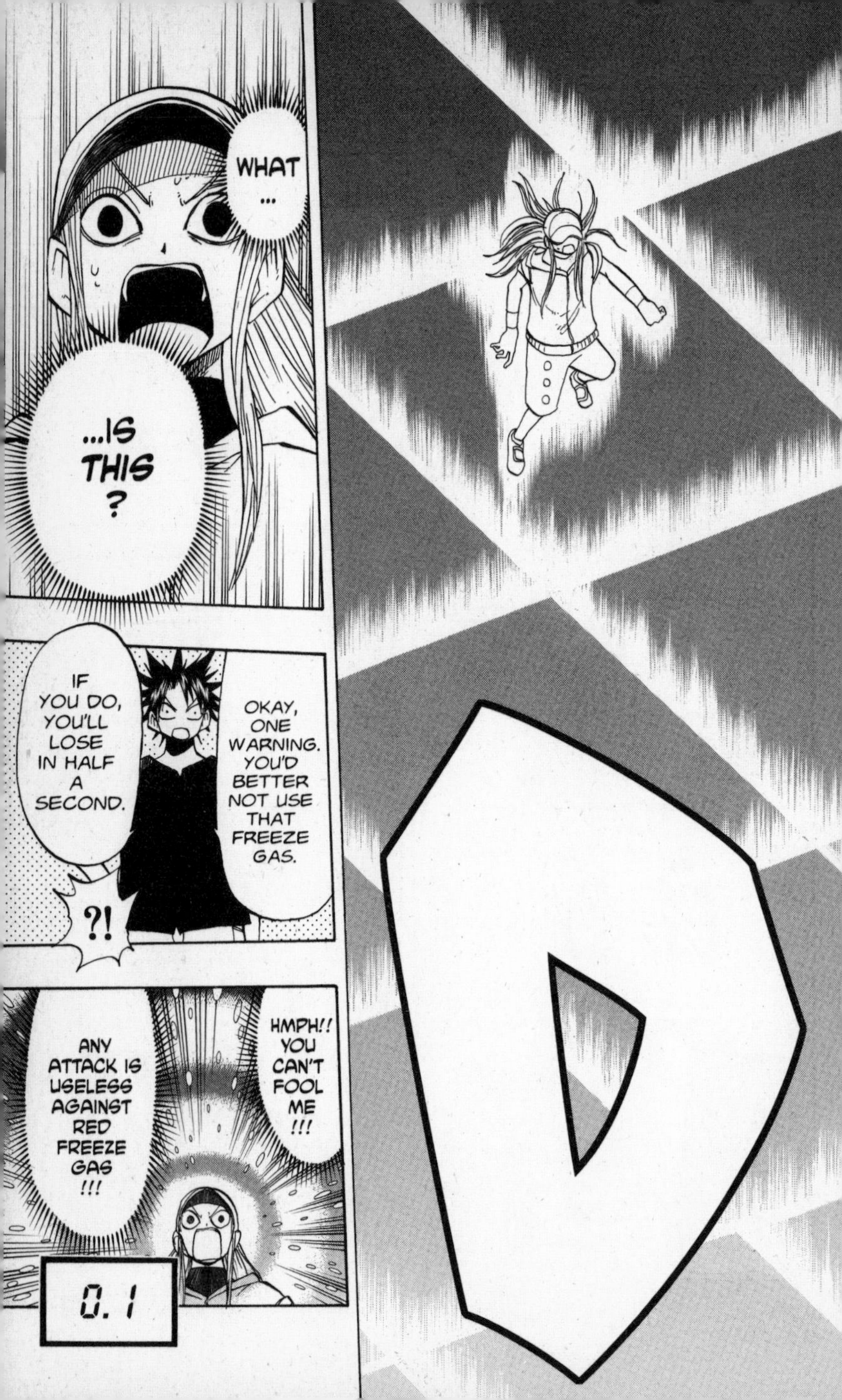
D
WHAT ...
...IS THIS ?
OKAY, ONE WARNING. YOU'D BETTER NOT USE THAT FREEZE GAS.
IF YOU DO, YOU'LL LOSE IN HALF A SECOND.
?!
HMPH!! YOU CAN'T FOOL ME !!!
ANY ATTACK IS USELESS AGAINST RED FREEZE GAS !!!
0.1

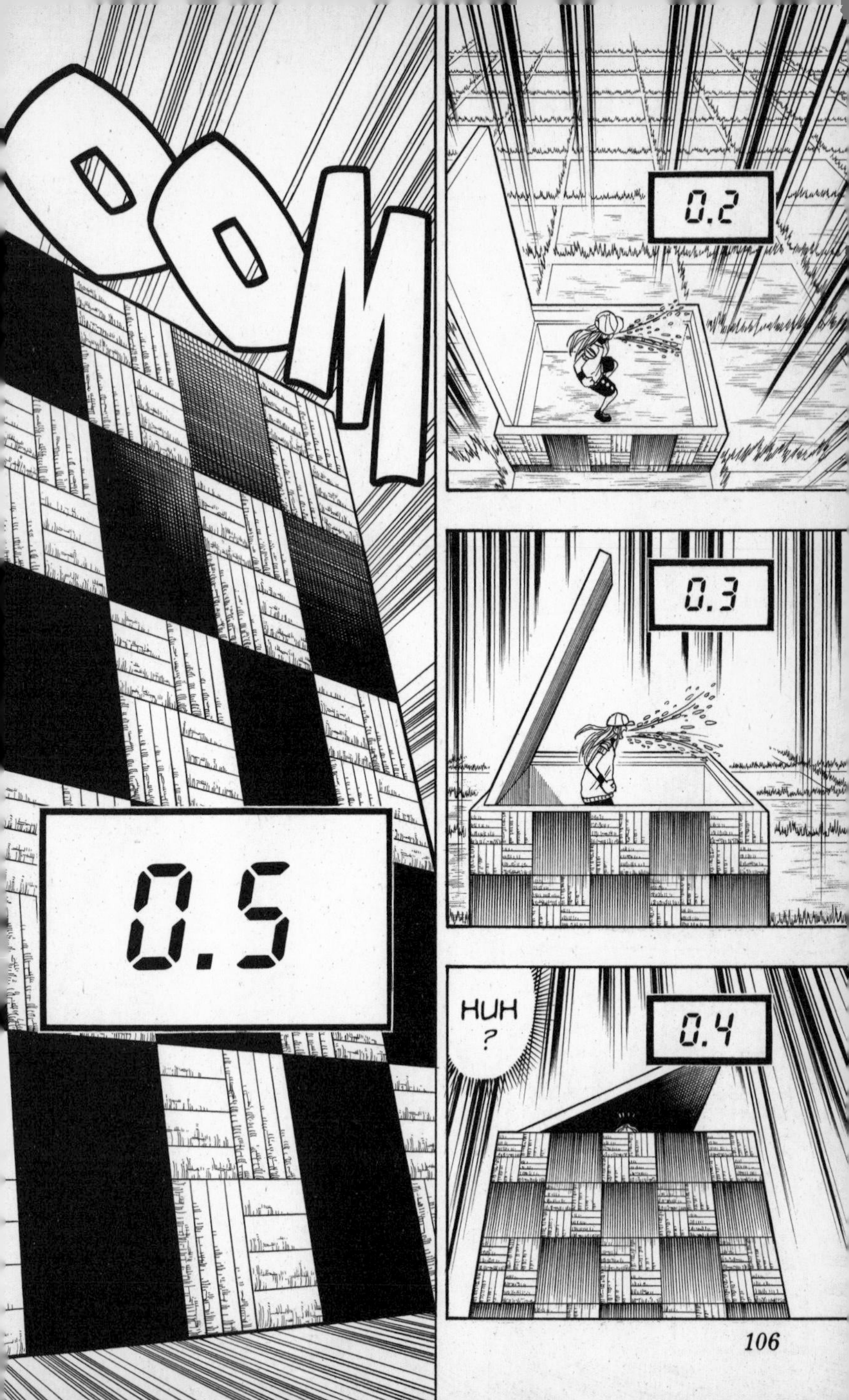
0.2
0.3
0.4
HUH ?
OOM
0.5

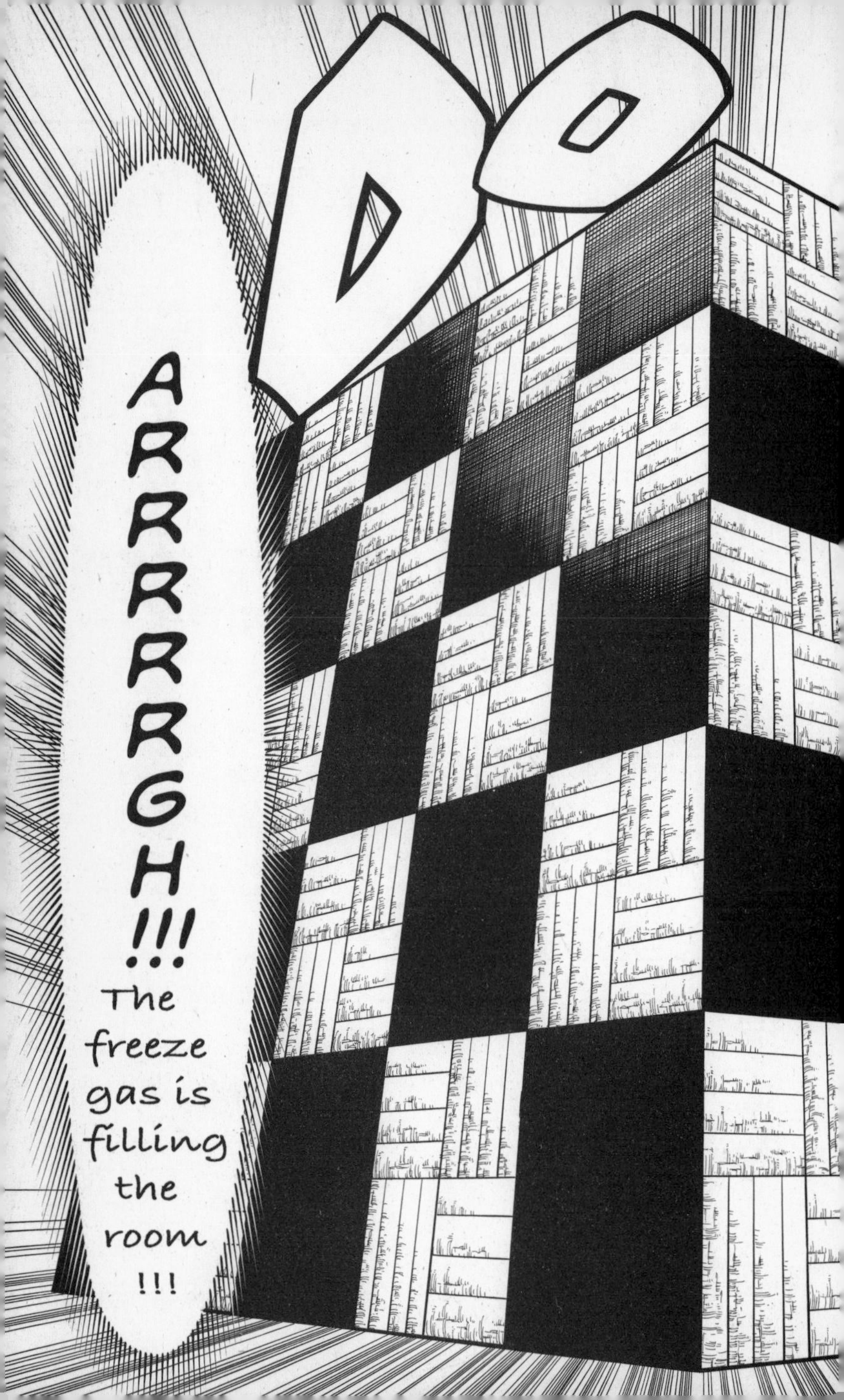
ARRRRGH!!! The freeze gas is filling the room!!!

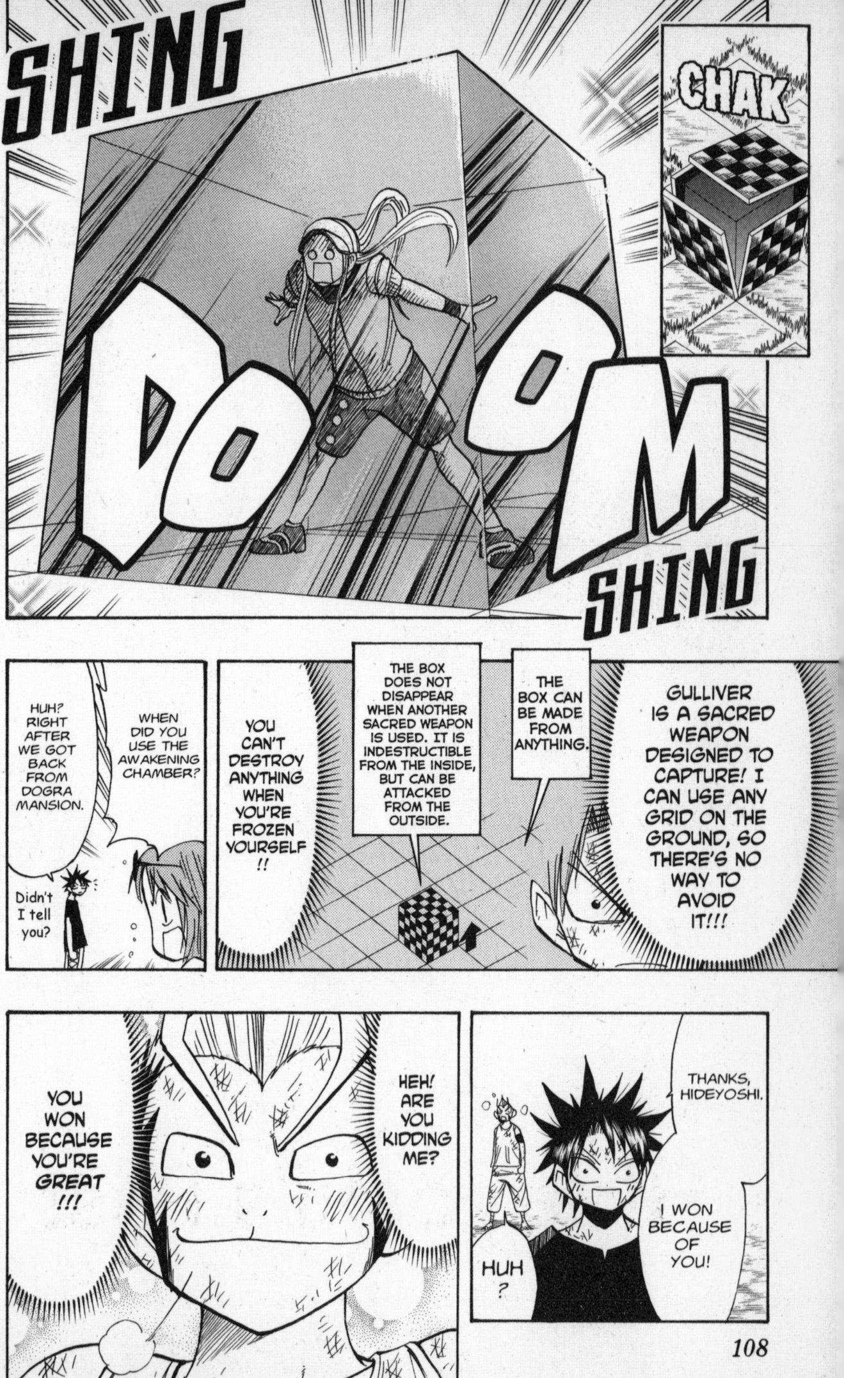
CHAK
SHING
DOOM
SHING
GULLIVER IS A SACRED WEAPON DESIGNED TO CAPTURE! I CAN USE ANY GRID ON THE GROUND, SO THERE'S NO WAY TO AVOID IT!!!
THE BOX CAN BE MADE FROM ANYTHING.
THE BOX DOES NOT DISAPPEAR WHEN ANOTHER SACRED WEAPON IS USED. IT IS INDESTRUCTIBLE FROM THE INSIDE, BUT CAN BE ATTACKED FROM THE OUTSIDE.
YOU CAN'T DESTROY ANYTHING WHEN YOU'RE FROZEN YOURSELF !!
WHEN DID YOU USE THE AWAKENING CHAMBER?
HUH? RIGHT AFTER WE GOT BACK FROM DOGRA MANSION.
Didn't I tell you?
THANKS, HIDEYOSHI.
I WON BECAUSE OF YOU!
HUH ?
HEH! ARE YOU KIDDING ME?
YOU WON BECAUSE YOU'RE GREAT !!!

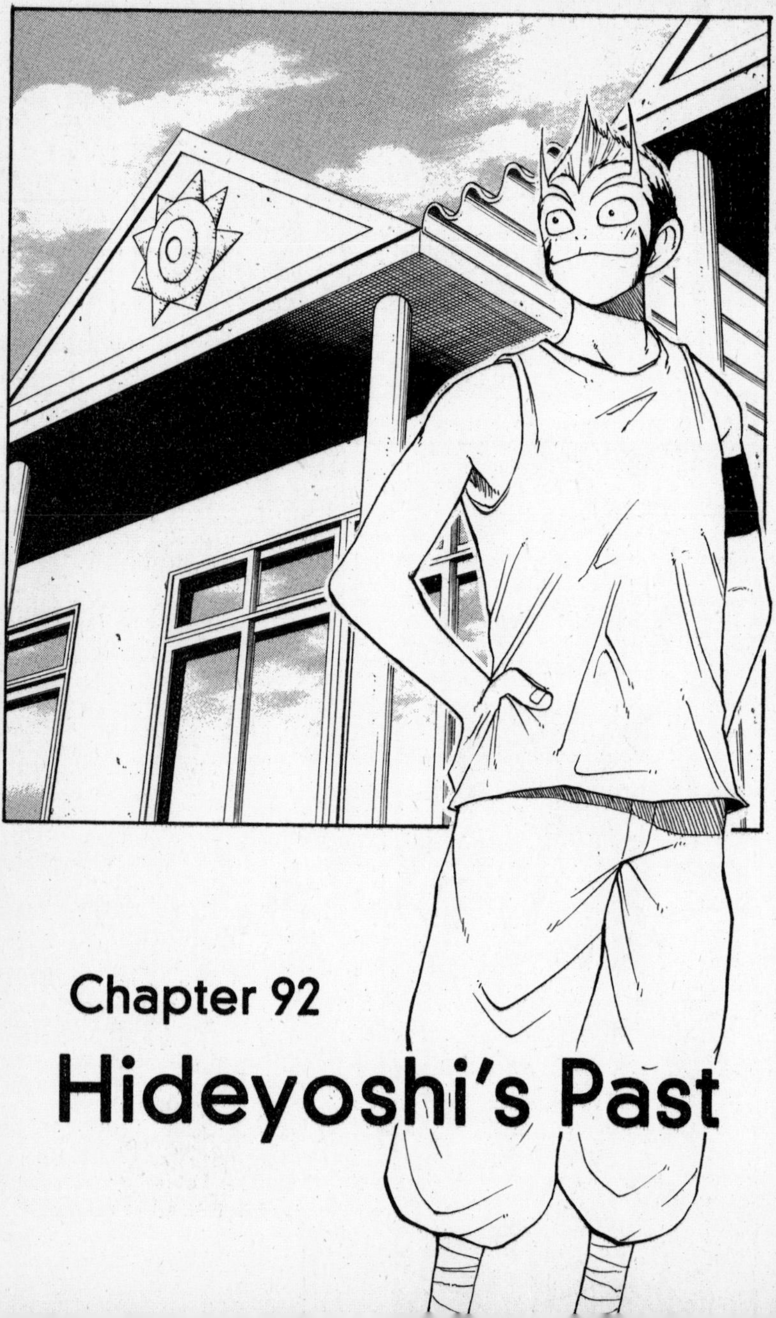
Chapter 92
Hideyoshi's Past

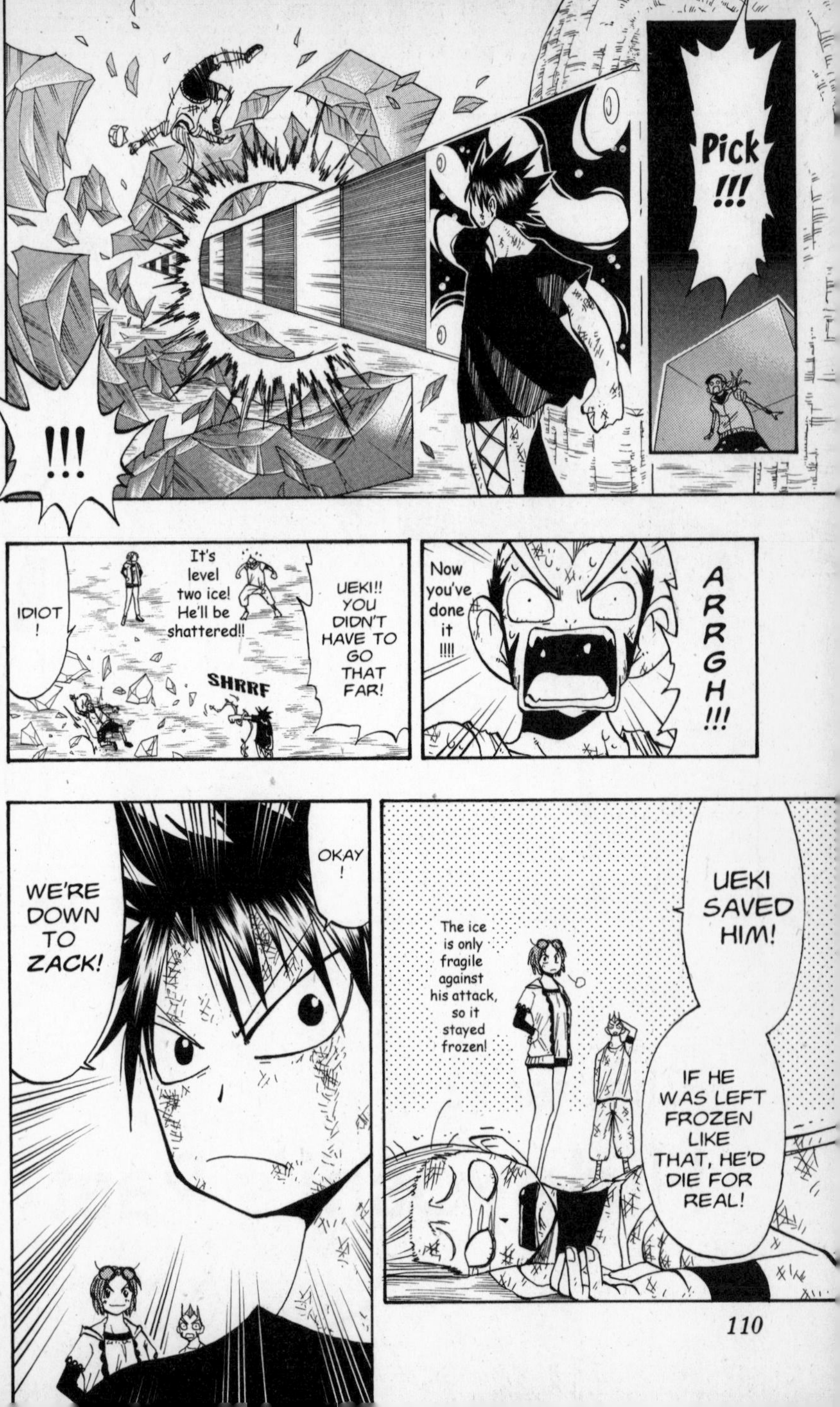
Pick !!!
!!!
ARRGH!!!
Now you've done it !!!!
UEKI!! YOU DIDN'T HAVE TO GO THAT FAR!
It's level two ice! He'll be shattered!!
SHRRF
IDIOT!
UEKI SAVED HIM!
The ice is only fragile against his attack, so it stayed frozen!
IF HE WAS LEFT FROZEN LIKE THAT, HE'D DIE FOR REAL!
OKAY!
WE'RE DOWN TO ZACK!

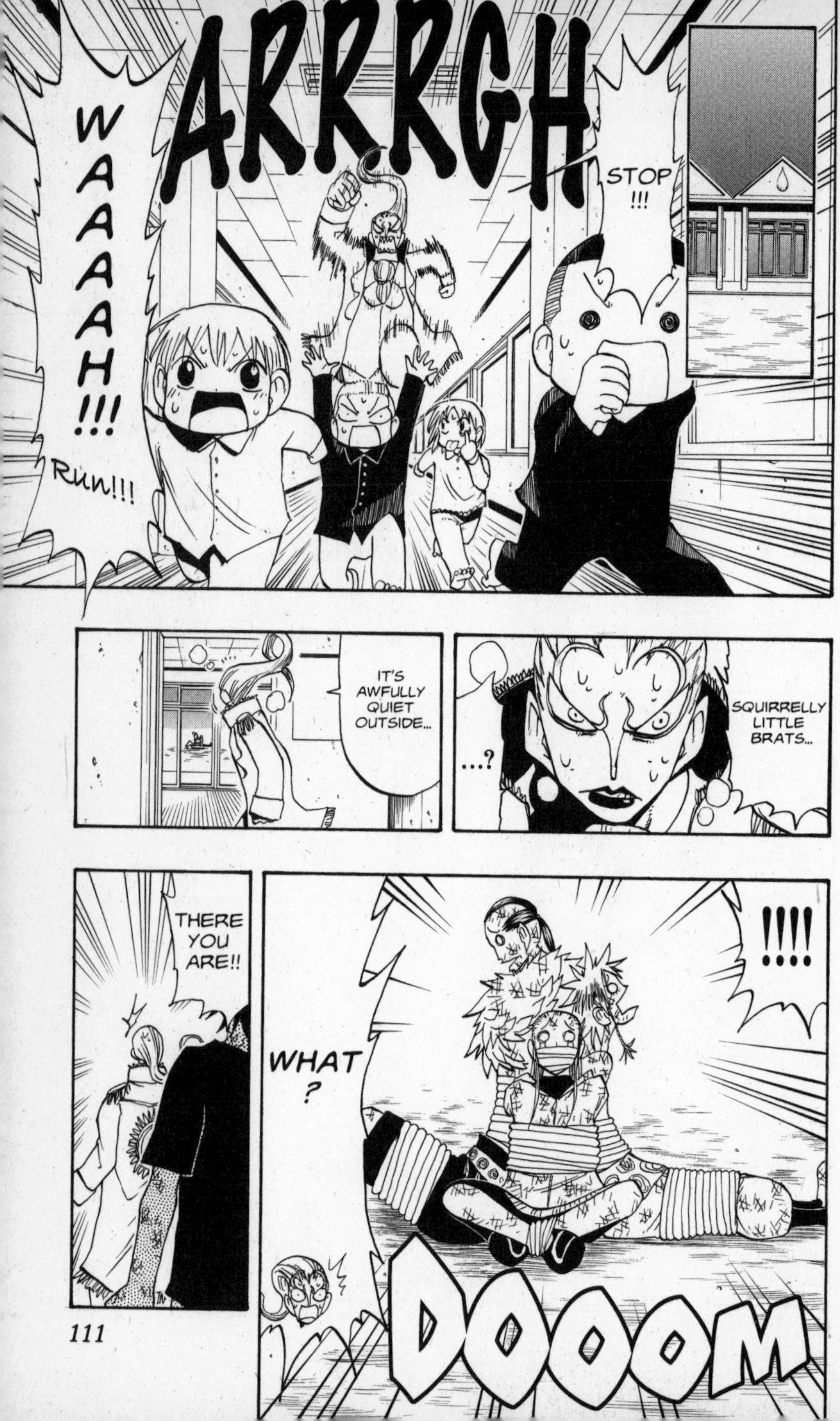
STOP !!!
ARRRGH
WAAAAAH!!!
Run!!!
SQUIRRELLY LITTLE BRATS...
...?
IT'S AWFULLY QUIET OUTSIDE...
!!!!
WHAT ?
DOOOM
THERE YOU ARE!!

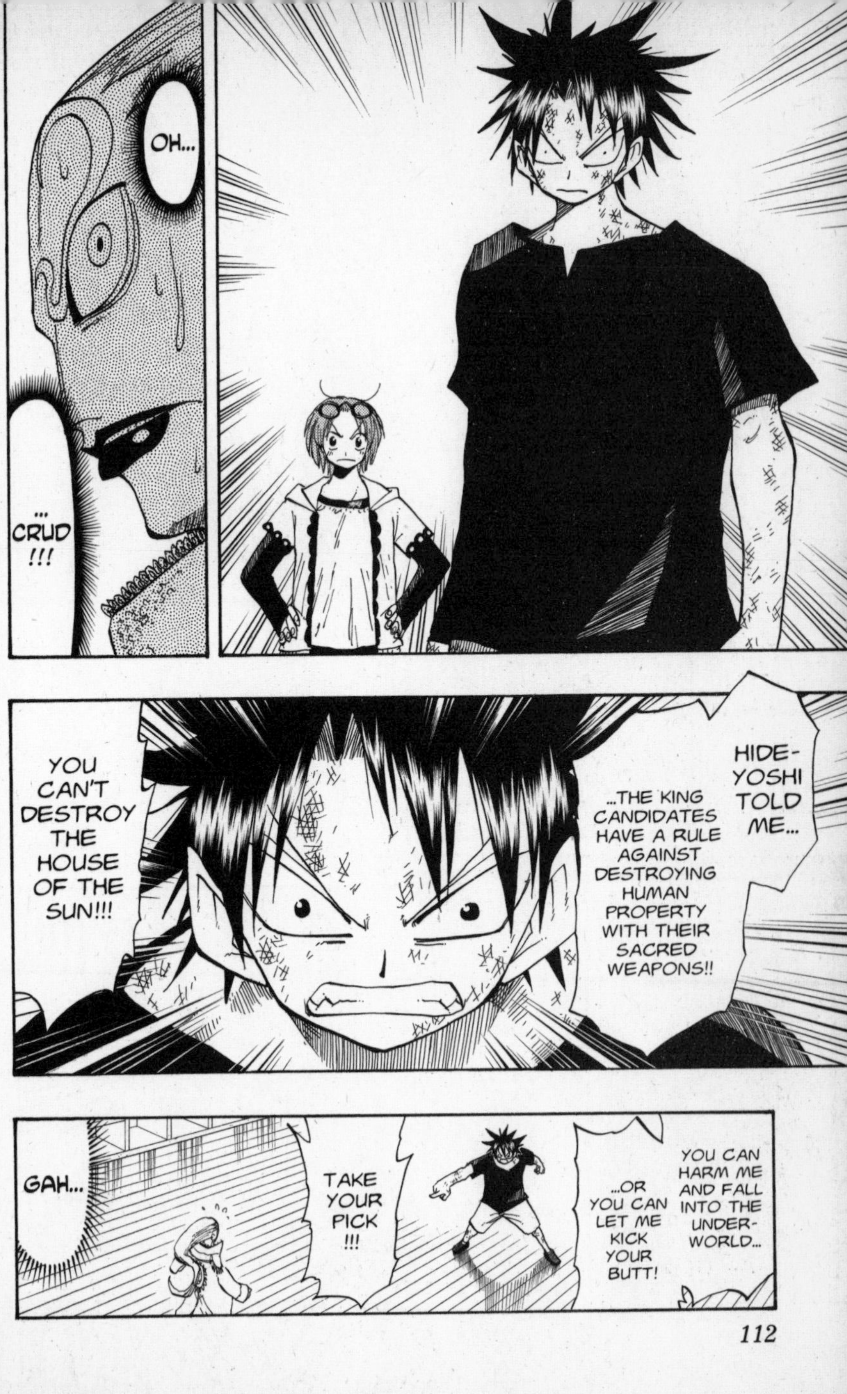
OH...
...CRUD!!!
HIDE-YOSHI TOLD ME...
...THE KING CANDIDATES HAVE A RULE AGAINST DESTROYING HUMAN PROPERTY WITH THEIR SACRED WEAPONS!!
YOU CAN'T DESTROY THE HOUSE OF THE SUN!!!
YOU CAN HARM ME AND FALL INTO THE UNDER-WORLD...
...OR YOU CAN LET ME KICK YOUR BUTT!
TAKE YOUR PICK!!!
GAH...

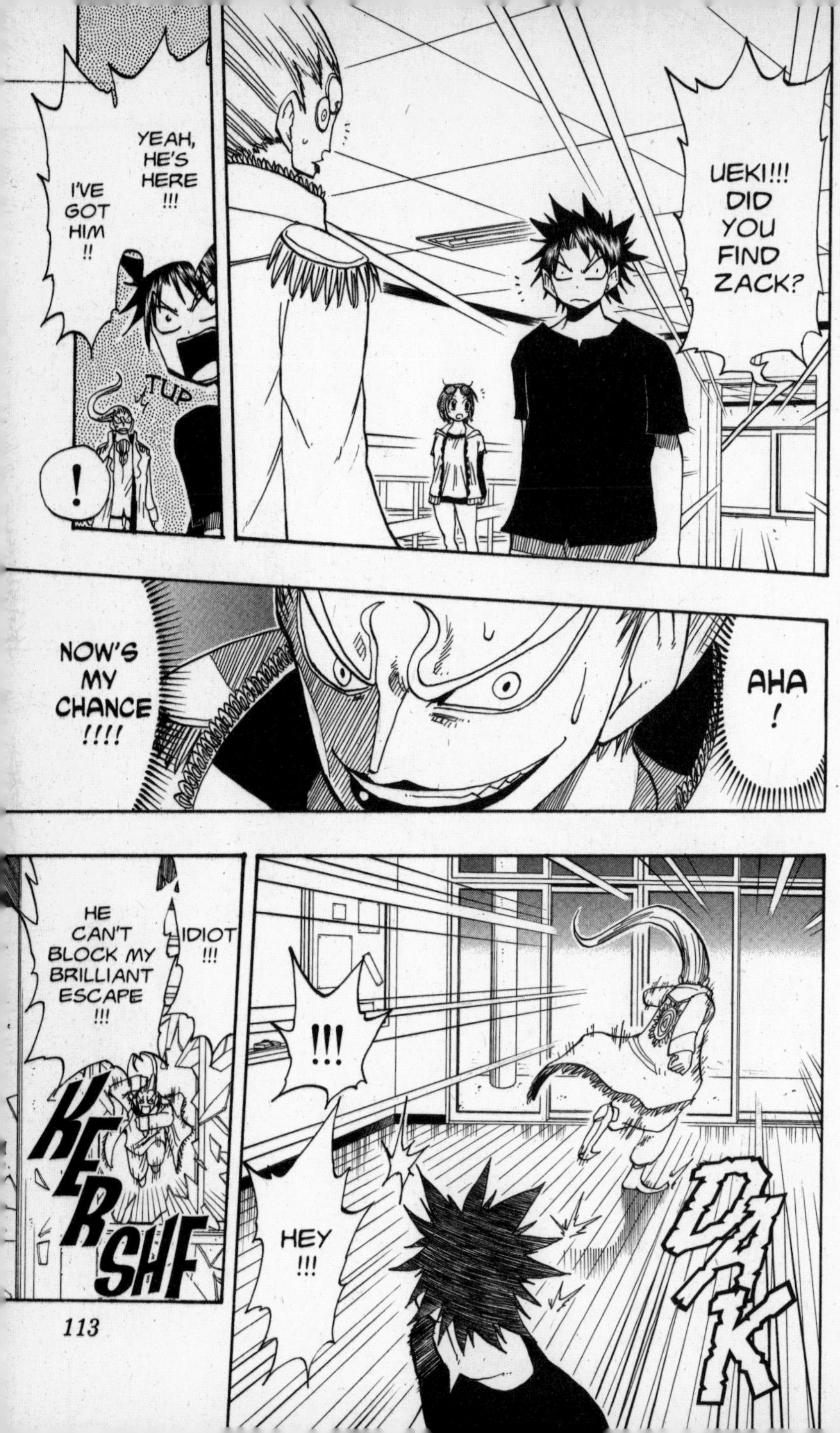
UEKI!!! DID YOU FIND ZACK?
YEAH, HE'S HERE !!!
I'VE GOT HIM !!
TUP
!
AHA !
NOW'S MY CHANCE !!!!
!!!
HEY !!!
DA
K
IDIOT !!!
HE CAN'T BLOCK MY BRILLIANT ESCAPE !!!
KERSHF

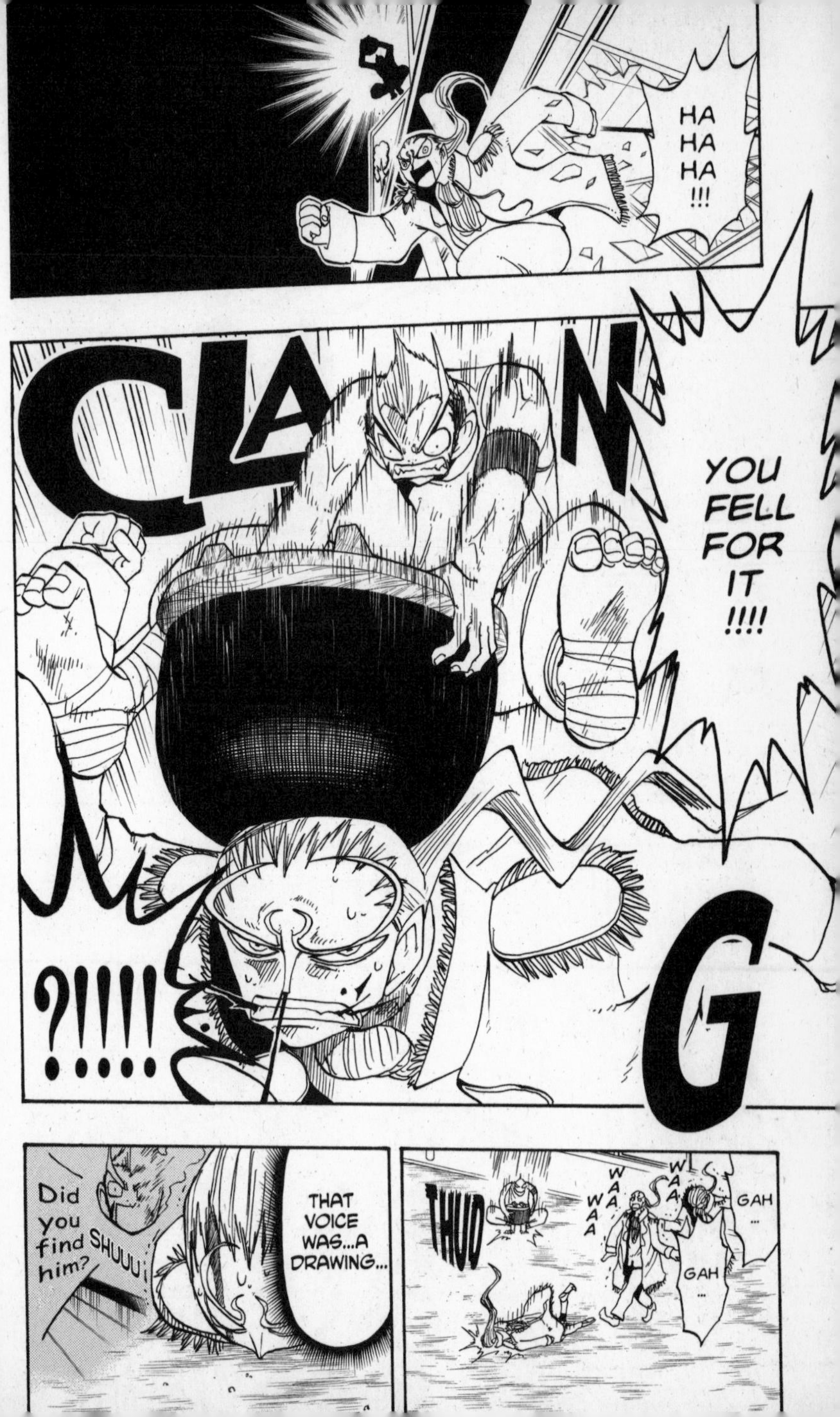
HA HA HA !!!
YOU FELL FOR IT !!!!
CLANG
?!!!!
Did you find him? SHUUU¡
THAT VOICE WAS...A DRAWING...
THUD
WAA WAA
WAA WAA
GAH ...
GAH ...

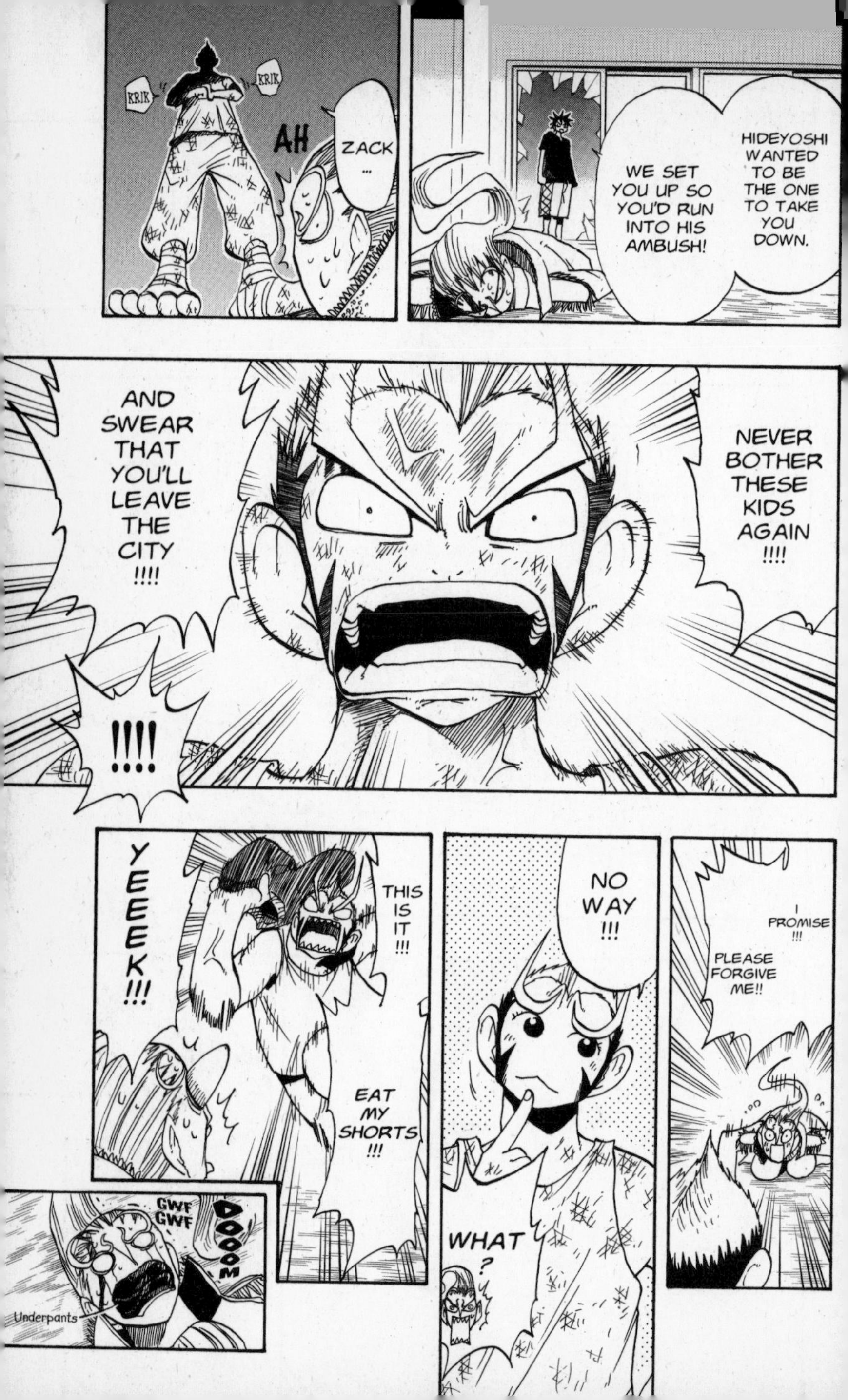
HIDEYOSHI WANTED TO BE THE ONE TO TAKE YOU DOWN.
WE SET YOU UP SO YOU'D RUN INTO HIS AMBUSH!
ZACK ...
AH
KRIK
KRIK
NEVER BOTHER THESE KIDS AGAIN !!!!
AND SWEAR THAT YOU'LL LEAVE THE CITY !!!!
!!!!
I PROMISE !!!
PLEASE FORGIVE ME!!
NO WAY !!!
WHAT ?
THIS IS IT !!!
YEEEK!!!
EAT MY SHORTS !!!
GWF GWF
DOOOM
Underpants

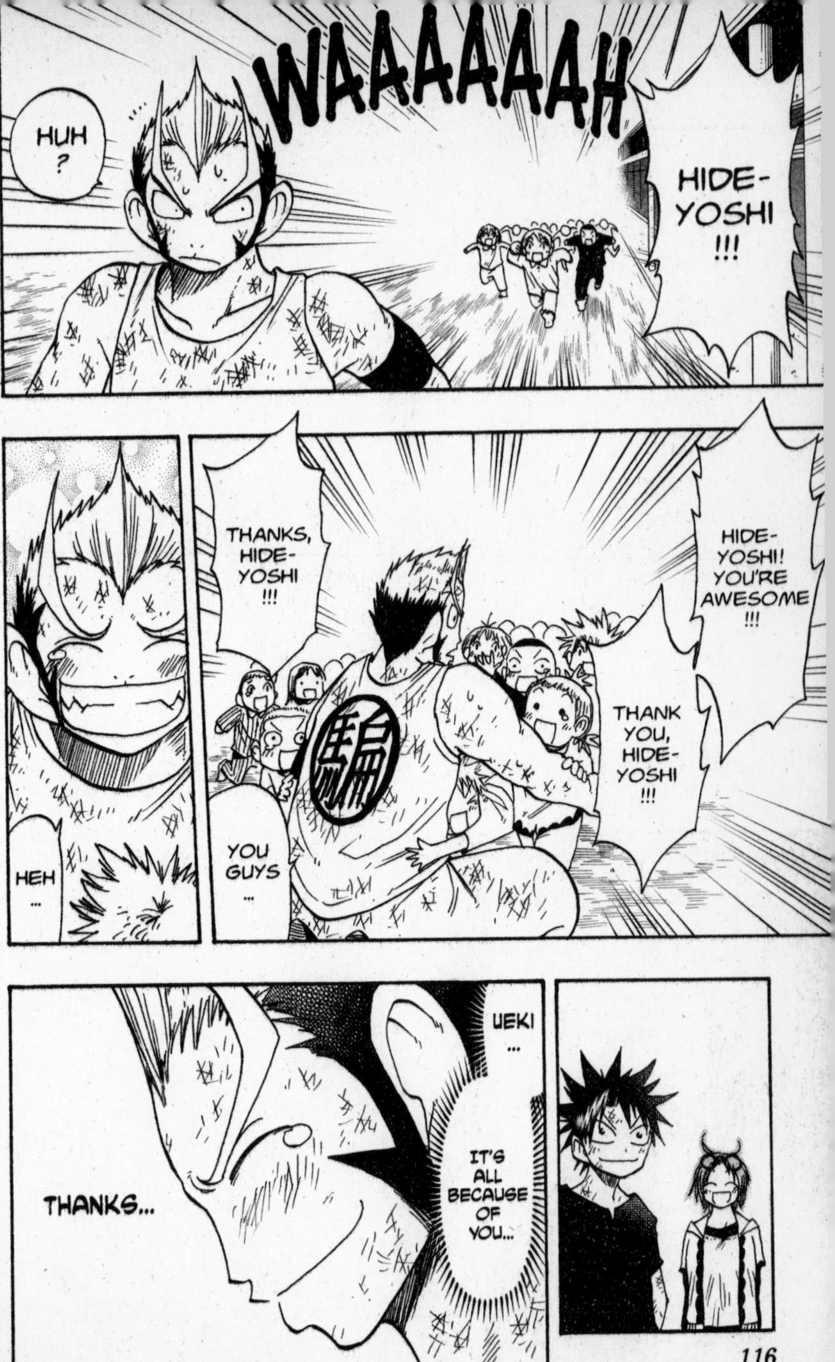
HIDE-YOSHI!!!
WAAAAAAH
HUH?
HIDE-YOSHI! YOU'RE AWESOME!!!
THANK YOU, HIDE-YOSHI!!!
THANKS, HIDE-YOSHI!!!
YOU GUYS...
HEH...
UEKI...
IT'S ALL BECAUSE OF YOU...
THANKS...

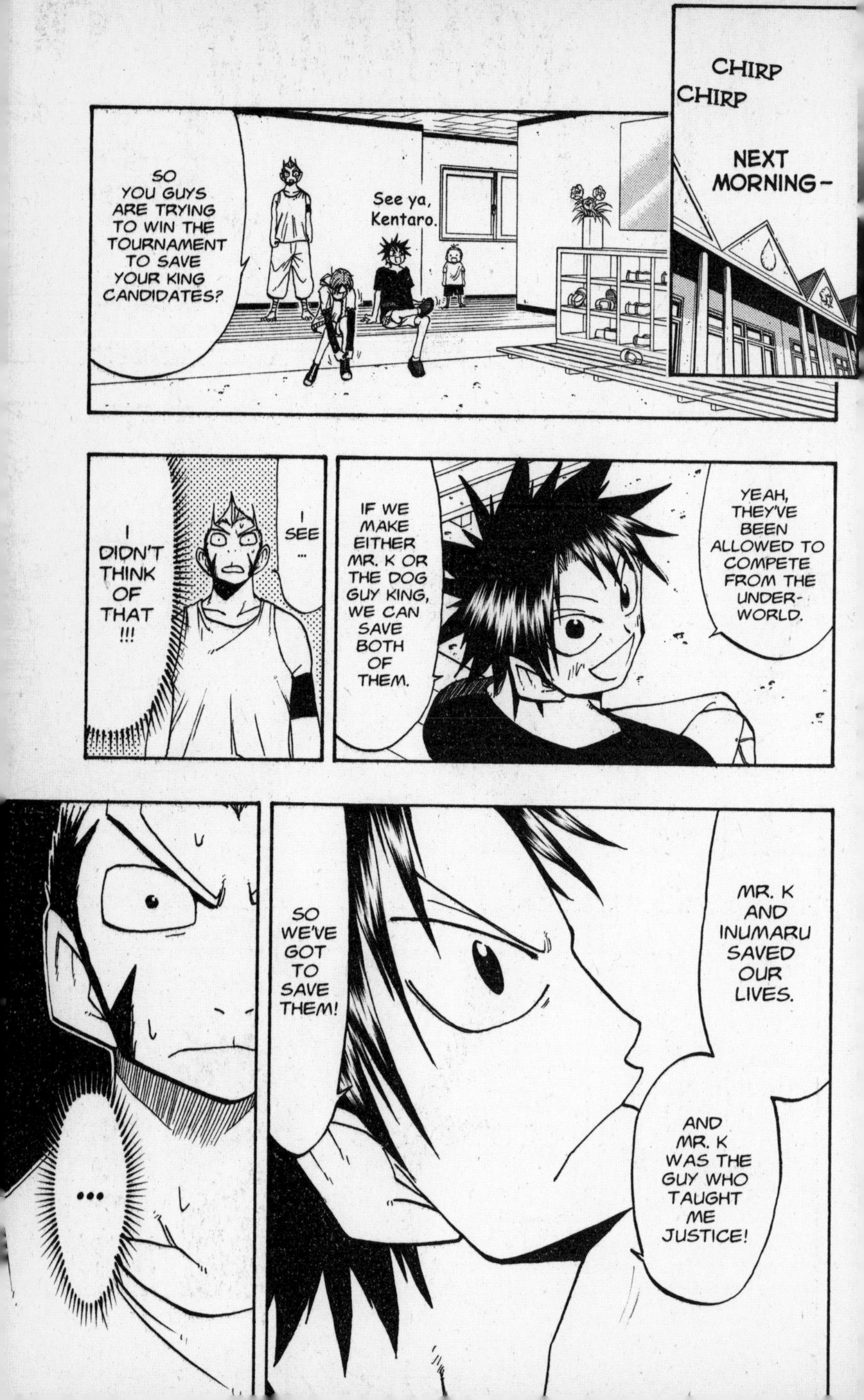
CHIRP CHIRP
NEXT MORNING-
See ya, Kentaro.
SO YOU GUYS ARE TRYING TO WIN THE TOURNAMENT TO SAVE YOUR KING CANDIDATES?
YEAH, THEY'VE BEEN ALLOWED TO COMPETE FROM THE UNDER-WORLD.
IF WE MAKE EITHER MR. K OR THE DOG GUY KING, WE CAN SAVE BOTH OF THEM.
I SEE ...
I DIDN'T THINK OF THAT !!!
MR. K AND INUMARU SAVED OUR LIVES.
AND MR. K WAS THE GUY WHO TAUGHT ME JUSTICE!
SO WE'VE GOT TO SAVE THEM!
...

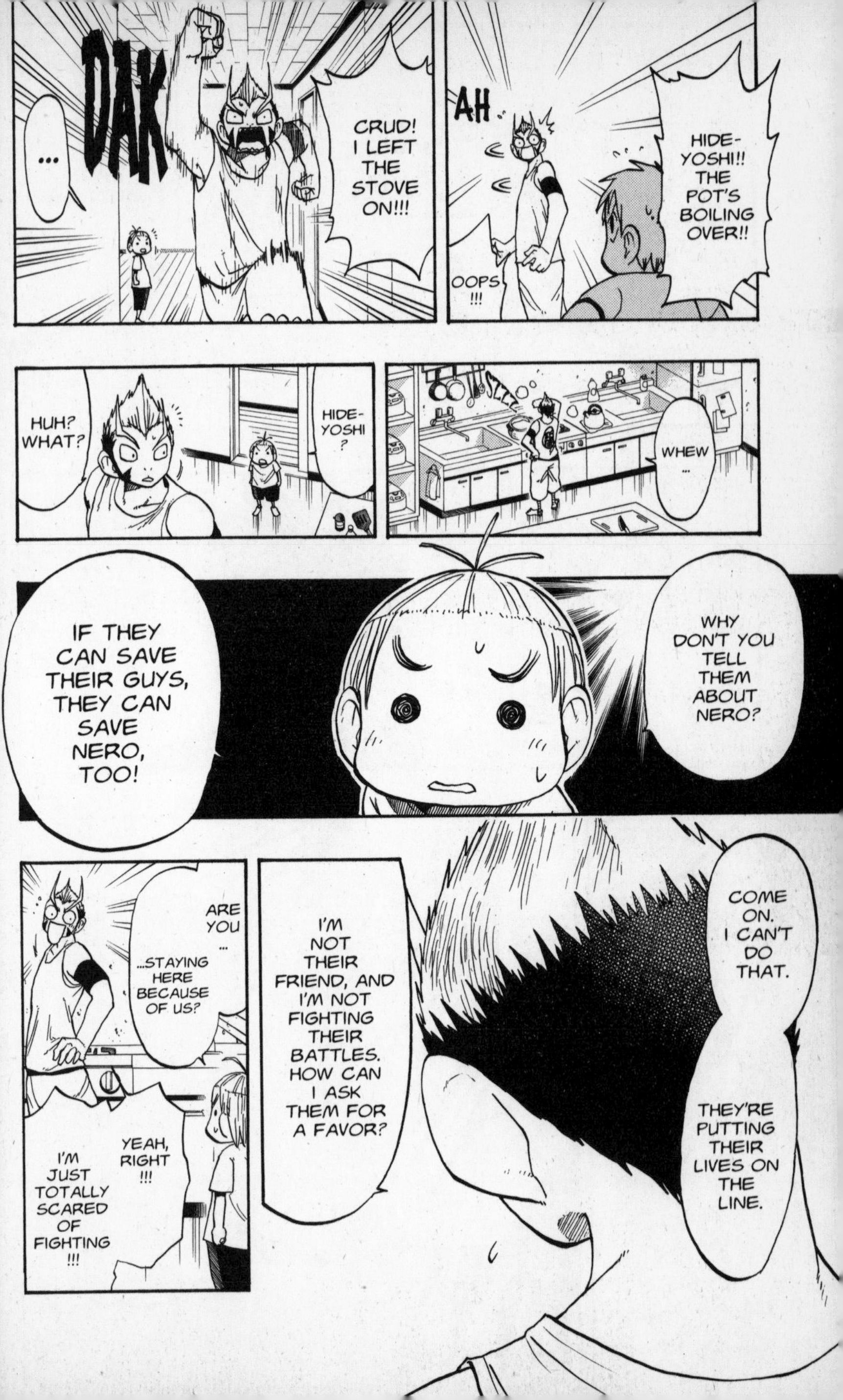
HIDE-YOSHI!! THE POT'S BOILING OVER!!
AH
OOPS!!!
CRUD! I LEFT THE STOVE ON!!!
DAK
...
WHEW ...
HIDE-YOSHI?
HUH? WHAT?
WHY DON'T YOU TELL THEM ABOUT NERO?
IF THEY CAN SAVE THEIR GUYS, THEY CAN SAVE NERO, TOO!
COME ON. I CAN'T DO THAT.
THEY'RE PUTTING THEIR LIVES ON THE LINE.
I'M NOT THEIR FRIEND, AND I'M NOT FIGHTING THEIR BATTLES. HOW CAN I ASK THEM FOR A FAVOR?
ARE YOU ...
...STAYING HERE BECAUSE OF US?
YEAH, RIGHT!!!
I'M JUST TOTALLY SCARED OF FIGHTING!!!

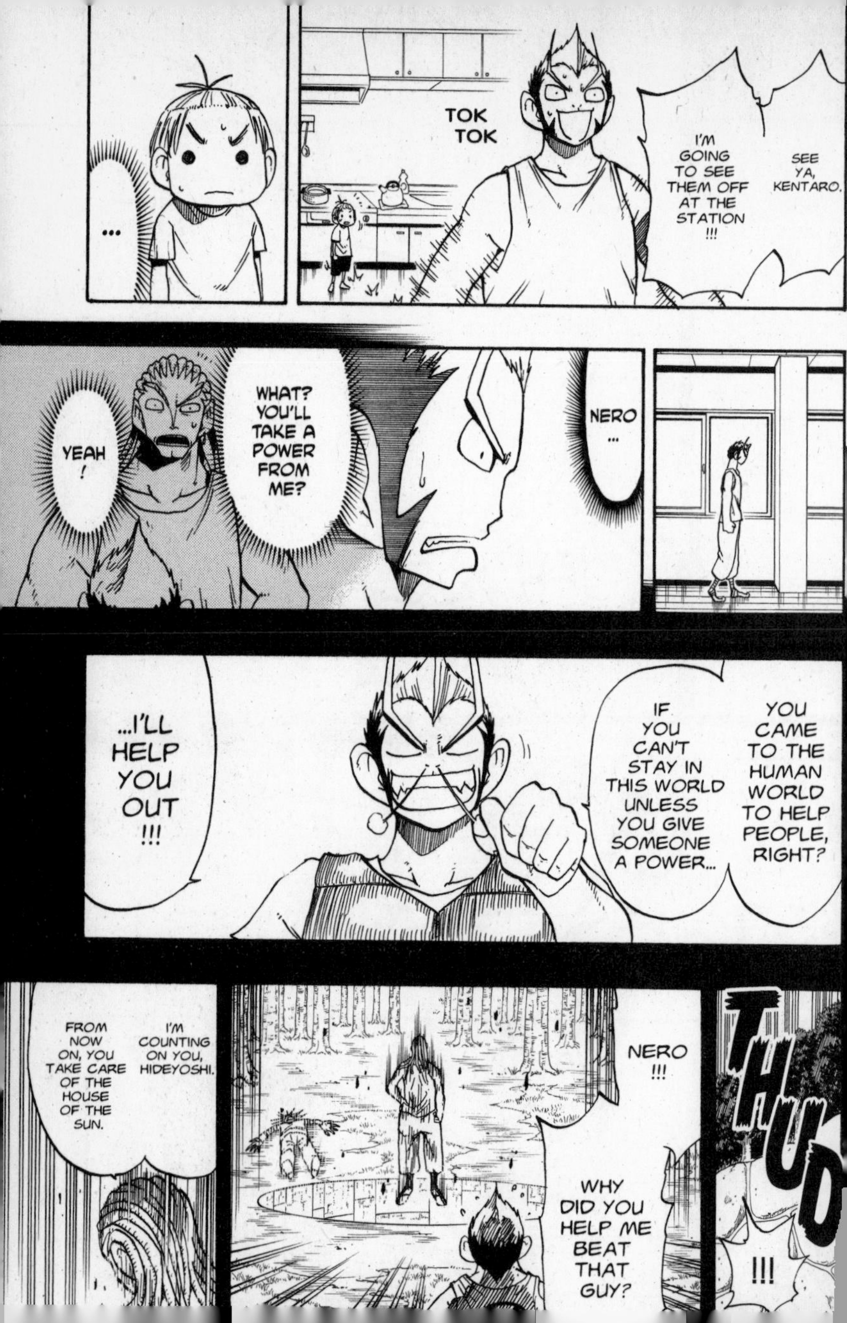
SEE YA, KENTARO.
I'M GOING TO SEE THEM OFF AT THE STATION !!!
TOK TOK
...
NERO ...
WHAT? YOU'LL TAKE A POWER FROM ME?
YEAH !
YOU CAME TO THE HUMAN WORLD TO HELP PEOPLE, RIGHT?
IF YOU CAN'T STAY IN THIS WORLD UNLESS YOU GIVE SOMEONE A POWER...
...I'LL HELP YOU OUT !!!
THUD
!!!
NERO !!!
WHY DID YOU HELP ME BEAT THAT GUY?
I'M COUNTING ON YOU, HIDEYOSHI.
FROM NOW ON, YOU TAKE CARE OF THE HOUSE OF THE SUN.

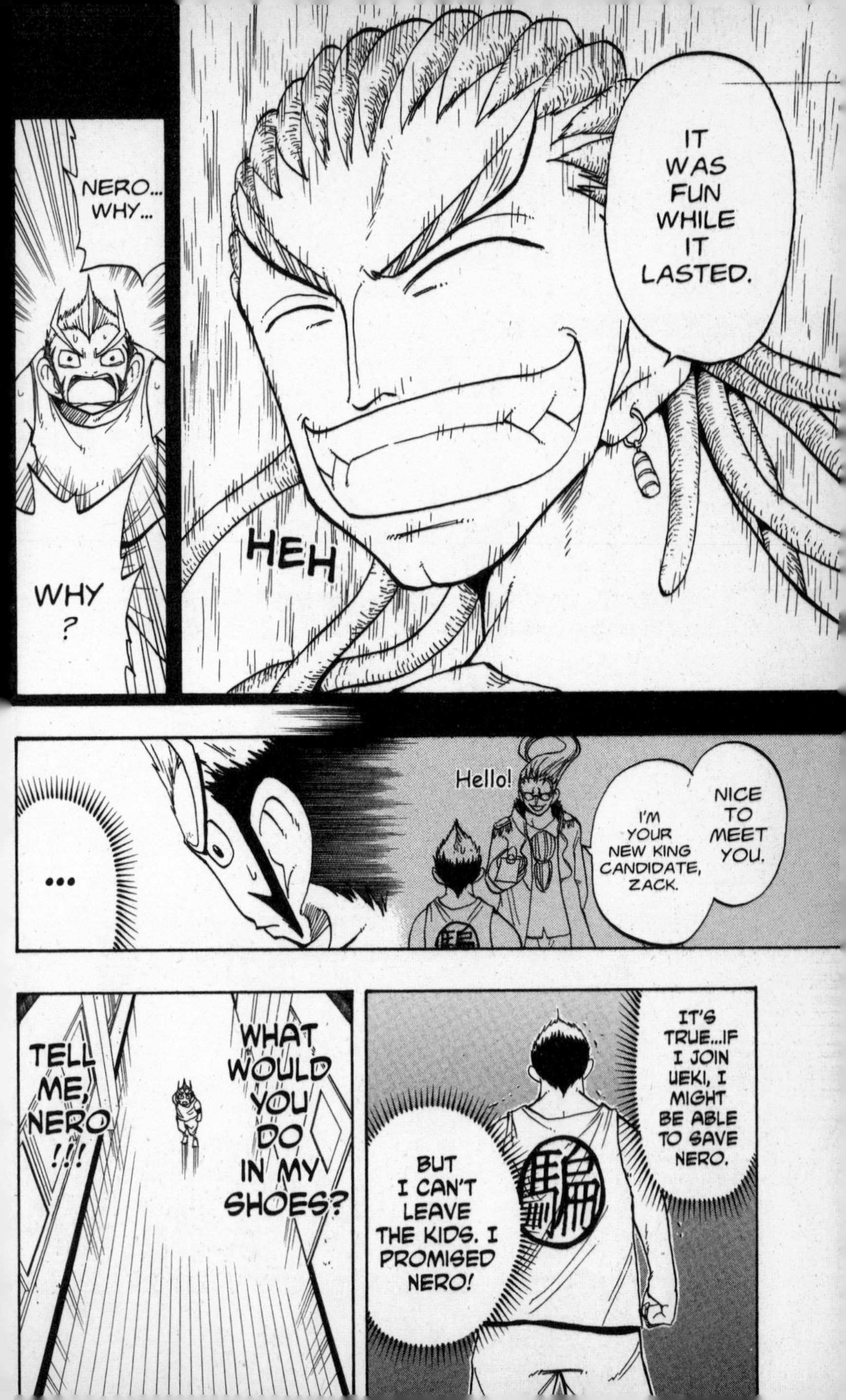
IT WAS FUN WHILE IT LASTED.
HEH
NERO... WHY...
WHY ?
NICE TO MEET YOU.
I'M YOUR NEW KING CANDIDATE, ZACK.
Hello!
...
IT'S TRUE...IF I JOIN UEKI, I MIGHT BE ABLE TO SAVE NERO.
BUT I CAN'T LEAVE THE KIDS. I PROMISED NERO!
WHAT WOULD YOU DO IN MY SHOES?
TELL ME, NERO !!!

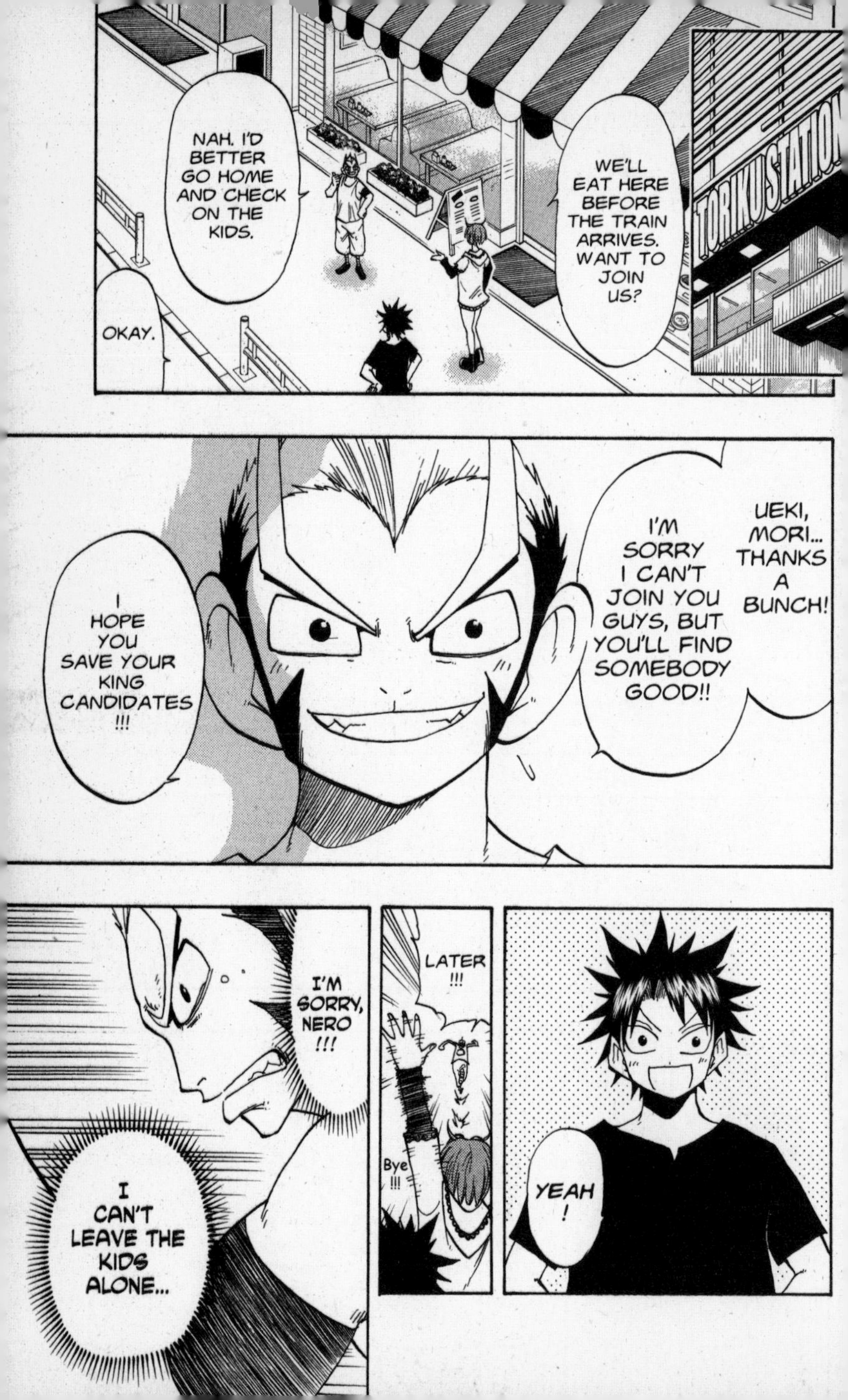
TORIKU STATION
WE'LL EAT HERE BEFORE THE TRAIN ARRIVES. WANT TO JOIN US?
NAH. I'D BETTER GO HOME AND CHECK ON THE KIDS.
OKAY.
UEKI, MORI... THANKS A BUNCH!
I'M SORRY I CAN'T JOIN YOU GUYS, BUT YOU'LL FIND SOMEBODY GOOD!!
I HOPE YOU SAVE YOUR KING CANDIDATES!!!
YEAH!
LATER!!!
Bye!!!
I'M SORRY, NERO!!!
I CAN'T LEAVE THE KIDS ALONE...

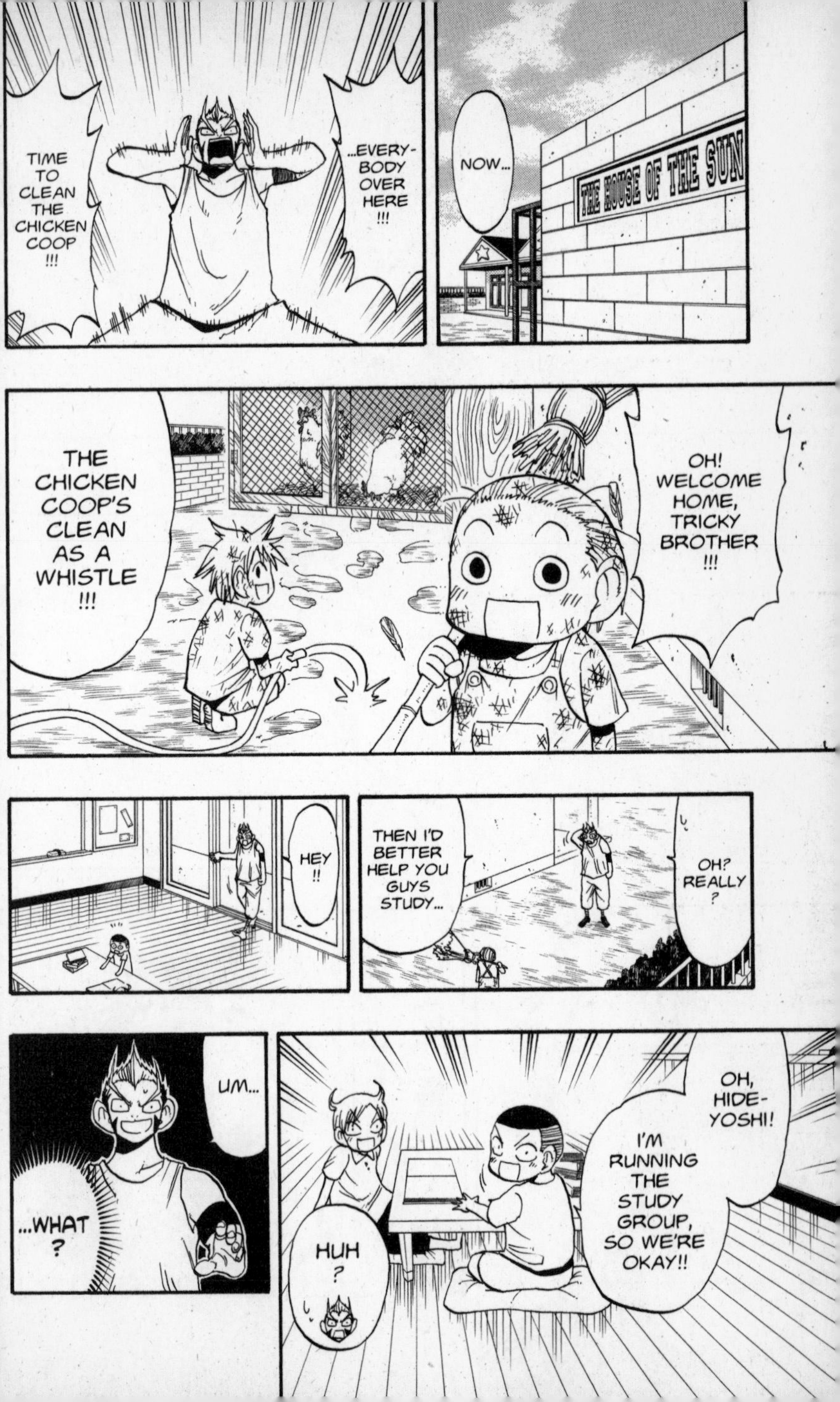
THE HOUSE OF THE SUN
NOW...
...EVERY-BODY OVER HERE!!!
TIME TO CLEAN THE CHICKEN COOP!!!
OH! WELCOME HOME, TRICKY BROTHER!!!
THE CHICKEN COOP'S CLEAN AS A WHISTLE!!!
OH? REALLY?
THEN I'D BETTER HELP YOU GUYS STUDY...
HEY!!
OH, HIDE-YOSHI!
I'M RUNNING THE STUDY GROUP, SO WE'RE OKAY!!
HUH?
UM...
...WHAT?

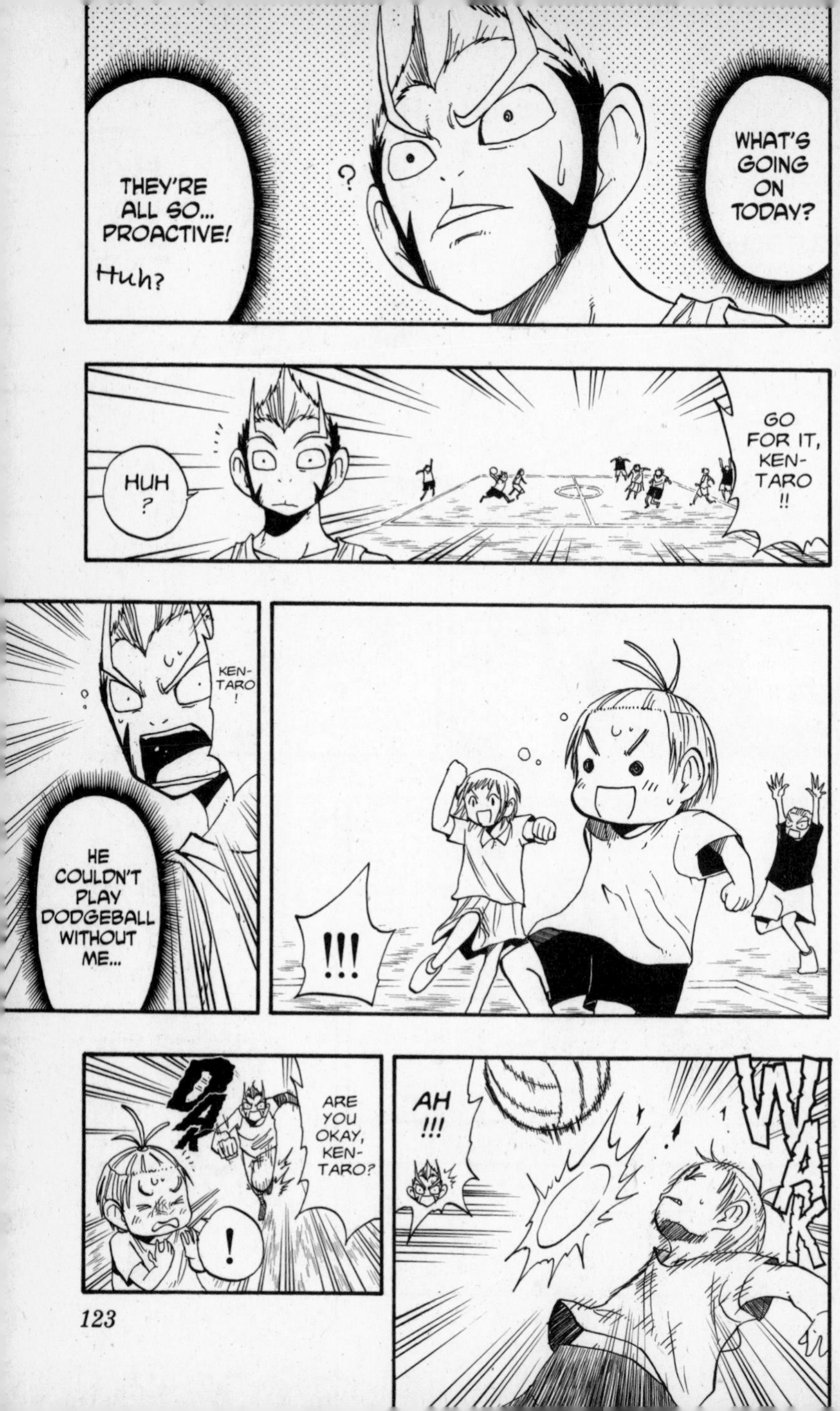
WHAT'S GOING ON TODAY?
THEY'RE ALL SO... PROACTIVE!
Huh?
GO FOR IT, KEN-TARO!!
HUH?
!!!
KEN-TARO!
HE COULDN'T PLAY DODGEBALL WITHOUT ME...
WAK
AH!!!
DA
ARE YOU OKAY, KEN-TARO?
!

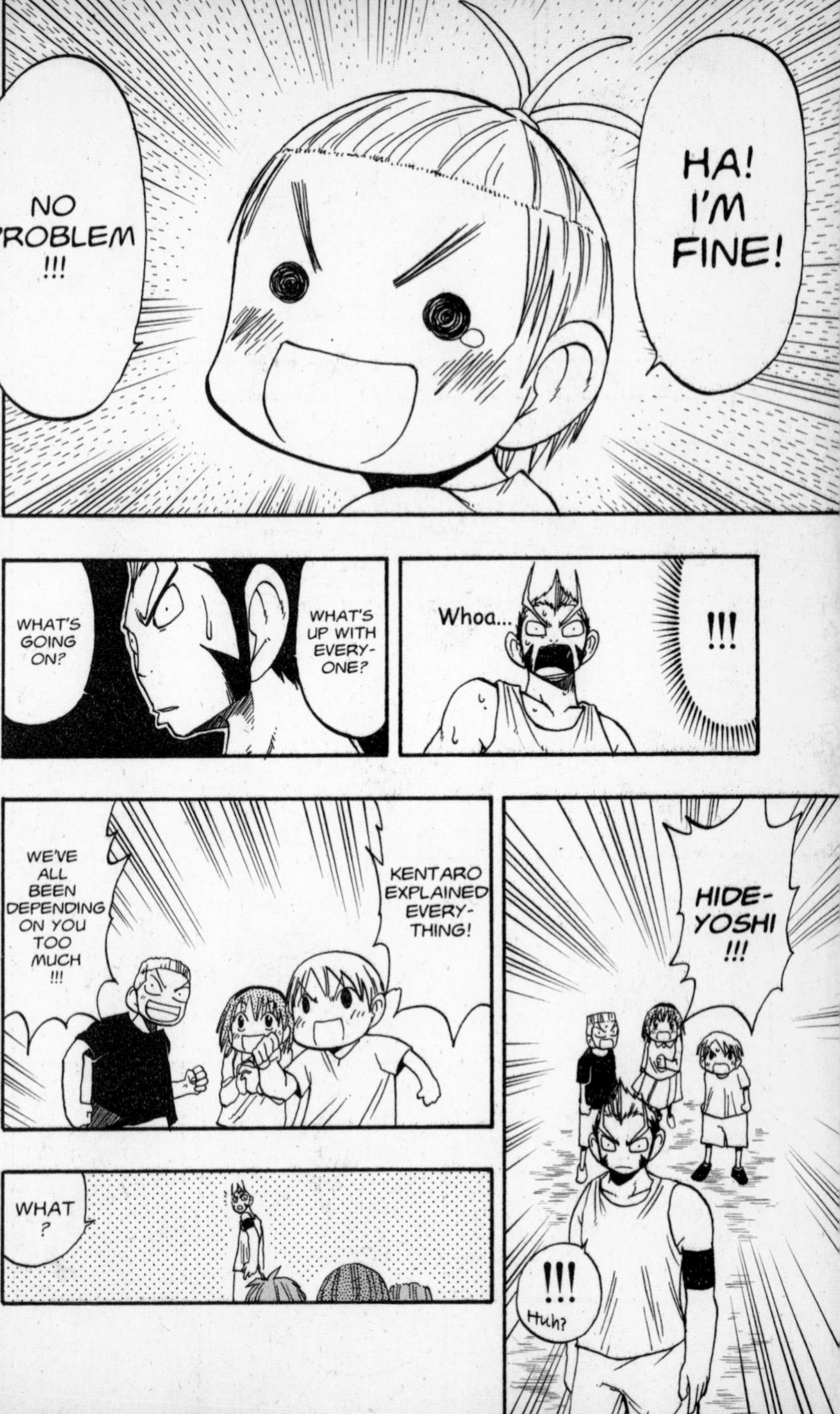
HA! I'M FINE!
NO PROBLEM!!!
!!!
Whoa...
WHAT'S UP WITH EVERY-ONE?
WHAT'S GOING ON?
HIDE-YOSHI!!!
!!!
Huh?
KENTARO EXPLAINED EVERY-THING!
WE'VE ALL BEEN DEPENDING ON YOU TOO MUCH!!!
WHAT?

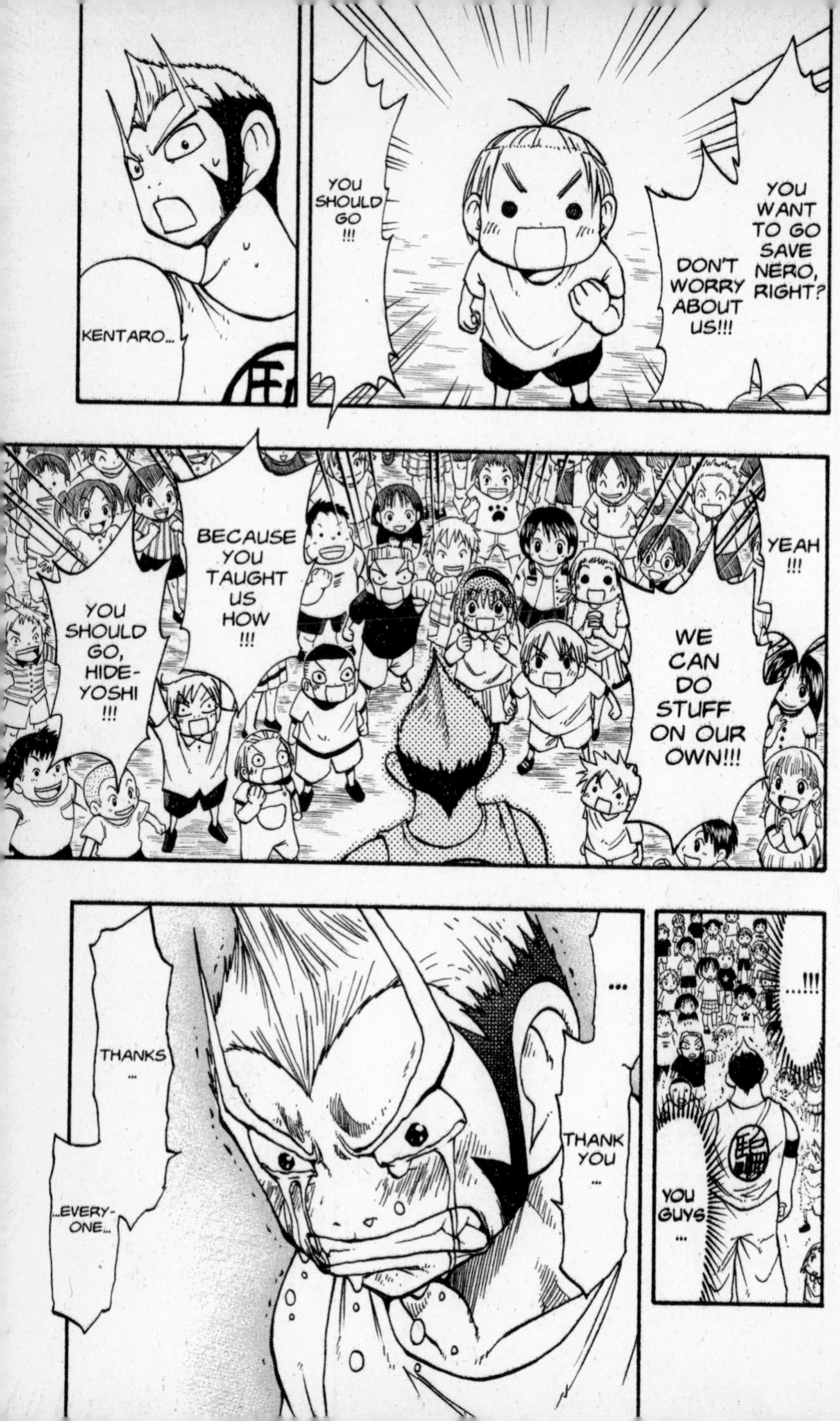
YOU WANT TO GO SAVE NERO, RIGHT?
DON'T WORRY ABOUT US!!!
YOU SHOULD GO !!!
KENTARO...
YEAH !!!
WE CAN DO STUFF ON OUR OWN!!!
BECAUSE YOU TAUGHT US HOW !!!
YOU SHOULD GO, HIDE-YOSHI !!!
...!!!
YOU GUYS ...
...
THANK YOU ...
THANKS ...
...EVERY-ONE...

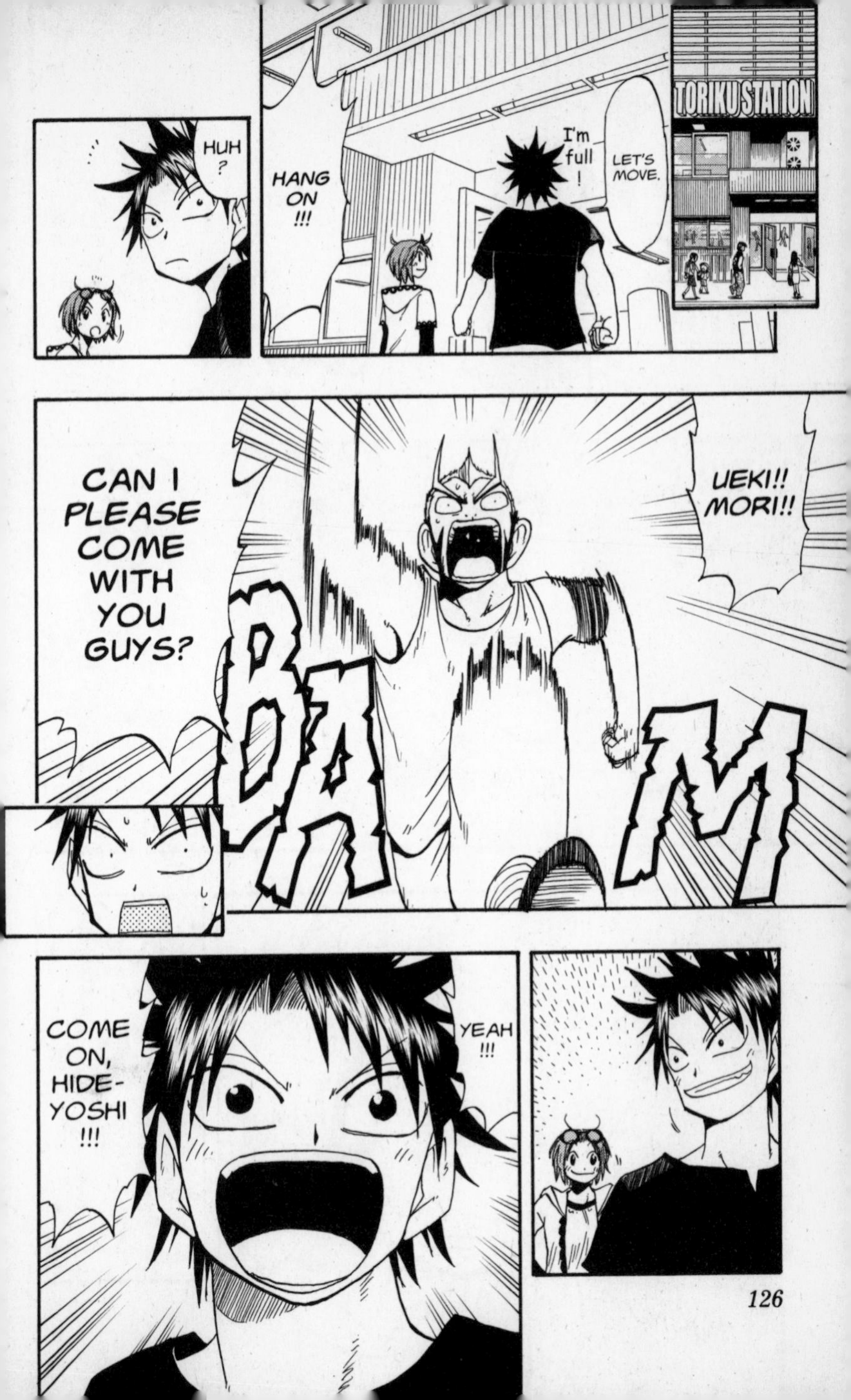
TORIKU STATION
I'm full !
LET'S MOVE.
HANG ON !!!
HUH ?
UEKI!! MORI!!
BAM
CAN I PLEASE COME WITH YOU GUYS?
YEAH !!!
COME ON, HIDE-YOSHI !!!

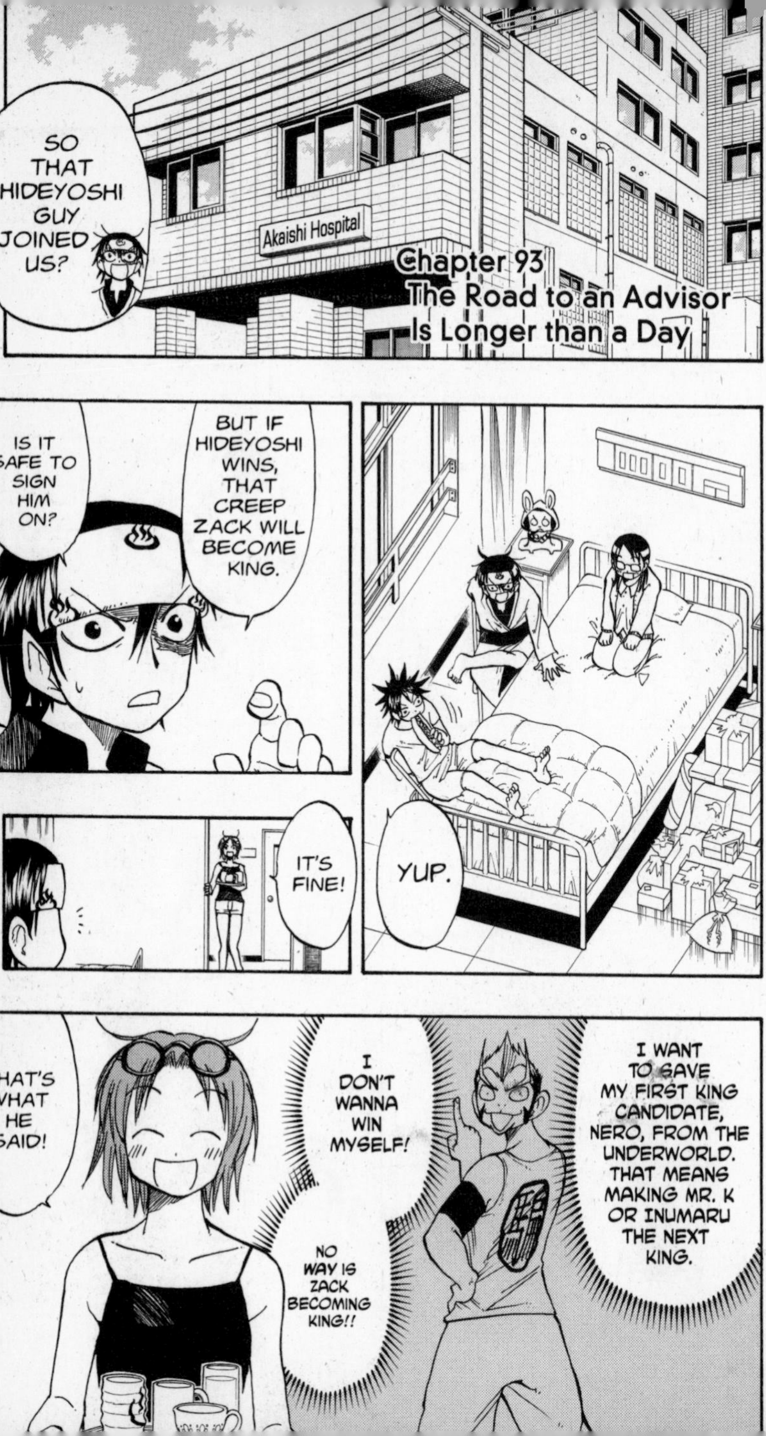
Chapter 93
The Road to an Advisor
Is Longer than a Day
Akaishi Hospital
SO THAT HIDEYOSHI GUY JOINED US?
YUP.
BUT IF HIDEYOSHI WINS, THAT CREEP ZACK WILL BECOME KING.
IS IT SAFE TO SIGN HIM ON?
IT'S FINE!
I WANT TO SAVE MY FIRST KING CANDIDATE, NERO, FROM THE UNDERWORLD. THAT MEANS MAKING MR. K OR INUMARU THE NEXT KING.
NO WAY IS ZACK BECOMING KING!!
I DON'T WANNA WIN MYSELF!
THAT'S WHAT HE SAID!

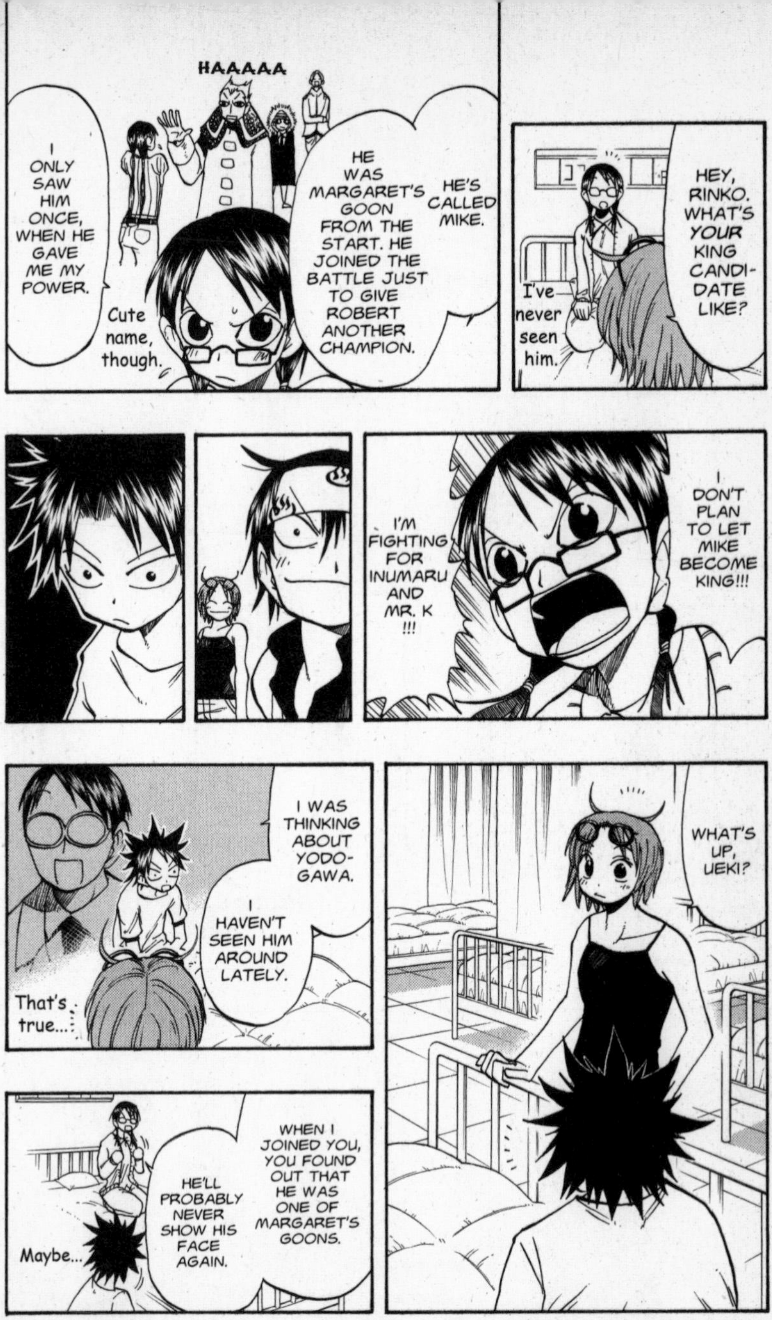
HEY, RINKO. WHAT'S YOUR KING CANDI-DATE LIKE?
I've never seen him.
HE'S CALLED MIKE.
HE WAS MARGARET'S GOON FROM THE START. HE JOINED THE BATTLE JUST TO GIVE ROBERT ANOTHER CHAMPION.
HAAAAA
I ONLY SAW HIM ONCE, WHEN HE GAVE ME MY POWER.
Cute name, though.
I DON'T PLAN TO LET MIKE BECOME KING!!!
I'M FIGHTING FOR INUMARU AND MR. K !!!
WHAT'S UP, UEKI?
I WAS THINKING ABOUT YODO-GAWA.
I HAVEN'T SEEN HIM AROUND LATELY.
That's true...
WHEN I JOINED YOU, YOU FOUND OUT THAT HE WAS ONE OF MARGARET'S GOONS.
HE'LL PROBABLY NEVER SHOW HIS FACE AGAIN.
Maybe...

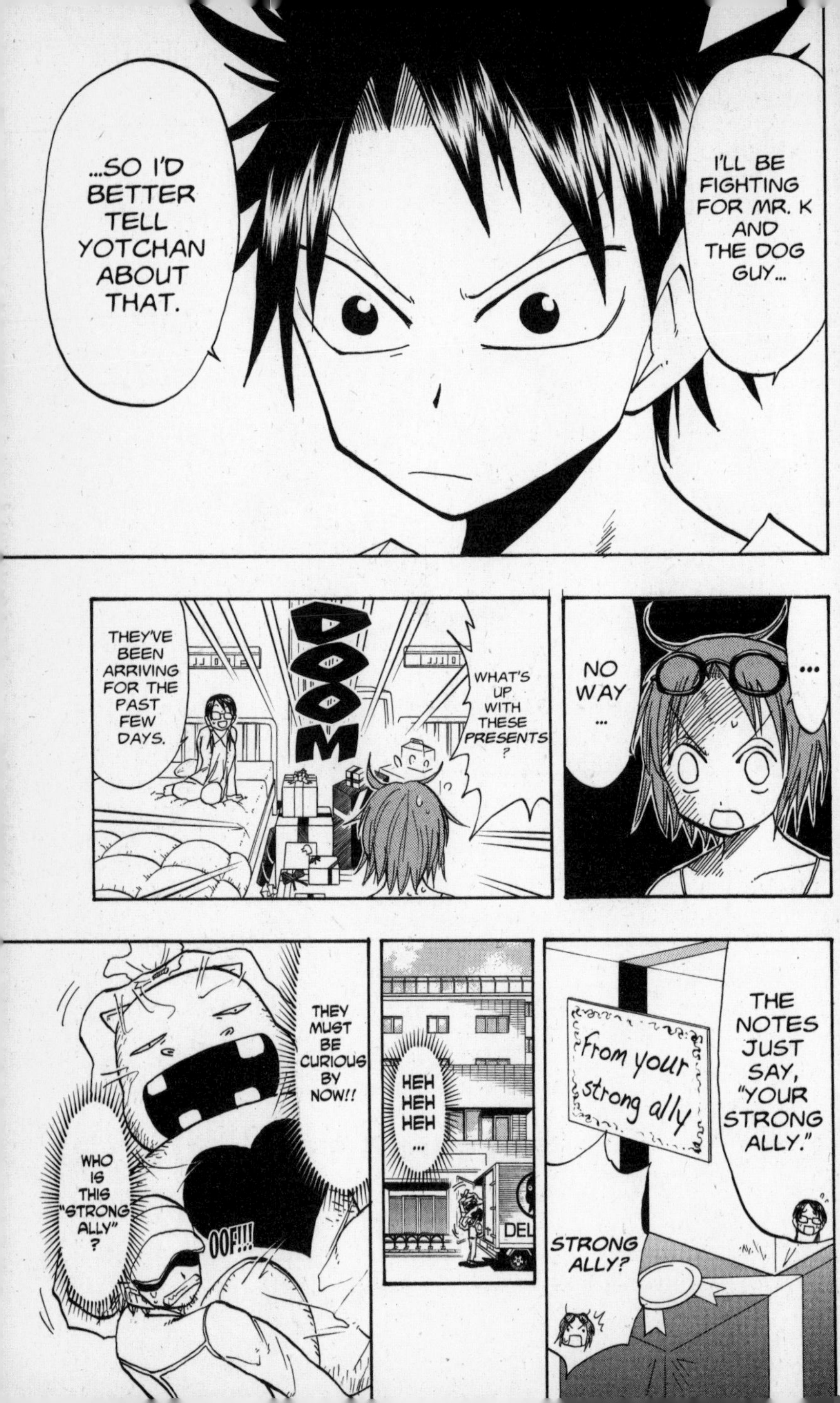
I'LL BE FIGHTING FOR MR. K AND THE DOG GUY...
...SO I'D BETTER TELL YOTCHAN ABOUT THAT.
NO WAY...
...
WHAT'S UP WITH THESE PRESENTS?
DOOM
THEY'VE BEEN ARRIVING FOR THE PAST FEW DAYS.
THE NOTES JUST SAY, "YOUR STRONG ALLY."
From your strong ally
STRONG ALLY?
HEH HEH HEH...
DEL
THEY MUST BE CURIOUS BY NOW!!
WHO IS THIS "STRONG ALLY"?
OOF!!!

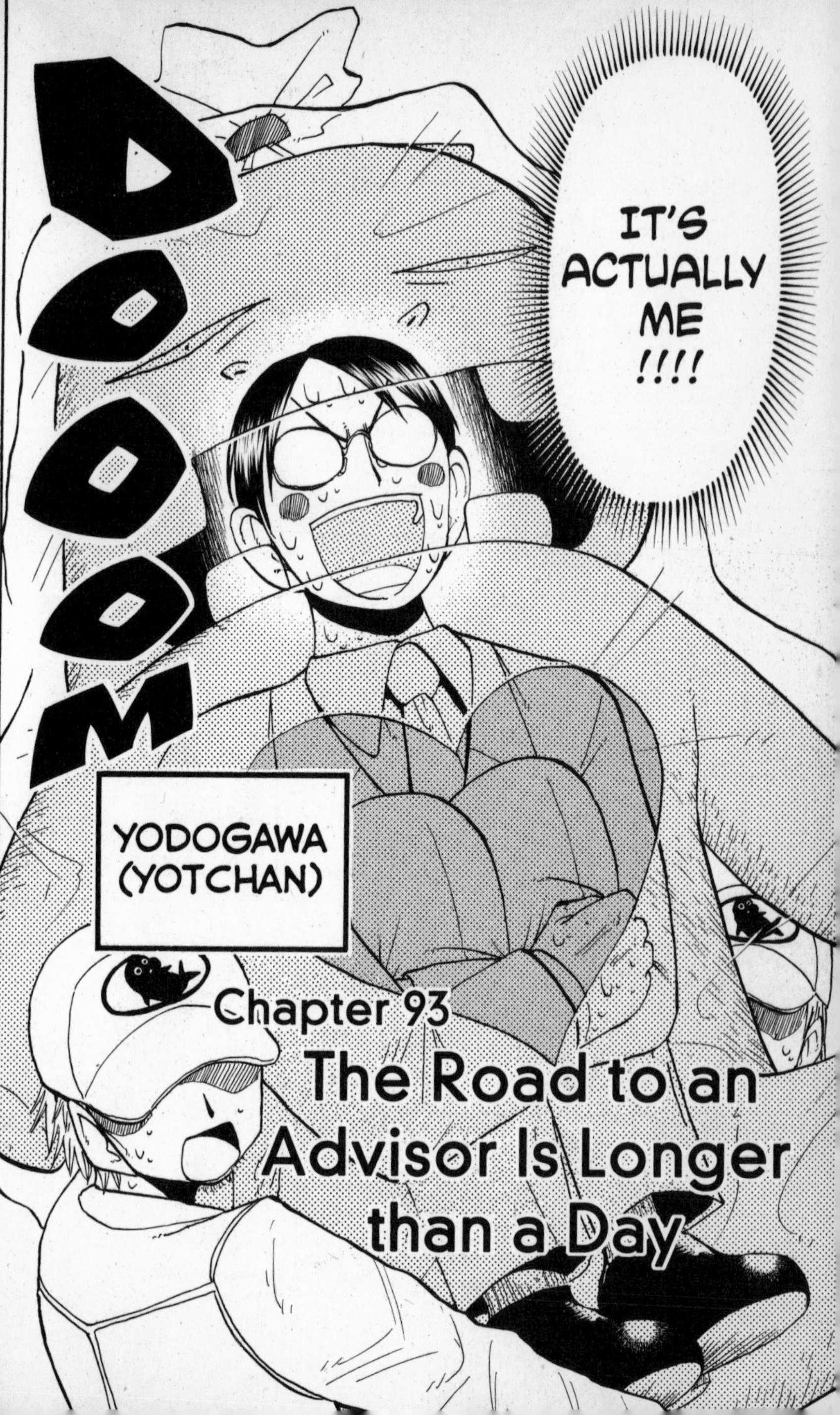
IT'S ACTUALLY ME !!!!
DOOOM
YODOGAWA (YOTCHAN)
Chapter 93
The Road to an Advisor Is Longer than a Day

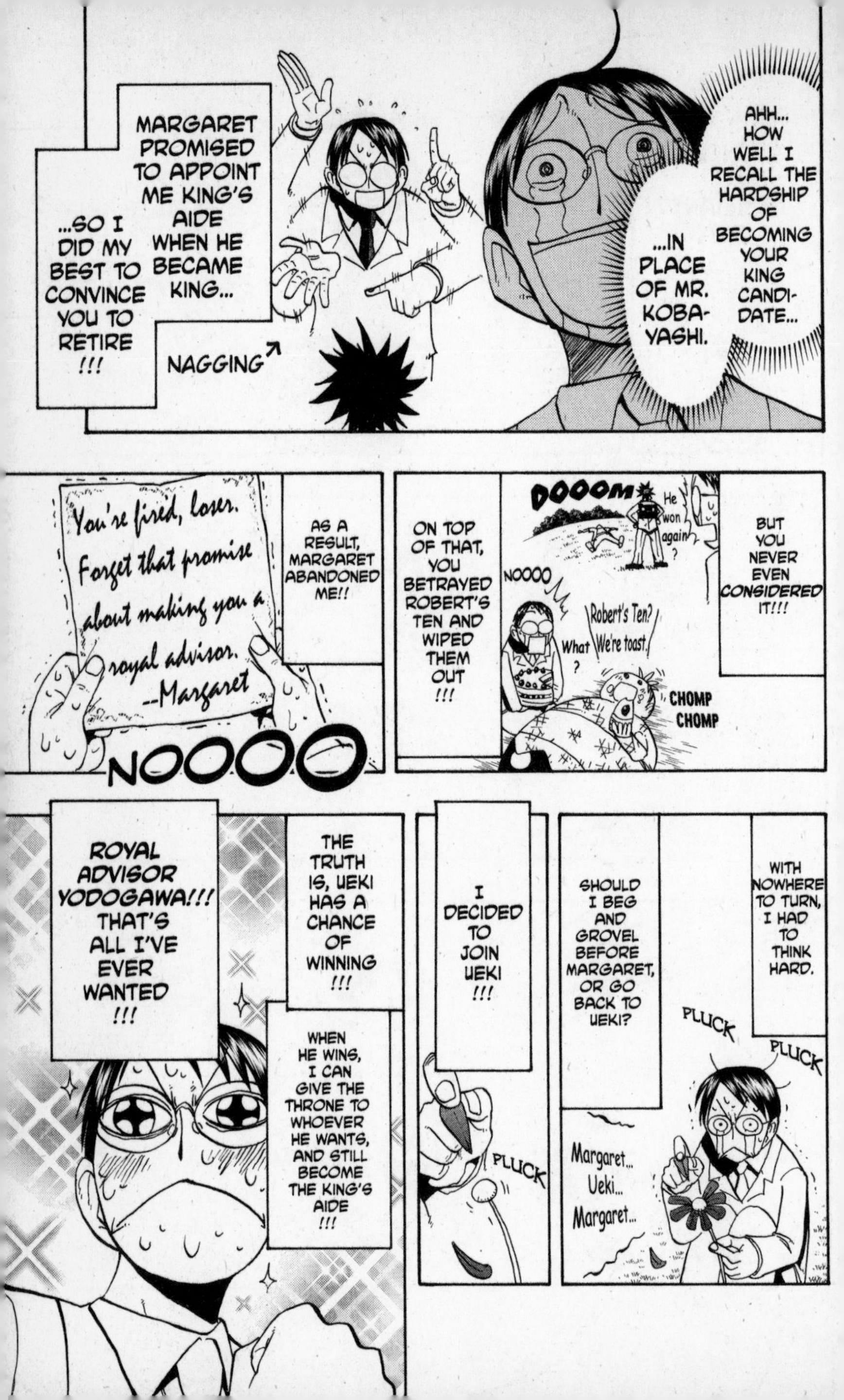
AHH... HOW WELL I RECALL THE HARDSHIP OF BECOMING YOUR KING CANDIDATE...
...IN PLACE OF MR. KOBAYASHI.
MARGARET PROMISED TO APPOINT ME KING'S AIDE WHEN HE BECAME KING...
...SO I DID MY BEST TO CONVINCE YOU TO RETIRE!!!
NAGGING
BUT YOU NEVER EVEN CONSIDERED IT!!!
DOOOM
He won again?
ON TOP OF THAT, YOU BETRAYED ROBERT'S TEN AND WIPED THEM OUT!!!
NOOOO
Robert's Ten?
We're toast.
What?
CHOMP CHOMP
AS A RESULT, MARGARET ABANDONED ME!!
You're fired, loser. Forget that promise about making you a royal advisor. --Margaret
NOOOO
WITH NOWHERE TO TURN, I HAD TO THINK HARD.
SHOULD I BEG AND GROVEL BEFORE MARGARET, OR GO BACK TO UEKI?
PLUCK
PLUCK
Margaret... Ueki... Margaret...
I DECIDED TO JOIN UEKI!!!
PLUCK
THE TRUTH IS, UEKI HAS A CHANCE OF WINNING!!!
WHEN HE WINS, I CAN GIVE THE THRONE TO WHOEVER HE WANTS, AND STILL BECOME THE KING'S AIDE!!!
ROYAL ADVISOR YODOGAWA!!! THAT'S ALL I'VE EVER WANTED!!!

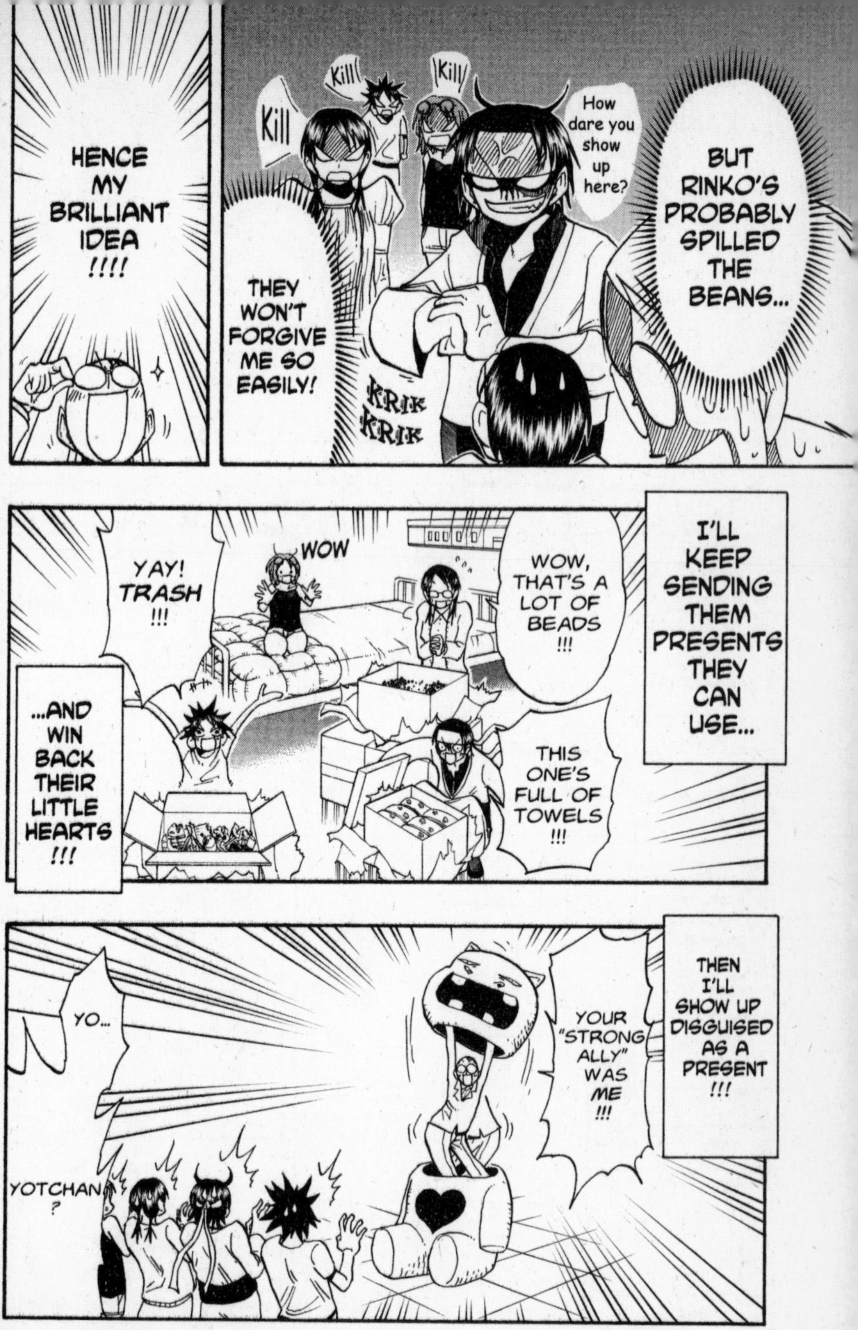
BUT RINKO'S PROBABLY SPILLED THE BEANS...
How dare you show up here?
Kill
Kill
Kill
THEY WON'T FORGIVE ME SO EASILY!
KRIK KRIK
HENCE MY BRILLIANT IDEA !!!!
I'LL KEEP SENDING THEM PRESENTS THEY CAN USE...
WOW, THAT'S A LOT OF BEADS !!!
THIS ONE'S FULL OF TOWELS !!!
WOW
YAY! TRASH !!!
...AND WIN BACK THEIR LITTLE HEARTS !!!
THEN I'LL SHOW UP DISGUISED AS A PRESENT !!!
YOUR "STRONG ALLY" WAS ME !!!
YO...
YOTCHAN ?

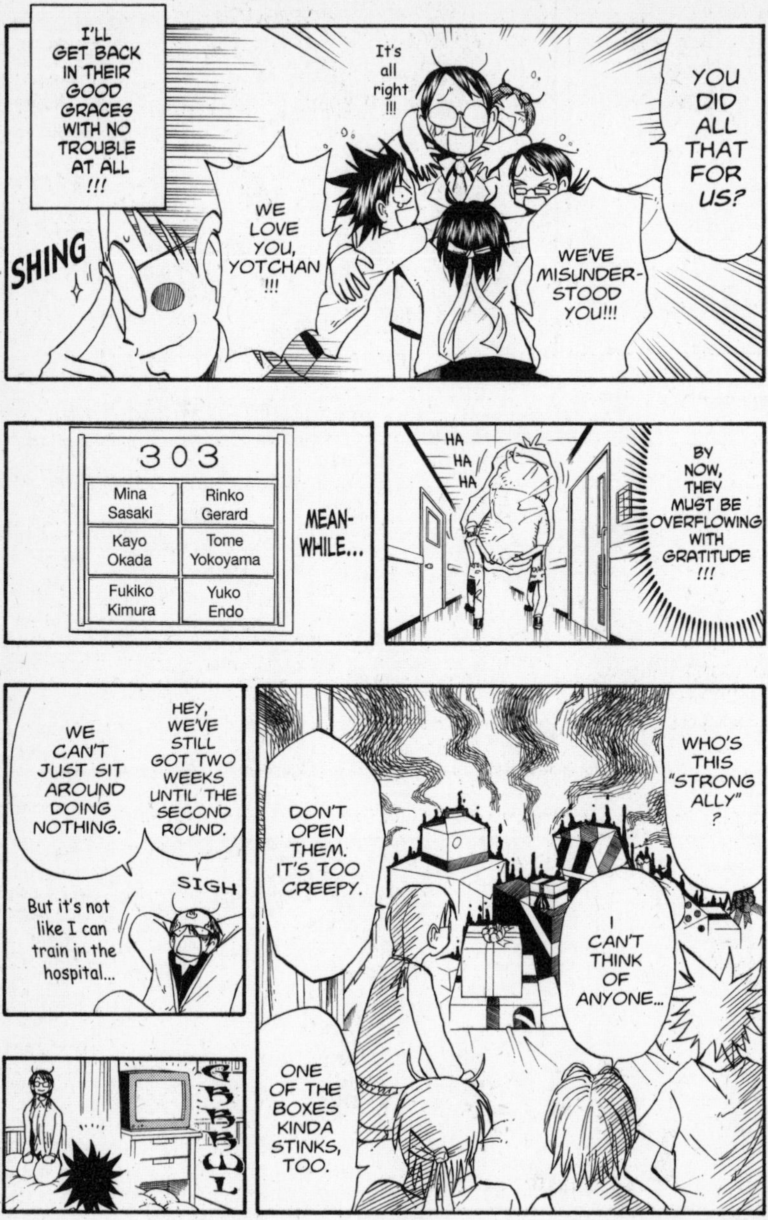
YOU DID ALL THAT FOR US?
WE'VE MISUNDER-STOOD YOU!!!
It's all right !!!
WE LOVE YOU, YOTCHAN !!!
I'LL GET BACK IN THEIR GOOD GRACES WITH NO TROUBLE AT ALL !!!
SHING
BY NOW, THEY MUST BE OVERFLOWING WITH GRATITUDE !!!
HA HA HA
MEAN-WHILE...
303
Mina Sasaki
Rinko Gerard
Kayo Okada
Tome Yokoyama
Fukiko Kimura
Yuko Endo
WHO'S THIS "STRONG ALLY" ?
I CAN'T THINK OF ANYONE...
DON'T OPEN THEM. IT'S TOO CREEPY.
ONE OF THE BOXES KINDA STINKS, TOO.
HEY, WE'VE STILL GOT TWO WEEKS UNTIL THE SECOND ROUND.
WE CAN'T JUST SIT AROUND DOING NOTHING.
SIGH
But it's not like I can train in the hospital...
GRRRWL

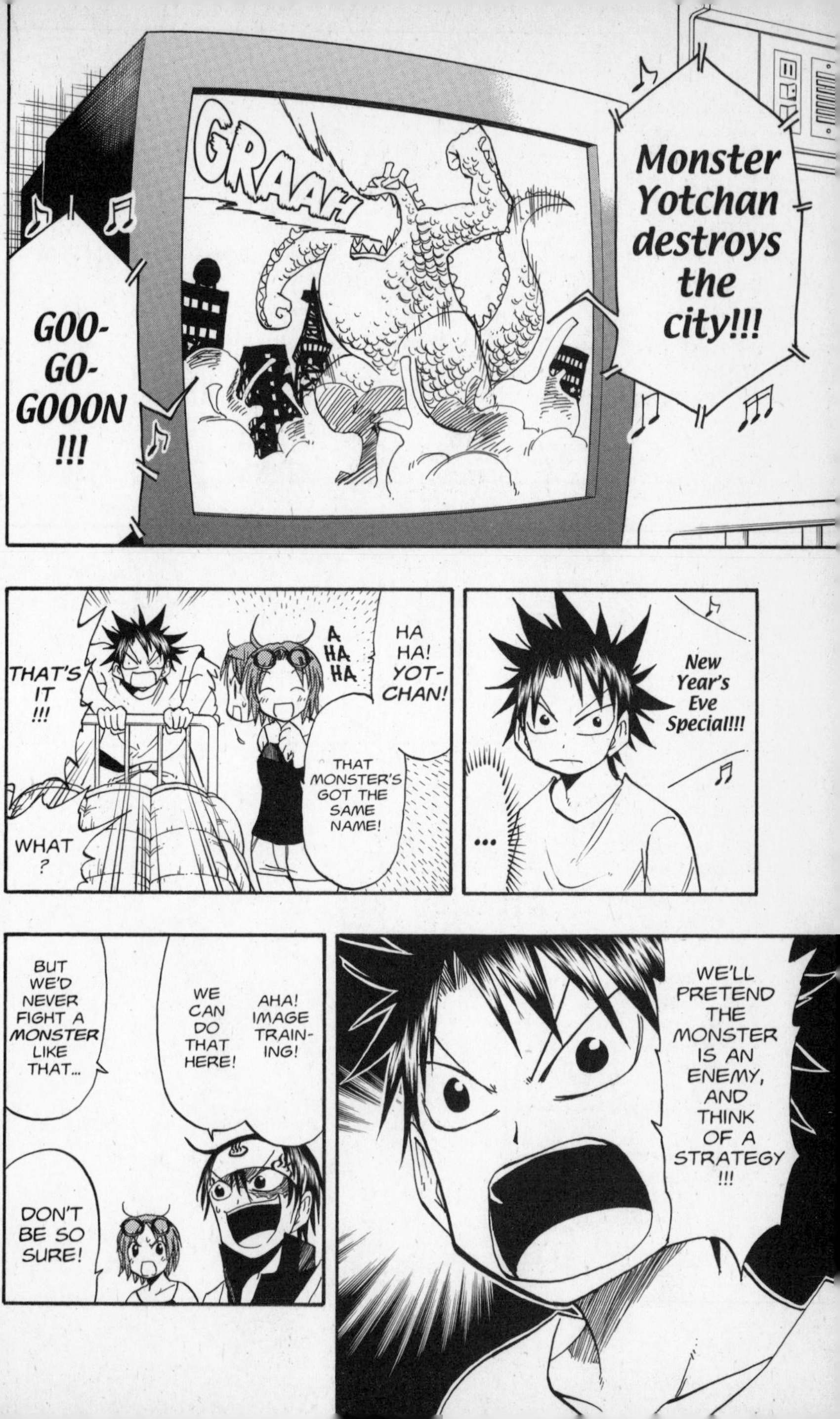
Monster Yotchan destroys the city!!!
GRAAAH
GOO-GO-GOOON!!!
New Year's Eve Special!!!
...
HA HA! YOT-CHAN!
A HA HA
THAT MONSTER'S GOT THE SAME NAME!
THAT'S IT!!!
WHAT?
WE'LL PRETEND THE MONSTER IS AN ENEMY, AND THINK OF A STRATEGY!!!
AHA! IMAGE TRAINING!
WE CAN DO THAT HERE!
BUT WE'D NEVER FIGHT A MONSTER LIKE THAT...
DON'T BE SO SURE!

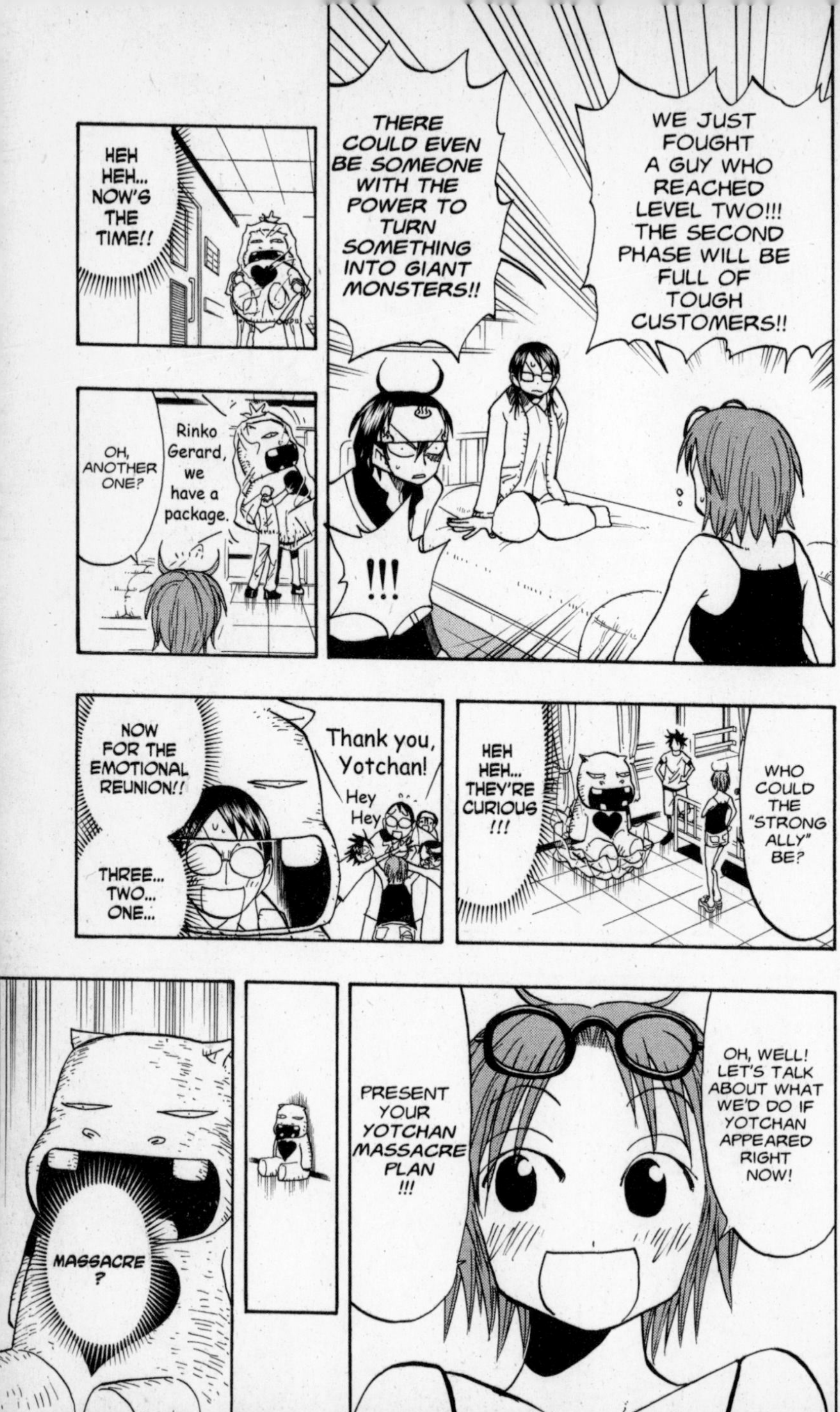
WE JUST FOUGHT A GUY WHO REACHED LEVEL TWO!!! THE SECOND PHASE WILL BE FULL OF TOUGH CUSTOMERS!!
THERE COULD EVEN BE SOMEONE WITH THE POWER TO TURN SOMETHING INTO GIANT MONSTERS!!
!!!
HEH HEH... NOW'S THE TIME!!
Rinko Gerard, we have a package.
OH, ANOTHER ONE?
WHO COULD THE "STRONG ALLY" BE?
HEH HEH... THEY'RE CURIOUS!!!
Thank you, Yotchan!
NOW FOR THE EMOTIONAL REUNION!!
Hey Hey
THREE... TWO... ONE...
OH, WELL! LET'S TALK ABOUT WHAT WE'D DO IF YOTCHAN APPEARED RIGHT NOW!
PRESENT YOUR YOTCHAN MASSACRE PLAN!!!
MASSACRE ?

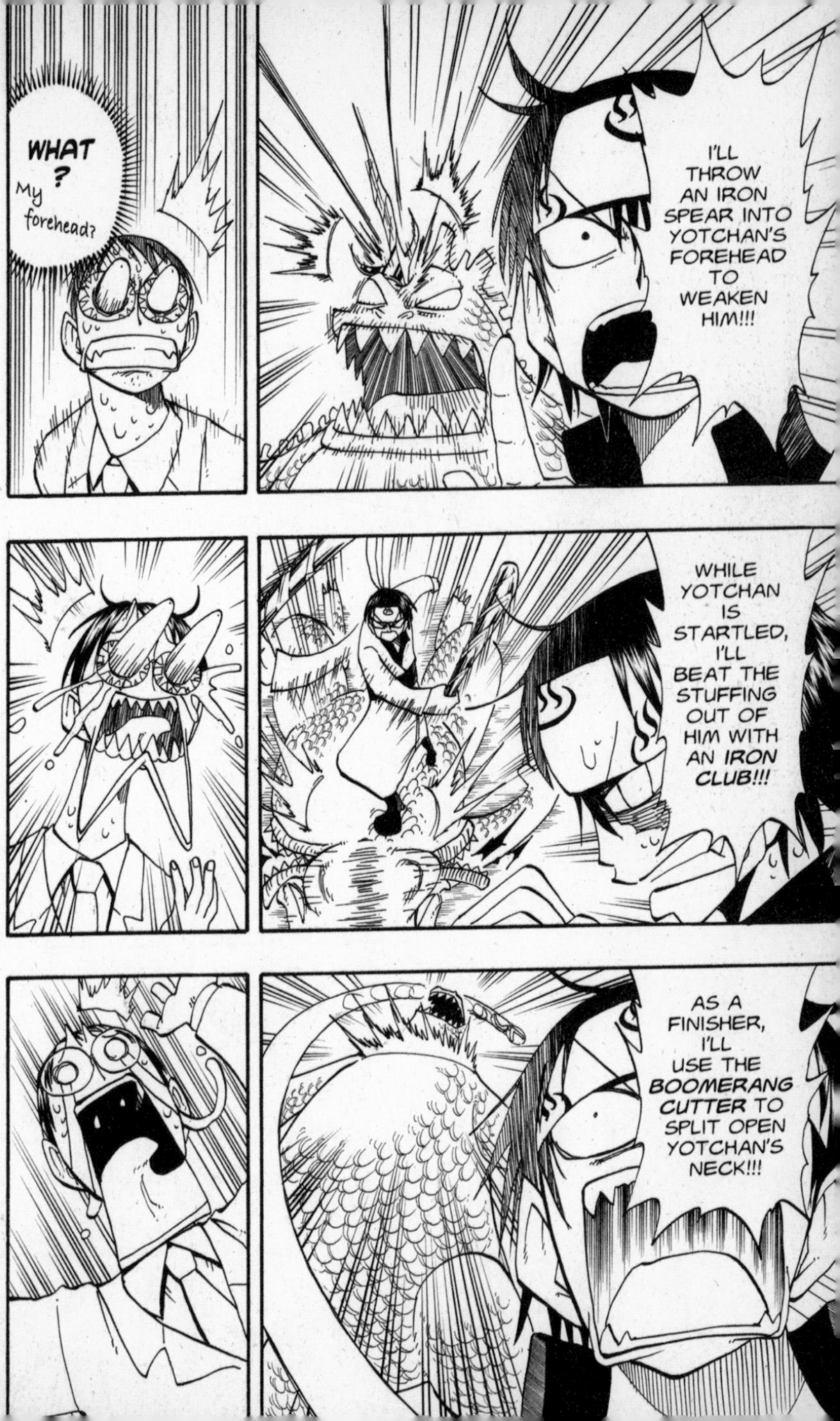
I'LL THROW AN IRON SPEAR INTO YOTCHAN'S FOREHEAD TO WEAKEN HIM!!!
WHAT?
My forehead?
WHILE YOTCHAN IS STARTLED, I'LL BEAT THE STUFFING OUT OF HIM WITH AN IRON CLUB!!!
AS A FINISHER, I'LL USE THE BOOMERANG CUTTER TO SPLIT OPEN YOTCHAN'S NECK!!!

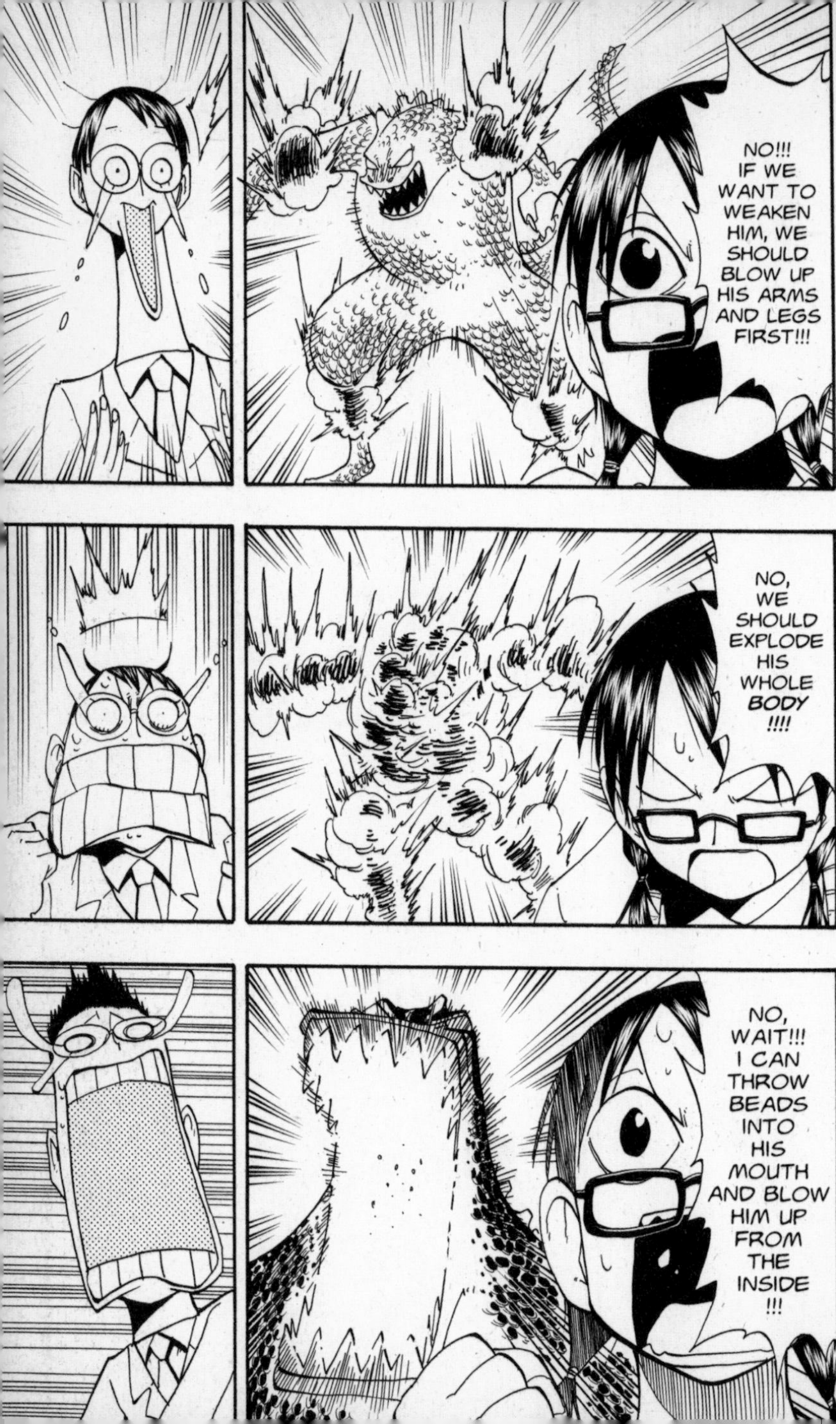
NO!!! IF WE WANT TO WEAKEN HIM, WE SHOULD BLOW UP HIS ARMS AND LEGS FIRST!!!
NO, WE SHOULD EXPLODE HIS WHOLE *BODY* !!!!
NO, WAIT!!! I CAN THROW BEADS INTO HIS MOUTH AND BLOW HIM UP FROM THE INSIDE !!!

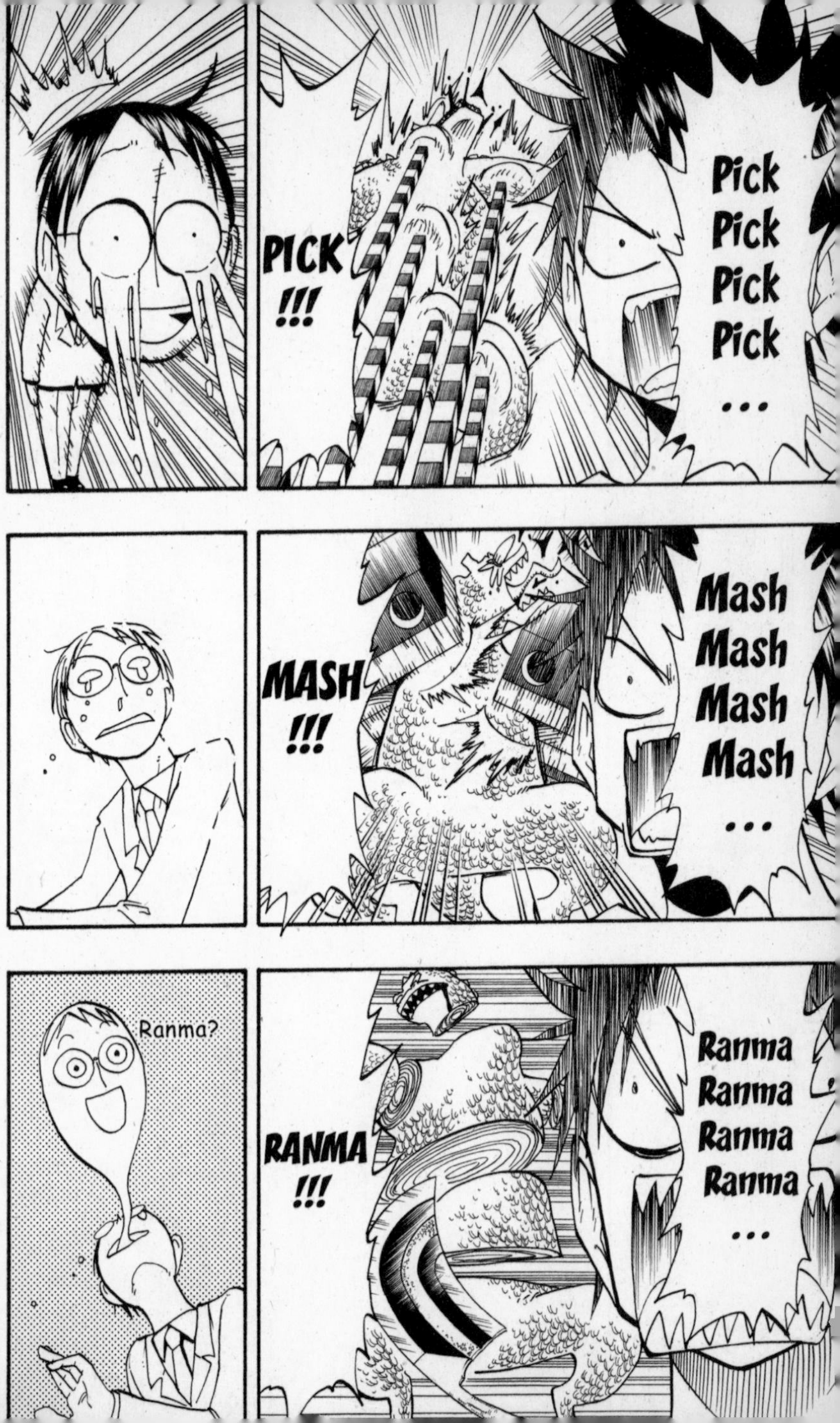
Pick Pick Pick Pick ...
PICK !!!
Mash Mash Mash Mash ...
MASH !!!
Ranma Ranma Ranma Ranma ...
RANMA !!!
Ranma?

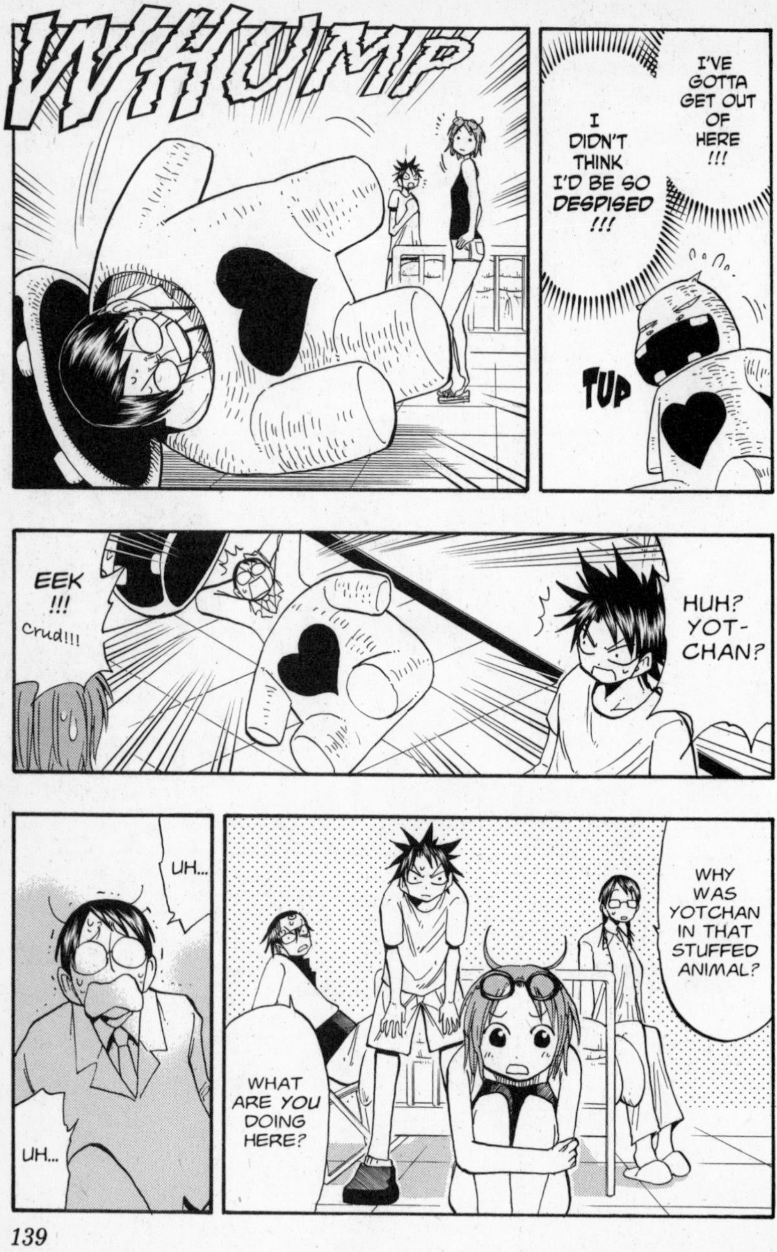
I'VE GOTTA GET OUT OF HERE !!!
I DIDN'T THINK I'D BE SO DESPISED !!!
TUP
WHUMP
HUH? YOT-CHAN?
EEK !!!
Crud!!!
WHY WAS YOTCHAN IN THAT STUFFED ANIMAL?
WHAT ARE YOU DOING HERE?
UH...
UH...

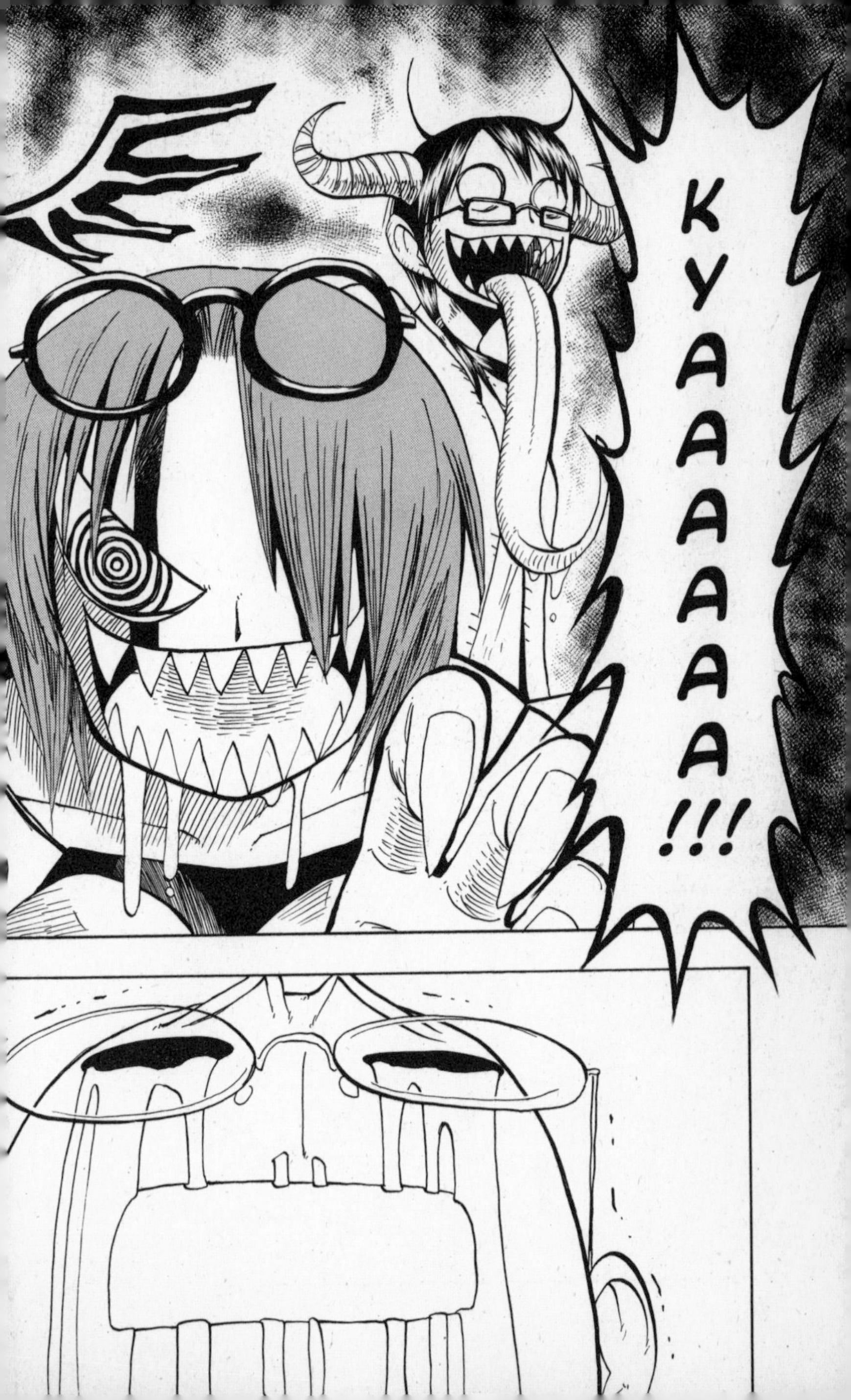
KYAAAAAAA!!!

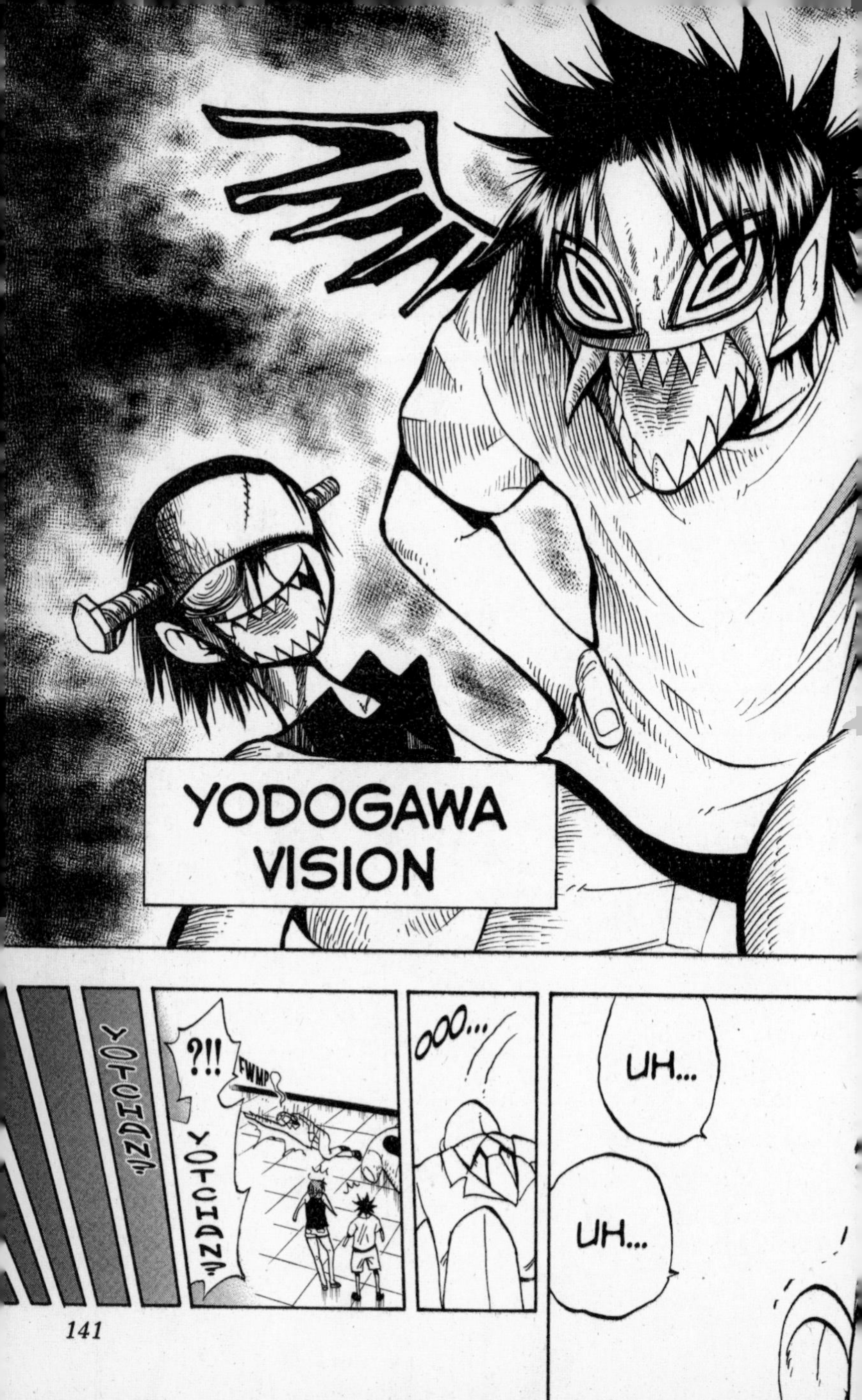
YODOGAWA VISION
UH...
UH...
OOO...
YOTCHAN!
?!!
FWMP
YOTCHAN!

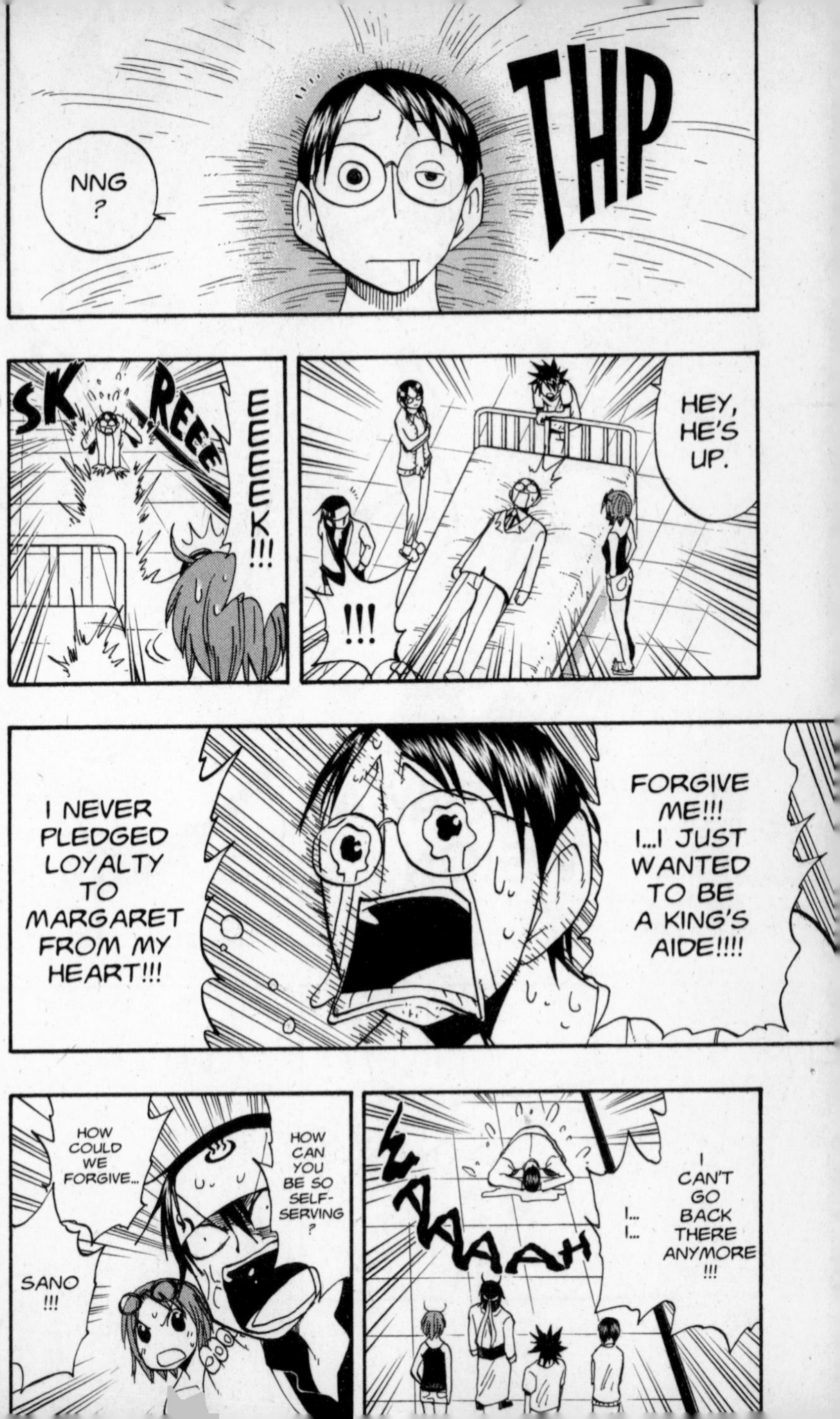
THP
NNG ?
HEY, HE'S UP.
!!!
EEEEEK!!!
SK REEE
FORGIVE ME!!! I...I JUST WANTED TO BE A KING'S AIDE!!!!
I NEVER PLEDGED LOYALTY TO MARGARET FROM MY HEART!!!
I CAN'T GO BACK THERE ANYMORE !!!
I... I...
WAAAAH
HOW CAN YOU BE SO SELF-SERVING ?
HOW COULD WE FORGIVE...
SANO !!!

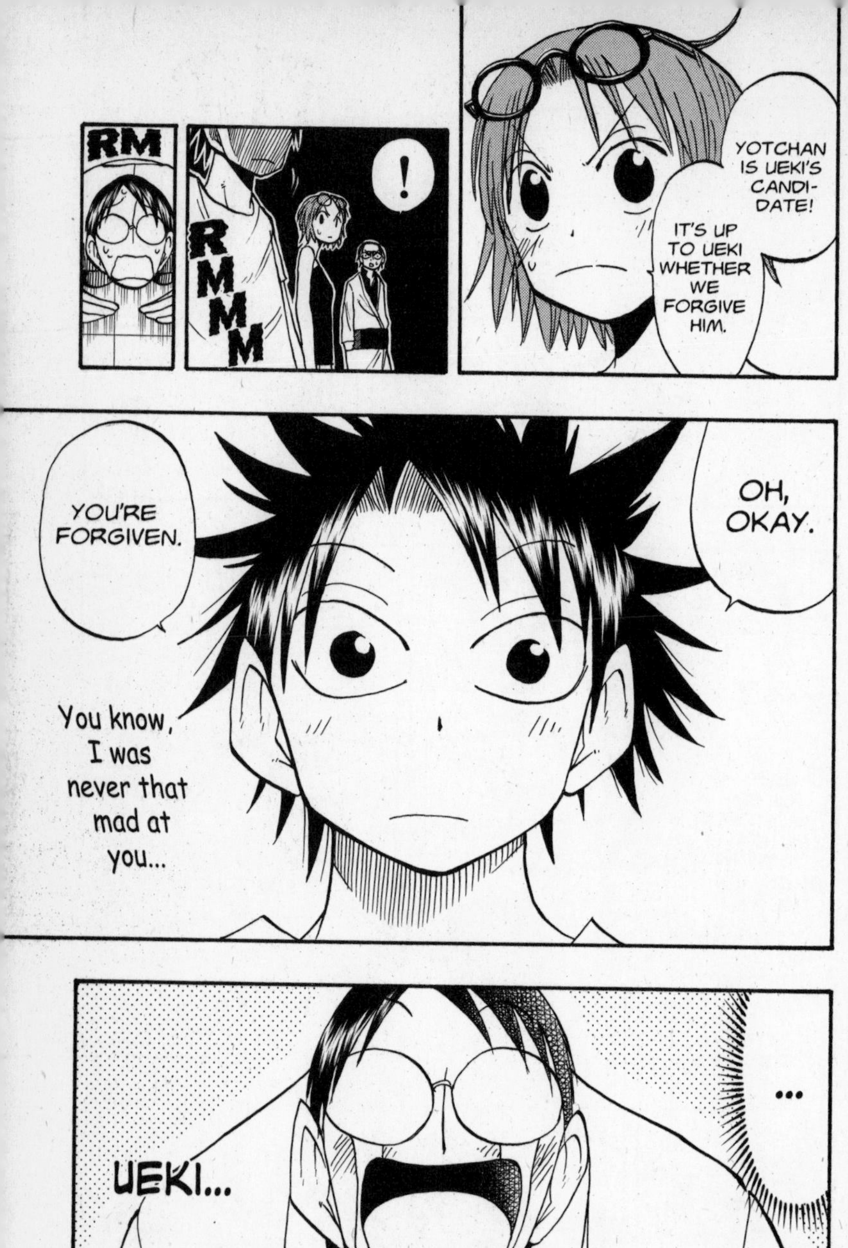
YOTCHAN IS UEKI'S CANDI-DATE!
IT'S UP TO UEKI WHETHER WE FORGIVE HIM.
!
RMMM
RM
OH, OKAY.
YOU'RE FORGIVEN.
You know, I was never that mad at you...
...
UEKI...

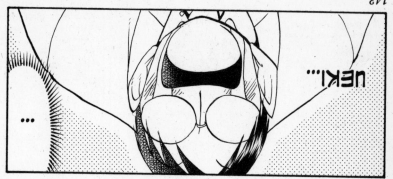

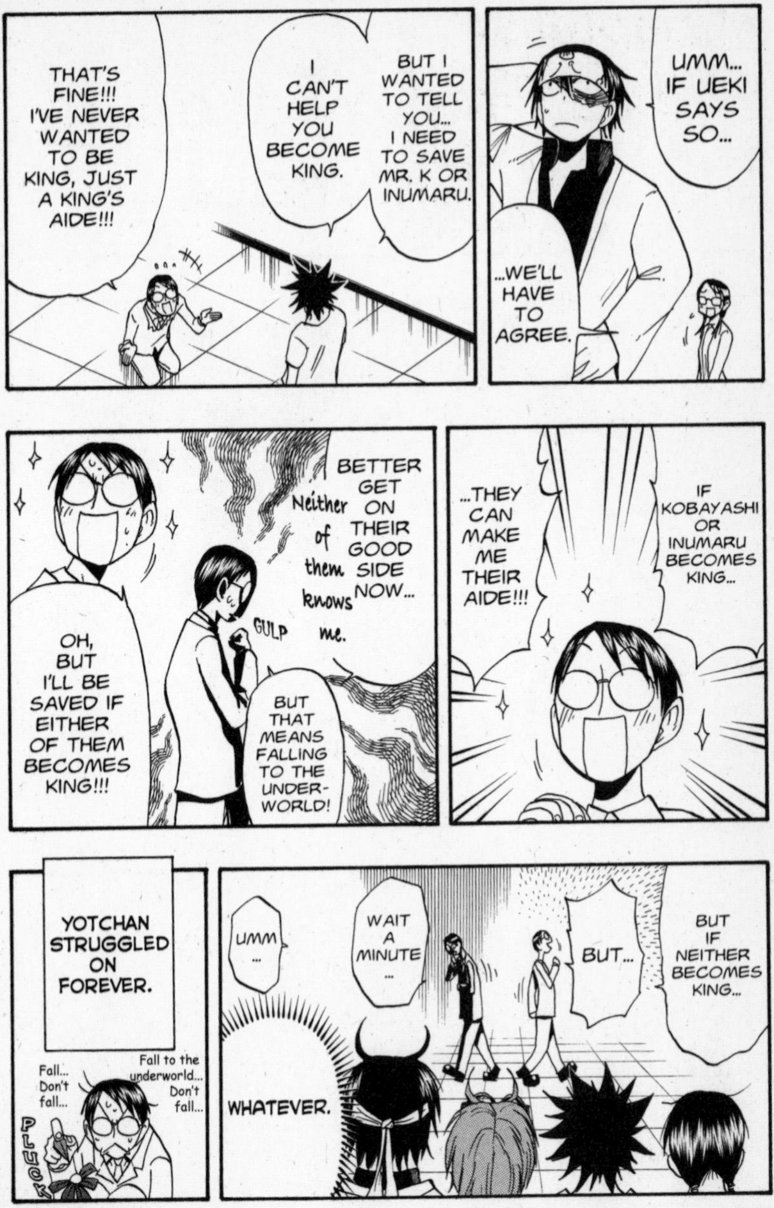
UMM... IF UEKI SAYS SO...
...WE'LL HAVE TO AGREE.
BUT I WANTED TO TELL YOU... I NEED TO SAVE MR. K OR INUMARU.
I CAN'T HELP YOU BECOME KING.
THAT'S FINE!!! I'VE NEVER WANTED TO BE KING, JUST A KING'S AIDE!!!
IF KOBAYASHI OR INUMARU BECOMES KING...
...THEY CAN MAKE ME THEIR AIDE!!!
BETTER GET ON THEIR GOOD SIDE NOW...
Neither of them knows me.
GULP
BUT THAT MEANS FALLING TO THE UNDER-WORLD!
OH, BUT I'LL BE SAVED IF EITHER OF THEM BECOMES KING!!!
BUT IF NEITHER BECOMES KING...
BUT...
WAIT A MINUTE ...
UMM ...
WHATEVER.
YOTCHAN STRUGGLED ON FOREVER.
Fall to the underworld... Don't fall...
Fall... Don't fall...
PLUCK

Chapter 94
The Final Awakening Chamber

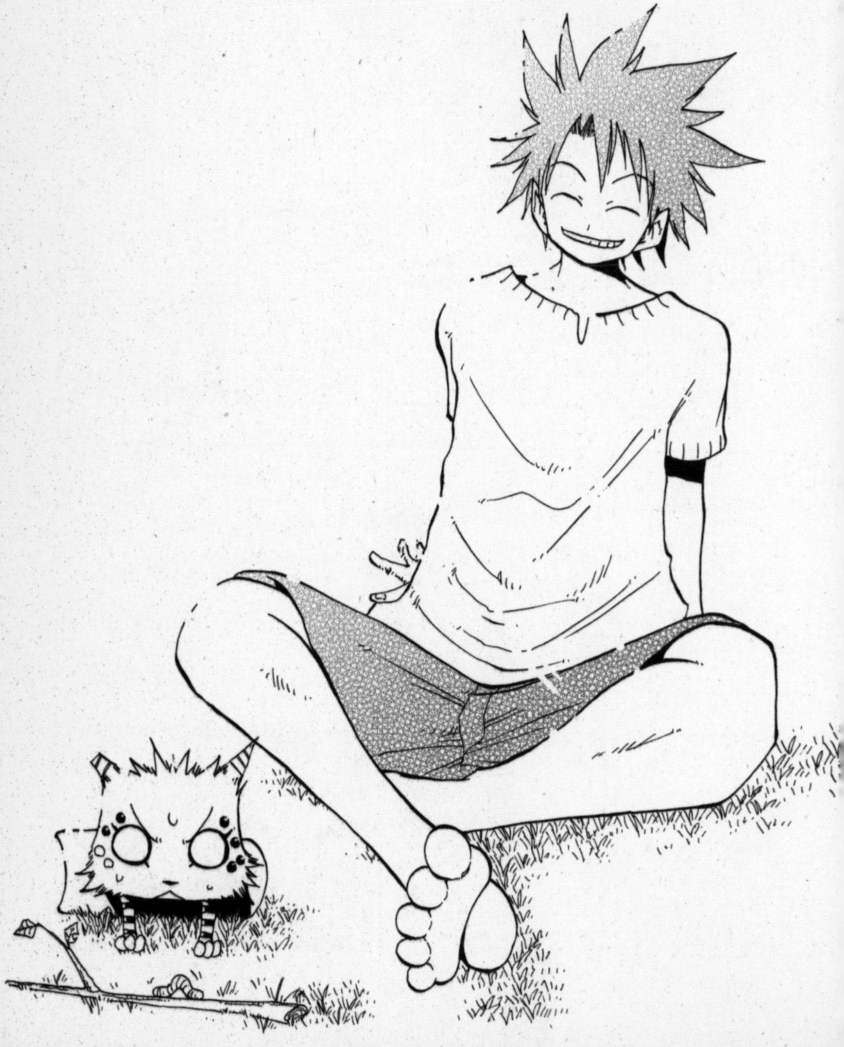

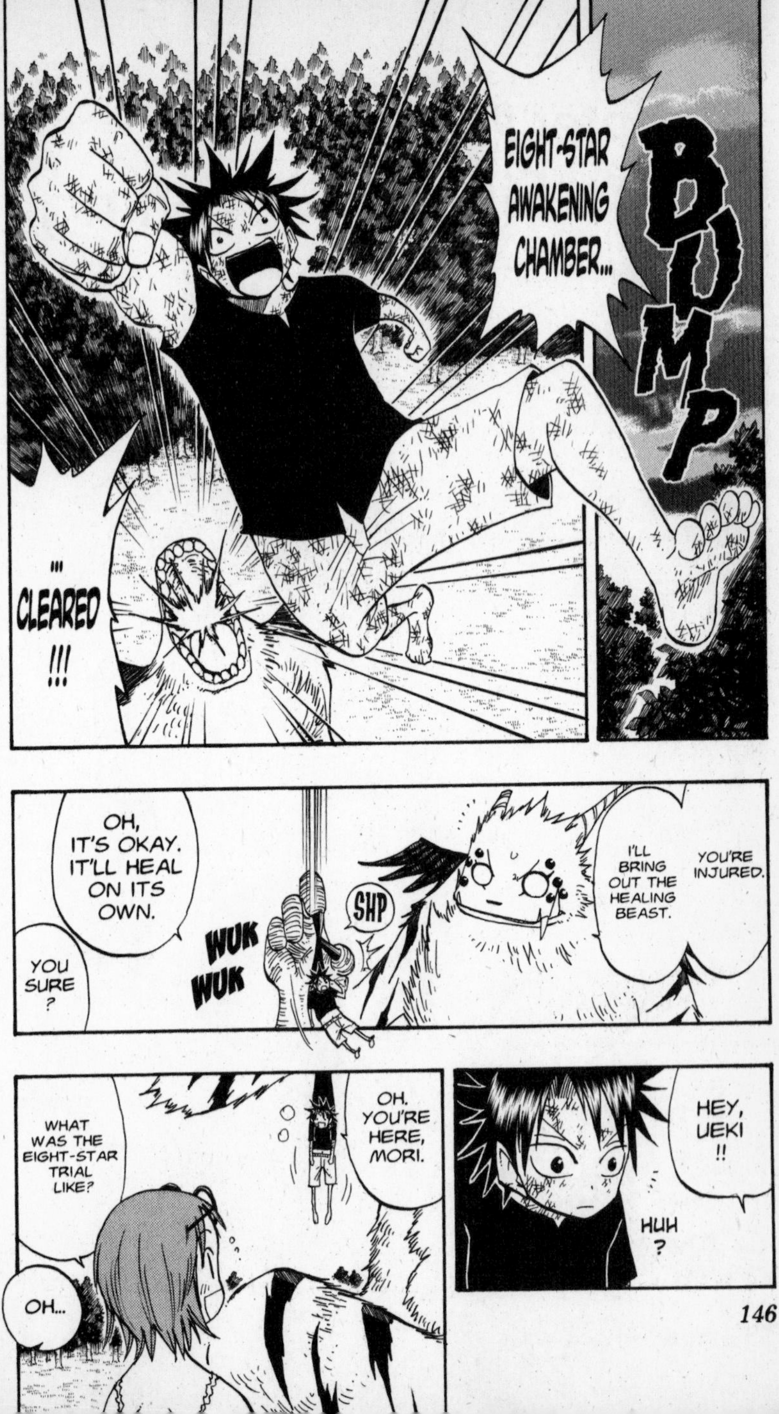
BUMP
EIGHT-STAR AWAKENING CHAMBER...
...CLEARED !!!
YOU'RE INJURED.
I'LL BRING OUT THE HEALING BEAST.
SHP
OH, IT'S OKAY. IT'LL HEAL ON ITS OWN.
WUK WUK
YOU SURE ?
HEY, UEKI !!
HUH ?
OH. YOU'RE HERE, MORI.
WHAT WAS THE EIGHT-STAR TRIAL LIKE?
OH...

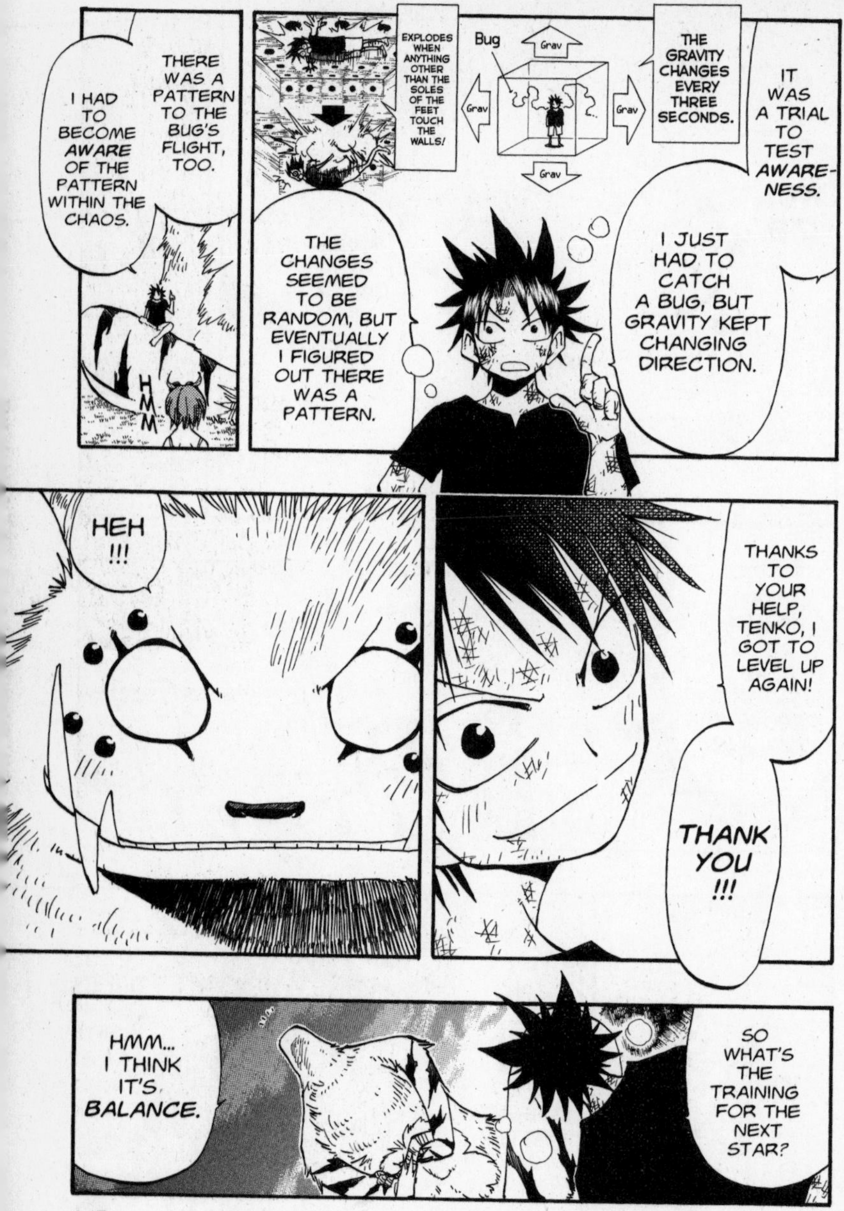
IT WAS A TRIAL TO TEST AWARENESS.
THE GRAVITY CHANGES EVERY THREE SECONDS.
Bug
Grav
Grav
Grav
Grav
EXPLODES WHEN ANYTHING OTHER THAN THE SOLES OF THE FEET TOUCH THE WALLS!
I JUST HAD TO CATCH A BUG, BUT GRAVITY KEPT CHANGING DIRECTION.
THE CHANGES SEEMED TO BE RANDOM, BUT EVENTUALLY I FIGURED OUT THERE WAS A PATTERN.
THERE WAS A PATTERN TO THE BUG'S FLIGHT, TOO.
I HAD TO BECOME AWARE OF THE PATTERN WITHIN THE CHAOS.
HMM
THANKS TO YOUR HELP, TENKO, I GOT TO LEVEL UP AGAIN!
THANK YOU !!!
HEH !!!
SO WHAT'S THE TRAINING FOR THE NEXT STAR?
HMM... I THINK IT'S BALANCE.

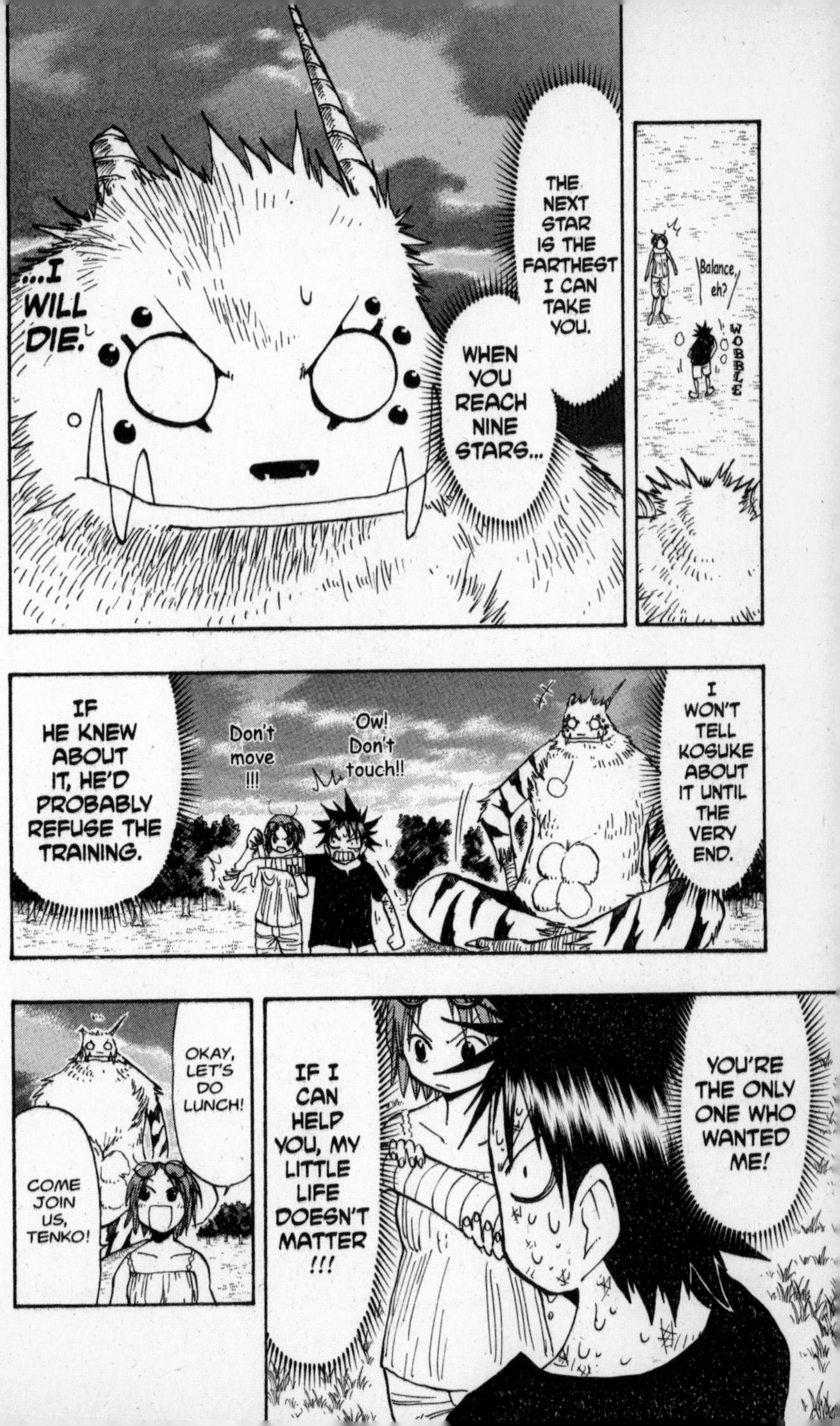
Balance, eh?
WOBBLE
THE NEXT STAR IS THE FARTHEST I CAN TAKE YOU.
WHEN YOU REACH NINE STARS...
...I WILL DIE.
I WON'T TELL KOSUKE ABOUT IT UNTIL THE VERY END.
Ow! Don't touch!!
Don't move !!!
IF HE KNEW ABOUT IT, HE'D PROBABLY REFUSE THE TRAINING.
YOU'RE THE ONLY ONE WHO WANTED ME!
IF I CAN HELP YOU, MY LITTLE LIFE DOESN'T MATTER !!!
OKAY, LET'S DO LUNCH!
COME JOIN US, TENKO!

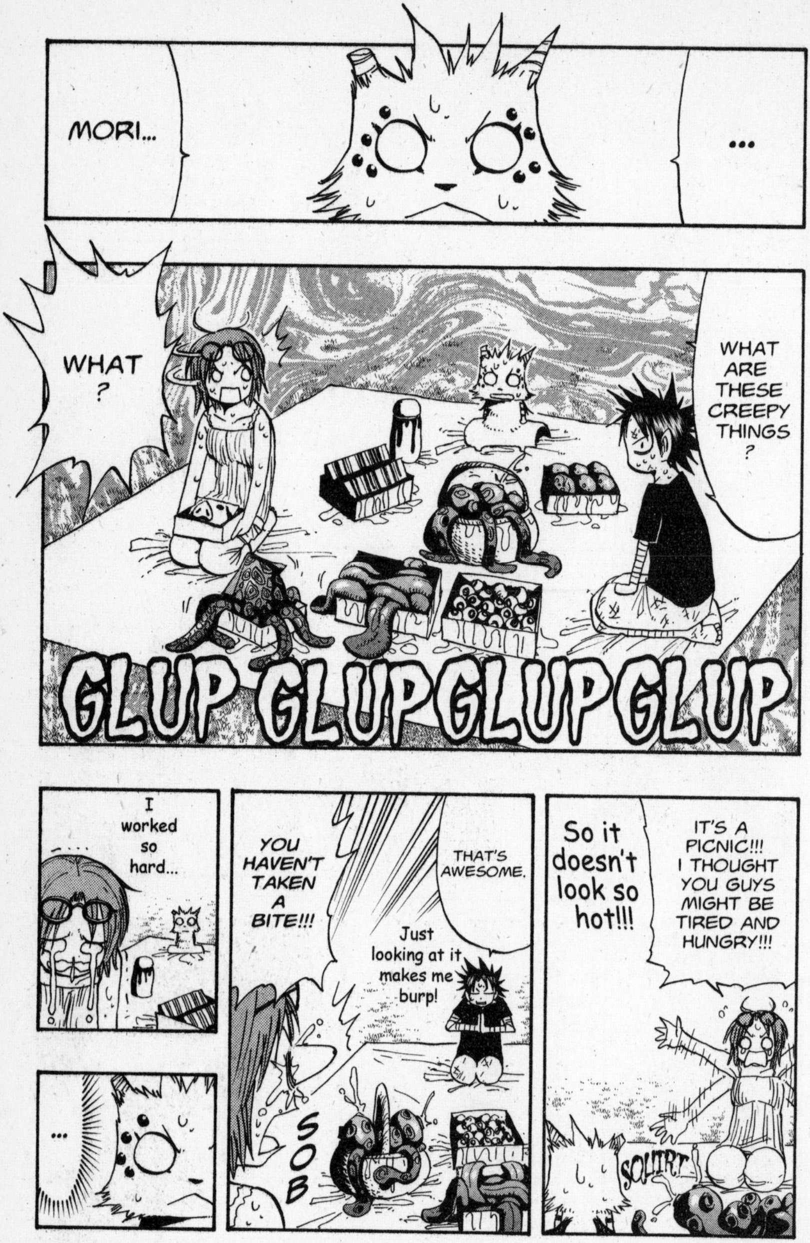
...
MORI...
WHAT ARE THESE CREEPY THINGS?
WHAT?
GLUP GLUP GLUP GLUP
IT'S A PICNIC!!! I THOUGHT YOU GUYS MIGHT BE TIRED AND HUNGRY!!!
So it doesn't look so hot!!!
SQUIRT
THAT'S AWESOME.
Just looking at it makes me burp!
YOU HAVEN'T TAKEN A BITE!!!
SOB
I worked so hard...
...
...

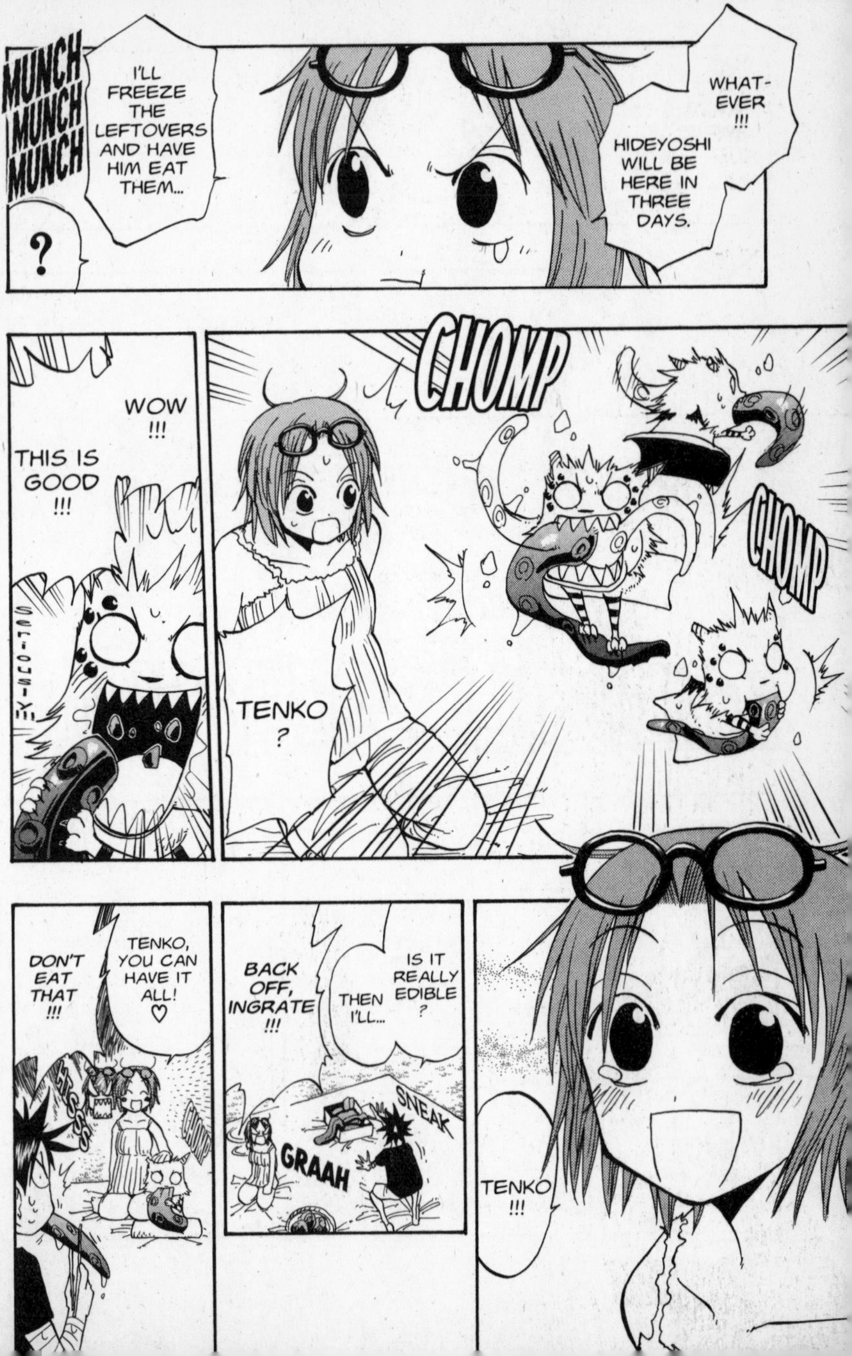
WHAT-EVER !!!
HIDEYOSHI WILL BE HERE IN THREE DAYS.
I'LL FREEZE THE LEFTOVERS AND HAVE HIM EAT THEM...
MUNCH MUNCH MUNCH
?
CHOMP
CHOMP
TENKO ?
WOW !!!
THIS IS GOOD !!!
SERIOUSLY!!
TENKO !!!
IS IT REALLY EDIBLE ?
THEN I'LL...
BACK OFF, INGRATE !!!
SNEAK
GRAAH
TENKO, YOU CAN HAVE IT ALL! ♡
DON'T EAT THAT !!!
HISSS

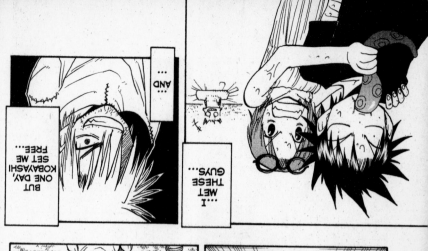

Wow! It's really good!!
Too late!!!
But it looks so...
Then don't eat it!!!
I NEVER DREAMED...
...THAT I'D HAVE ORDINARY DAYS LIKE THIS.
THOUSANDS OF YEARS AGO, WHEN I WAS LITTLE...
...I USED TO SPEND DAYS LIKE THIS WITH THE CELESTIALS.
BUT I GREW AND GREW, AND WHEN I BECAME A NUISANCE, I WAS JAILED ON FALSE CHARGES.
I ACCEPTED THAT MY LIFE WAS OVER.
BUT ONE DAY, KOBAYASHI SET ME FREE...
...AND...
...I MET THESE GUYS...

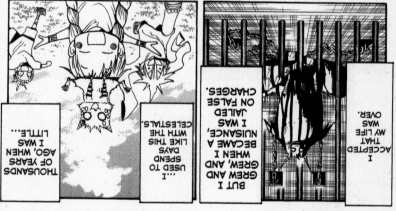

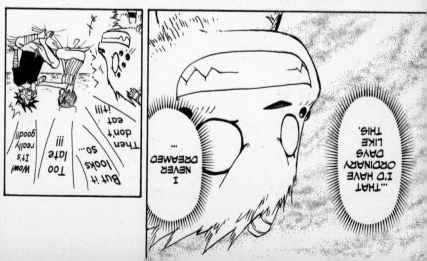

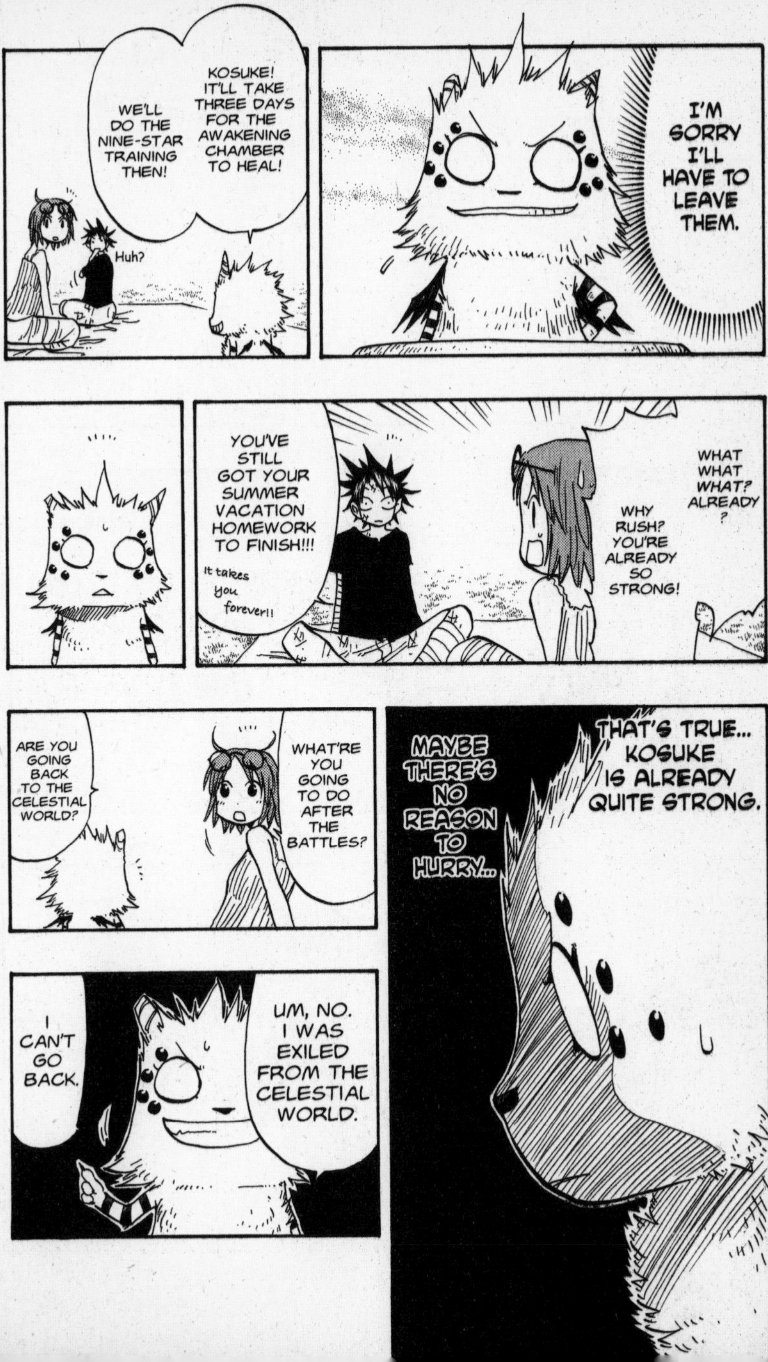
I'M SORRY I'LL HAVE TO LEAVE THEM.
KOSUKE! IT'LL TAKE THREE DAYS FOR THE AWAKENING CHAMBER TO HEAL!
WE'LL DO THE NINE-STAR TRAINING THEN!
Huh?
WHAT WHAT WHAT? ALREADY?
WHY RUSH? YOU'RE ALREADY SO STRONG!
YOU'VE STILL GOT YOUR SUMMER VACATION HOMEWORK TO FINISH!!!
It takes you forever!!
WHAT'RE YOU GOING TO DO AFTER THE BATTLES?
ARE YOU GOING BACK TO THE CELESTIAL WORLD?
UM, NO. I WAS EXILED FROM THE CELESTIAL WORLD.
I CAN'T GO BACK.
THAT'S TRUE... KOSUKE IS ALREADY QUITE STRONG.
MAYBE THERE'S NO REASON TO HURRY...

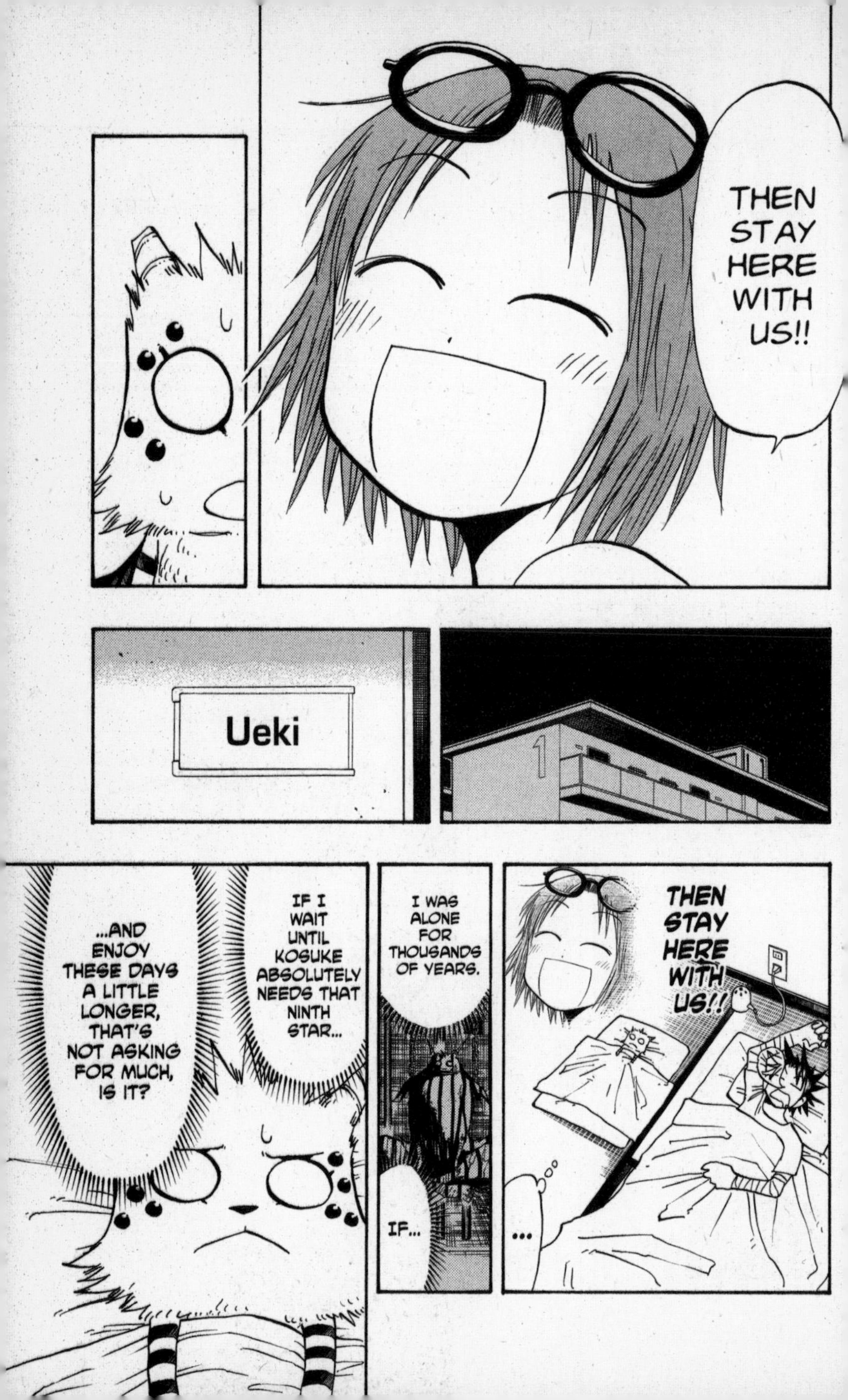
THEN STAY HERE WITH US!!
Ueki
THEN STAY HERE WITH US!!
...
I WAS ALONE FOR THOUSANDS OF YEARS.
IF...
IF I WAIT UNTIL KOSUKE ABSOLUTELY NEEDS THAT NINTH STAR...
...AND ENJOY THESE DAYS A LITTLE LONGER, THAT'S NOT ASKING FOR MUCH, IS IT?

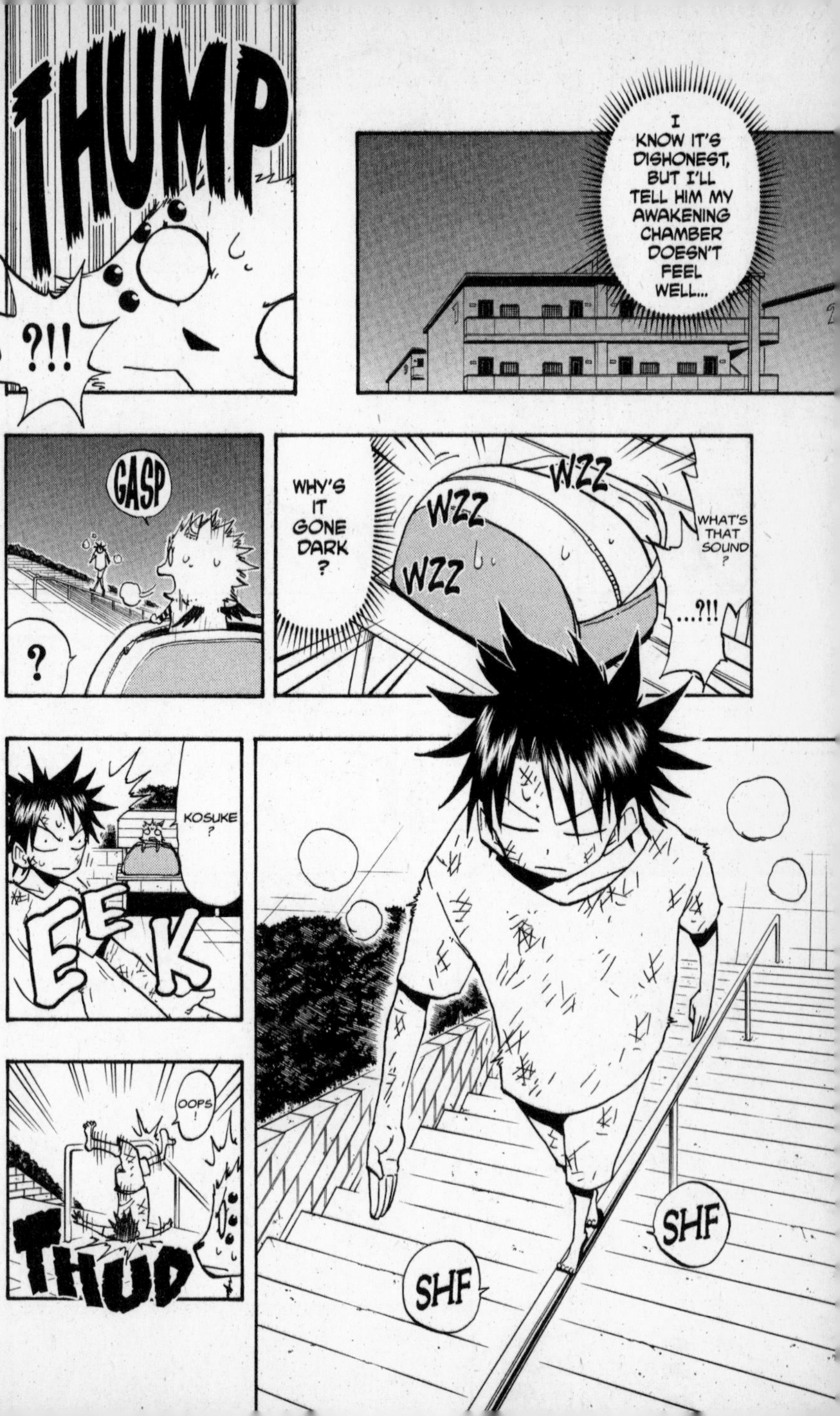
I KNOW IT'S DISHONEST, BUT I'LL TELL HIM MY AWAKENING CHAMBER DOESN'T FEEL WELL...
THUMP
?!!
WHY'S IT GONE DARK?
WZZ
WZZ
WZZ
WHAT'S THAT SOUND?
...?!!
GASP
?
SHF
SHF
KOSUKE?
EEK
OOPS!
THUD

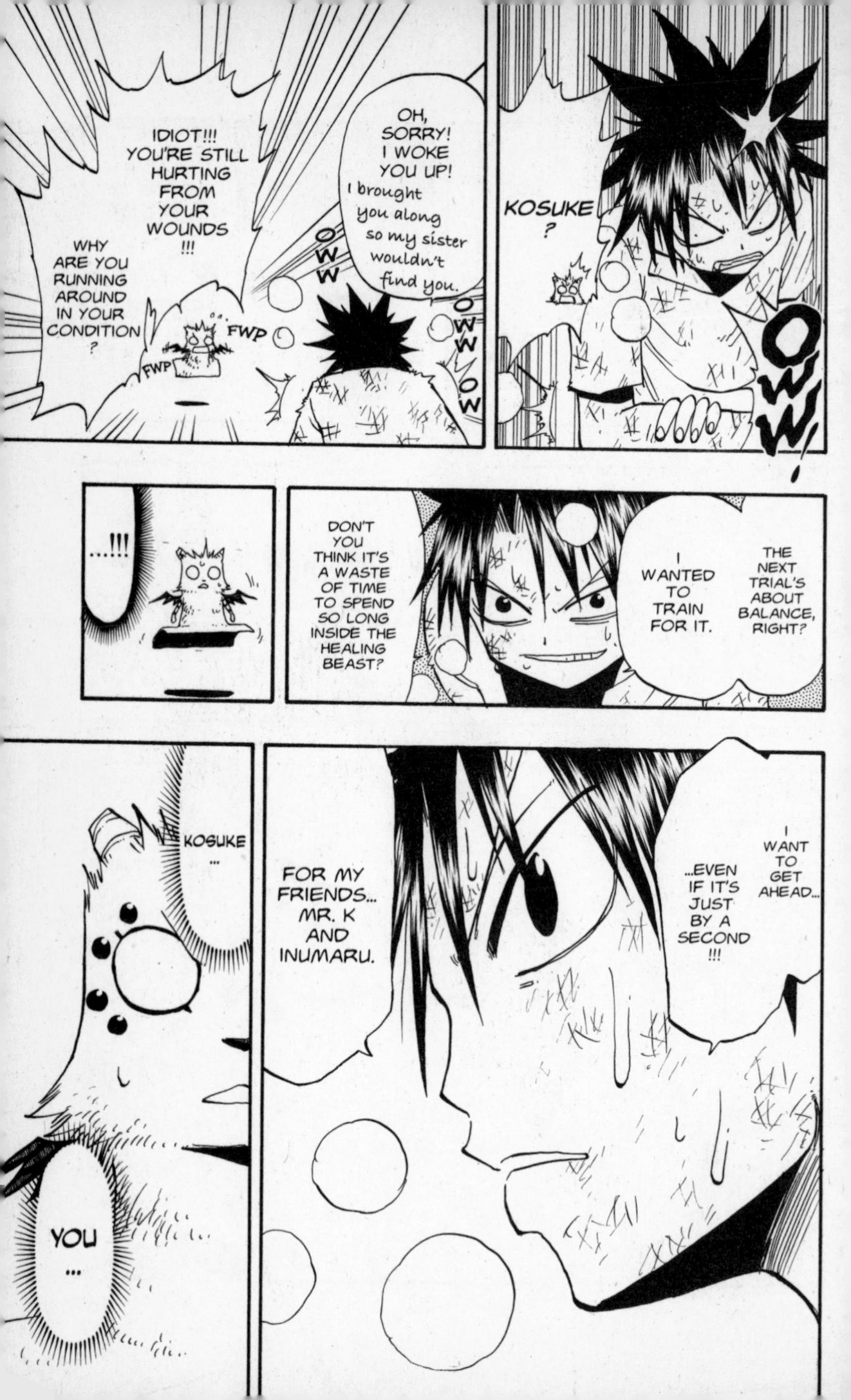
OWW!
KOSUKE?
OWWOWW
OWW
OH, SORRY! I WOKE YOU UP!
I brought you along so my sister wouldn't find you.
IDIOT!!! YOU'RE STILL HURTING FROM YOUR WOUNDS!!!
WHY ARE YOU RUNNING AROUND IN YOUR CONDITION?
FWP
FWP
THE NEXT TRIAL'S ABOUT BALANCE, RIGHT?
I WANTED TO TRAIN FOR IT.
DON'T YOU THINK IT'S A WASTE OF TIME TO SPEND SO LONG INSIDE THE HEALING BEAST?
...!!!
I WANT TO GET AHEAD...
...EVEN IF IT'S JUST BY A SECOND!!!
FOR MY FRIENDS... MR. K AND INUMARU.
KOSUKE...
YOU...

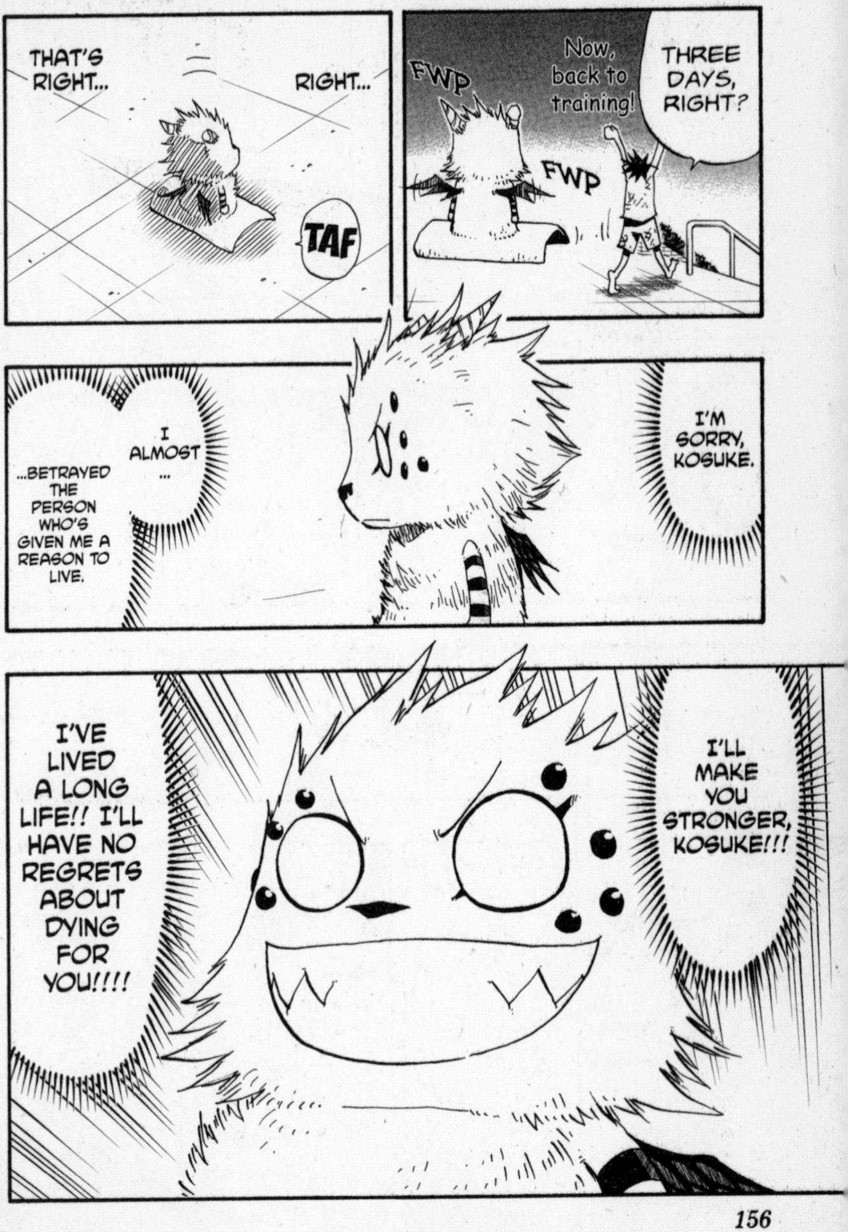
THREE DAYS, RIGHT?
Now, back to training!
FWP
FWP
RIGHT...
THAT'S RIGHT...
TAF
I'M SORRY, KOSUKE.
I ALMOST ...
...BETRAYED THE PERSON WHO'S GIVEN ME A REASON TO LIVE.
I'LL MAKE YOU STRONGER, KOSUKE!!!
I'VE LIVED A LONG LIFE!! I'LL HAVE NO REGRETS ABOUT DYING FOR YOU!!!!

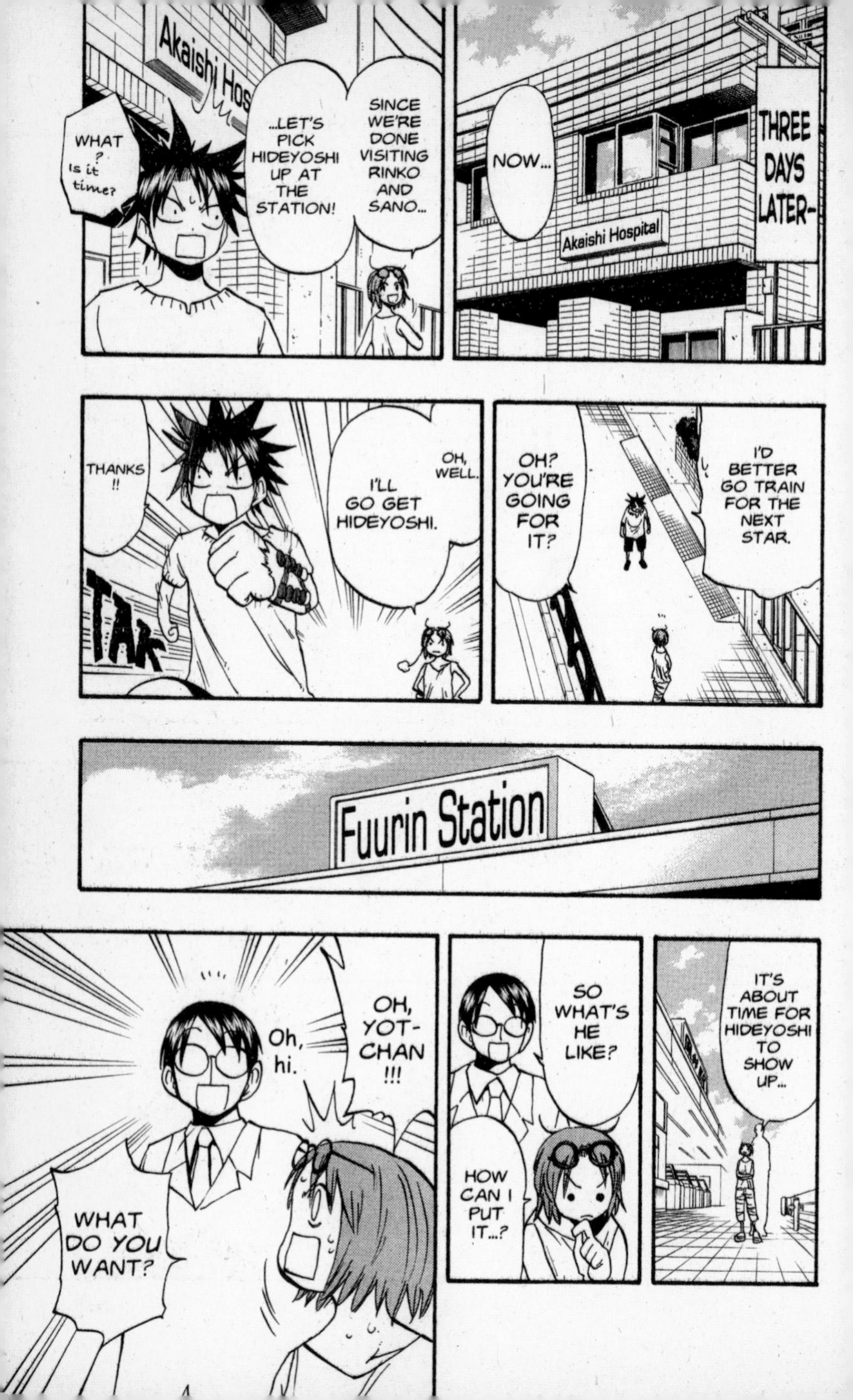
THREE DAYS LATER-
Akaishi Hospital
NOW...
SINCE WE'RE DONE VISITING RINKO AND SANO...
...LET'S PICK HIDEYOSHI UP AT THE STATION!
Akaishi Hos
WHAT? Is it time?
I'D BETTER GO TRAIN FOR THE NEXT STAR.
OH? YOU'RE GOING FOR IT?
OH, WELL.
I'LL GO GET HIDEYOSHI.
THANKS!!
TAK
Fuurin Station
IT'S ABOUT TIME FOR HIDEYOSHI TO SHOW UP...
SO WHAT'S HE LIKE?
HOW CAN I PUT IT...?
OH, YOT-CHAN!!!
Oh, hi.
WHAT DO YOU WANT?

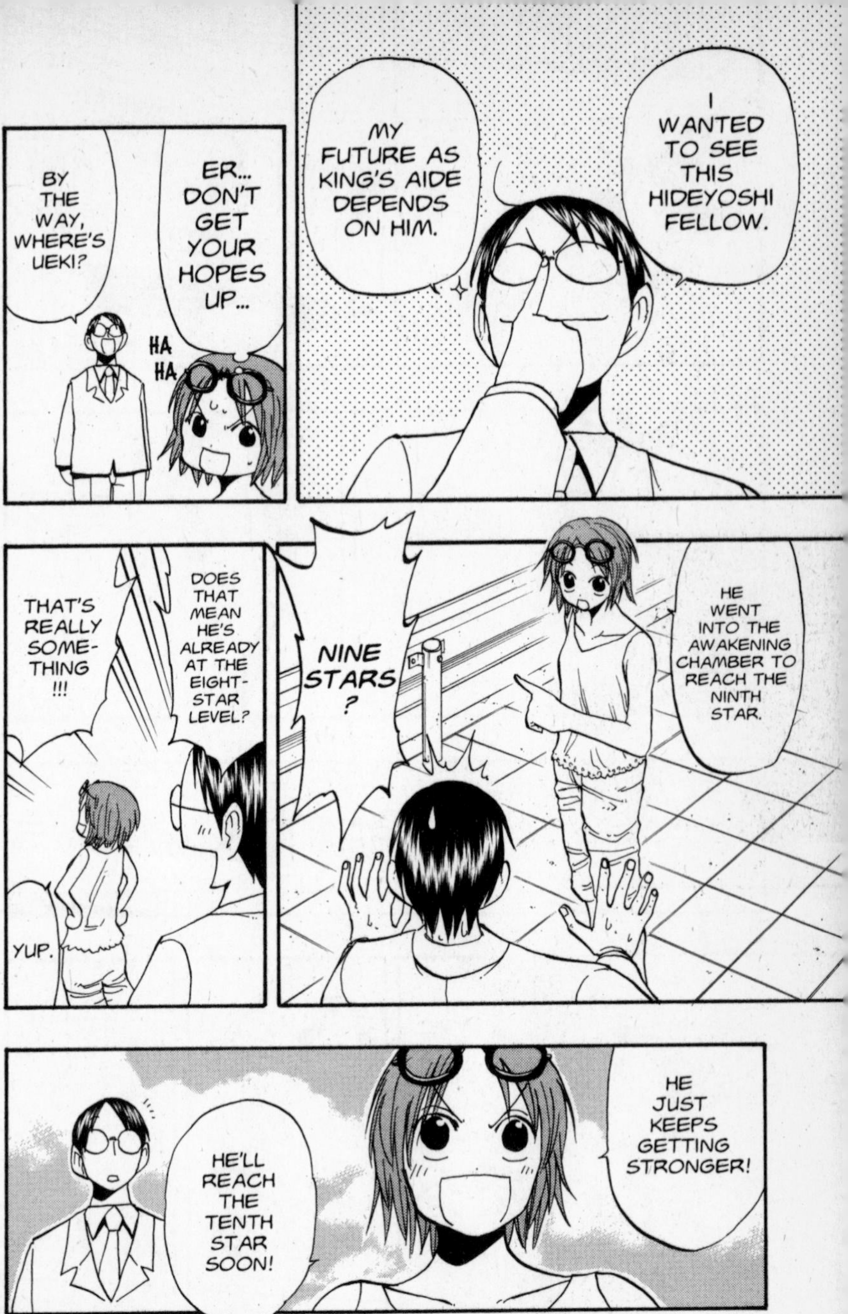
I WANTED TO SEE THIS HIDEYOSHI FELLOW.
MY FUTURE AS KING'S AIDE DEPENDS ON HIM.
ER... DON'T GET YOUR HOPES UP...
HA HA
BY THE WAY, WHERE'S UEKI?
HE WENT INTO THE AWAKENING CHAMBER TO REACH THE NINTH STAR.
NINE STARS?
DOES THAT MEAN HE'S ALREADY AT THE EIGHT-STAR LEVEL?
THAT'S REALLY SOME-THING!!!
YUP.
HE JUST KEEPS GETTING STRONGER!
HE'LL REACH THE TENTH STAR SOON!

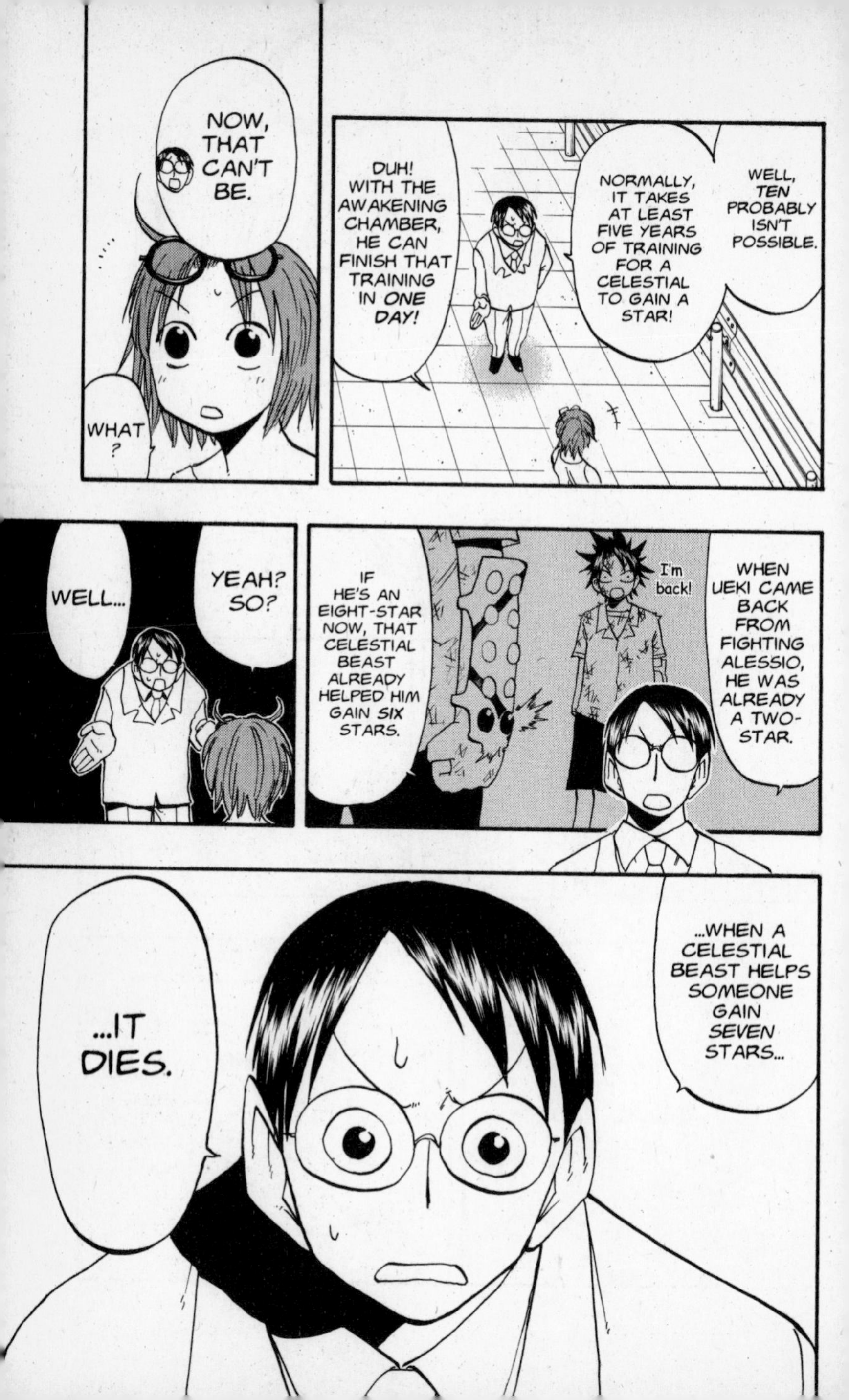
WELL, TEN PROBABLY ISN'T POSSIBLE.
NORMALLY, IT TAKES AT LEAST FIVE YEARS OF TRAINING FOR A CELESTIAL TO GAIN A STAR!
DUH! WITH THE AWAKENING CHAMBER, HE CAN FINISH THAT TRAINING IN ONE DAY!
NOW, THAT CAN'T BE.
...
WHAT?
WHEN UEKI CAME BACK FROM FIGHTING ALESSIO, HE WAS ALREADY A TWO-STAR.
I'm back!
IF HE'S AN EIGHT-STAR NOW, THAT CELESTIAL BEAST ALREADY HELPED HIM GAIN SIX STARS.
YEAH? SO?
WELL...
...WHEN A CELESTIAL BEAST HELPS SOMEONE GAIN SEVEN STARS...
...IT DIES.

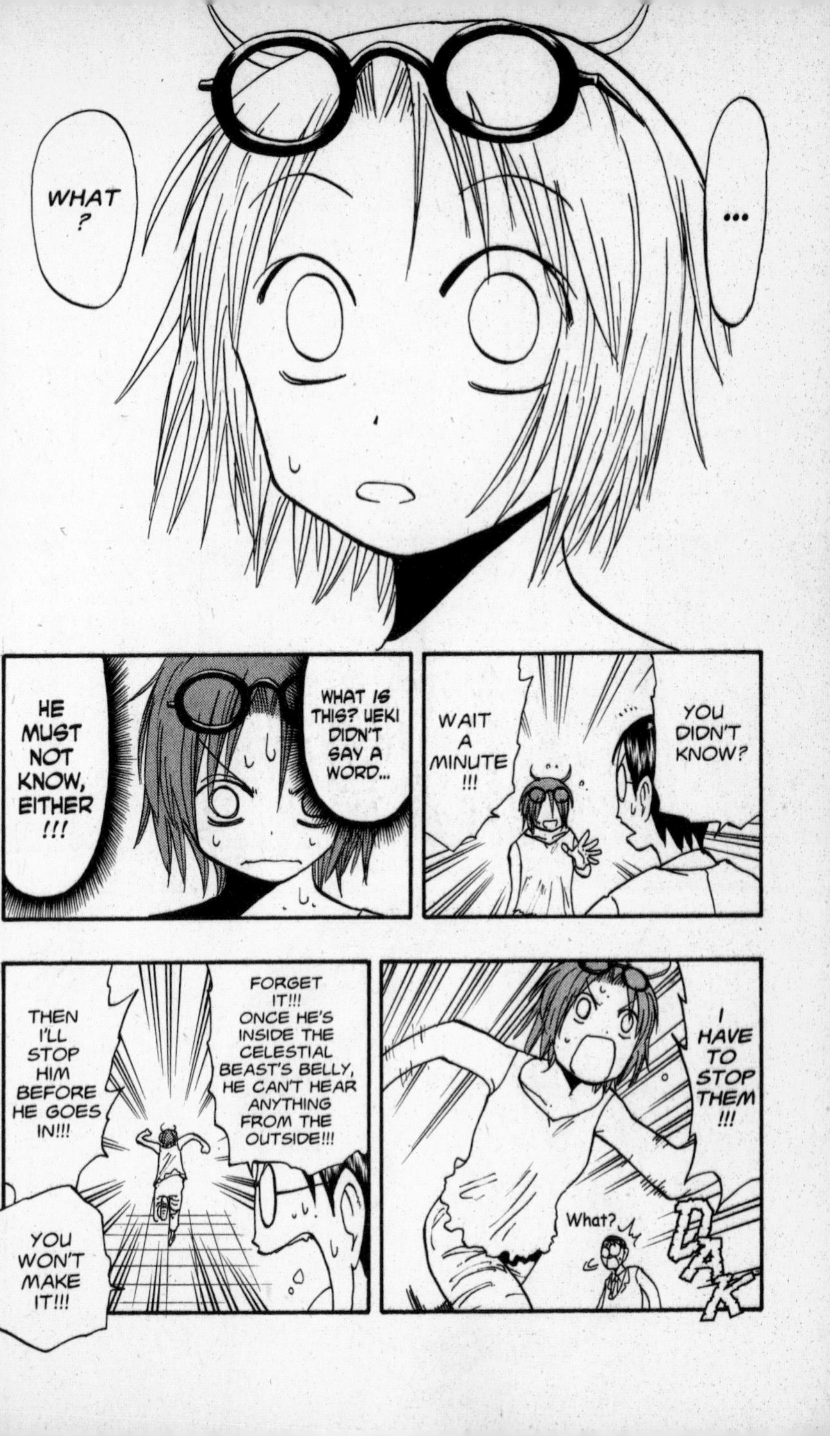
...
WHAT ?
YOU DIDN'T KNOW?
WAIT A MINUTE !!!
WHAT IS THIS? UEKI DIDN'T SAY A WORD...
HE MUST NOT KNOW, EITHER !!!
I HAVE TO STOP THEM !!!
What?
DAK
FORGET IT!!! ONCE HE'S INSIDE THE CELESTIAL BEAST'S BELLY, HE CAN'T HEAR ANYTHING FROM THE OUTSIDE!!!
THEN I'LL STOP HIM BEFORE HE GOES IN!!!
YOU WON'T MAKE IT!!!

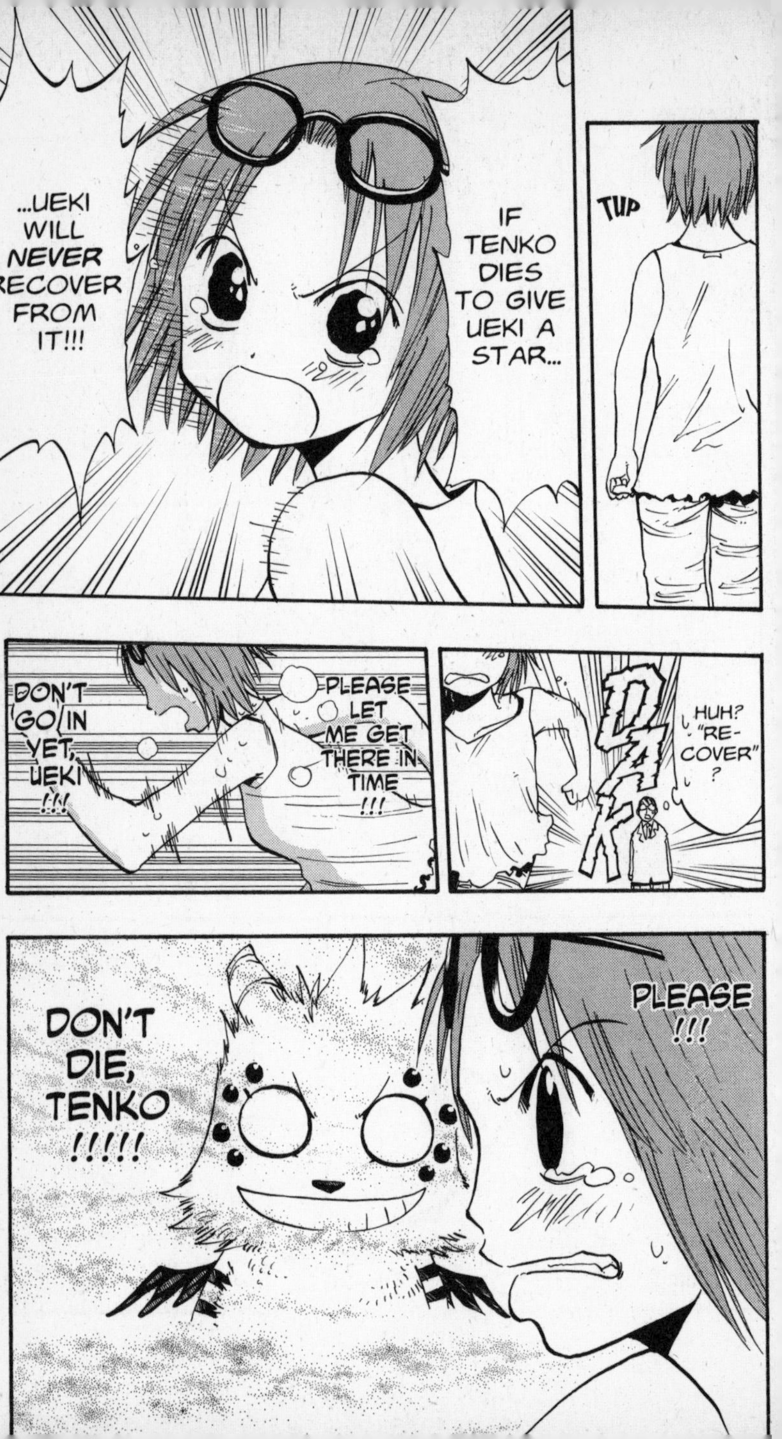
TUP
IF TENKO DIES TO GIVE UEKI A STAR...
...UEKI WILL NEVER RECOVER FROM IT!!!
HUH? "RE-COVER"?
DAK
PLEASE LET ME GET THERE IN TIME!!!
DON'T GO IN YET, UEKI!!!
PLEASE!!!
DON'T DIE, TENKO!!!!!

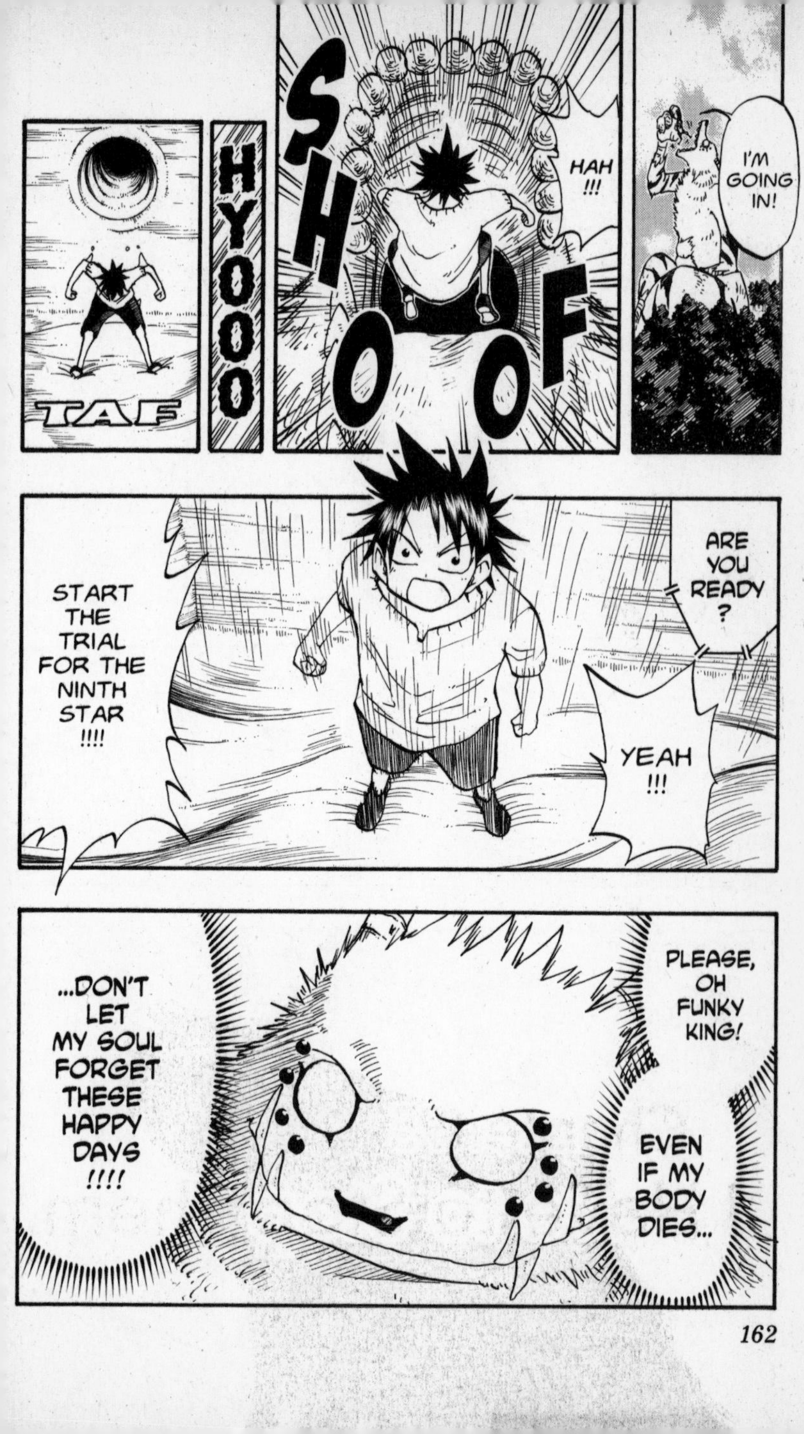
I'M GOING IN!
HAH !!!
SHOOF
HYOOO
TAF
ARE YOU READY ?
YEAH !!!
START THE TRIAL FOR THE NINTH STAR !!!!
PLEASE, OH FUNKY KING!
EVEN IF MY BODY DIES...
...DON'T LET MY SOUL FORGET THESE HAPPY DAYS !!!!

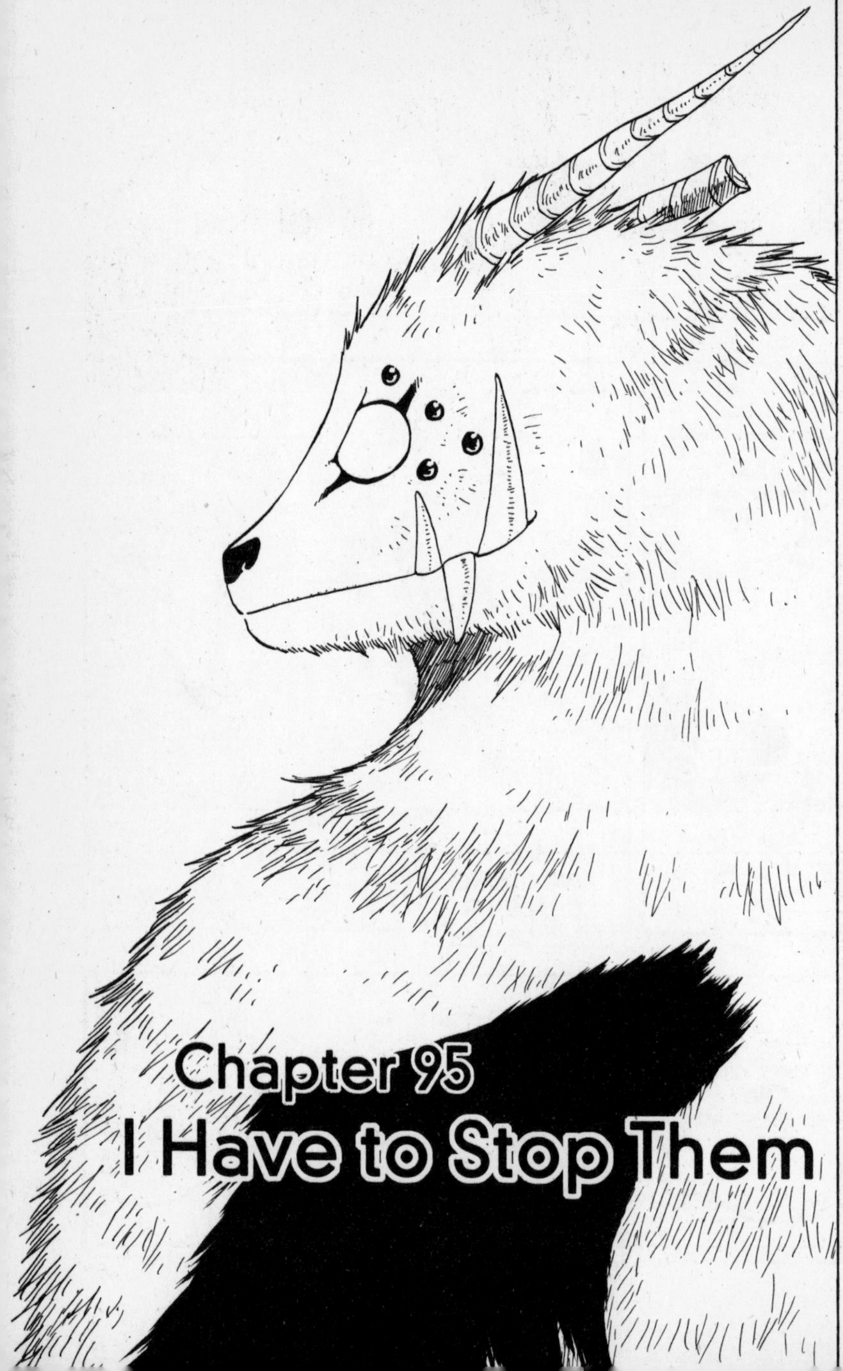
Chapter 95
I Have to Stop Them

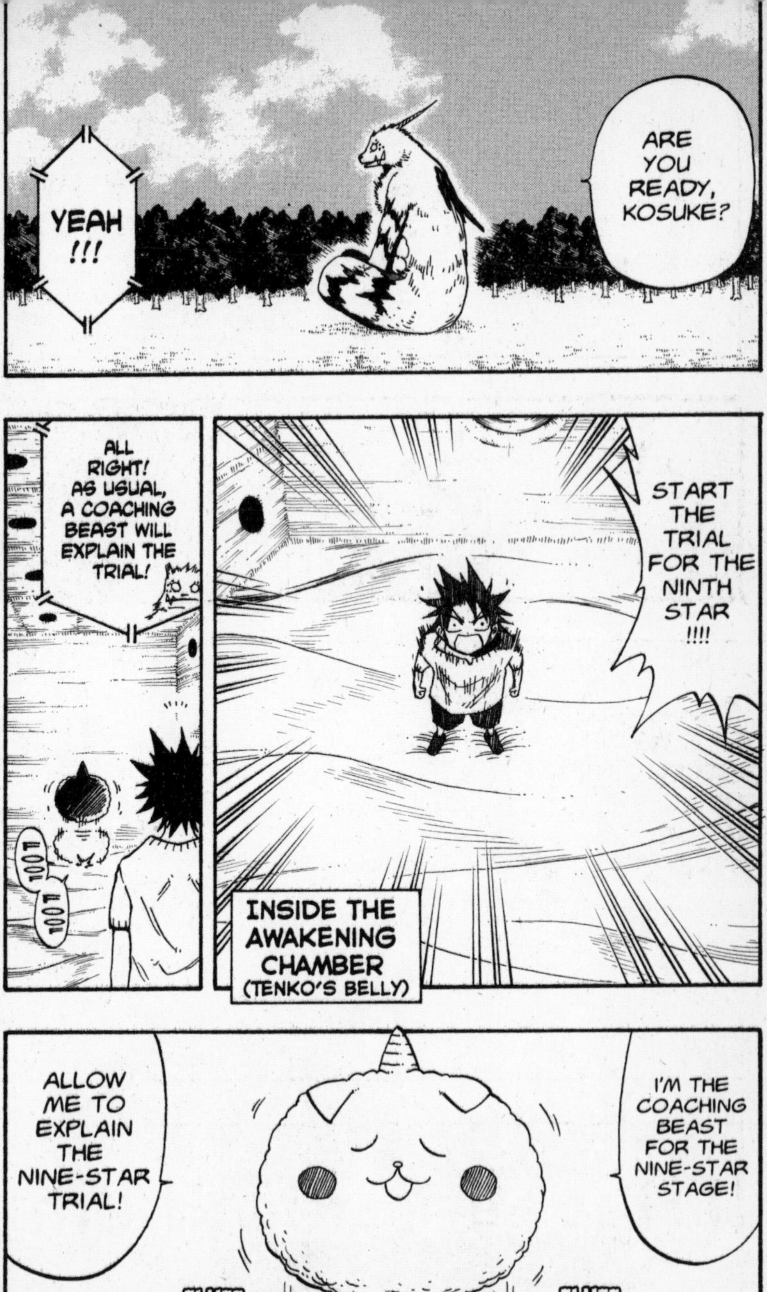
ARE YOU READY, KOSUKE?
YEAH !!!
START THE TRIAL FOR THE NINTH STAR !!!!
INSIDE THE AWAKENING CHAMBER (TENKO'S BELLY)
ALL RIGHT! AS USUAL, A COACHING BEAST WILL EXPLAIN THE TRIAL!
I'M THE COACHING BEAST FOR THE NINE-STAR STAGE!
ALLOW ME TO EXPLAIN THE NINE-STAR TRIAL!
FLUFF
FLUFF

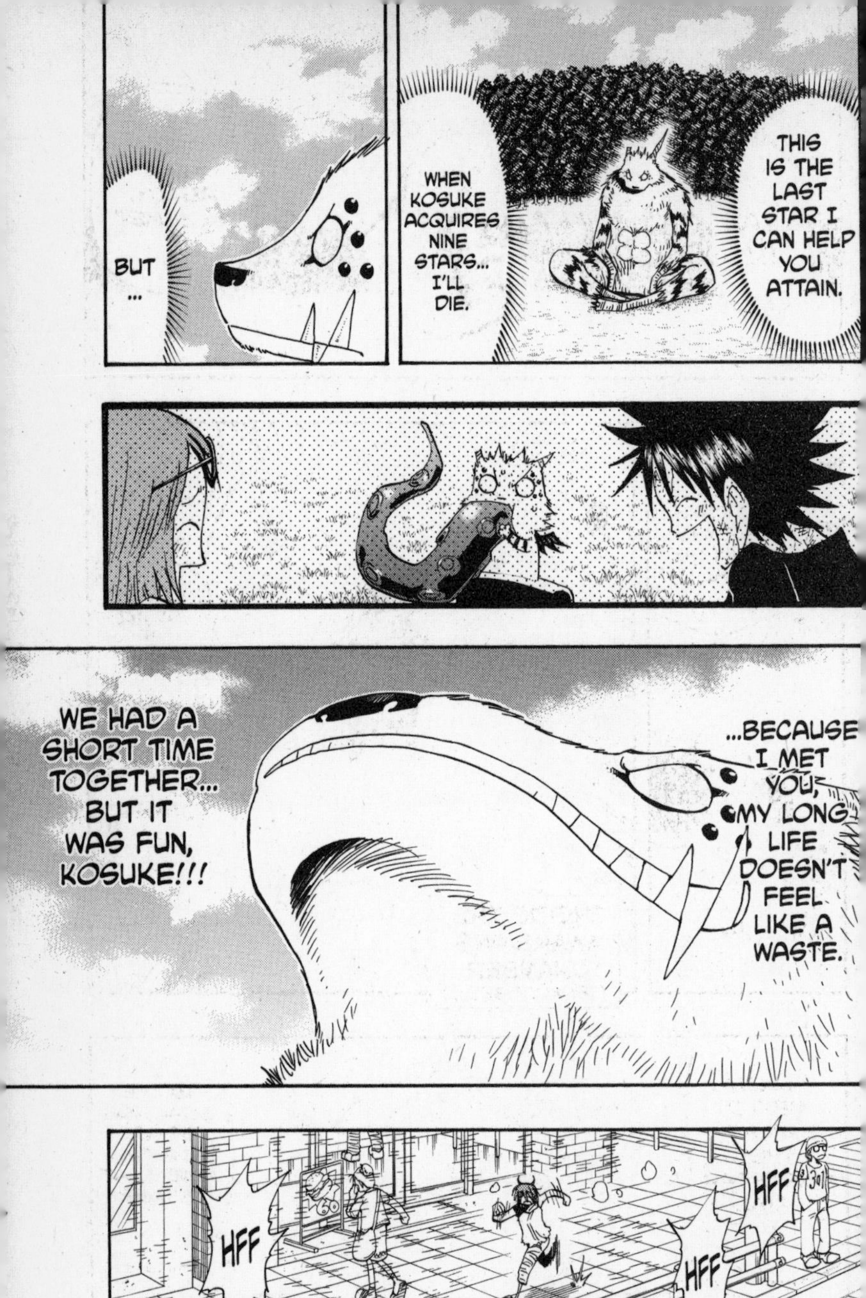
THIS IS THE LAST STAR I CAN HELP YOU ATTAIN.
WHEN KOSUKE ACQUIRES NINE STARS... I'LL DIE.
BUT ...
...BECAUSE I MET YOU, MY LONG LIFE DOESN'T FEEL LIKE A WASTE.
WE HAD A SHORT TIME TOGETHER... BUT IT WAS FUN, KOSUKE!!!
HFF
HFF
HFF
301

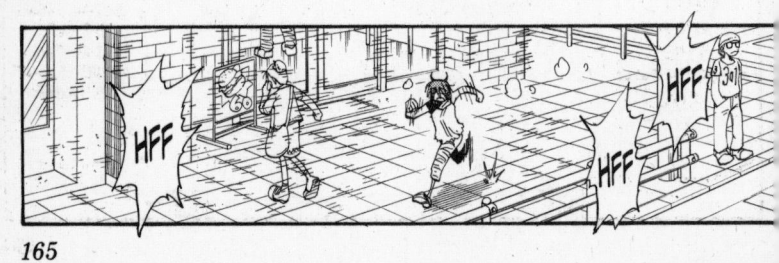

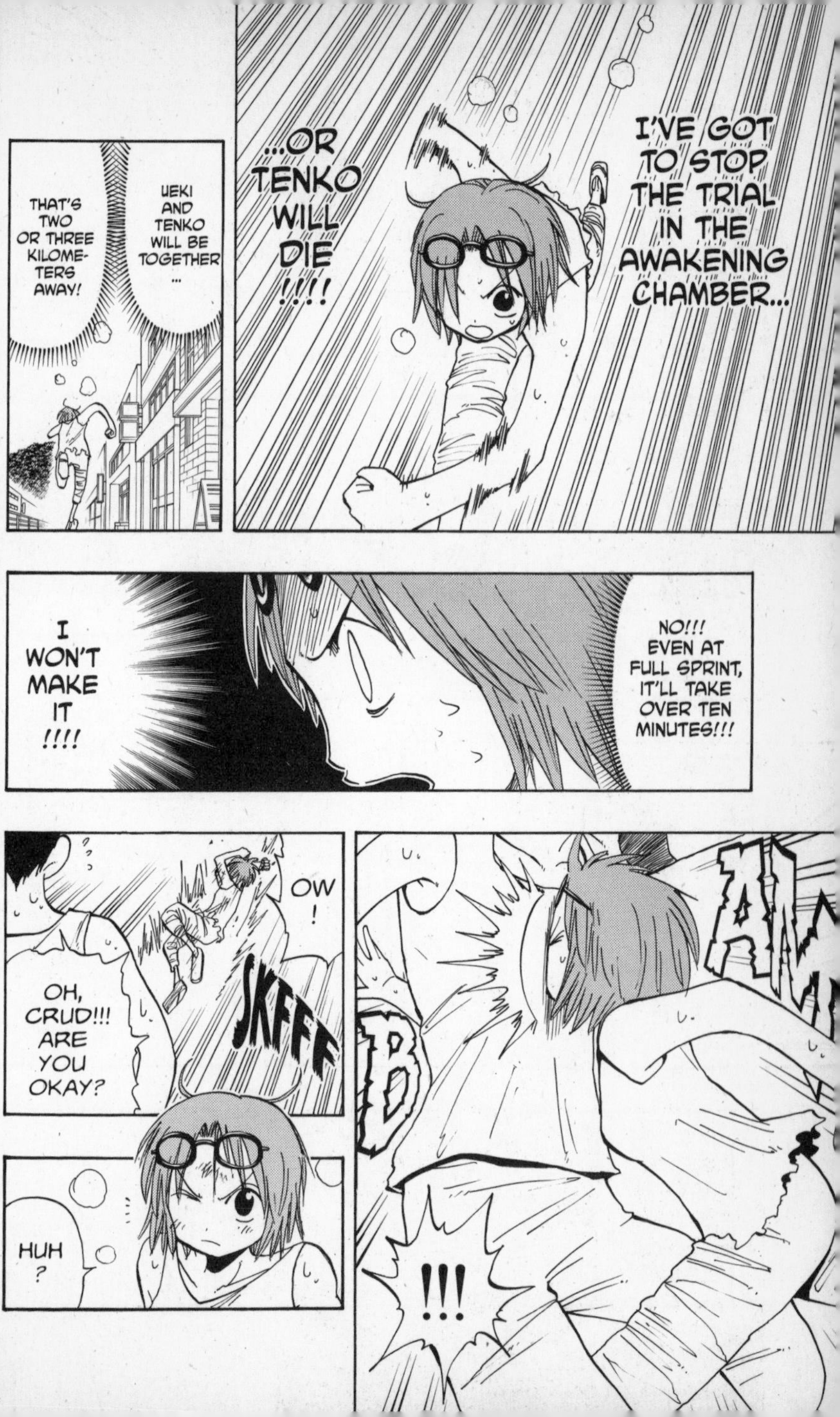
I'VE GOT TO STOP THE TRIAL IN THE AWAKENING CHAMBER...
...OR TENKO WILL DIE !!!!
UEKI AND TENKO WILL BE TOGETHER ...
THAT'S TWO OR THREE KILOMETERS AWAY!
NO!!! EVEN AT FULL SPRINT, IT'LL TAKE OVER TEN MINUTES!!!
I WON'T MAKE IT !!!!
!!!
OW !
SKFFF
OH, CRUD!!! ARE YOU OKAY?
HUH ?

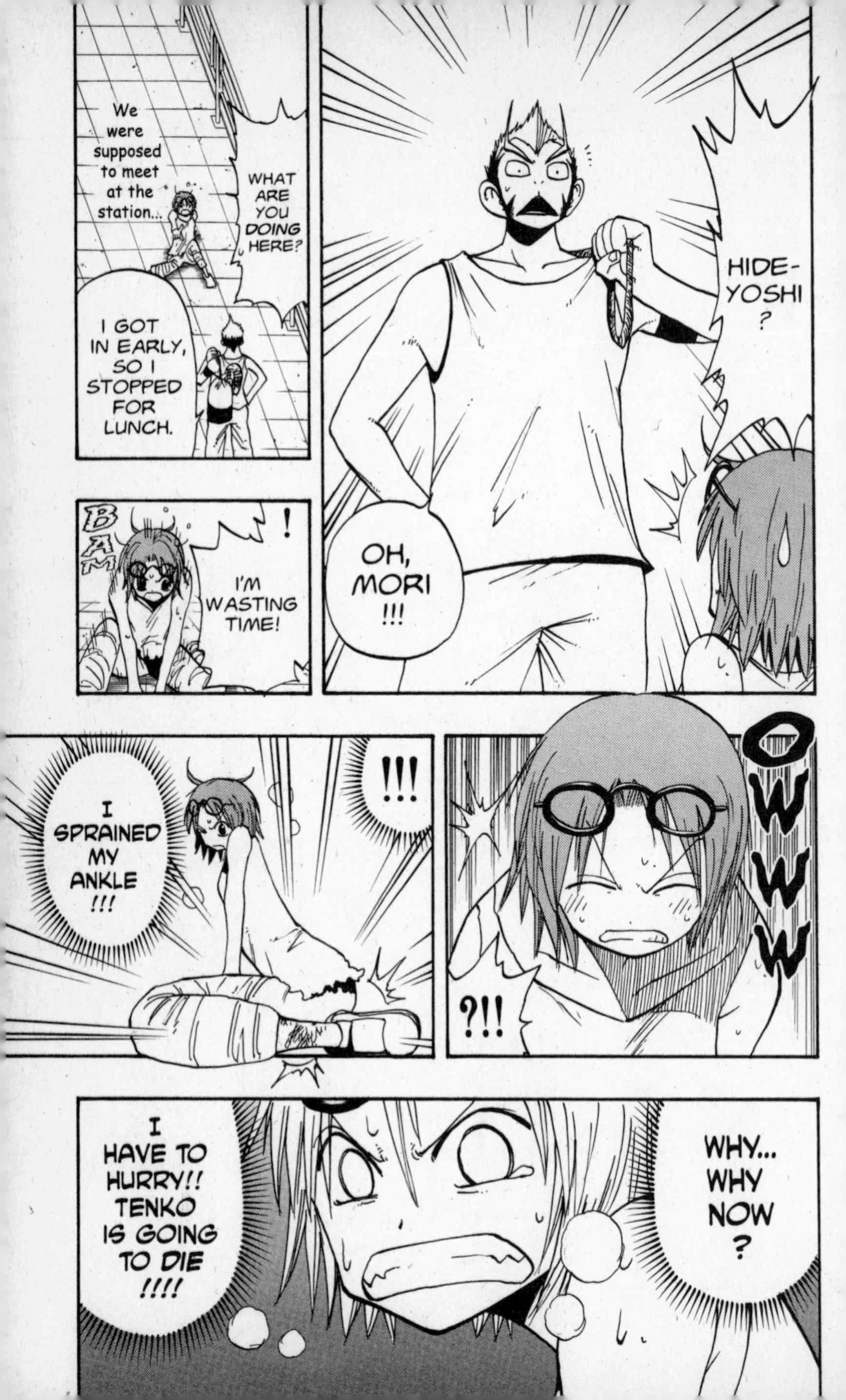
HIDE-YOSHI?
OH, MORI!!!
WHAT ARE YOU DOING HERE?
We were supposed to meet at the station...
I GOT IN EARLY, SO I STOPPED FOR LUNCH.
!
BAM
I'M WASTING TIME!
OWWW
?!!
!!!
I SPRAINED MY ANKLE!!!
WHY... WHY NOW?
I HAVE TO HURRY!! TENKO IS GOING TO DIE!!!!

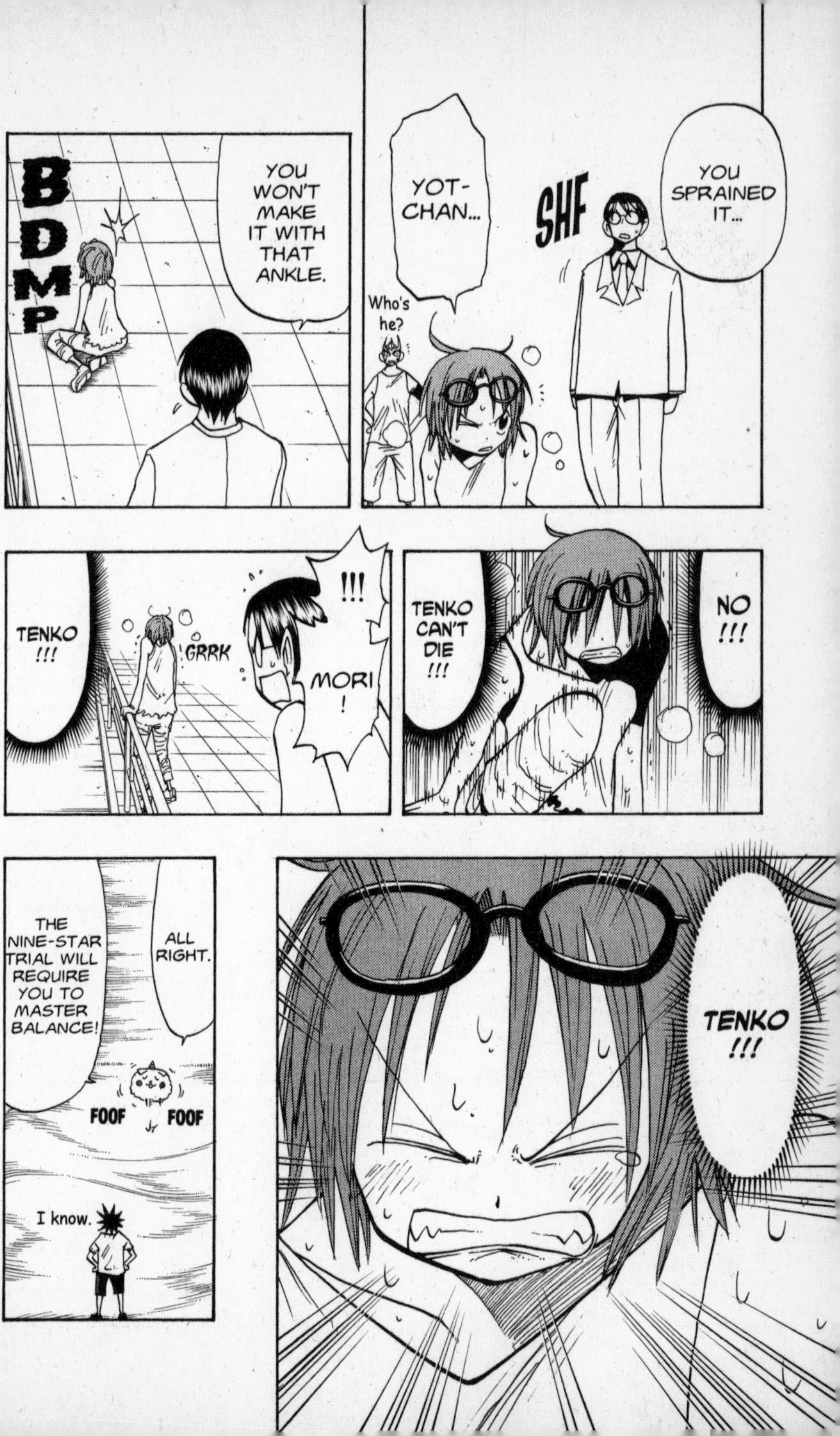
YOU SPRAINED IT...
SHF
YOT-CHAN...
Who's he?
YOU WON'T MAKE IT WITH THAT ANKLE.
BDMP
NO !!!
TENKO CAN'T DIE !!!
!!!
MORI !
GRRK
TENKO !!!
TENKO !!!
ALL RIGHT.
THE NINE-STAR TRIAL WILL REQUIRE YOU TO MASTER BALANCE!
FOOF
FOOF
I know.

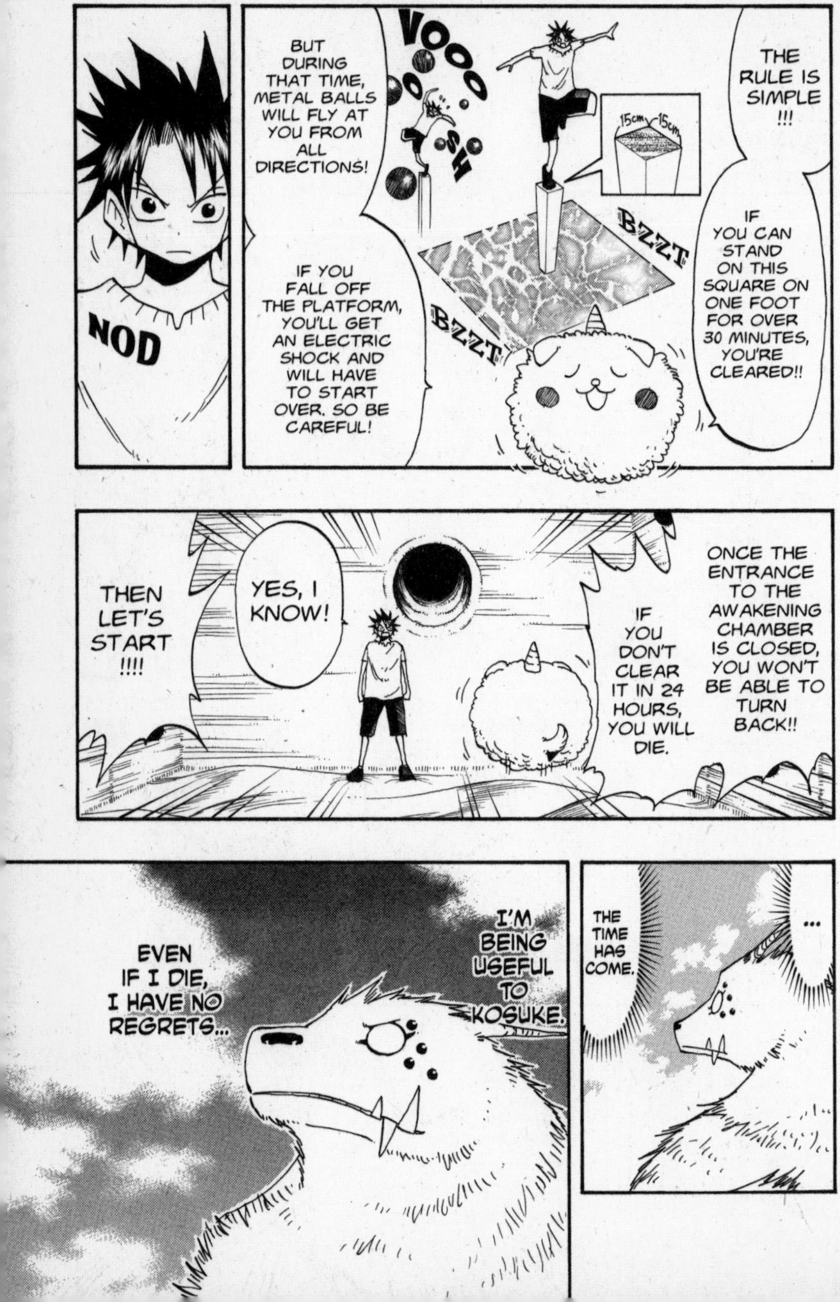
THE RULE IS SIMPLE !!!
15cm 15cm
IF YOU CAN STAND ON THIS SQUARE ON ONE FOOT FOR OVER 30 MINUTES, YOU'RE CLEARED!!
BZZT
BZZT
VOOOOSH
BUT DURING THAT TIME, METAL BALLS WILL FLY AT YOU FROM ALL DIRECTIONS!
IF YOU FALL OFF THE PLATFORM, YOU'LL GET AN ELECTRIC SHOCK AND WILL HAVE TO START OVER. SO BE CAREFUL!
NOD
ONCE THE ENTRANCE TO THE AWAKENING CHAMBER IS CLOSED, YOU WON'T BE ABLE TO TURN BACK!!
IF YOU DON'T CLEAR IT IN 24 HOURS, YOU WILL DIE.
YES, I KNOW!
THEN LET'S START !!!!
...
THE TIME HAS COME.
I'M BEING USEFUL TO KOSUKE.
EVEN IF I DIE, I HAVE NO REGRETS...

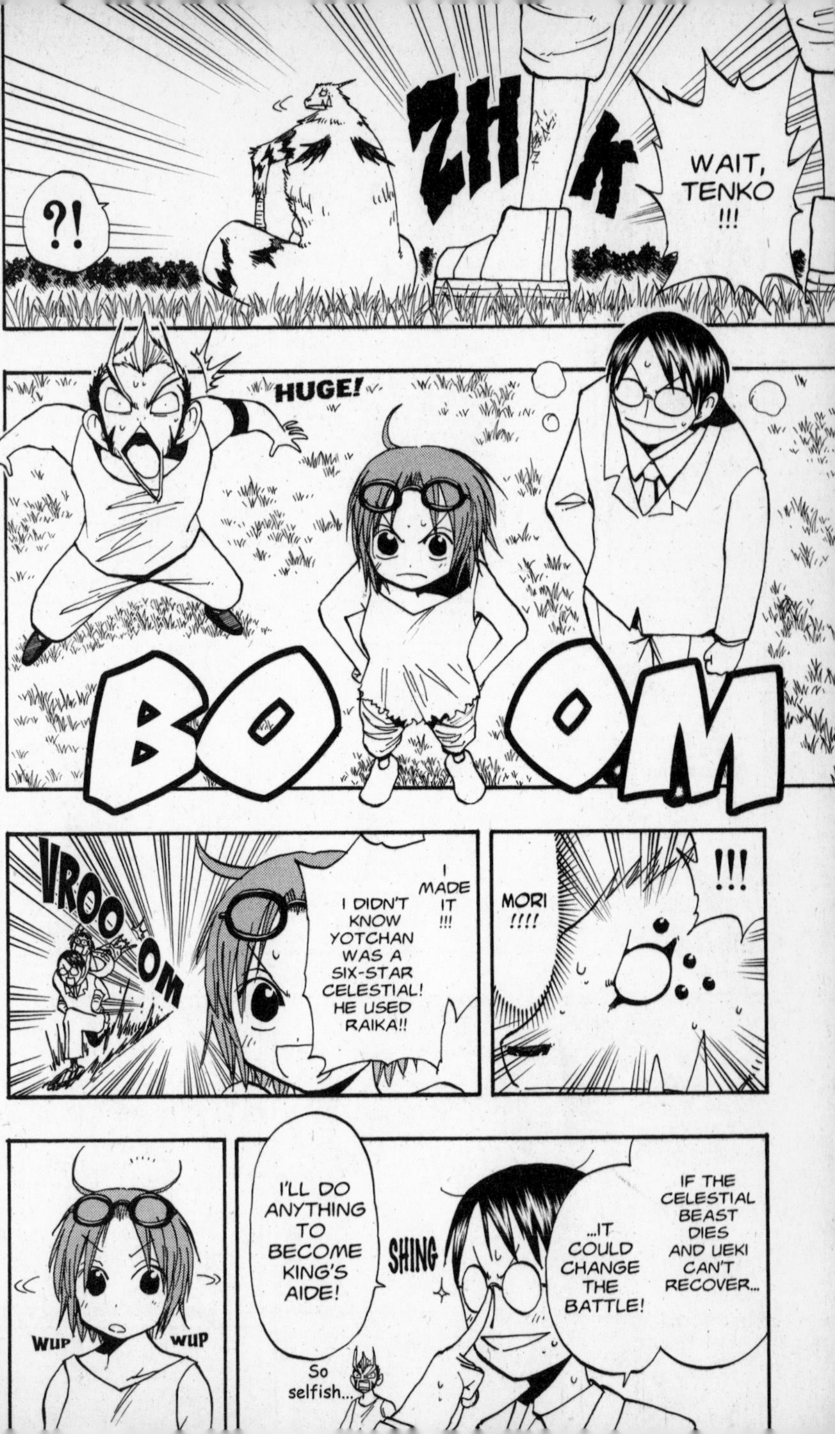
WAIT, TENKO !!!
ZHA
?!
HUGE!
BOOM
!!!
MORI !!!!
I MADE IT !!!
I DIDN'T KNOW YOTCHAN WAS A SIX-STAR CELESTIAL! HE USED RAIKA!!
VROOOM
IF THE CELESTIAL BEAST DIES AND UEKI CAN'T RECOVER...
...IT COULD CHANGE THE BATTLE!
SHING
I'LL DO ANYTHING TO BECOME KING'S AIDE!
So selfish...
....
WUP WUP

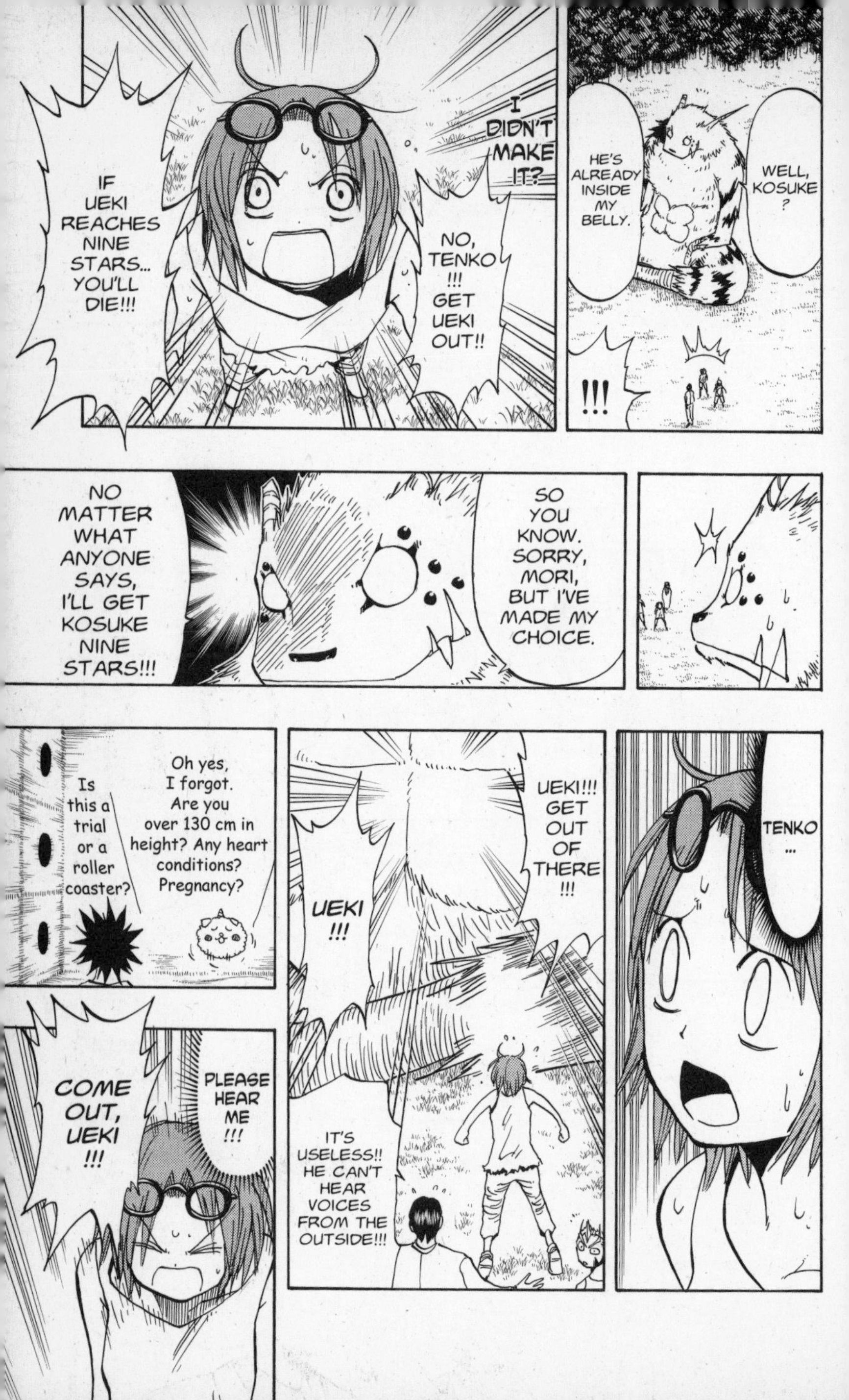
WELL, KOSUKE ?
HE'S ALREADY INSIDE MY BELLY.
!!!
I DIDN'T MAKE IT?
NO, TENKO !!! GET UEKI OUT!!
IF UEKI REACHES NINE STARS... YOU'LL DIE!!!
SO YOU KNOW. SORRY, MORI, BUT I'VE MADE MY CHOICE.
NO MATTER WHAT ANYONE SAYS, I'LL GET KOSUKE NINE STARS!!!
TENKO ...
UEKI!!! GET OUT OF THERE !!!
UEKI !!!
IT'S USELESS!! HE CAN'T HEAR VOICES FROM THE OUTSIDE!!!
Oh yes, I forgot. Are you over 130 cm in height? Any heart conditions? Pregnancy?
Is this a trial or a roller coaster?
COME OUT, UEKI !!!
PLEASE HEAR ME !!!

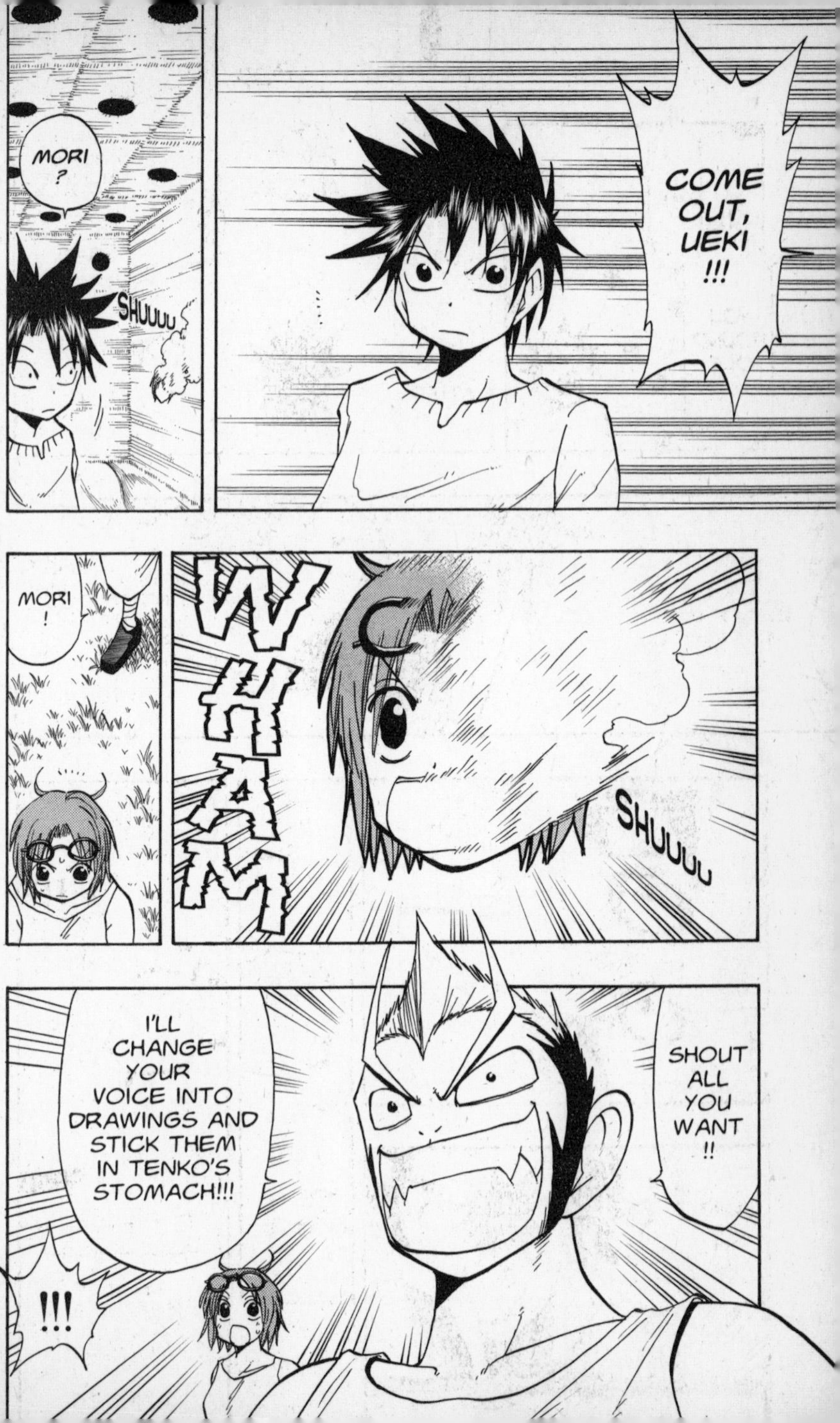
COME OUT, UEKI !!!
MORI ?
SHUUUU
WHAM
SHUUUU
MORI !
SHOUT ALL YOU WANT !!
I'LL CHANGE YOUR VOICE INTO DRAWINGS AND STICK THEM IN TENKO'S STOMACH!!!
!!!

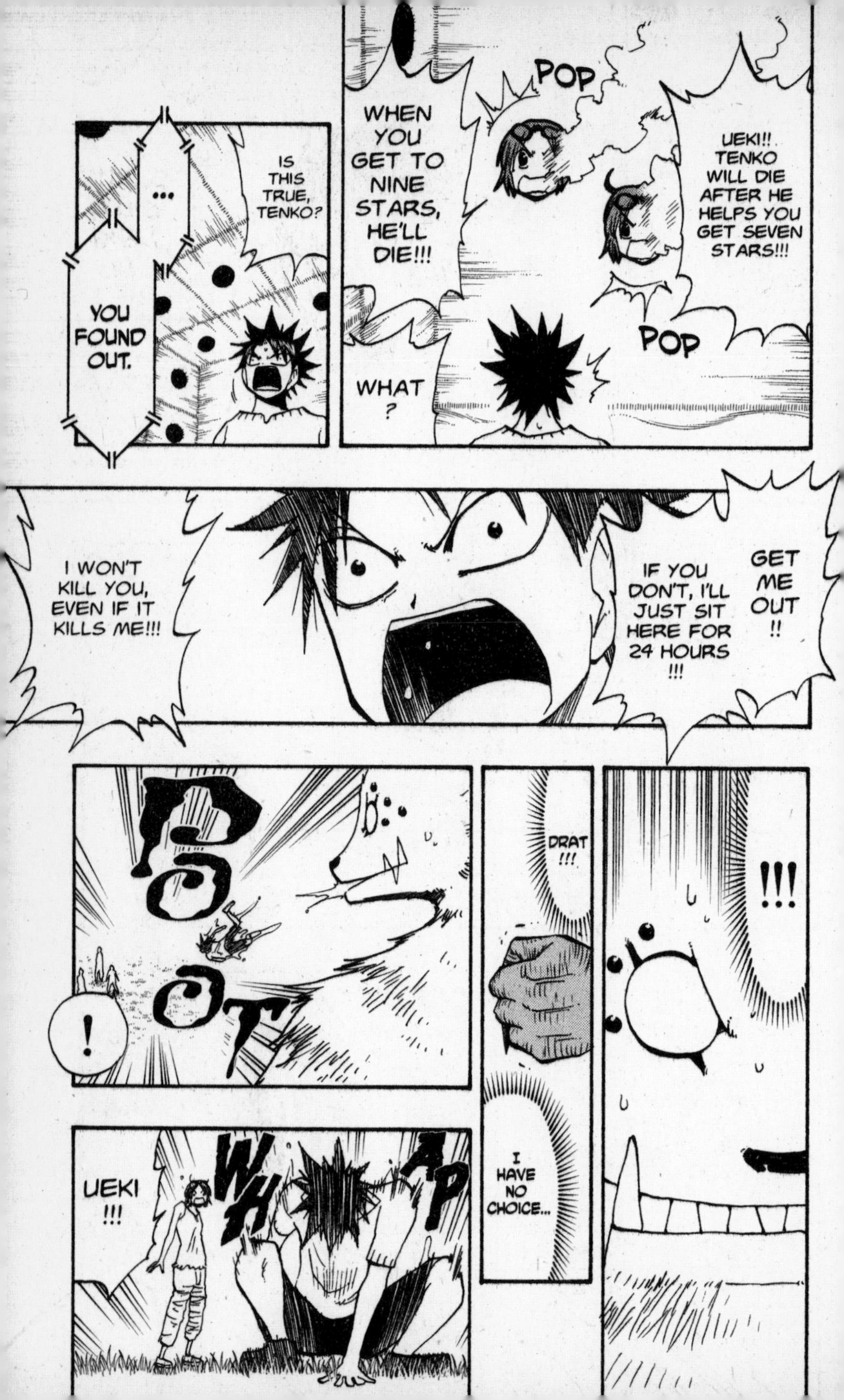

POP
UEKI!! TENKO WILL DIE AFTER HE HELPS YOU GET SEVEN STARS!!!
WHEN YOU GET TO NINE STARS, HE'LL DIE!!!
POP
WHAT ?
IS THIS TRUE, TENKO?
...
YOU FOUND OUT.
GET ME OUT !!
IF YOU DON'T, I'LL JUST SIT HERE FOR 24 HOURS !!!
I WON'T KILL YOU, EVEN IF IT KILLS ME!!!
!!!
DRAT !!!
I HAVE NO CHOICE...
BOOT
!
WHAP
UEKI !!!

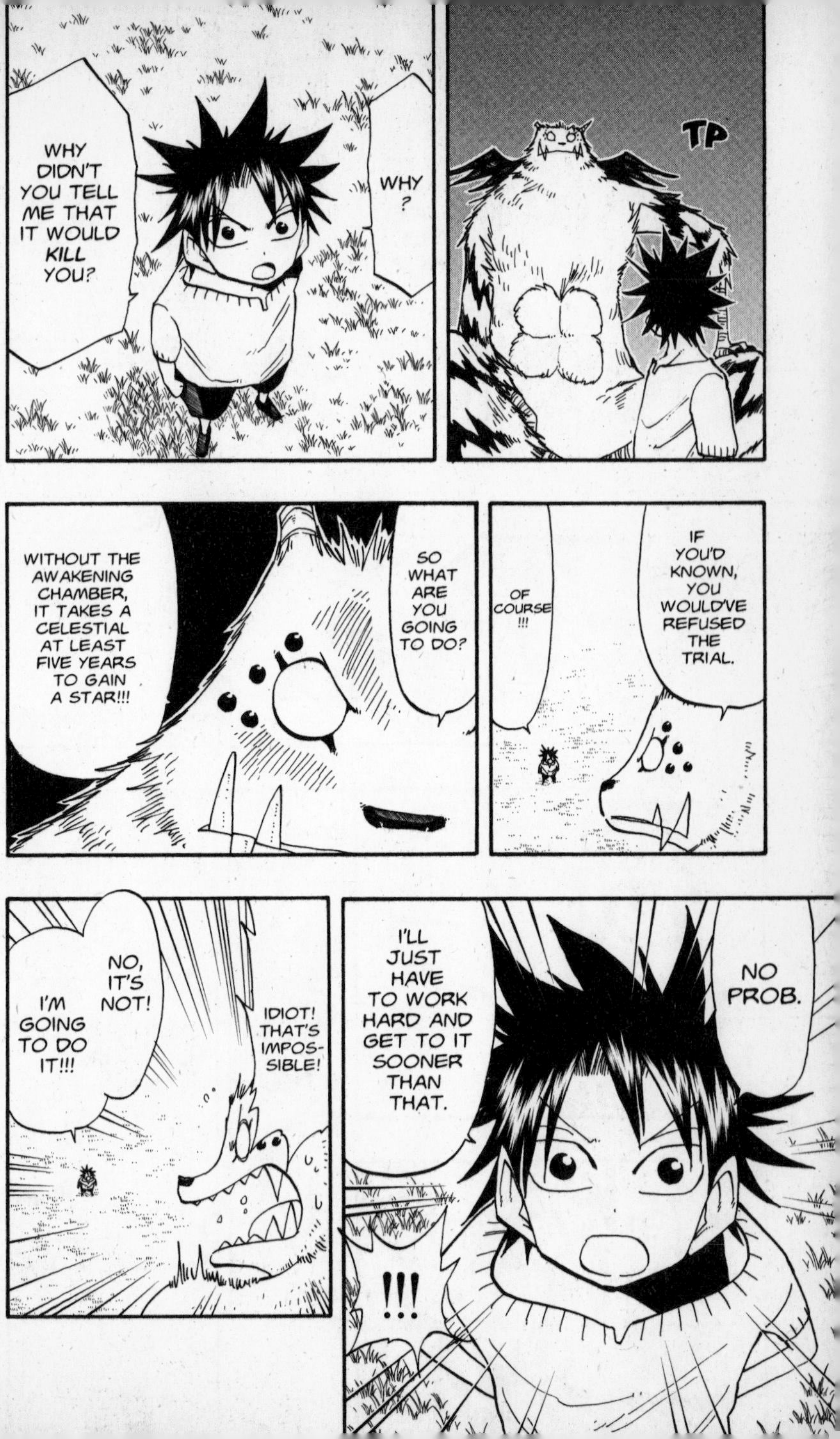
TP
WHY?
WHY DIDN'T YOU TELL ME THAT IT WOULD KILL YOU?
IF YOU'D KNOWN, YOU WOULD'VE REFUSED THE TRIAL.
OF COURSE!!!
SO WHAT ARE YOU GOING TO DO?
WITHOUT THE AWAKENING CHAMBER, IT TAKES A CELESTIAL AT LEAST FIVE YEARS TO GAIN A STAR!!!
NO PROB.
I'LL JUST HAVE TO WORK HARD AND GET TO IT SOONER THAN THAT.
!!!
IDIOT! THAT'S IMPOS-SIBLE!
NO, IT'S NOT!
I'M GOING TO DO IT!!!

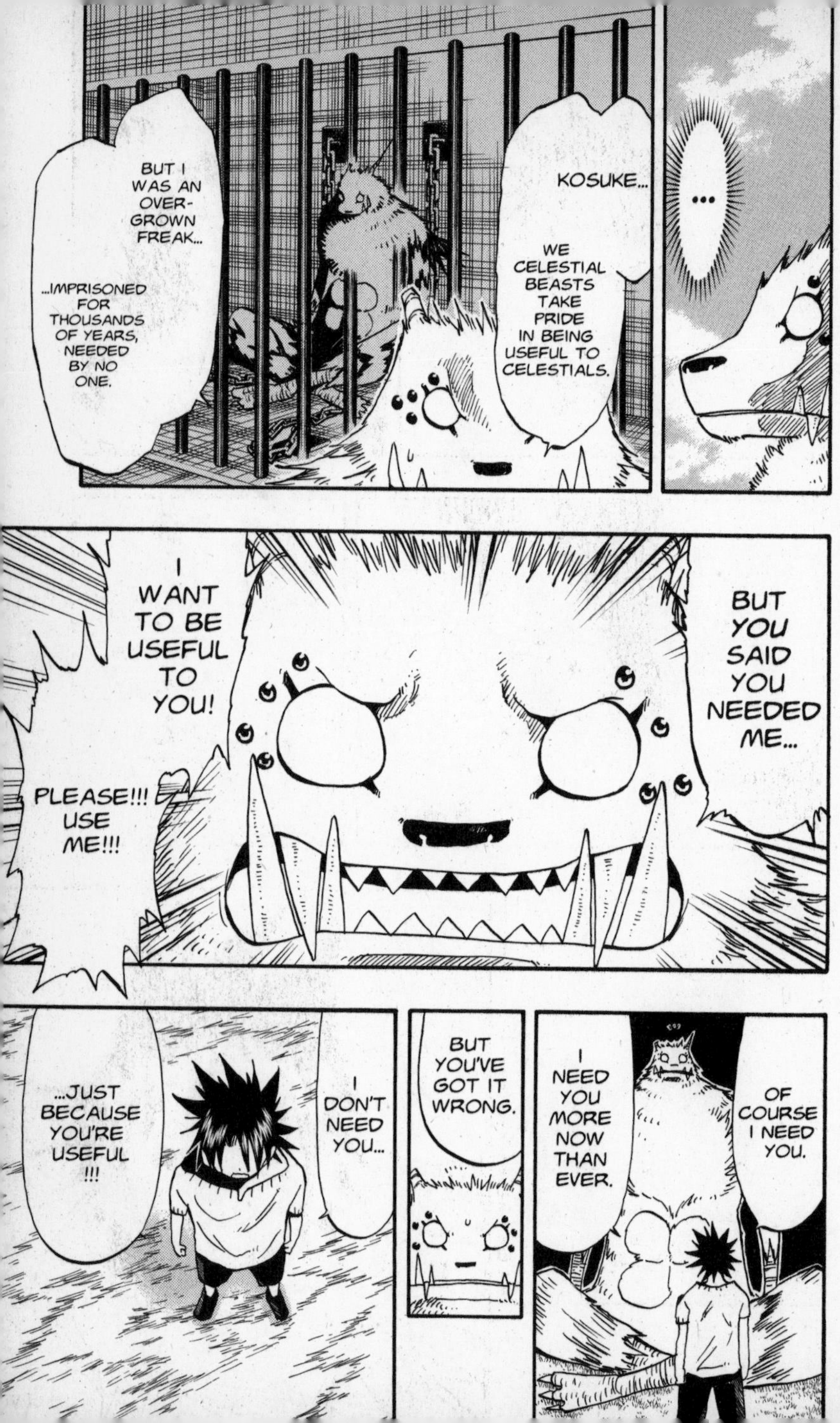
...
KOSUKE...
WE CELESTIAL BEASTS TAKE PRIDE IN BEING USEFUL TO CELESTIALS.
BUT I WAS AN OVER-GROWN FREAK...
...IMPRISONED FOR THOUSANDS OF YEARS, NEEDED BY NO ONE.
BUT YOU SAID YOU NEEDED ME...
I WANT TO BE USEFUL TO YOU!
PLEASE!!! USE ME!!!
OF COURSE I NEED YOU.
I NEED YOU MORE NOW THAN EVER.
BUT YOU'VE GOT IT WRONG.
I DON'T NEED YOU...
...JUST BECAUSE YOU'RE USEFUL !!!

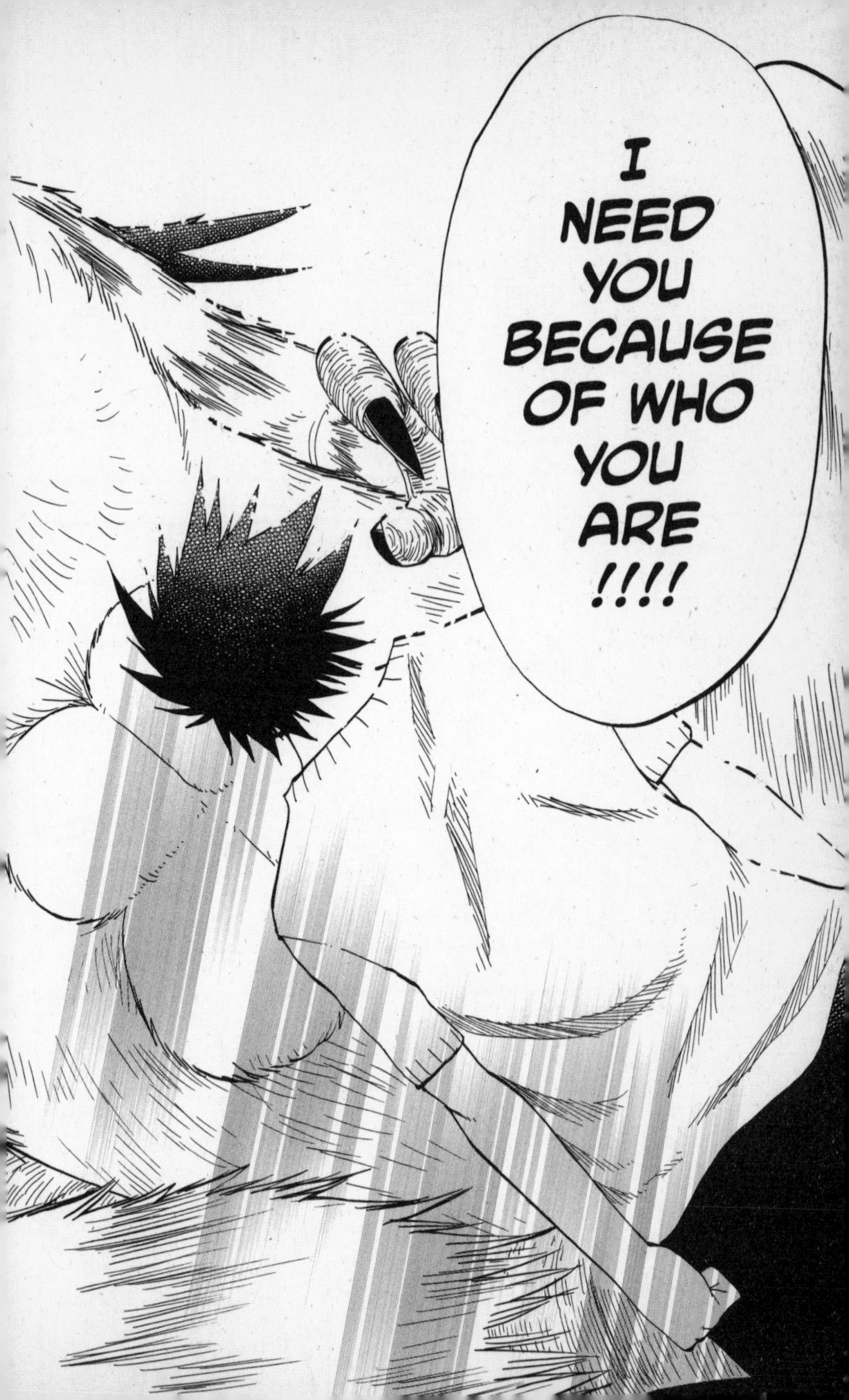
I NEED YOU BECAUSE OF WHO YOU ARE!!!!

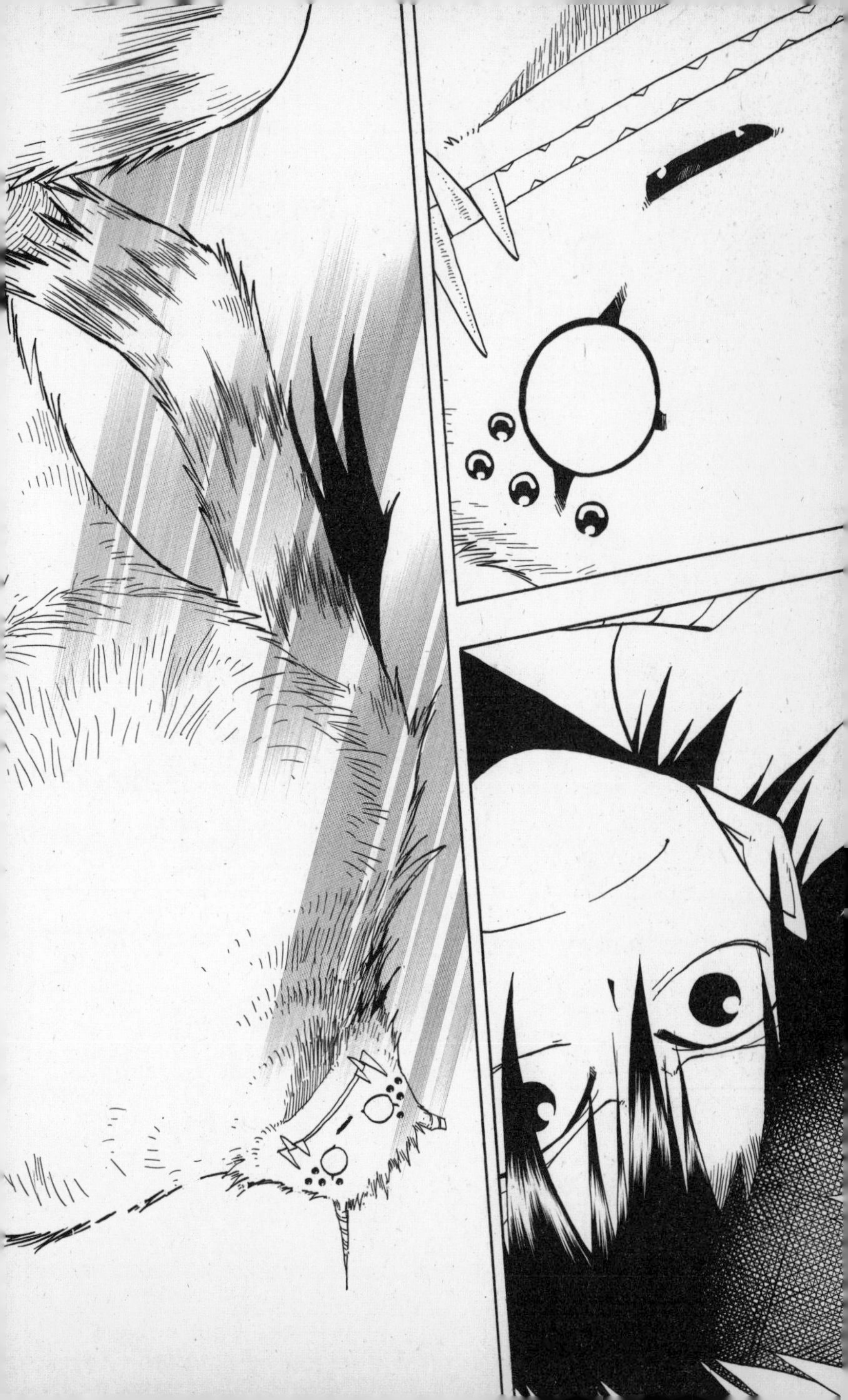

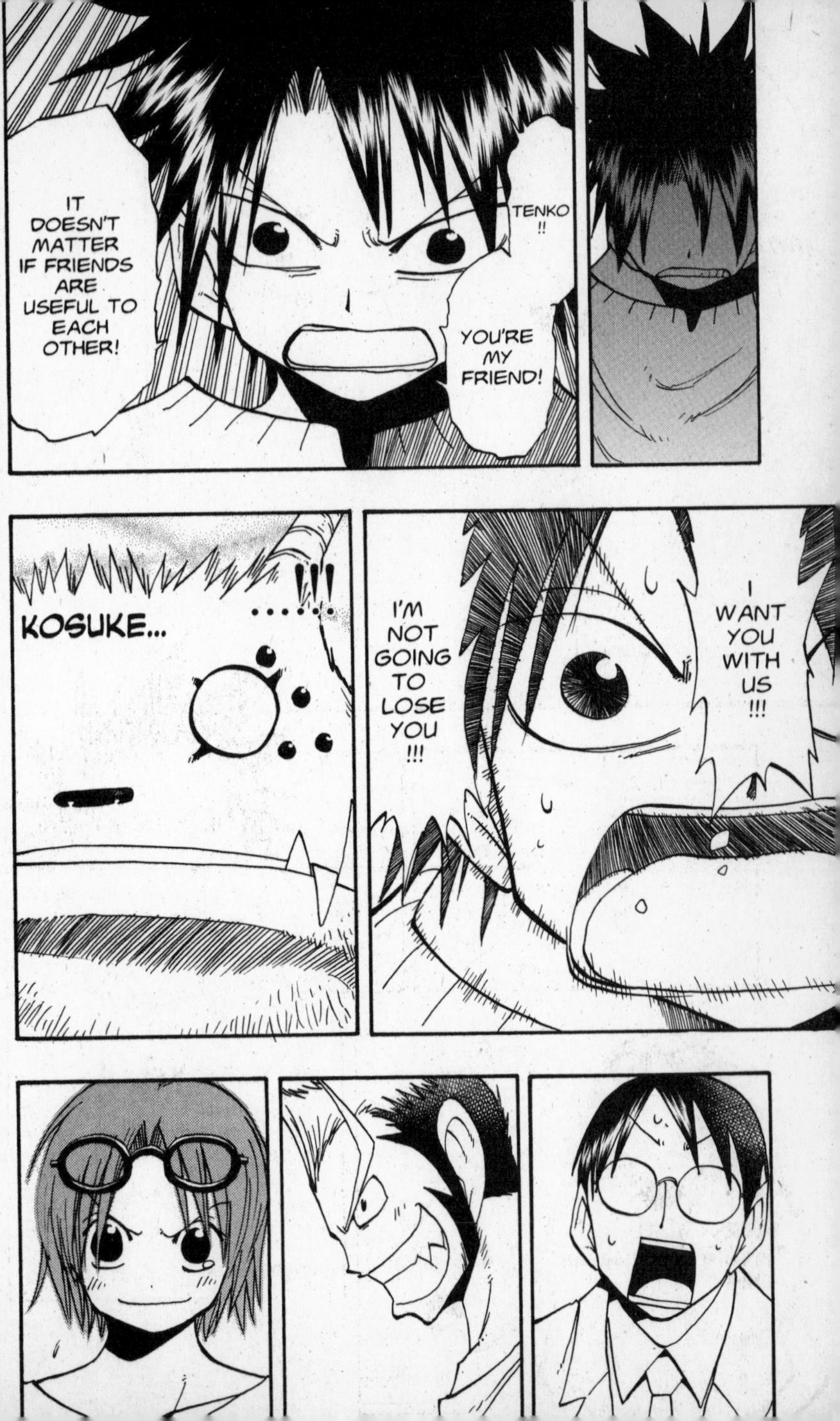
TENKO !!
YOU'RE MY FRIEND!
IT DOESN'T MATTER IF FRIENDS ARE USEFUL TO EACH OTHER!
I WANT YOU WITH US !!!
I'M NOT GOING TO LOSE YOU !!!
......!!!
KOSUKE...

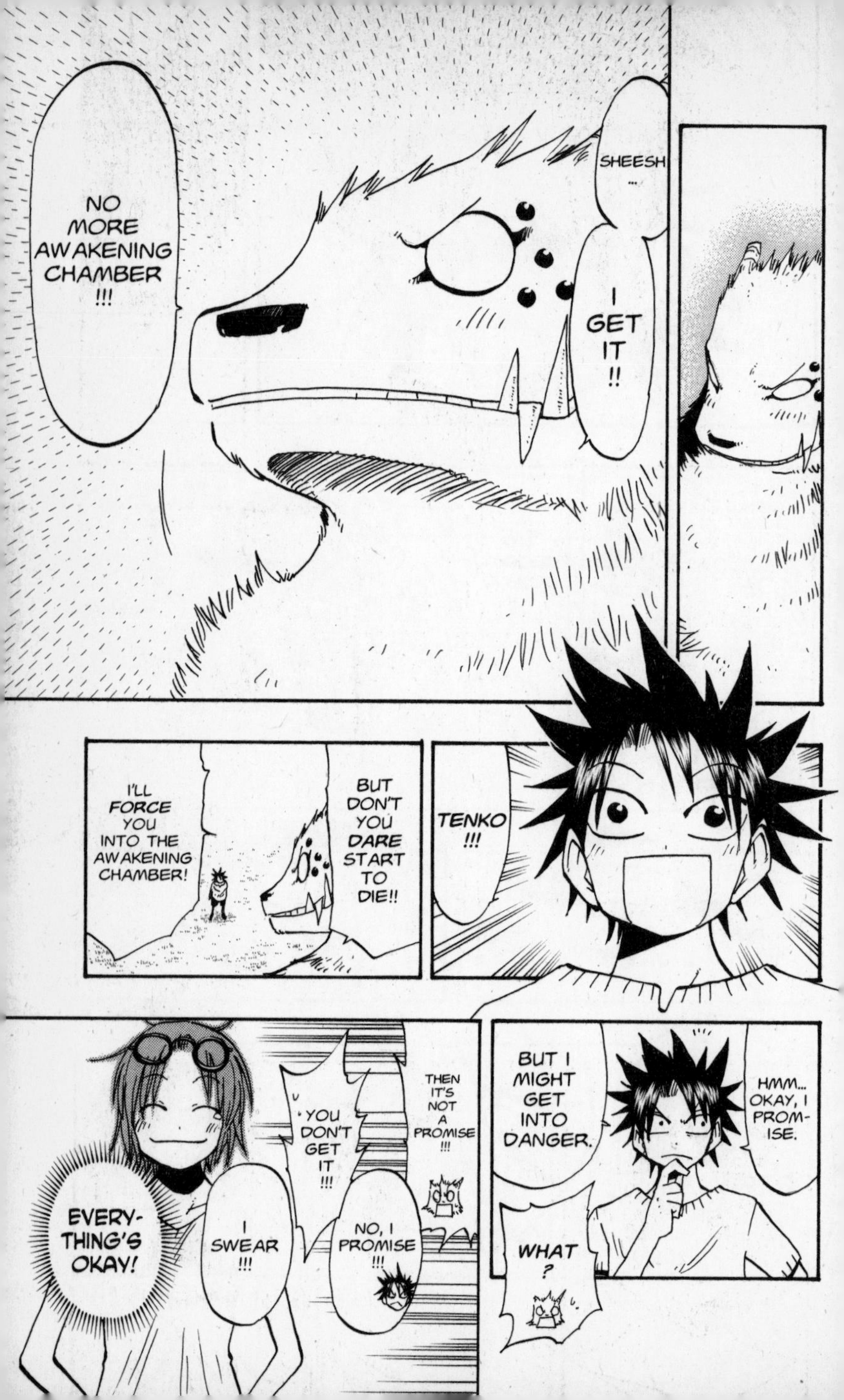
SHEESH...
I GET IT!!
NO MORE AWAKENING CHAMBER!!!
TENKO!!!
BUT DON'T YOU DARE START TO DIE!!
I'LL FORCE YOU INTO THE AWAKENING CHAMBER!
HMM... OKAY, I PROM-ISE.
BUT I MIGHT GET INTO DANGER.
WHAT?
THEN IT'S NOT A PROMISE!!!
NO, I PROMISE!!!
YOU DON'T GET IT!!!
I SWEAR!!!
EVERY-THING'S OKAY!

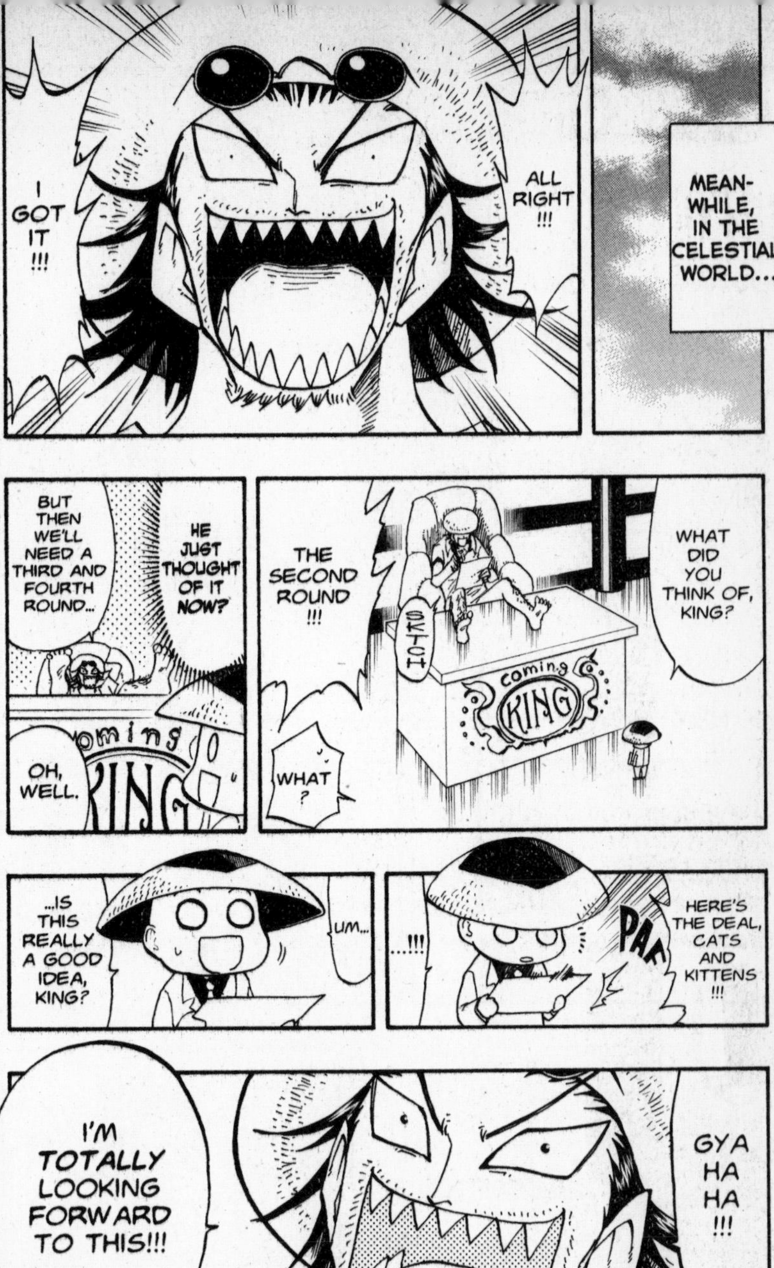
MEAN-WHILE, IN THE CELESTIAL WORLD...
ALL RIGHT!!!
I GOT IT!!!
WHAT DID YOU THINK OF, KING?
THE SECOND ROUND!!!
SKETCH
WHAT?
HE JUST THOUGHT OF IT NOW?
BUT THEN WE'LL NEED A THIRD AND FOURTH ROUND...
OH, WELL.
HERE'S THE DEAL, CATS AND KITTENS!!!
PAF
...!!!
UM...
...IS THIS REALLY A GOOD IDEA, KING?
GYA HA HA!!!
I'M TOTALLY LOOKING FORWARD TO THIS!!!

End of Volume 10

SPECIAL EXTRA FEATURE

AI MORI'S... UEKI'S SACRED WEAPON RESEARCH FILE

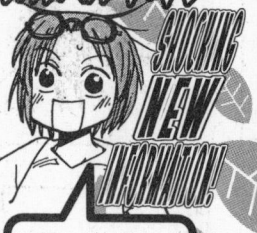

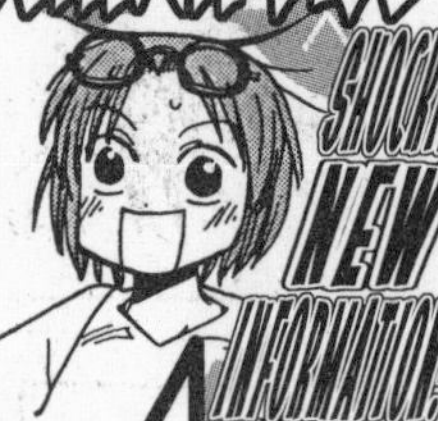
SHOCKING NEW INFORMATION!
I'M REVEALING MY RESEARCH ON SACRED WEAPONS! BUT I WAS VERY SURPRISED THAT UEKI WAS A CELESTIAL...

WHAT IS A SACRED WEAPON?

IT'S A WEAPON USED BY CELESTIALS. THERE ARE 10 TYPES. A CELESTIAL'S STRENGTH CAN VARY FROM ONE TO TEN STARS, AND THEY LEARN TO USE ONE WEAPON FOR EVERY LEVEL THEY GAIN.

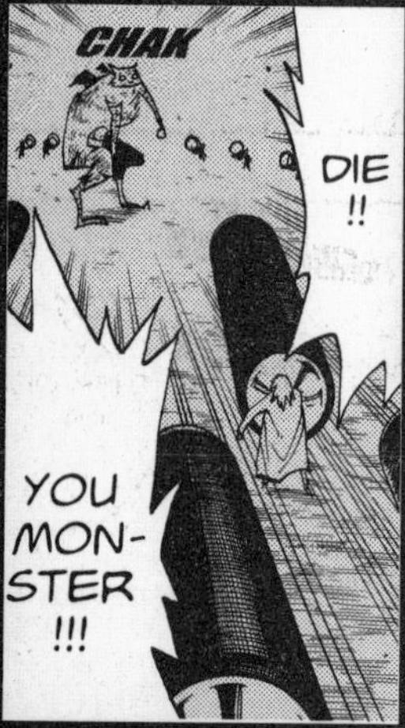
CHAK
DIE !!
YOU MON-STER !!!

CELESTIALS ATTACKING TENKO WITH KUROGANE. UNLIKE UEKI'S VERSION, THEIR SACRED WEAPONS COME STRAIGHT OUT OF THEIR HANDS.

WHAT IS THE DIFFERENCE BETWEEN A NORMAL SACRED WEAPON AND UEKI'S?

UEKI IS A NEO-CELESTIAL, COMBINING HIS POWER OVER TREES WITH HIS SACRED WEAPONS. COMBINED WITH TREES, HIS WEAPONS BECOME GIGANTIC!

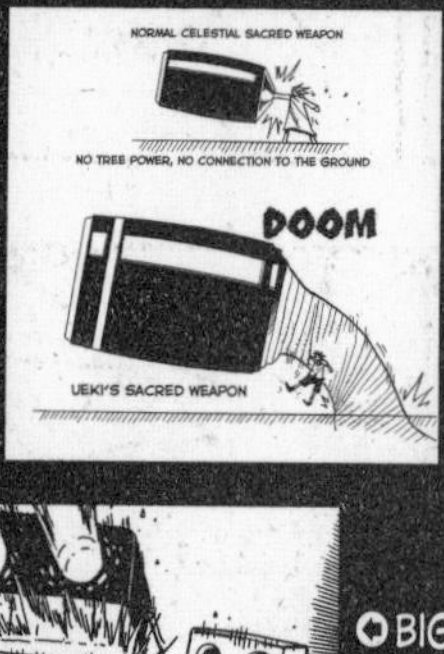
NORMAL CELESTIAL SACRED WEAPON
NO TREE POWER, NO CONNECTION TO THE GROUND
DOOM
UEKI'S SACRED WEAPON

TREE POWER! THE WEAPON IS ROOTED TO THE GROUND TO SUPPORT ITS HUGE SIZE.

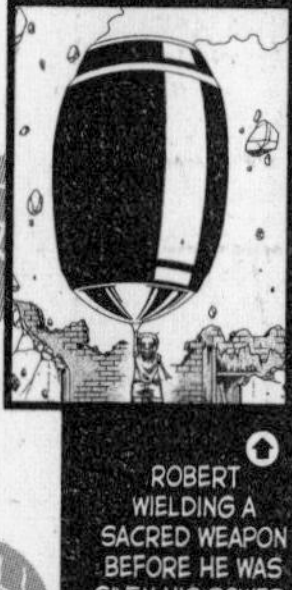

ROBERT WIELDING A SACRED WEAPON BEFORE HE WAS GIVEN HIS POWER. IT'S A NORMAL SACRED WEAPON.

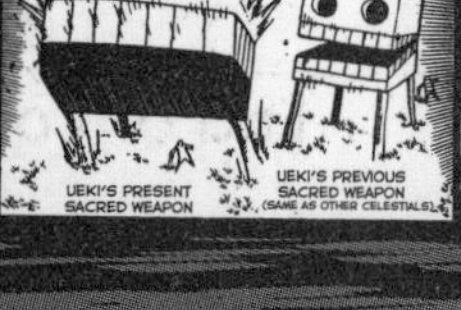
UEKI'S PRESENT SACRED WEAPON
UEKI'S PREVIOUS SACRED WEAPON (SAME AS OTHER CELESTIALS)

BIGGER AND BETTER!

FILE. 1

One-Star Sacred Weapon Neo-celestial version

Kurogane

THE FIRST SACRED WEAPON THAT UEKI GAINED. IT'S A CANNON-SHAPED WEAPON THAT FIRES HUGE BULLETS. UEKI COMBINES IT WITH A TREE, SO THE BULLET IS MADE OUT OF WOOD. IT'S THE MOST BASIC OF THE WEAPONS. ONE CAN USE IT JUST BY BEING AWARE THAT ONE IS A CELESTIAL.

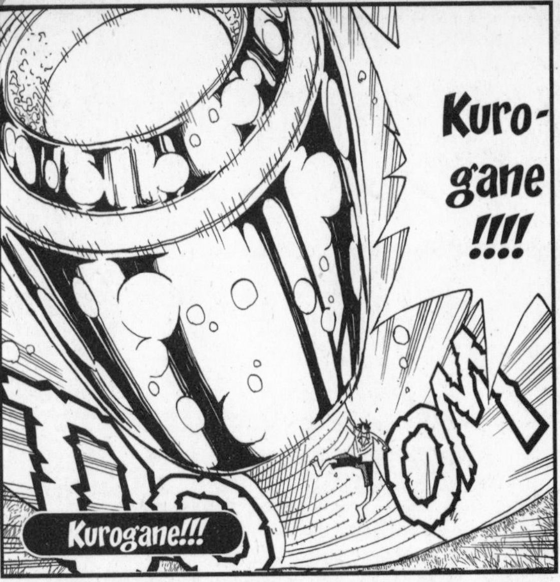
Kuro-
gane
!!!!
Kurogane!!!

KUROGANE AFTER UEKI'S AWAKENING AS A NEO-CELESTIAL. THE DESIGN HAS CHANGED, AND THE POWER HAS INCREASED EXPONENTIALLY!

NORMAL VERSION

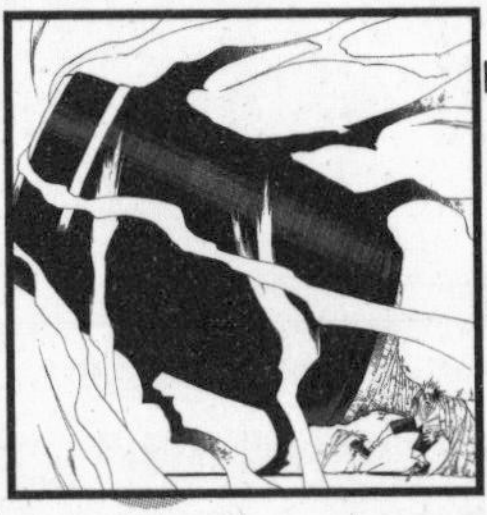

KUROGANE BEFORE UEKI BECAME A NEO-CELESTIAL.

KEY TO LEARNING
AWARENESS

ENEMIES KNOCKED OUT
ALESSIO NIKO

THE KEY TO LEARNING IS TO BE AWARE OF BEING A CELESTIAL. UEKI BROUGHT OUT KUROGANE THE MOMENT HE SHOUTED.

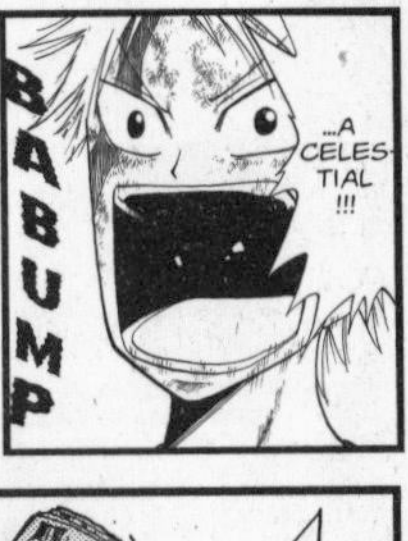
BABUMP
...A CELESTIAL !!!

IT CAN CHANGE DIRECTIONS! BUT IT LOOKS LIKE IT REQUIRES TREMENDOUS STRENGTH, SINCE IT'S SO HEAVY.

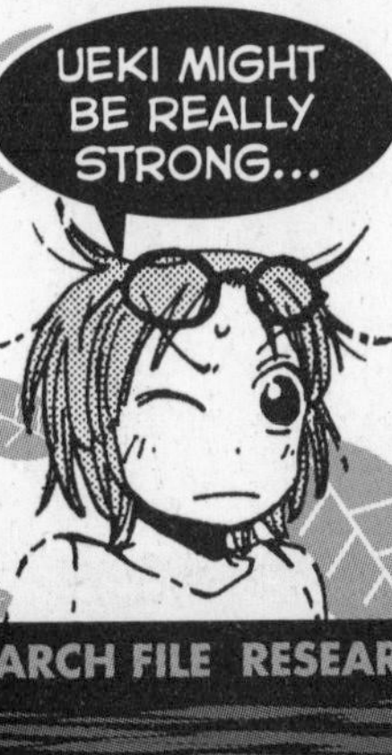
UEKI MIGHT BE REALLY STRONG...

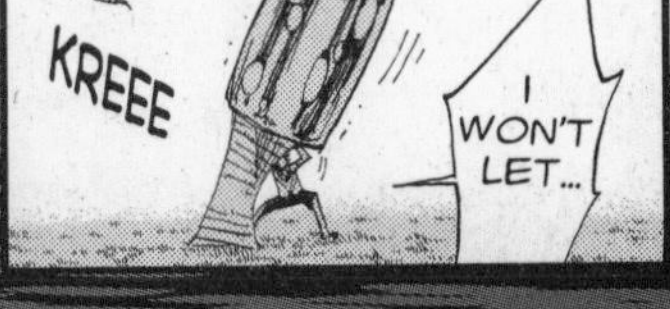
KREEE
I WON'T LET...

RESEARCH FILE RESEARCH FILE RESEARCH FILE RESEARCH FILE

FILE. 2

Two-Star Sacred Weapon Neo-celestial version

Hood

A DEFENSIVE SACRED WEAPON THAT ACTS AS A SHIELD!! THE KEY TO LEARNING IS "ENDURANCE." A SOUL THAT CAN ENDURE ANYTHING BECOMES A CELESTIAL'S DEFENSE.

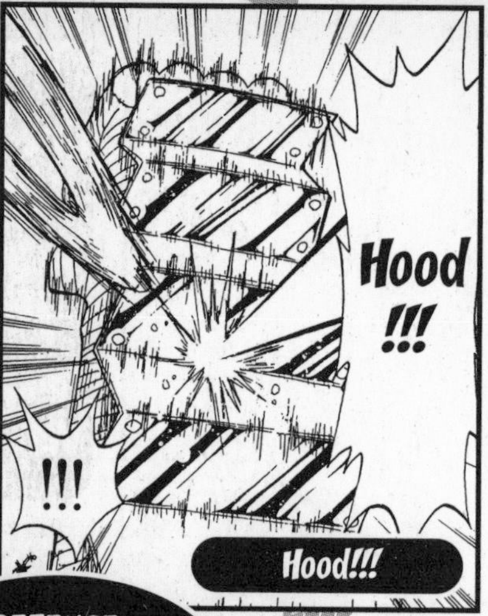

Hood !!!
!!!
Hood!!!

HOOD AFTER UEKI BECAME A NEO-CELESTIAL. IT'S LARGER, WITH MORE DURABILITY. THE DEFLECTING PORTION LOOKS DIFFERENT, TOO.

KEY TO LEARNING

ENDURANCE

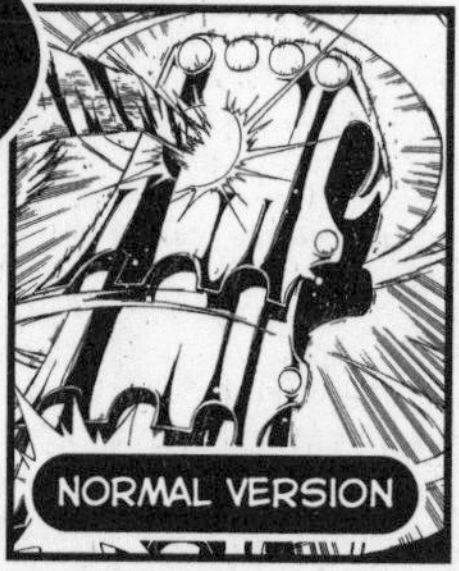

NORMAL VERSION

DEFLECT ENEMY ATTACKS BY SUMMONING IT!

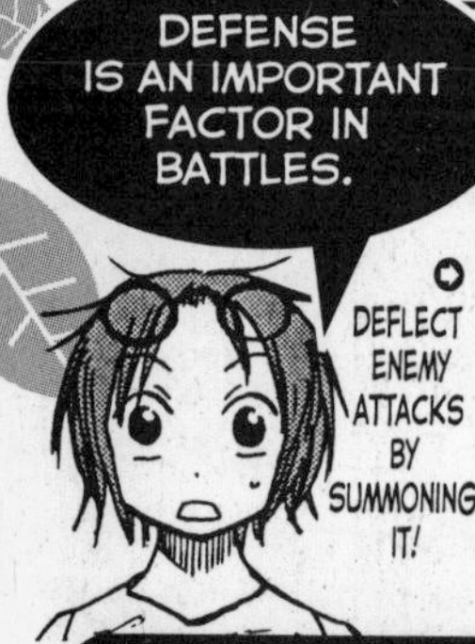

DEFENSE IS AN IMPORTANT FACTOR IN BATTLES.

CHECK POINT

A SACRED WEAPON'S STRENGTH CAN BE CONTROLLED!!

I'M NOT SURE IF UEKI REALIZES IT, BUT DEPENDING ON THE TARGET, HE SEEMS TO ADJUST THE POWER OF HIS WEAPONS!

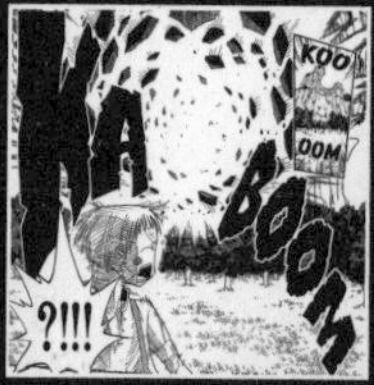

KOO
DOM
KA BOOM
?!!!

A FULL-POWER KUROGANE CAN EVEN BLOW AWAY MOUNTAINS! INCREDIBLE POWER...

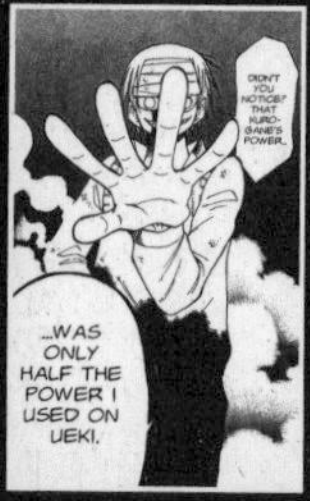

DIDN'T YOU NOTICE? THAT KURO-GANE'S POWER...
...WAS ONLY HALF THE POWER I USED ON UEKI.

SOMEONE AT ROBERT'S LEVEL SEEMS TO BE ABLE TO FREELY ADJUST THE POWER OF THE SACRED WEAPONS!

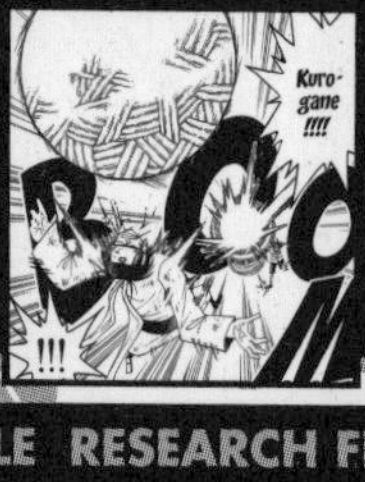

Kuro-gane !!!!
!!!

WHEN HE SHOT AT SANO. SEEMS WEAK.

RESEARCH FILE RESEARCH FILE RESEARCH FILE RESEARCH FILE

FILE. 3

Three-Star Sacred Weapon Neo-celestial version

Ranma

A HUGE SWORD-LIKE WEAPON THAT ATTACKS THE ENEMY BY SLASHING. THE KEY TO LEARNING IS "FOCUS." IT'S SIMILAR TO JAPANESE SWORDSMANSHIP, WHICH STRESSES BLOCKING OUT ALL DISTRACTIONS. RANMA SEEMS TO BE EXTRA SHARP COMPARED TO A NORMAL SWORD.

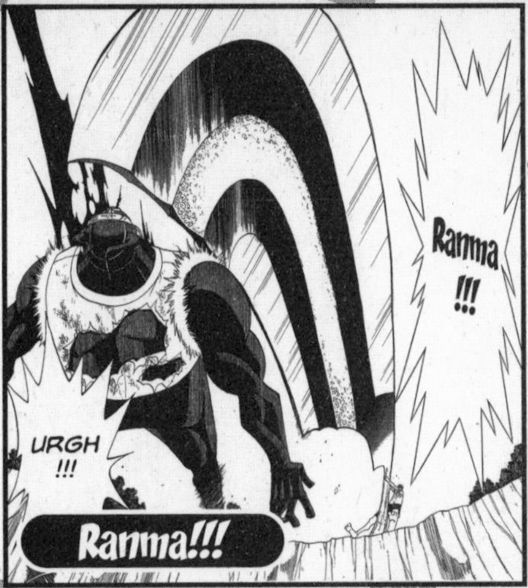
Ranma !!!
URGH !!!
Ranma!!!

THE FIRST TIME UEKI USED RANMA WAS AFTER BECOMING A NEO-CELESTIAL, SO I'VE NEVER SEEN A NORMAL RANMA. IT CUT THROUGH THE ARMOR OGRE WAS WEARING, EVEN THOUGH IT DIDN'T BUDGE AGAINST RINKO'S BEADS.

KEY TO LEARNING	ENEMIES DEFEATED
FOCUS	OGRE

CHECK POINT

WHAT IS THE AWAKENING CHAMBER?

AN ORGAN INSIDE TENKO THAT ALLOWS CELESTIALS TO LEVEL UP IN A SHORT AMOUNT OF TIME.

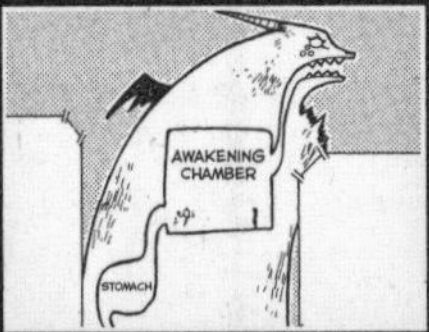
AWAKENING CHAMBER
STOMACH

CELESTIALS WHO ENTER ARE FACED WITH TRIALS. UNLESS A TRIAL IS FINISHED WITHIN 24 HOURS, THE CELESTIAL IS DIGESTED!!

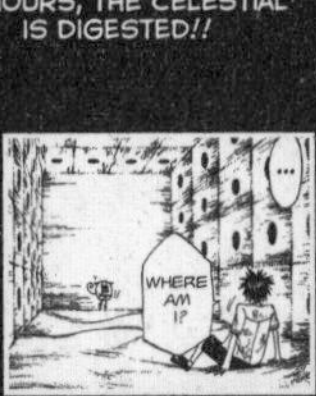
...
WHERE AM I?

THE TRIAL IS DIFFERENT FOR EACH STAR.

CHECK POINT

AWAKENING CHAMBER FOR THREE STARS.

FIND THE SPEAR WORM FROM WITHIN THE SPEARS AND KILL IT.

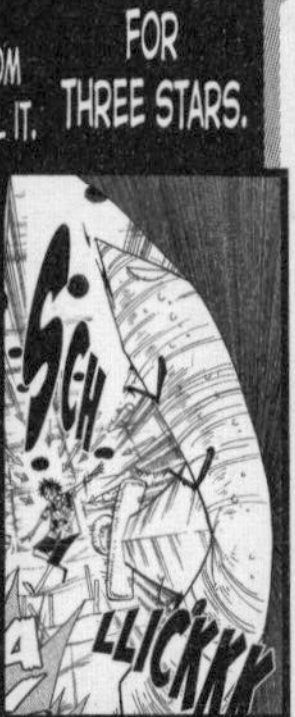
SCH
LLICKKK

IT CAN BE CLEARED ONCE ONE LEARNS TO FOCUS!!

A COACHING BEAST ACTS AS A GUIDE.

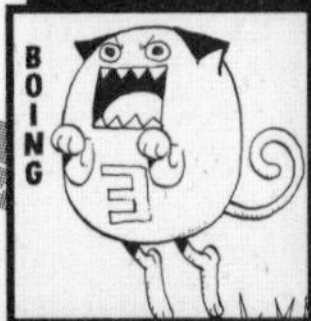
BOING

FILE. 4

Four-Star Sacred Weapon Neo-celestial version

Mash

A WEAPON THAT CRUSHES WITH GREAT POWER!! IT'S SHAPED LIKE A CUBE, AND IT CRUSHES WITH ITS MOUTH. THE KEY TO LEARNING IS "EXERTION." IT'S A POWER-BASED WEAPON THAT REQUIRES THE EXERTION OF GREAT FORCE!!

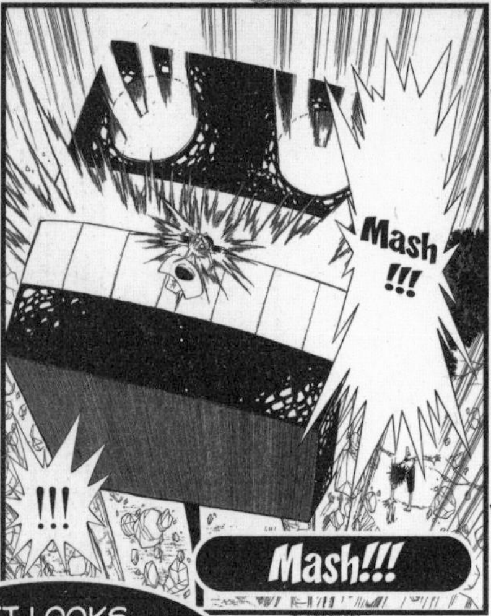
Mash !!!
!!!
Mash!!!

THE NEO VERSION IS HUGE, INCREASING THE RANGE. THE DIRECTION IT FACES CAN BE CHANGED.

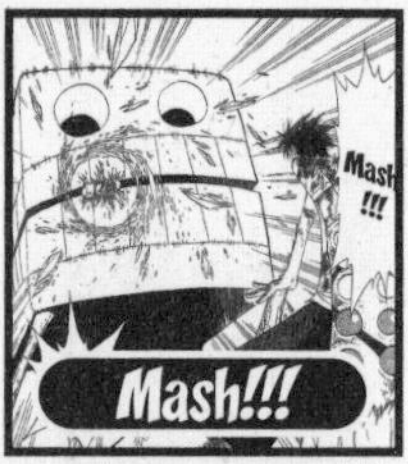
Mash !!!
Mash!!!

THE SIZE AND COLOR DIFFERS FROM THE NEO VERSION.

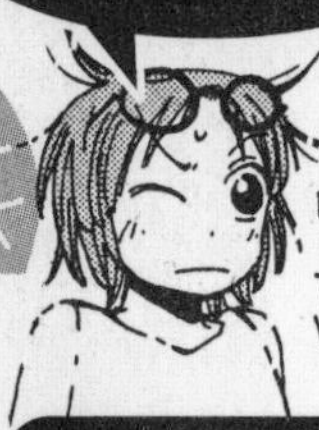
IT LOOKS PAINFUL TO GET CAUGHT IN THERE!!

KEY TO LEARNING

EXERTION

ENEMIES DEFEATED

DON
MARCO
BECKY
MYOJIN
YAKUZA BOSS
SAMEJIMA
GODA
YOSHIMOTO
MAMUSHIBARA
KIRISAKI
CHUN
MURANAKA
J

CHECK POINT

FOUR-STAR AWAKENING CHAMBER

TRIAL TO PUT ALL STRENGTH INTO AN ATTACK. CLEARED WHEN FULL FORCE IS EXERTED.

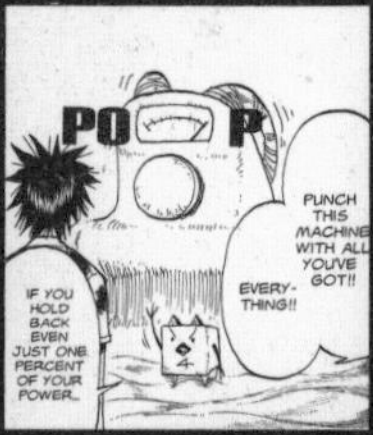
POP
PUNCH THIS MACHINE WITH ALL YOU'VE GOT!!
EVERY-THING!!
IF YOU HOLD BACK EVEN JUST ONE PERCENT OF YOUR POWER...

THE COACHING BEAST IS DIFFERENT FOR EACH STAR.

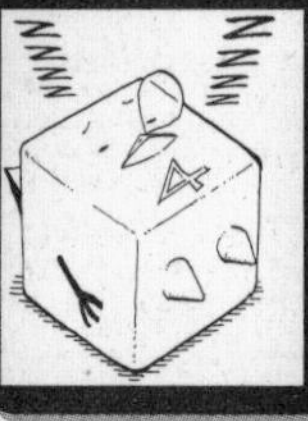
NNNN
NNNN

HIT THIS MACHINE WITH FULL STRENGTH. IT REFLECTS THE FORCE PUT IN!

FILE. 5

Five-Star Sacred Weapon

Pick

A SACRED WEAPON THAT USES THRUST!! IT EXERTS A STRONGER FORCE THAN MASH ON A SINGLE POINT. THE KEY TO LEARNING IS "CONCENTRATION," MEANING THAT THIS WEAPON CAN'T BE USED UNLESS ONE LEARNS TO CONCENTRATE ALL POWER ON ONE POINT. UEKI USES IT FOR MANY THINGS BESIDES ATTACK, MAKING IT A FLEXIBLE TOOL!!

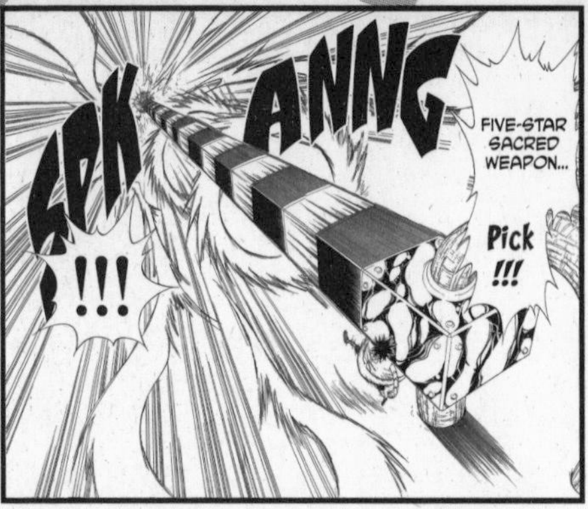
FIVE-STAR SACRED WEAPON...
Pick !!!
SPK ANNG !!!

UEKI'S PICK IS ONCE AGAIN LARGER THAN A NORMAL CELESTIAL'S! (EVEN INUMARU SAYS SO!) LIKE HIS OTHER WEAPONS, IT'S STABILIZED WITH A ROOT. IT'S A LONG, STICK-SHAPED WEAPON THAT FIRES STRAIGHT AT THE ENEMY!

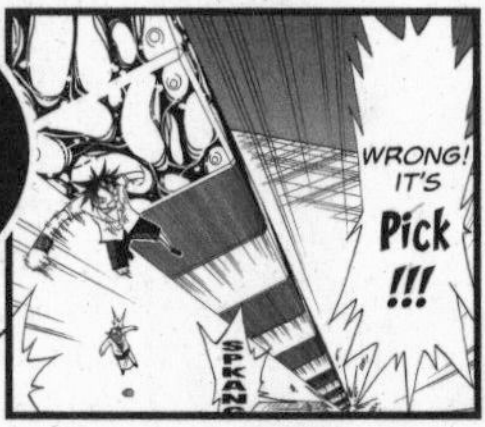
WRONG! IT'S
Pick !!!

WHEN UEKI FIRES AT THE GROUND, HE CAN FLY! HE WAS INSPIRED TO USE PICK AS A POLE VAULT.

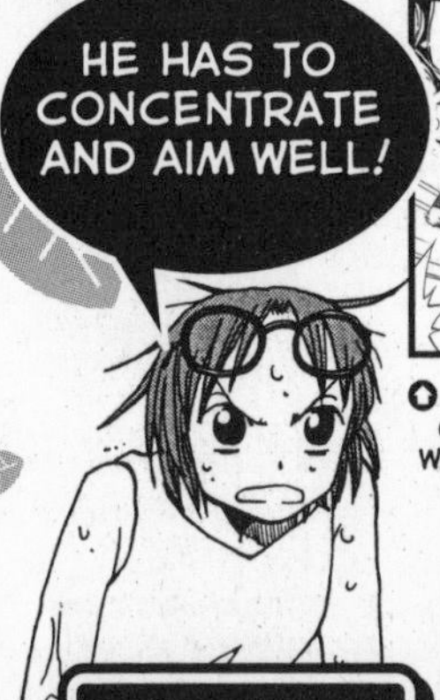
HE HAS TO CONCENTRATE AND AIM WELL!

KEY TO LEARNING

CONCENTRATION

DEFEATED ENEMIES

YUNPAO
NIKO
MARIO

CHECK POINT FIVE-STAR AWAKENING CHAMBER

IT SEEMS THE TRAINING REQUIRED "CONCENTRATION." THERE ARE NO FURTHER DETAILS.

IS HE ALWAYS SMOKING A PIPE?

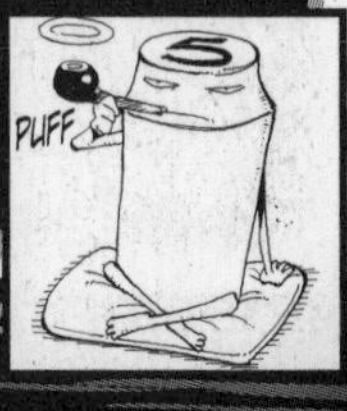
PUFF

FILE. 6

Six-Star Sacred Weapon

Raika

HIGH-SPEED TRANSPORTATION WEAPON. EFFECTIVE IN DEFENSE OR OFFENSE. THE KEY TO LEARNING IS "FORESIGHT." IT CAN'T BE USED UNLESS ONE CAN READ AN OPPONENT'S MOVES AND CHANGING BATTLE CONDITIONS.

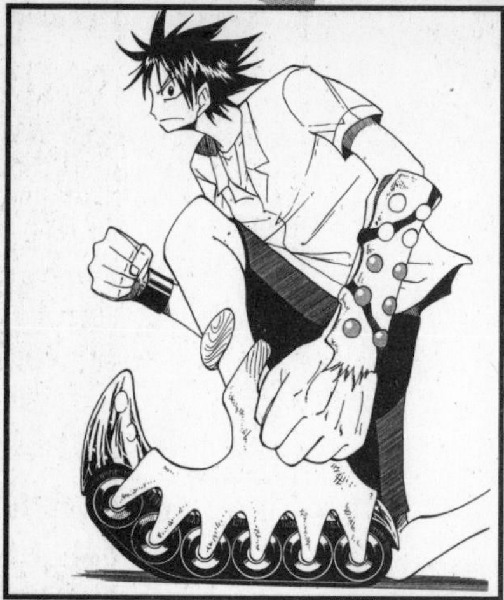

IT'S SHAPED LIKE A PAIR OF INLINE SKATES. A BRANCH WRAPS AROUND THE LEG, ALLOWING SUPER-HIGH-SPEED MOVEMENT.

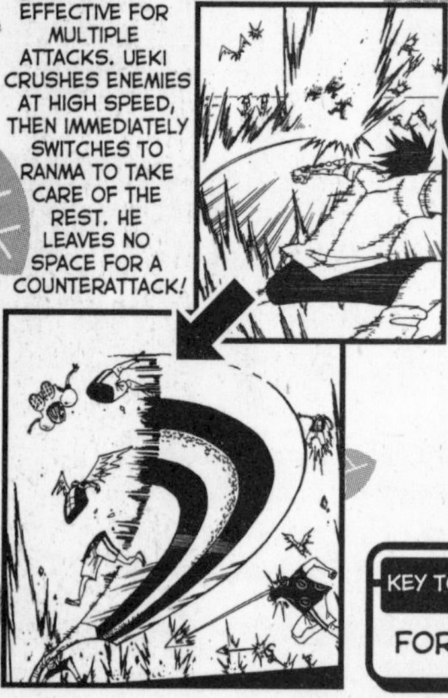

RAIKA IS EFFECTIVE FOR MULTIPLE ATTACKS. UEKI CRUSHES ENEMIES AT HIGH SPEED, THEN IMMEDIATELY SWITCHES TO RANMA TO TAKE CARE OF THE REST. HE LEAVES NO SPACE FOR A COUNTERATTACK!

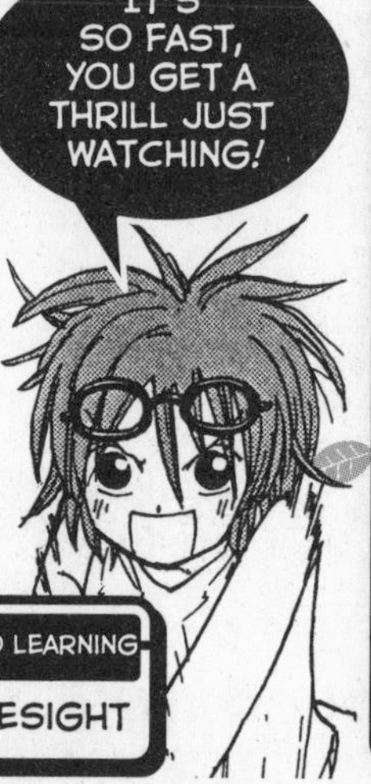
IT'S SO FAST, YOU GET A THRILL JUST WATCHING!

KEY TO LEARNING

FORESIGHT

CHECK POINT SIX-STAR AWAKENING CHAMBER

THE TRIAL REQUIRES TRAINING IN "FORESIGHT." THE COACHING BEAST HAS NEVER BEEN REVEALED UNTIL NOW!

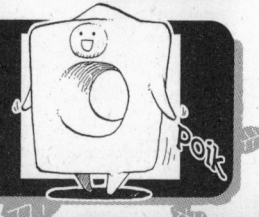

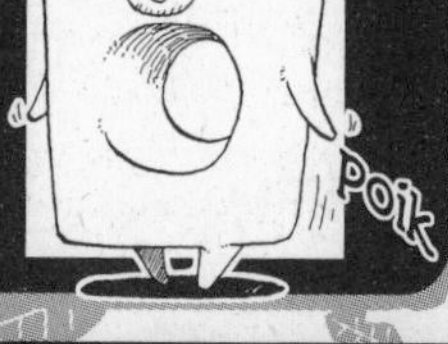
Poik

FILE. 7

Seven-Star Sacred Weapon

Gulliver

THIS SACRED WEAPON CAN CAPTURE ANY TARGET, ALLOWING FOR ATTACKS THAT CAN'T MISS. THE KEY TO LEARNING IS "MAINTENANCE," REQUIRING THE USER TO KEEP MAINTAINING A HOLD ON THE ENEMY.

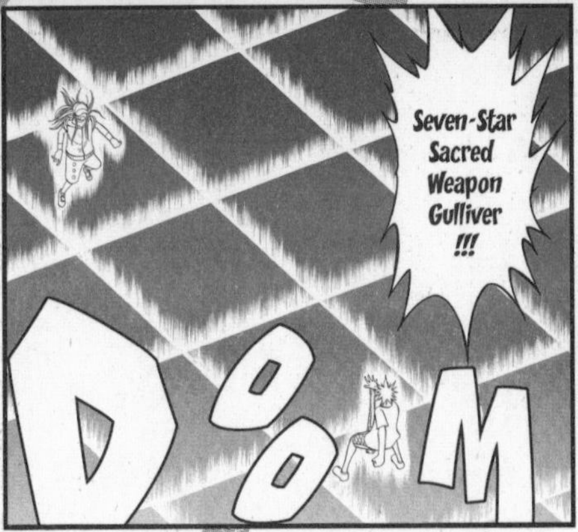
Seven-Star Sacred Weapon Gulliver !!!
DOOOM

A BOX CAN APPEAR ANYWHERE ON THE GRID, SO THE ENEMY HAS NO WAY OF AVOIDING IT. IT TAKES HALF A SECOND TO CAPTURE THE TARGET! NO PLACE TO RUN!

THE BOX SHOOTS UP AND THE LID CLOSES. NO WAY OUT!!

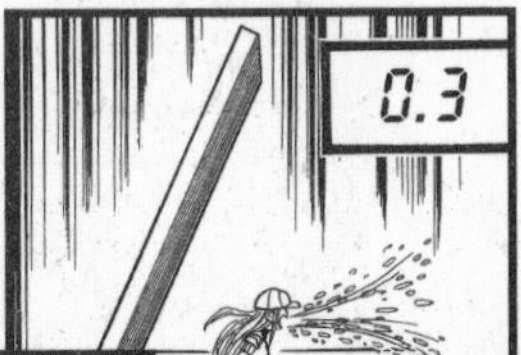
0.3

CAPTURE COMPLETE. INDESTRUCTIBLE FROM THE INSIDE, BUT VULNERABLE TO ATTACK FROM THE OUTSIDE!!

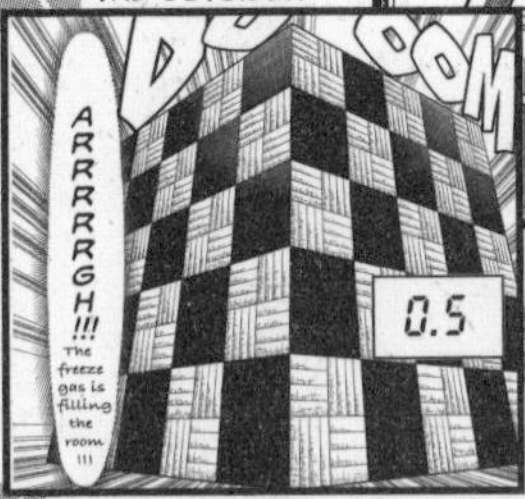
DOOOM
ARRRRRGH!!!
The freeze gas is filling the room !!!
0.5

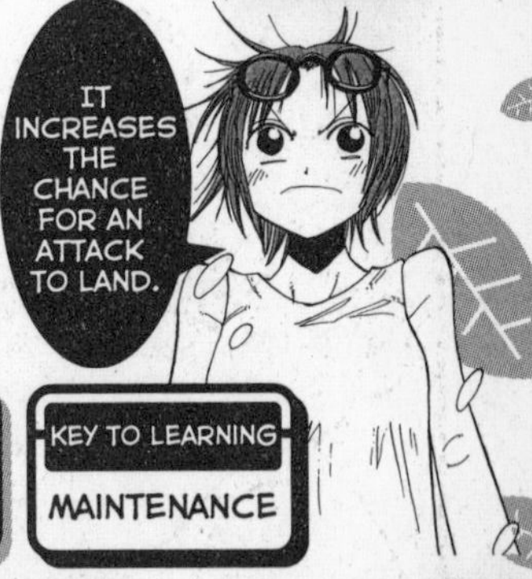
IT INCREASES THE CHANCE FOR AN ATTACK TO LAND.

DEFEATED ENEMIES	KEY TO LEARNING
KAPUSHO	MAINTENANCE

CHECK POINT SEVEN-STAR AWAKENING CHAMBER

I DON'T KNOW THE DETAILS, BUT "MAINTENANCE" WAS REQUIRED FOR THIS TRIAL. THIS COACHING BEAST HAS NEVER BEEN SEEN BEFORE!

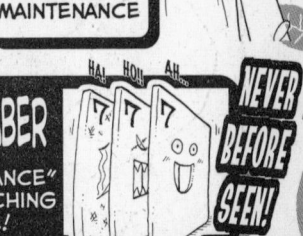

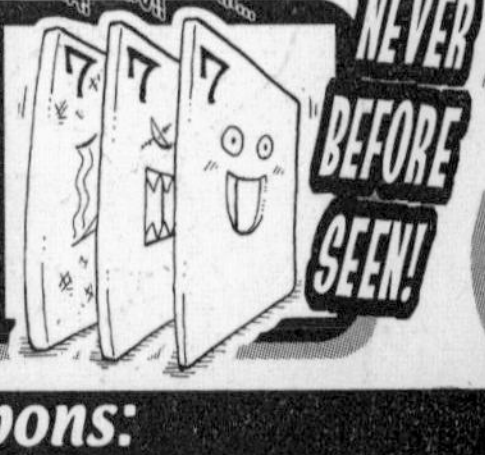
HA! HO!! AH...
NEVER BEFORE SEEN!

There are other sacred weapons: Eight-star "Namihana," Nine-star "Seiku," and Ten-star "Archenemy"!

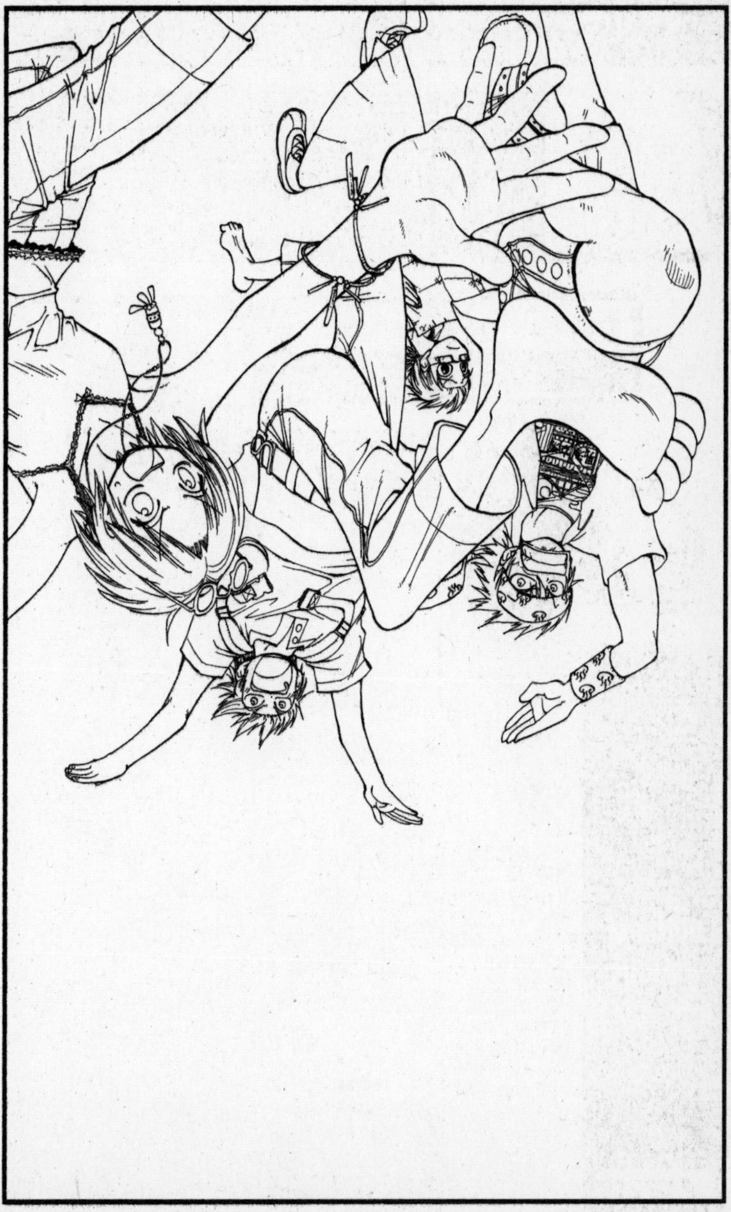

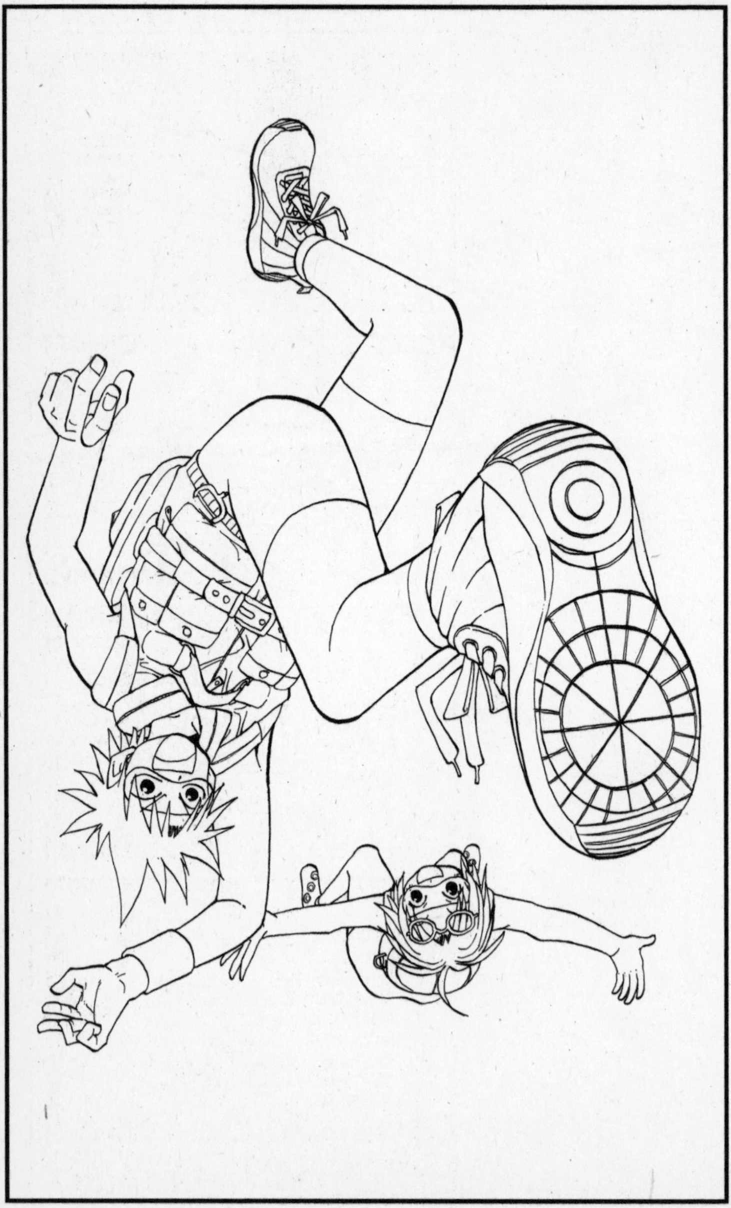

DIFFERENT LAWS 10

WHEN I HAVE TO FINISH WORK IN A HURRY AND FEEL PSYCHOLOGICALLY CORNERED ...
I NEED TO REARRANGE MY ROOM !!
BOOM
... I'LL SAY SOMETHING LIKE THIS.
ONCE I START REARRANGING ...
I SHOULD CLEAN WHILE I'M AT IT!
... I'LL SAY SOMETHING LIKE THIS.
AND ONCE I START CLEANING ...
OH, MY GRADUATION ALBUM!
Those were the days!
RRRRRR
... I'LL GET DISTRACTED LIKE THIS.
HOW'S THE WORK COMING ALONG? (EDITOR)
ERK
um
ER
... STEADILY ...
THE LAW OF DIGGING A DEEPER HOLE!!!

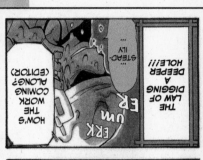

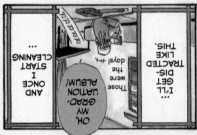

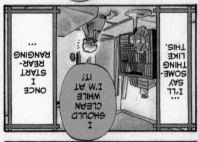

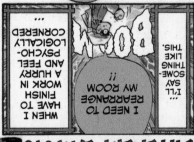